THE GIRLHOOD OF

CLARA SCHUMANN

(CLARA WIECK AND HER TIME)

BY

FLORENCE MAY

AUTHOR OF "THE LIFE OF JOHANNES BRAHMS"

WITH PORTRAIT

Travis & Emery

Florence May.

The Girlhood Of Clara Schumann: Clara Wieck And Her Time.

First published Edward Arnold, London, 1912.

Republished Travis & Emery 2009.

Published by

Travis & Emery Music Bookshop

17 Cecil Court, London, WC2N 4EZ, United Kingdom.

(+44) 20 7240 2129

neworders@travis-and-emery.com

Hardback: 978-1-84955-036-9 Paperback: 978-1-84955-037-6

Florence May (1845-1923), English pianist and author.

She studied with Clara Schumann and later under Brahms, which made her well positioned to write about them both.

Her biographies are well researched and also provide an insight to music of her time.

This edition was written in the 1910s but not published till 1948.

More details available from
- Stanley Sadie: The New Grove Dictionary of Music and Musicians.

THE GIRLHOOD OF CLARA SCHUMANN

CLARA WIECK.
From a lithograph by C. Brand, in the possession of the Gesellschaft der Musikfreunde, Vienna.

THE GIRLHOOD OF
CLARA SCHUMANN

(CLARA WIECK AND HER TIME)

BY

FLORENCE MAY

AUTHOR OF "THE LIFE OF JOHANNES BRAHMS"

WITH PORTRAIT

LONDON

EDWARD ARNOLD

1912

PREFACE

IN placing before English-speaking readers an account of the
girlhood of the famous pianist whose art and personality
are vividly remembered by the older generation of the music-
lovers of to-day, I can in no wise claim that I am able to offer
any hitherto unpublished particulars of biographical interest.
For the main facts of that portion of my work which deals
with the personal events of Clara Wieck's life I am indebted
to the first volume of Berthold Litzmann's "Clara Schumann,
ein Künstlerleben" (three volumes), which, founded on the
diary and correspondence of the great artist, is, from the purely
biographical point of view, exhaustive.   There is, however,
another standpoint from which Frau Schumann's early career
may be studied ; one that has been left unconsidered by Litzmann and that was, perhaps, necessarily excluded from the
scope of his work by the mere bulk of the personal material at
his command, yet of great interest to music-lovers : the standpoint of musical history.   The years covered by Clara Wieck's
activity as a pianist coincide with a clearly-defined period in
the progress both of creative and executive art, with the developments of which her achievement stood in distinctive and
important relation.   To show precisely what that relation was
is one of the main purposes of the following pages.   This part
of the subject has not, so far as I am aware, been discussed
in any previously published work, and its treatment has
involved considerable search in original records.

The presentation, side by side with Clara's story, of an account of Robert Schumann's youthful aims and advancing successes, of the circumstances under which he produced the works for pianoforte solo completed at the date of his marriage —which include practically all those that have made his name famous in this domain—and their brief characterisation have seemed to me to belong essentially to my subject as a whole. For matters of fact in this connection I have made use of Clara Schumann's "Jugendbriefe von Robert Schumann," Gustav Jansen's "Robert Schumanns Briefe" (Neue Folge, zweite Ausgabe) and "Die Davidsbündler," and Wasielewski's "Robert Schumann, Eine Biographie" (vierte Ausgabe).

That Friedrich Wieck, generally remembered chiefly as the tyrannical father who opposed his daughter's marriage, appears in these pages as an enlightened musician of his time and the creator of his daughter's great career would, I believe, have been approved by Frau Schumann herself,* and that I have ventured to think there is something to be said from Wieck's point of view as to the exigencies of his position as Clara's father during the earlier years of her attachment, may, perhaps, be held justified in the opinion of impartial readers of my work.

I have brought my narrative to a close with the date of Clara's marriage because the distinctively historical character of Frau Schumann's career, which has been but little recognised up to the present time, was definitely established during her girlhood. The progress of her maturity served, indeed, to emphasise and develop, but not to change, the most essential feature of her early artistic activity ; whilst in her case, as in others, a detailed account of the successes of the mature executive artist could scarcely fail to produce on the mind of the reader the impression of repetition.

* " I must say with pain that my father has never been recognised as he deserved."—Litzmann, iii. 434 ; see also *ibid.*, 302.

I am indebted for much valuable information to Alfred Dörffel's " Geschichte der Gewandhauskonzerte in Leipzig," compiled from the original records preserved in the society's archives. I have, further, consulted on various points Grove's " Dictionary of Music and Musicians," Hanslick's " Geschichte des Konzertwesens in Wien," Karasowski's " Friedrich Chopin," Kohut's " Friedrich Wieck," La Mara's " Liszt's Briefe," Mendelssohn's " Briefe," Frau Moscheles' " Aus Moscheles' Leben," Ramann's " Franz Liszt als Kunstler und Mensch " and Riemann's " Musiklexikon."

References to newspaper records and other authorities not mentioned in this list will be found in the text or in footnotes.

My thanks are due to Dr. Eusebius Mandyczewski, Archivar to the Gesellschaft der Musikfreunde, Vienna, for permission to reproduce the portrait of Clara Wieck in the Society's possession.

F. M.

South Kensington, S.W.
January, 1912.

CONTENTS

CHAPTER I

1785–1819

CHAPTER II

1819–1828. Ætat up to 9 Years *

CHAPTER III

1828–1829. Ætat 9–10 Years

CHAPTER IV

1830–1831. Ætat 10–11 Years

* All the age indications appearing in this table refer to Clara.

CHAPTER XI

1836. ÆTAT 16 YEARS

CHAPTER XII

1836–1837. ÆTAT 17 YEARS

CHAPTER XIII

1837. ÆTAT 17–18 YEARS

CHAPTER XIV

1837–1838. ÆTAT 18 YEARS

CHAPTER XV

1838. ÆTAT 18 YEARS

CHAPTER XVI

1838–1839. ÆTAT 18–19 YEARS

CHAPTER XVII

1839. ÆTAT 19 YEARS

CHAPTER XVIII

1839–1840. ÆTAT 19–21 YEARS

CHAPTER XIX

1840–1907

THE GIRLHOOD OF CLARA SCHUMANN

CHAPTER I

1785–1819

Friedrich Wieck—School and university career—Life as a private tutor—
He settles in Leipzig as a pianoforte teacher—Marriage with Marianne
Tromlitz—Begins to do business as a pianoforte dealer—The development of the pianoforte—Dawn of musical romanticism—The great
composer-pianists—Frau Marianne Wieck—Birth of Clara (September 13
.1819).

" HE has devoted too much time to music," Rector Benedict
had written in the otherwise laudatory certificate that
was handed to Carl Friedrich Gotthelf Wieck on the termination of his school career at the gymnasium of Torgau in 1803,
and from the point of view not only of the Rector, but of the
young man's parents, the qualification was undoubtedly justified.

That Friedrich possessed great musical aptitude had been
an admitted fact since his early boyhood; but it was a fact in
which neither his father, a respectable tradesman of Pretzsch,
in Saxony, nor his mother, a simple pastor's daughter, had
seen particular reason to rejoice. Things were not as they
had been with the good merchant. His affairs, once flourish-
ing, had begun to decline before Friedrich, who was born
August 18, 1785, had counted many summers, whilst one
child quickly succeeded another, to confront the parents with
life problems of a more elementary character than that of
the cultivation of their eldest son's special gift. It happened,
however, that Friedrich gave early promise of capacity in more
than one direction, and that his clear intelligence, tenacity of
will, and confidence in his own youthful purposes secured for

him the help of a patron who sent him in due time to be
educated in the neighbouring town of Torgau. The assistance
which this friend was able to afford was not extensive. It
provided the lad with a lodging, but not with the wherewithal
to keep body and soul together. For some little while he
subsisted almost entirely on the bread and butter which his
mother sent him by the driver of a wagon that had regular
business on the road between Pretzsch and Torgau, the meagre
fare being supplemented on Saturdays by a basin of hot soup
spared from his landlord's table ; but gradually Friedrich
made a few friends, and the time came when he was invited
once a week to dine with Advocate Schulze. "This cheered
me, weakly and sensitive as I was, and the good food which
I enjoyed—generally roast mutton with beans or peas—revived
and strengthened me during the best part of a summer." Later
on the extreme hardship of this struggling student life was
more appreciably mitigated. Friedrich obtained a place at a
free dinner-table that was provided by a few kind-hearted
citizens of Torgau for some of the poor scholars of the gymnasium; he was able to earn a few pence every week by
teaching Meister Petzhold's little daughter to read, and Herr
Oberförster von Löben was even moved to give him a monthly
allowance of a gulden (about one shilling and eightpence), a
sum which Friedrich, taught by necessity, knew how to lay
out to the best possible advantage.

The young student was debarred by circumstances outside
his control from the enjoyment of such moderate cultivation of
his musical talent as might have been afforded it had he been
a member of the school choir. Even if his voice had been
stronger than it was, delicate health would have prevented
him from joining in the processional street singing that was
a generally recognised function of the German choristers of
the period, its punctual performance at whatever season being
subject to no considerations of weather. But if Friedrich
found himself shut out from an advantage that was within
easy reach of some of his less gifted companions, his unconquerable will recognised such an obstacle only as a further
incentive to the creation of his own opportunities. He made
acquaintance with Town-musician Nitzsche, who allowed

him to scrape on a fiddle or 'cello in company with the
musicians of a dancing class that was held at Nitzsche's
house. He attracted the notice of Organist Klint, who, finding that he desired to become not only a player, but a composer
of dance-tunes, encouraged and set him further on his way
by giving him some hints on musical theory. Chance made
him the possessor of an old table clavier, on which he practised diligently, and the height of his ambition seemed within
measurable distance of realisation when his kind friend the
Oberförster engaged the celebrated pianoforte teacher Milchmayer, court musician to his Highness the Elector of Bavaria,
to give lessons at his house, and invited his favourite to come
and listen to them. Friedrich eagerly availed himself of this
privilege, and exercised his power of improving opportunity
to such good advantage that Milchmayer was impressed by
his earnestness and good-naturedly devoted a few hours to
his special instruction. The half-dozen lessons he thus obtained
gave Wieck an insight into some of the elementary principles
of the art of pianoforte playing, and, assisting his keen
intelligence with an impulse in the right direction, were
remembered by him in after-life as having been amongst
the factors that enabled him gradually to work out the
method of instruction which placed him amongst the foremost
pianoforte teachers of Germany.

Many laborious years were to intervene, however, before
Friedrich found himself in a position to concentrate his best
energies on the calling in which he was destined to achieve
eminence. His first choice of a vocation was guided by
circumstances which, combining with the generally favourable result of his studies at Torgau, enabled him to follow
his mother's cherished wish. He matriculated in November,
1804, as *studiosus theologiæ* at the University of Wittenberg,
his anticipations of the future being, perhaps, cheered by
remembrance of the traditional recognition accorded by the
Lutheran Church to music as the handmaid of religion and by
hope that the profession of divinity might bring him facilities
of its own for the study of his beloved art. Three years of
conscientious work at Wittenberg enabled him to pass his
final examinations honourably, if not brilliantly; but the

expectation formed by his friends of his immediate appointment to a preachership remained unfulfilled, and it was not
long before he was induced by the pressure of daily need to
adopt the only alternative open to him. His trial sermon,
delivered at St. Sophia's Church, Dresden, was the last he
preached. He abandoned theology and accepted employment
as a teacher.

It is significant of the sterling worth and stubborn force of
character innate in Wieck that he should have found it
possible, as a youth of twenty-two, fresh from three years'
enjoyment of the freedom of German university life, not
only to submit patiently to the limitations inseparable from
the position of tutor in a private family, but to dedicate himself
with enthusiasm to the performance of his new duties. He
was enabled to do so, not because he underestimated his own
value, but from the very fact that an unfailing respect for
himself and the dignity of his office gave him a certain
equanimity under petty trials that might have upset the
nerve of a man of less arrogant nature. Evidence of the
earnest view he took of his obligations is to be found in a
short essay on education, entitled, "Weekly Notes on his
pupil Emil von Metzradt," written by him in the early part
of his tutor's career, in which he set forth, for the information
of the boy's parents and his own satisfaction, the principles
that guided his activity as a teacher. It is certain that his
conscientious thoroughness gained him the affectionate respect
of his pupils, though his vein of sarcastic humour and his
occasional intolerance of defects, from which his own boyhood
had been immune, may have prevented his winning their entire
confidence.

"I am far from pretending that I have found the philosopher's stone," he says, " or that I am capable of giving ideal
training and instruction, but I may claim that I have carefully
studied the business of teaching, to which I must devote a
short part of my life, without blindly attaching myself to any
so-called system, whether of ancient or modern time ; the best
means, as I believe, of approaching the wise middle path,
which is not always easily discovered. I venture, therefore,
to put down some of my thoughts on this subject. Should

they prove too crude, or even erroneous, may they remain buried in these pages!" Wieck sets forth his ideas under the three headings: physical, intellectual, and moral training. Strongly insisting, under the first, on the necessity for the young of frequent and enjoyable open-air exercise, he declares himself, under the second, equally opposed to the systems of forcing and of unduly delaying the work of actual education. "Herr Campe," he writes, "maintains in one of his treatises —and with much plausibility—that school lessons and reading, of whatever kind, are injurious to children of Emil's age; that cultivation of the child's mind by means of books should not be begun before the age of ten. I do not presume to contradict Councillor Campe, yet I find myself convinced of the contrary in Emil's case. He, as a lively child, is forgetful, careless, volatile, and impatient, and his power of attention can be developed only if he is distracted as little as possible, when at work, by his surroundings. How can this be better accomplished than by keeping his eyes fixed on his book or multiplication table? Or is nature, the child's temperament, to be allowed entirely its own way? . . .

"It is true one must have method; one must not merely be able to drill the pupil, but must take pleasure in one's calling, cultivate an animated manner, and have the power of interesting the pupil in his work. My principle is: teach a talented child anything he can understand and that attracts him, if it is likely to be useful in contributing to his development, without being over-anxious about his age. . . ."

With regard to moral education, "the most important, my maxim is: make it your central aim to train the child to become a good man, for this is the highest goal of humanity. The manifest power of the Christian faith to this end will be denied only by those who seem to have no religion at all. If it be said that children should be taught no religion before the age of ten because they cannot understand it earlier, I would say: religion, and especially in the case of children, should be a matter not merely of the understanding, but also of the heart. And again: the ideas of God, religion, and virtue are, as it were, innate in the young, innocent mind, and so much a part of it that these things will vibrate in answer to the slightest touch. Is it not better to bend the tree while it is young? to guide the heart and teach it right while it is still tender and pure? True, one must be circumspect. An over-anxious religious training, and especially frequent tedious moralising, or premature instruction in the positive doctrines of Christianity, may easily lead to irreligion. . . .

"This little essay," he concludes, probably in allusion to some candid remarks on Emil contained in the paper, "may be taken as evidence of my love for my honourable calling, for my pupil, and for truth, whose service has ever been my chief endeavour. I only desire that my words may be received in a spirit as frank as that in which they have been written, and that my heart, which is incapable of flattery and hypocrisy, may not be misjudged, even as it does not misjudge others. This would be my sufficient reward."

Although Wieck made a valuable musical acquaintance at the house of his first employer, Baron von Seckendorf, in the person of the pianoforte teacher Adolf Bargiel, with whom he formed an intimacy that was not without influence on his future career, further opportunities for the pursuit of his artistic studies did not readily present themselves in the years during which he occupied successive posts as a tutor, and at the age of twenty-five he had never heard an important public concert. All things come, however, to him who waits. He was able to attend two "academies," as concerts were then frequently called, given at Erfurt under Spohr's direction in August, 1811, and from this time was not entirely debarred from the enjoyment of listening to good music. That his first experience of this new delight was remembered by him as marking an epoch in his life may be inferred from the circumstance that a copy of the programme of August 15th, which included a Beethoven symphony and one of Spohr's duets for two violins, played by the composer with Konzertmeister Matthäi of Leipzig, was found, after his death, preserved amongst other mementos.

Friedrich's thoroughgoing devotion to his duties by no means rendered him insensible to the attraction of feminine society, and the monotony of his tutor's existence was broken by several transient romantic episodes before he made the

acquaintance of the lady who was to become his wife. He
met his destiny in the year 1814, in the person of the youthful
Marianne Tromlitz, who belonged to a musical family of the
town of Plauen, where her father occupied a position as
cantor. Her grandfather, Johann Georg Tromlitz, called to
Leipzig a few years later than our present date to fill the
part of first flutist in the Gewandhaus orchestra, was not
only a distinguished performer, but a well-known composer
for his instrument, and Marianne herself had inherited an
artistic temperament and musical talent which had been
developed to some account. Wieck's interest was soon
attracted to her, and his quickly-formed admiration strengthened his growing impatience of the restrictions incidental to
life in another man's house and his desire to establish himself
in an independent position. He found his opportunity on the
occasion of an illness that threatened his eyesight and caused
him to visit Leipzig for medical treatment. His "cure"
turned out to be a somewhat lengthy business, and it chanced
that the renewal of a former intimacy with Police-President
Streubel, an enthusiastic music-lover who had been his fellow-
student at Wittenberg, was the means of procuring him a
kind reception in some of the musical circles of the town. An
introduction to the famous critic Rochlitz, editor of the
Allgemeine Musikalische Zeitung, was followed by results that
offered particular encouragement to his artistic dreams. Rochlitz had known struggle in his youth, and had been obliged,
like Wieck, to renounce theology for tutorship. Interested to
find that the younger man had passed through difficulties
similar to those of his own early career, and attracted by his
earnestness, he offered, after listening indulgently to some of
Wieck's little songs, to publish one of them in the supplement
to a forthcoming number of his periodical, and even promised
to mention his name to the great Carl Maria von Weber, then
resident at Prague as conductor of the opera and the object
of Wieck's unbounded veneration.

"It will give me pleasure to accept Herr Wieck's songs,"
writes Weber to Rochlitz in the course of a letter dated March
14, 1815; "I regard it as a privilege that I, by my work
and endeavour, should have power to influence an upward-

striving mind and help it in its progress towards the good and the beautiful. Pray convey to him in anticipation my best thanks for this proof of his esteem."

A glance at the song of eight bars entitled "Romance," which duly appeared in the *Allgemeine Musikalische Zeitung* of April 19, 1815, does not suggest that the tutor's talent for composition was of a pronounced order, whilst perusal of the detailed criticism written by Weber a few months later for Wieck's benefit and at his request, of a set of songs numbered as Op. 7, and of a review of the same works published in the *Zeitung* of October 4, leads to the conclusion that his self-guided theoretical studies had furnished him up to this period with but a modicum of exact technical knowledge. As a matter of fact his further attempts as a composer do not—with exception of some books of technical exercises—call for serious consideration, but must be regarded merely as a further indication of the energetic spirit that delighted to try its powers in various branches of art. Wieck was, however, well satisfied with his immediate success, which convinced him that he would be able gradually to make a place for himself in the musical world, and he had not been long in Leipzig before he decided to settle there permanently, hoping to become known in time as a pianoforte teacher, a musical essay writer, a composer of songs and dances—in such capacity, in short, as would give him the status of a professional musician. He soon felt that he would be justified in bringing home a wife to share his opening prospects, and his marriage with Marianne Tromlitz, which was one of ardent affection on both sides, took place May 23, 1816, a few days after the bride had completed her nineteenth year. Thus, at the mature age of nearly thirty-one, Wieck had succeeded by sheer force of character in reaching the threshold of a career the indirect influence of which is still felt in some of the high places of art.

Evidence of the ready acceptance accorded to the Wiecks by the leading musical circle of Leipzig is afforded by the records of the Gewandhaus subscription concerts, which show that during the winter immediately following their marriage—1816–17—Marianne frequently appeared on the famous platform as a solo singer of small parts. In a general review of the earlier half of the season contained in the *Allgemeine Musikalische Zeitung* of February 26, 1817, we read : "Madame Wieck, the young wife of a resident pianoforte teacher, was heard on several occasions as second, and in Mozart's Requiem as first, soprano, and showed that she possesses, together with a resonant and agreeable voice, considerable skill, certainty, and industry." Similar favourable mention is made of later performances in March and April, and it is probable that Frau Marianne's performances, whilst contributing something towards the payment of housekeeping expenses, were of still greater indirect value to her husband by making his name more widely familiar and thus confirming the footing he had gained in Leipzig. Friedrich was no mere visionary, and the struggles of his youth, victorious as they had been in the best sense of the word, had served to strengthen his natural force of character. Side by side with his long-cherished dream of achieving some kind of artistic distinction, there dwelt within him a clear sense of his practical duties, which was accentuated in the second year of his marriage by the prospect that Marianne would shortly become a mother. Keenly desirous of placing the future of his family life upon a substantial basis, he resolved to seize a favourable opportunity and to accept from his friend Streubel the loan of a sufficient sum of money to enable him to establish himself in a double business that was attractive to him. He moved, early in 1818, to a house known as the " Hohe Lilie," situated in the new Neumarkt, where he opened a musical lending library, and, as soon as his arrangements were sufficiently complete, began to trade cautiously as a pianoforte dealer.

Many a man facing the responsibilities of family life and conscientiously bent on achieving a modest pecuniary success, who found himself obliged to enter on an apprenticeship to business under the burden of a considerable debt and at a period when his first youth was already behind him, might have been tempted to forget early dreams of personal distinction in the pursuit of fortune. Wieck, however, was not so constituted. Though not gifted with the imperious imagination which dominates the life of the genuinely creative artist, compelling him to surrender himself at all costs to its supreme need of expression, he had within him the enthusiasm for ideal aims which is of the essence of poetry, and he could never have sacrificed these for the attainment of mere worldly ease. If, perceiving that he could not keep the wolf from his door by the exercise of his musicianship only, he was able to turn his attention with characteristic energy to business, this was because he regarded his lending library as a valuable assistance to his private pursuit of art, and because he studied the pianofortes which passed through his hands, carefully noting their merits and defects, with the special object of perfecting his mechanical knowledge of the instrument around which his ambition was gradually concentrating itself into definite shape.

The period of Wieck's early residence in Leipzig is an interesting one in the history of the pianoforte. Less than fifty years had elapsed since Clementi (1752–1832), crowning the efforts and successes of famous makers of the eighteenth century, had published three sonatas (1773) composed with special view to its capabilities, thus advancing to a distinctive existence an instrument that had hitherto been regarded merely as one amongst other claviers. The remaining quarter of the century had witnessed the gradual displacement of the harpsichord from its traditional position as the concert clavier *par excellence*. A brilliant group of musicians rose to eminence—Clementi himself, Dussek, Cramer, Woelfl, Hummel, and others—who associated their art in a special manner with the instrument upon which the rivalry of the most eminent makers of Europe had become centred, and to it Beethoven dedicated many early fruits of the genius that was to secure for it a yet more glorious future. At the dawn of the nineteenth century the triumph of the pianoforte as the universally accepted instrument of the concert-room and the chamber was complete ; and the next two and a half decades, which produced the sonatas of Beethoven's second and third periods, gave it immortality. Nor was this all. The first quarter of the nineteenth century saw the rise of a coming phase of musical art. Whilst Beethoven was engaged upon the transcendent works of his later years, amongst which the five pianoforte sonatas, from Op. 101 onwards, occupy a prominent position; whilst he was quickening the forms of Haydn and Mozart with the tremendous energy of a new inspiration—an inspiration that can never grow old because it gives expression to the upward-striving instincts of mankind at large—the earliest personal notes were sounded of a new romanticism, in the development of which the piano-forte was to play an important part: the romanticism that was to fascinate music-lovers of succeeding generations in the works of Chopin, Mendelssohn, and Schumann. Weber's (1786–1826) "Concertstück" and "Invitation to the Waltz" mark the definite beginning of this new era in the literature of the pianoforte, for which the way had been prepared by much of the same master's previous activity; while the best nocturnes of his Irish contemporary, John Field (1782–1837), the inventor of a form to which Chopin was to give perman-ence, are hardly surpassed in their quality of delicate poetry, fragile though they be, by the Polish master's more developed pieces in the same style.

The great pianists of the day, the majority of them being musicians in the full meaning of the word—trained musicians, that is to say, of more or less genuine creative power—were divided into two groups which respectively represented the "Vienna" and "Clementi" schools of pianistic art. Each cultivated beauty and variety of tone; with varying method, indeed, but with like enthusiasm. The "Vienna" school—founded on the light action of the celebrated instruments by Stein and Streicher of which in 1818 Hummel, Steibelt, and Czerny, and, a little later, Moscheles, were the leading repre-sentatives—was especially admirable for purity and equality of tone, with power of minute tone-shading; for clearness, light-ness, and rapidity of execution, and for elegance of style; but was deficient in poetic capacity, and therefore in the first principle of enduring artistic life. Its innate tendency towards the superficial became more pronounced as, with the growth of the century, the public benefit-concerts of merely performing virtuosi increased in number, and it was largely responsible for the extraordinary favour accorded for many years to the pro-ductions of Herz, Döhler, and other writers of glittering commonplace or vapid sentimentality. The popularity of the

" Vienna " or " bravura " school declined with the advance of public interest in genuine art, to which, from the early thirties, Mendelssohn's influence greatly contributed.

The " Clementi " school was based upon the so-called " English " action of the pianofortes made by Broadwood, by Clementi himself, who founded the firm known later on as Collard and Collard, and by Erard of Paris, who gradually introduced into its mechanism individualities of his own. The particular features of this school, connected with the deep fall of the keys of the English instruments, were fullness and roundness, as well as variety of tone, and sustained singing power : the power, in short, of expression. Its inherent poetic capacity attracted to its principles the support of those amongst the great player-composers of the day who were essentially tone poets, and around the name of its founder, Clementi, pianist, composer, and teacher, and the originator of much that is best in the pianist's art of the twentieth century, must be associated those of Dussek, Field, Cramer, Ferdinand Ries, Ludwig Berger, and of Beethoven.

There is abundant evidence to show that Wieck followed the signs of his time with eager interest, keeping his mind open for the appreciation of whatever they might denote of import to the welfare of musical art, and especially the art of the pianist, to the service of which he had resolved to devote his future. From the very beginning of his career as a pianoforte teacher his principles were in accord with those of the Clementi school, and this in spite of the fact that he could have had little practical acquaintance with the English instruments, and, up to the winter of 1820–21, which was passed by Clementi in Leipzig, no opportunity of personal intercourse with the great pianist himself or either of his direct pupils. The influence of personal association, indeed, might well have drawn him in the other direction, if he had been a man of less independent mind, since his most important transactions as a dealer were carried on with the makers of Vienna, and his business visits to the imperial capital enabled him, as time went on, to form agreeable friendships with some of its most prominent musicians.

The Wiecks' first child, a daughter, who was christened

Adelheid, died in infancy. It became likely before long, however, that the blank left in the affections of the father and
mother would be filled, and the unborn infant became the
subject of Friedrich's most ardent longings and dreams. If, as
he hoped, his second child should also be a girl, she should be
set apart and dedicated from her birth to the service of the
divine art. Whatever talent, whatever knowledge, influence,
power, were his by Heaven's free gift or his own painful
acquirement, should be consecrated with all the devotion that
was in him to her training. She should become a shining
star in the musical firmament, a star of the first magnitude,
whose glory should make many a lesser light dim, and through
her radiance the name Wieck should yet become a name to
conjure with from one end of Europe to the other.   .

The child was born September 13, 1819, and it happened
that the first condition necessary for the accomplishment of
the father's purpose was fulfilled by the event. The longed-for
baby proved to be a girl, and was christened Clara Josephine,
her father's old friend Streubel being one of the sponsors.

No mention of Marianne's name occurs in the annals of
musical Leipzig during the two or three years that immediately succeeded her modest successes as a vocalist. She
worked as a teacher, accepting pupils for singing or the
pianoforte as they were offered her, and, by her husband's
desire, devoted an hour or two every day to pianoforte practice.
She had had lessons from Friedrich in her girlhood, and since
her marriage had again become his pupil. It was not for long
that she remained a very willing one. She was of an affectionate disposition, free from the absorbing ambition which was
Wieck's ruling passion, but possessed a strong will of her own
that would not yield to Friedrich's hard determination in
regard to matters as to which they were not agreed. Sharp
differences of opinion became more and more frequent between
the husband and wife, which, never thoroughly reconciled, were
but too ominous of the future. All the more striking, therefore, are the facts that the lessons were persevered in for
several years, and with such good result that on the departure
of Friedrich Schneider, a prominent musician and the leading
resident pianist of Leipzig, to fill a post at Dessau, Wieck's

rapidly acquired influence in musical circles enabled him to take advantage of the opening thus afforded to younger talent for the benefit of Marianne, who appeared at the Gewandhaus concert of October 10, 1821, with Ries's pianoforte concerto in E flat. Her success, combined with her position as Wieck's wife, was sufficient to procure her a similar engagement in the course of each of the two following seasons, and she played Dussek's concerto in E flat and Field's in A flat respectively on October 6, 1822, and December 13, 1823. It is a circumstance to be noted that her performances on all three occasions associated her name and, in a still more real sense, that of her husband, with the Clementi school, "the school of pianoforte singers," as it has sometimes been called.

It may be taken for granted that the public testimony of his worth as a teacher afforded by his wife's progress as a pianist gratified Friedrich, in spite of the constant dissensions between himself and Marianne which forced their lives ever farther asunder. Probably, however, his deepest satisfaction in her creditable achievements was derived from the good augury they afforded him as to the future of his hopes for his little girl. If he had been under some illusion when he proposed to Marianne that they should renew the relation of teacher and pupil which had brought them together as lovers, no long experience was necessary to dissipate it. Even if her talent had been of a more robust order than it proved, the obvious duties of her position as a young wife and mother would have presented difficulties in the way of its thorough development which her natural temperament was calculated not only to confirm, but to render insuperable. She had only moderate leisure for pianoforte practice, and inclination did not tempt her to try to make more. Her third appearance on the Gewandhaus platform was her last in public. Three little brothers arrived to keep Clara company—Alwin, born August 27, 1821; Gustav, January 31, 1823; and Viktor, February 22, 1824—whose names have but a passing interest in our story. Alwin was trained as a violinist and obtained a recognised position as an orchestral player; Viktor died before completing his fourth year.

CHAPTER II

1819—1828

Clara—Wieck and his wife separate—Wieck's success in Leipzig—His relations with Vienna—Clara becomes her father's pupil—The "Logier" system—Wieck as a pianoforte teacher—Clara's musical progress—Her first appearance in public—Wieck's second marriage.

NO sign of the precocity which is the frequent accompaniment of unusual musical talent was apparent in the little Clara during her earliest years of childhood. At the age of four she could neither speak nor understand speech, but was a quiet, solitary little maiden, absorbed, seemingly, in a mysterious inner life of her own, the nature of which might only be conjectured from the wistful expression of the large, dark eyes that gave attraction to her face, framed in an abundance of dark glossy hair, in spite of its want of child-like animation. Both father and mother were loving parents, though Friedrich could not be demonstrative even of his best affections, and Marianne had little time to devote to the caressing fondness that makes the happiness of a sensitive child. Who knows how early the little girl may have become dimly conscious of the jarring discords in the home life that were to deprive her of a mother two days before she completed her fifth year? Wieck separated from his wife after a union of eight years, a few months after her third and last appearance at the Gewandhaus subscription concerts, and on May 12, 1824, Marianne returned to her parents in Plauen, taking with her her daughter and baby son Viktor. Clara was to be brought back to Leipzig later in the year, the law court having assigned her, from the age of five, to the guardianship of her father. Frau Wieck very shortly afterwards became the wife of Adolf Bargiel, whom we have already mentioned as a pianoforte teacher and one of Wieck's early and intimate friends.

When Clara returned on September 17, 1824, to her father's house in Little Salt-street (Salzgässchen), Leipzig, to which he had moved in 1821, she came to a home which, if it were managed now and hereafter on lines of simple economy, was already to some extent a distinguished one in its degree. Though Wieck had not as yet made any great way as a teacher, his success in business had exceeded his expectations. His debt to Streubel was diminishing year by year, and he was able to look forward with confidence to a time when he should begin to accumulate some little capital of his own. He had at this date placed his musical circulating library under the care of an excellent manager, Bartolf Senff, the future founder of the publishing house of this name, but he continued personally to superintend his affairs as a dealer, and with so much enterprise and ability that his pianoforte warehouse had come to be accepted as the best in Leipzig, and the instruments required for the Gewandhaus subscription concerts were chosen as a matter of course—preferably those of Andreas Stein—from his show-rooms. His reputation as a man well acquainted with Leipzig circles, whose goodwill was therefore worth cultivation, was gradually spreading beyond the boundaries of his adopted town ; composers and executants of European fame sought his opinion on the prospects and business of their concerts more and more frequently as events proved it a safe one to follow, and his house was becoming a recognised meeting-place for established musical notabilities and rising aspirants to fame. A letter addressed to Wieck by Carl Czerny, dated May 9, 1824, may be of interest here, not only as showing the cordiality of his relations with one of the prominent musicians of Vienna, but as referring to the culminating event—the first performance of the ninth symphony—in the life of Beethoven, of whose pianoforte works the tiny girl about to commence her apprenticeship to art was to become a famous interpreter :—

" MOST ESTEEMED HERR VON WIECK,*—My silence is to be

* Analogous to the English custom of addressing letters to men with the courtesy title of Esquire was the old Viennese usage of adding the word *von*, in itself a sign of nobility, to the names of educated citizens of the middle class.

attributed not only to want of time but also to my determination not to write to you, valued friend, until after Beethoven's
long expected concert. His friends overcame a number of
real and imaginary difficulties and sent him, and even published, a memorial signed by many prominent art lovers, and
at last, the day before yesterday, the revered master gave us
the opportunity of hearing some of his newest compositions
in the Kärnthner theatre. The concert began with an
overture [Die Weihe des Hauses] given a few years since at
the opening of a suburban theatre, but quite new to me,
which, though perhaps claiming our admiration less than
Beethoven's other works in point of *originality*, is marked out
by its splendid development, fugato nearly throughout, as
almost a companion piece to Mozart's ' Zauberflöte ' overture.
This was unanimously acknowledged, and proves that the great
master is still striving to make fresh discoveries in the pro-
fundities of counterpoint. The *Kyrie* from his new Mass, that
has already met with such satisfactory recognition abroad,
followed, in D major ; indescribably effective and perhaps the
most successful setting ever composed to this text. In the
next following *Credo* was a fugue, the mere hearing of which
nearly took my breath away ($\frac{3}{2}$ time and very difficult), the
most dazzling feature of the work, which places the great
composer by the side of Handel and Sebastian Bach whilst
abating nothing of his unapproachable originality. The third
selection from the Mass (*Agnus Dei* and *Donna nobis*) seemed
less satisfactory, and the modest listener must reserve judgment of it until after repeated hearings. In conclusion his
newest and perhaps greatest symphony was performed. Here
no description is possible after a first hearing. The opening
movement dazzles the ear, just as a too fearless glance at the
sun, the eye. The scherzo, incontestably the greatest movement of its kind in existence, roused the whole house to
stormy, involuntary bursts of interrupting applause, which was
renewed after the divinely beautiful adagio, and would have
reached its climax if—the finale had been an entirely instrumental movement. The idea of introducing Schiller's ' Ode
to Joy ' set as a chorus, though beautifully conceived and
developed—but at too great length—would have been more

3

appropriate for a special fantasia. Beethoven is so great, he stands so entirely alone as an instrumental composer, that voices perhaps confine rather than inspire him. The numerous but select public showed an indescribable, but worthy and reverent enthusiasm, and proved that it is surpassed by no public in the world in its feeling for really great works of art. The large orchestra covered itself with glory and perspiration, and Umlauf conducted at Beethoven's side with a fire and devotion that do him honour both as man and artist. The programme is to be repeated next Friday in the large Redoubtensaal. . . .

" You will probably have heard particulars of the impression made on us last autumn by Moscheles and Kalkbrenner. Both pleased and entertained our public, yet not so irresistibly as to prevent one from discovering the natural limitations of their talent. Moscheles' two new concertos are very good and fulfil their aim. His playing has become more solid and may approach Hummel's perfection if his individuality should allow it. Imagination is his weak side. Kalkbrenner's playing is a finished, so to say, classical, mechanism ; his concerto in D minor pleased without making a striking impression.

" Your most sincere friend,

" CARL CZERNY."

"It seems to me only natural that Moscheles should have used an instrument by Lescher, as he has patronised him before. He extemporised once on the ruins of the English pianoforte that belonged to Beethoven (as Graf would not let him have one of his)—with more honour to the player than the instrument. Have you not been scandalised by the shocking praise my little rogue and pupil Liszt is receiving in Paris? He is overwhelmed with profit and honour and procures me the most brilliant offers in case of my going there.

" . . . Kalkbrenner played on a Graf piano. Not one of the million tones which he produced was lost, and yet no one was moved to tears. . . . The great pianoforte makers must be in despair if they wish to satisfy all these finger heroes." *

* First published by Kohut in his " Friedrich Wieck." Translated by the author from the original letter in the possession of Fräulein Marie Wieck. The oft-described scene which was witnessed at the

No time was lost by Wieck, after he had received his little daughter back into his own hands, in setting about the prosecution of the plans he had formed for her future. He commenced Clara's regular musical training on September 18th, the day after her return from Plauen, and from that time for a period of fourteen years devoted his best energies to the development of her powers and the establishment of her fame, objects which, as time went on, were found to be directly or indirectly promoted by other branches of his activity.

Feeling, perhaps, the deficiencies of his own hardly accomplished training and scanty musical experience, he had, during the first years of his professional life in Leipzig, taught the pianoforte on the " Logier " system, so called after the name of its founder—a musician of French extraction resident in Ireland—which was extraordinarily popular for a few years from 1815 onwards in some of the teaching circles of Dublin and London, and a little later, of Berlin, Leipzig, and other continental towns.   Three of its especial features were : The use of the chiroplast, a machine invented by Logier which was supposed to assist children in the acquirement of a good position of the hand and fingers on the keyboard ; a peculiar custom of class lessons which consisted in the simultaneous practice, by a number of learners, of a series of short studies of ascending difficulty, written for the purpose, of which the easier and slower were repeated over and over again by the beginners, whilst pupils who had made some progress went on to the more difficult and rapid numbers according to their powers ; progressive instruction in elementary theory and harmony in immediate association with the early teaching of the pianoforte.   Spohr, who was present, in 1820, at a meeting of one of Logier's London classes, speaks with approbation in his autobiography of the results attained by the

end of Beethoven's concert described in Czerny's letter must ever be remembered as perhaps the most profoundly touching of which musical annals have to tell. The immortal master, now stone deaf, stood, as he had stood through the performance of his transcendent work, by the conductor's side, with his back to the audience, unconscious of the enthusiasm that had been excited by his divine genius, until one of the singers, Mademoiselle Unger, touched him and caused him to look round to see the applause that he could not hear.

simultaneous practice of more than twenty children between the ages of seven and ten, and expresses unmitigated astonishment at the readiness with which even the youngest pupils worked out the difficult paper exercises that he set as a test of their powers. The system, as such, had its day and was heard of no more, but whatever it may have contained of real worth survived in the teaching of its more intelligent early supporters, of whom Friedrich Wieck was one of the foremost. He especially incorporated into his own method, gradually formed as his experience became matured, that most valuable characteristic of Logier's, the immediate combination of theory with practice in the teaching of the pianoforte to beginners; and thus educated his youngest pupils not merely as future executants, but as incipient musicians.

The training that was to produce such happy results in the case of little Clara was marked, from its earliest stages, by humanity and imaginative insight. Wieck set himself in the first place to awaken the musical sensibility which, as he fondly hoped, might be latent in the child; and from the moment when it began to declare itself he aimed at directing its development by means correspondent with the processes of natural growth, striving to prepare his little daughter for the career, not of a youthful prodigy, but of a soundly equipped artist.

A judicious use of the Logier class system on a scale adapted to her age helped the five-year-old Clara over some of her peculiar difficulties. After a few weeks' preparation, Wieck supplemented her practice of the little five-finger exercises of the first position, that had been carried on every day under his guidance, by associating her with two other children and teaching the little party of three to apply in class lessons the separate instruction by which he carried each pupil from point to point of progress. The advantage derived by Clara from this youthful companionship was soon apparent in her increased power of talking and of understanding what was said to her, and from this period, whilst her general development proceeded rapidly, the signs of her natural musicality became constantly more pronounced. She readily learnt by ear the progressive tunes which her father wrote for her use, and retained them in her memory with unconscious ease. Five-finger exercises, the major and minor scales, and the triads with their inversions formed, in addition to these tunes, the material of her studies during her first year of training— in the second half of which the class lessons, having served their purpose, were discontinued—and they were learnt and practised without either help or hindrance from printed music book.

It was part of Wieck's method to exercise a beginner for a very considerable time on the pianoforte before beginning the teaching of written notes; an order of procedure no doubt partly dictated by a wise desire to make the early stages of instruction pleasant to the learner, but which had an essential and intimate connection with the method as a whole, and with its author's conception of what a teacher's aim should be: the continuous direction of the pupil's physical and mental capacity along certain lines of growth, leading inevitably, in the case of even but moderate talent, to some amount of healthy artistic fruition. The earliest immediate means by which the great end was to be pursued by the teacher were: to induce in the pupil, whilst establishing in his fingers the beginning of an intimate acquaintance with the keyboard, the habit, which should gradually become automatic, of keeping his hands in good position and of striking the keys with a correct movement of each and every finger; to assist the development of his musical ear and, therewith, of his inner imaginative appreciation of musical tone and rhythm; to make clear to him, as far as possible, the theoretical basis underlying each important step of his progress in pianoforte practice.

These main objects were followed by Wieck, during the first two years of Clara's musical training, with the unbroken logic that his position as her father made possible, and with a devotion to the child's best interests that has rarely been witnessed under similar circumstances, and the results were rapid and certain. Whilst all forcing was carefully avoided, the little pupil felt constantly encouraged by her childish consciousness of her own progress, and was never disappointed or delayed by having to go back over a false step in the course of her instruction. She began to play from notes in the

autumn of 1825, soon after completing her sixth year, and after
a few months was able to learn all her new pieces from book,
advancing step by step from easy duets and solos to suitable
works, or arrangements of works, for four hands by Czerny,
Cramer, Müller, Mozart, Moscheles, Field, and even Weber.
Arrived at a certain point, it became her duty to supplement
her hour's daily lesson by practising alone every day at
intervals for a length of time which was gradually increased
to two hours in all.

The beginning of 1827 marked a period in her advance.
Two years and a half of Wieck's skilful and prudent training
of fingers and brain had produced definite signs that promised
well for the future. The fingers had acquired a sensible
amount of strength, certainty, and individuality; little Clara
was beginning to have a " touch "; her ear had considerably
developed in its perception of pitch; whilst her knowledge of
keys and chords not only extended from the principal triads—
tonic, dominant, and subdominant—to the diminished sevenths
of every key, but allowed her to modulate from one key to
another as she was desired. Such good progress was rewarded
by outward and visible signs of her father's approbation.
Clara was permitted, and even required, to lengthen her
practice time, part of which was devoted, as a matter of
course, to finger exercises, scales, and other progressive fundamental work, and was further promoted to the study of a
concerto, Hummel in G major, Op. 73. With this she progressed so satisfactorily that in a few months' time she was
able to begin another, Mozart in E flat; and the event of
the year was reached on September 9, a few days before her
eighth birthday, when she performed the last named work
before an invited audience, accompanied by a band of eight
instruments, in which Concertmeister Matthäi, already mentioned as of the Gewandhaus orchestra, played first violin.
From this date she took her place as the child pianist of her
father's circle and became a familiar and favourite figure at
private musical gatherings at home or elsewhere, to the programmes of which she frequently contributed; sometimes
joining her father in a pianoforte duet, sometimes playing a
solo, and occasionally undertaking the important rôle of

pianist in some concerted work of chamber music suited to her powers. A fortnight's holiday visit to Dresden, made in Wieck's care, in the summer of 1828, afforded opportunity for the exercise of her talent before some of the music lovers of the Saxon capital, and on October 20 of the same year she made her first public appearance at a concert given by a Fräulein Perthaler of Graz in the Leipzig Gewandhaus. On this important occasion she performed the treble of a pianoforte duet with her father's favourite professional pupil, already known in Leipzig as an excellent pianist, with whom she had been in the habit of playing at home, and under these reassuring circumstances, went through her part with all desirable aplomb, creating a most favourable impression. The critic of the *Allgemeine Musikalishe Zeitung* wrote concerning the event: "It was with particular pleasure that we listened to the performance of the very talented, nine-year-old Clara Wieck, with whom was associated Demoiselle Emilie Reichold, in Kalkbrenner's variations for four hands on a march from ' Moses.' Under the guidance of her experienced father, who is especially distinguished by his knowledge of the art of pianoforte playing and the enthusiasm with which he devotes himself to its furtherance, her future may be anticipated with the highest hopes."

The story of an adventure, recalled occasionally by Frau Schumann in after years, and related by Litzmann, which went near to mar the success of the evening, seems to bring clearly before the mind the childish presence of the dark-eyed maiden in white who stood, eager and unconscious, ready to make her entrance into the great world for which she had been destined before her birth and in which she was to fulfil an illustrious career. Clara, ready dressed for the concert and summoned for the start, entered a strange coach that was standing before the house door and in which some other children were seated, and was driven away in the wrong direction some minutes before the mistake could be rectified. Overtaken by the Gewandhaus carriage and arriving, at length, terribly frightened and in tears, at the concert hall, she was met by her father, who, giving her a sugar plum, quieted her excitement with the words: "I quite forgot to tell you that every one is carried off by strangers before playing for the first time in public, Clärchen ! ''

Clara had now been for four years her father's pupil, and if Wieck, contemplating her musical progress with unmixed pride, felt that her successful *début* at the Gewandhaus warranted him in looking forward with some assurance to the fulfilment of his special hopes for her future, he had reason to be well satisfied also with the course of her general development both of body and mind. Her early difficulties surmounted, she became a healthy, lively child, fond of the society of young companions, especially of those who were somewhat her senior, full of interest in what went on around her, accepting without question the fact that music was her particular business in life, and happy in the varied occupation and privilege it brought her. She showed early signs of the possession of a strong will, but, though occasionally inclined to question even her father's ordinances, yielded him on the whole the exact obedience that he demanded, and that resulted naturally from the peculiar tie existing between them. Wieck, as we have seen, was rarely demonstrative of affection, but Clara lived in all his thoughts and deeds and filled his heart and his life. In the spring of 1827, to which we have referred as marking a period in her musical training, he began to keep a diary in her name, bringing it up to date by noting down the particular events of her eight years of life from the day of her birth. The work—which is prefaced by the following words in his writing : '' My diary, begun by my father, May 7, 1827, and to be continued by Clara Josephine Wieck:'' and which was so continued until a very few weeks before Frau Schumann's death—contains occasional laconic reference to Clara's shortcomings, inserted, no doubt, with a view to her edification and improvement. An unusually grave situation seems to have arisen shortly after her appearance at the Gewandhaus : '' My father, who has long vainly hoped for a change of mood on my part, remarked again to-day that I am still so idle, negligent, unmethodical, self-willed, &c., especially in pianoforte playing and practising . . . that he tore the copy [of Hünten's variations] in pieces before my eyes, and from to-day will not give me another lesson, and I may only play the scales, Cramer's Études L. 1, and Czerny's exercises on the shake." * This severe sentence was recalled six days later on Clara's solemn promise of amendment, and we may be certain that the small offender was not the only person to feel relieved at the reconciliation.

Clara, who attended school with fair regularity from the age of six, was, as might be expected, quick and intelligent at her ordinary lessons, but it was recognised that her musical studies were of paramount importance and that other subjects must give way to them if necessary. She was mistress of a considerable répertoire of tunes before beginning the study of the alphabet, and was already versed in the writing of notes when she was first set to the tracing of her German pot-hooks. Wieck was indeed too intelligent and farseeing to withhold from his daughter the advantages of an ordinary schoolgirl's education, but neither during her childhood nor afterwards did he encourage in her a taste for books. "My father never allowed me to read," Frau Schumann once said to the present author, with, perhaps, a tinge of regret in her tone. There is no doubt that Wieck acted in this matter from conviction and that his conduct was partly guided by care for Clara's health. He never lost sight of the fact that effective musical practice makes demands upon the various mental and bodily powers that are hardly equalled by those of any other study ; that the training of the young musician involves the simultaneous exercise, for several hours daily, not only of eyes, ears, and fingers, but of intellect and ima-gination ; and that, if musical and not merely mechanical results are to be obtained, the work must be done when the faculties are fresh and the attention alert and interested. He never allowed Clara " to practise herself to death musically " ; i.e., to dull her artistic sensibility by long-continued labour at technical difficulties ; nor did he permit her to come to her practice fatigued or preoccupied with other pursuits. A great part of her recreation time was passed out of doors, and Clara, who was a capital walker, had no reluctance to over-come when the hour arrived for the open-air exercise that formed so important a part of the routine prescribed by the

* Litzmann's " Clara Schumann," i. 16.

master of the household for all its members. If, as she grew older, books had little share in the formation of her tastes, their place was to a considerable extent supplied not only by visits to the concert-room and theatre, with both of which she became familiar at a very early age, but by the special circumstances of her daily life. Whilst her father success-fully aimed at keeping her an unspoiled child through the natural years of childhood, her mind could not fail to receive a decisive impress from the frequent personal contact with men and women of distinction that was secured to her by her early recognised talent.

It seems likely that, possessed not only of unusual intelli-gence, but of very strong affections that craved the satis-faction of the outward signs of love, Clara may have been subdued at times, child as she was, by a longing for the mother and the mother's tenderness that were absent from her life. With all her vivacity there was a suggestion of melancholy about her that answered to the pathetic ex-pression of her eyes, and to which her father refers in the diary as " a strange tendency not to take pleasure in the present . . . seldom to appear satisfied." Her first little letter was written to her mother in Berlin, and whom, as she grew older, she kept well informed of her doings, though she was not spared from home to visit her. So far as an absent mother's place can be filled, it was faithfully supplied to Clara by her father's second wife, Clementine Fechner, whom he married in 1828 at the age of forty-three, when his little girl was nearly nine. This lady, twenty years younger than her husband, belonged to a family of distinguished culture. Her father, a pastor, was esteemed for the exceptional liberality of his views, and her two brothers became eminent, each in his own line: Eduard, who was long resident in Paris, as a painter ; and Gustav Theodor, a university professor of Leipzig, as a thinker and philosopher. A few lines, written by Wieck a fortnight after his marriage, to Andreas Stein, hint at some of the causes which induced him to risk the chances of matri-mony a second time :—

" DEAR FRIEND,—I was married on July 3rd to my dear Clementine Fechner, and we went to Dresden the next day—

yesterday we returned, and to-day I write to beg for your congratulations on the sudden event. I had been considering the matter for three years and had been wholly unable to make a choice. My children, my house, and I myself will now, if I mistake not, be splendidly cared for." *

This marriage was a thoroughly happy one. Clementine adapted herself in every respect to her husband's wishes, cared for her stepchildren with untiring affection, and was as proud of Clara's talent as Wieck himself could desire. She had three children of her own : Clemens, who died at the age of two, Marie, and Cecilia. Marie succeeded Clara as her father's pupil and became an eminent pianist.

* Kohut's " Friedrich Wieck."

CHAPTER III

1828–1829

Robert Alexander Schumann—Early manifestation of musical and literary talent—Schooldays—A student of law at the university of Leipzig—His pianoforte lessons from Wieck—First meeting with Clara—He leaves Leipzig—Paganini.

AS may be inferred from the notice of Clara's *début* quoted, in the last chapter, from the *Allgemeine Musikalische Zeitung*, Wieck had, at this time, quite made good his title to be considered one of the best pianoforte teachers of Leipzig, and letters addressed to him by the parents or friends of pupils who came from a distance to profit by his tuition show that he proved, not only an invaluable instructor, but a very kind friend, to the young people who were placed more or less under his temporary guardianship. His personal association with the Gewandhaus had been maintained, after his separation from his first wife, through the successful performances of Fräulein Emilie Reichold, who, after her first appearance in the winter of 1826 with Beethoven's E flat concerto, was heard regularly once or twice a year at the great subscription concerts until her marriage and retirement in 1830; and his frequent journeys on the business of his pianoforte trade, during which he never lost sight of his plans for Clara's future, had given him insight into the circumstances of German musical circles, and procured him influential acquaintances likely to be useful when the time should be ripe for the fuller development of his favourite designs.

It happened in the summer of 1828 that a highly-gifted young musical amateur who was keeping his first term as a law student at the university of Leipzig offered himself as a pupil to the genial teacher and was accepted by him. The youth in question, Robert Alexander Schumann, born June 8, 1810, at Zwickau, in Saxony, was the son of a bookseller, Friedrich August Gottlob Schumann, of literary taste and ability, and was, perhaps, as little suited for his destined vocation as ever any young man who has been required by parent or guardian to master the dry details of Roman and Saxon law, and of other unattractive branches of German jurisprudence. Imaginative and emotional, enthusiastic and impulsive, sensitive and reserved, shrinking from contact with the commonplaces of life, a born poet, and dominated by the poet's irresistible need of expression, the circumstances of his early youth had been ill adapted to prepare him for the exercise of the self-repression, or, indeed, positive self-abnegation, which must have been the condition of his successful pursuit of a study in the highest degree distasteful to him. As the youngest and most gifted of a family of five children, attractive, generous, and keenly affectionate, he had been from infancy the admired darling of the home circle and its intimates, and the early signs he showed of the possession of literary and musical talent gave him, as he grew towards youth, something of the position of a local celebrity. He learned the pianoforte from his seventh year of a musician, Baccalaureus Kuntsch, who occupied an official position in Zwickau, and soon made sufficient progress to be able to follow a natural impulse to compose at the instrument. At the age of twelve he directed a small orchestra formed from among his playmates, supplementing it when necessary on the pianoforte, and preparing arrangements of easy works, and occasionally an original composition, for its use. His extempore pianoforte playing was a source of ever-increasing delight to the few privileged friends before whom he consented to perform, whilst his frequent musical contributions to the weekly entertainments arranged by the pupils of the Zwickau gymnasium, which he attended from his tenth year, were accepted, as he grew older, as the most brilliant features of the functions.

He was barely fifteen when his music teacher, whose influence he had long outgrown, refused to give him any more lessons, and shortly after this event his father opened negotiations with Carl Maria von Weber in pursuance of the boy's desire to be trained as an artist. They were abandoned, however, probably in deference to his mother's strongly expressed opinion, and from this time for a period of several years Robert's musical development was guided by the promptings of his talent, aided only by the opportunities he derived from his intimacy in the few musical houses to be found in Zwickau ; notably in that of Herr Carl Erdmann Carus, a distinguished amateur violinist. In this gentleman's circle, where the names of Haydn, Mozart, and Beethoven were cherished as those of household gods, he was able to breathe the congenial atmosphere of musical family life that was absent from his home, and in the Carus's house he first heard and took part in performances of many of the great works of chamber music, a domain he was one day to enrich with original treasure.

Side by side with Robert's absorbing affection for the ideal tone world in which he had thus from earliest childhood found expression for his thoughts, there had grown in him a natural love of letters which, nourished from the abundant store of literature at his command in the bookshop, and encouraged by his father's warmest sympathy, had impelled him not only to the habitual cultivation of his mind by reading, but also to a rather precocious exercise of his powers in authorship. He wrote little comedies in verse for home production in his ninth year and made his first appearance in print in his fifteenth, contributing to one of his father's publications : " Picture Gallery of the Most Famous Men of all Nations and Epochs." As time went on he amused himself by translating from the classics, produced many original songs and occasional poems, and made considerable progress with a work on the æsthetics of musical art. At sixteen he drew up the statutes of a " literary association " which he formed with some of his schoolfellows for the study of German literature. At the meetings, generally held under his presidency, biographies of great men and masterpieces of poetry and prose were read aloud, obscure passages discussed, and poems proposed for criticism. That Robert regarded the society not only as a source of pleasure and instruction, but as a possible training-school for the profession of letters, may be inferred from a remark contained in his paper of laws : " Uz, Cramer, Kleist, Hagedorn, and other great men whose names will be inscribed in golden letters in the history of German literature, were produced from similar societies."

The early death of his only sister Emilie in 1826 made a profound impression on his imagination, and the loss of his good father a few months later produced in him a tempest of feeling that prevented him for a while from deriving solace from his favourite pursuits :—

" The whole year went by as a dream," he wrote later in his memorandum book. " Two beloved beings were torn from me. . . . I railed then at destiny ; now I can contemplate everything more calmly, and see, I acknowledge it openly, that destiny has been justified. . . . I have experienced much—I have learnt to know life. In a word, I have become inwardly clearer." *

His first acquaintance with the writings of Jean Paul Richter, some of whose works were read aloud during the summer of 1827 at the meetings of the literary association, marked the beginning of an epoch in Robert's existence. Recognising in the spirit and form of this master's style a close affinity with his own nature, he gave himself up unreservedly to the fascination of his discovery, and henceforward Jean Paul became a leading influence in his life. How essentially such an affinity was grounded in his own nature is shown by the fact that the influence of his acquaintance with Jean Paul's writings on his own literary style is to some extent anticipated in his early memorandum books, the contents of which, notwithstanding their immaturity of diction, frequently exhibit a striking resemblance to the manner of the famous romanticist. The reading of "Hesperus," " Titan," &c., confirmed and developed a natural tendency, and the letters written by Robert to his friend Flechsig immediately after his first perusal of these works are already veritable Jean-Pauliads in which the whimsical caprice, the extravagant sentimentality, and the redeeming undercurrent of ironical humour that characterise the author's style are successfully reproduced.

* Wasielewski's " Robert Schumann," 4th edition, p. 24.

Robert at seventeen had already more than once sacrificed at the altar of feminine charm, but the two girls, Nanni Patsch and Liddy Hemper who were alternately the more or less unconscious objects of his adoration seem rather to have been representative lay figures necessary for the exercise of his poetic sensibility than objects of his serious affection, and it was not long before their images were obscured to his fancy through his introduction to Frau Agnes Carus, a relation of his Zwickau friends, who, as an amateur vocalist of exceptional gifts, excited in him an enthusiastic platonic admiration of which he darkly hints in his letters to Flechsig. That he did not as yet take himself very seriously in such matters is evident in the tone of persiflage that runs through his confidences to his friend :—

"My poetic mill," he writes in July, 1827, "is standing quite still at present. Either there is too much water, so that the wheels are disturbed and prevented from grinding well-formed poetic twopenny rolls, or there is no water to set the wheels in motion. To be enabled to climb the sunny Pindus one must have a friend, a beloved, and—a glass of champagne. I no longer have either of the three here. Liddy is a narrow-hearted soul . . . if one could turn her into the white marble Anadyomene of a Carlsbad spring every true and fine connoisseur of art must declare her to be a female beauty, but she must be of stone—she must not speak. . . . I have not concealed from you or others that she pleases me—I believe I loved her—but I only knew her form, from which the roseate imagination of youth generally draws conclusions as to the soul. I have, therefore, no longer a beloved, but I am now forming other ideals. *Perhaps* I may explain this point to you by word of mouth. . . . Nanni was, indeed, the most glorious maiden. If I cherish the flames of a glowing love for her with less ardour than formerly, they have passed into the still, sacred glow of a divine friendship, esteem, a sort of Madonna reverence." *

As, with the approaching termination of his school career, the question of his future vocation became pressing, Robert's sense of the irreparable loss he had sustained by his father's

* "Jugendbriefe," p. 4.

death was painfully revived. His mother, the daughter of a provincial pastor, conventional in her ideas and of inconsiderable culture, had habitually petted and spoiled him in small things, but, without appreciation for the exceptional quality of his gifts, was unable in this all-important matter to rise above the prejudices in which she had been educated. She was inflexible in her determination that her favourite child, who evidently had no turn for business, should choose one of the learned professions, in either of which she hoped he might earn a competence; a determination that was acquiesced in by her elder sons, now in partnership as booksellers, and steadily supported by Robert's guardian, a well-to-do merchant of Zwickau. The result was a foregone conclusion. Robert, whose gentle personality had obtained for him the pet name of "Fridolin," by which he was known to the friends of the Carus household, had been accustomed to get his own way in the family circle by means of affectionate persuasion, harmless jest, or quiet persistence, and found himself incapable of sustaining a serious conflict with those he loved best. He agreed to study law, and after successfully passing his final school examination and matriculating as *studiosus juris* at the university of Leipzig, he settled down in lodgings with Flechsig, already a student of theology at the same seat of learning, though he shrank from the prospect before him with an aversion that was deepened by his consciousness of having committed himself to the first step in a course of life sacrifice. If his mother allowed herself to entertain any doubt as to the future success of her plans, she can hardly have been reassured by the contents of a letter dated May 21, 1828, that she received from him a few days after his arrival in Leipzig :—

"Where can I find nature here ? " he says ; " no valley, no hill, no forest where I can give myself up to my own thoughts; no place where I can be alone unless I am bolted into my own room, underneath which there is constant noise and confusion. It is this that prevents me from being contented. And then there is the eternal inward struggle against the selection of a study. Cold jurisprudence, which crushes one at the very beginning with its icy definitions, cannot satisfy

4

me; medicine I will not, and theology I cannot, choose. I am thus in perpetual conflict with myself, and look in vain for a guide capable of telling me what I ought to do. And yet—it cannot be helped. I must stick to jurisprudence; cold and dry as it is, I *will* overcome, and if a man only *will* he can accomplish anything. Philosophy and history shall, at any rate, be included among my principal studies. Enough of the subject. All will be well, and I will not look forward with dismal apprehension to a future which may be so happy if I do not waver. . . ."

But nature proved stronger than good resolutions, never, perhaps, very rigorously entertained. Robert found one or two congenial spirits among the university students, young men with tastes and enthusiasms similar to his own; he joined a Burschenschaft, or students' society, which enabled him to greet an acquaintance occasionally in the club-room or on the fencing-ground; he took lessons in fencing; he attended lectures on philosophy and was attracted, by what he heard, to the study of Kant, Fichte, and Schelling; and he listened outside the door of the lecture-room on one or two occasions to part of a discourse by the learned professor of jurisprudence. Herewith the tale of his academic pursuits is complete. He worked—but at music; played, composed, derived fresh inspiration from the performances he heard at private assemblies of the university professor, Dr. Carus, and especially from the singing of this gentleman's wife, Frau Agnes, and, after making Wieck's acquaintance at their house, took full advantage of the opportunities for musical enjoyment it afforded him. That his playing, though it was the playing of an amateur, made a striking impression at this period on those qualified to judge of it may be inferred from a few words written to his mother in August :—

"I am a good deal with Wieck, my pianoforte teacher, and have daily opportunity at his house of becoming acquainted with the most distinguished musicians of Leipzig. I often play duets with the best pianiste, Demoiselle Reichold, and shall, perhaps, perform a concerto for four hands with her at one of the great winter concerts." *

* " Jugendbriefe," p. 33.

Wieck did not, indeed, remain long in doubt as to the musical endowments of his new pupil, who soon became an extraordinary favourite with him, in spite of the fact that Robert, who had never been properly grounded in the elements of his beloved art, or shown himself willing to persevere even in such fundamental study as Kuntsch had been capable of advising, proved extremely restive when his present master insisted on the necessity of restraint in his performances, and demanded of him the careful, deliberate practice of mechanism in all its details as the indispensable preliminary to finished artistic performance.   Wieck administered his counsels with invariable kindness and patience, if with undeviating firmness; and, exceptionally indulgent in this case, scarcely showed resentment when Robert gave vent to his irritation by sending excuses for his absence on several successive lesson days. Even after the wayward pupil had become partially convinced of the good results to be obtained by methodical finger-training, he was not to be persuaded to avail himself of the moderate amount of theoretical instruction which his master combined with practical teaching, but, in spite of occasional good resolutions, continued to extemporise and compose in complete ignorance of the laws of harmony and thorough bass; in his own words, " as a simple pupil of nature." His productive activity in this capacity was considerable during his first year at Leipzig, in the course of which he completed numerous songs with pianoforte accompaniment, solos and duets for pianoforte, and a quartet for pianoforte and strings. When it is added that he held weekly meetings in his rooms for the practice of chamber music and the discussion of musical matters, it will be clear that little time or energy can have remained at his disposal for application to the study of law. The death of Schubert, whose songs and published pianoforte works had become known to him in the autumn of 1827, shortly after his first acquaintance with the writings of Jean Paul, and who had since lived in his heart by the side of the famous author, affected him as that of a personal friend, moving him even to tears; and one of the great events of his first year in Leipzig was his performance with his friends Knorr and Täglichsbeck, after very special practice, of the master's E flat Trio before a select party of guests, among whom Wieck stood foremost.

The relation of master and pupil between Wieck and young Schumann, the continuance of which, in spite of its difficult moments, had been rendered possible by mutual appreciation and regard, was terminated by Wieck in February, 1829, on account of the pressure of his engagements, and in view of the fact that his pupil would, in any case, soon take a long farewell of Leipzig. Robert had persuaded himself that he would be better able to adjust his mind to legal study if he could carry it on for a time under the celebrated jurist and well-known musical amateur, A. F. J. Thibaut, university professor of Heidelberg. The town was attractive to his fancy from its romantic situation and its convenient position as a point of departure for Switzerland and Italy, countries in which he hoped one day to travel. He had succeeded in winning both his mother and his guardian to the opinion that the desired change of residence would be favourable to his advance in professional knowledge, and was to proceed to Heidelberg in May, with the special object of profiting by Thibaut's lectures on Roman law and the Pandects, branches which the famous jurist was supposed to treat with peculiar insight and lucidity.

It seems, on first thoughts, not a little surprising that no mention of Clara is to be found in the letters written by Robert during his early visit to Leipzig; but deliberate study of his published correspondence affords an adequate explanation of the circumstance. Whilst he was naturally prone to view outward events through the medium of emotion, he was, at nineteen, passing through an acute stage of his *Sturm und Drang* period, and was without the strengthening influence that might have been supplied him by regular work in a congenial field of labour for the attainment of a definite end. For the moment, torn by the struggle between the unconquerable instinct that attracted him to art and the consciousness that he was not doing his duty by his mother, he was entirely self-engrossed and unable to feel sustained interest in what did not immediately concern his own affairs and feelings. Clara's life was passed in a daily routine of

school-work, musical study, and open-air exercise; she was
too young a child to be made the subject of sentimental
outpourings, whilst Robert in his present dilemma was
capable of little else. Yet a sentence in a letter of many
years later, in which Robert recalls his first meeting with
Clara—who, a little girl, sitting at a table laboriously writing
a copy, looked at him furtively now and again with big
dark eyes—seems to suggest that some subtle wave of
sympathy may have passed between them even at this
early date. It can hardly be doubted, at any rate, that the
proof which was constantly afforded him of the excellence
of Wieck's method by Clara's rapid progress, and by the
charm which already distinguished her playing, had its influence on his mind and helped to convince him of the
value of systematic training. He diligently applied himself
after leaving Leipzig to the practice of mechanism, and
pursued it later on with an ardour that brought calamity
in its train.

Newspaper announcements early in 1829 that arrangements
had been made for the first North German concert tour of
the violinist Nicolo Paganini, then about twenty-five years
of age, were welcomed by artists and amateurs of Dresden,
Leipzig, and Berlin with the excited interest that followed
the movements of this extraordinary man throughout his
public career, and that especially resulted in this instance
from the reports of the phenomenal triumphs achieved by him
in Vienna in the spring of the preceding year. The first
four concerts of the northern tour, given in the Dresden court
theatre, created the expected sensation, and the news which
spread through the audience assembled for the Leipzig
Gewandhaus concert of February 12th, that Paganini had
arrived in the town with his manager that very afternoon,
and had put up at the Hôtel de France—but only *en route*
for Berlin—excited a general eager desire to hear him without
delay. Wieck, whose usual strong interest in musical men
and matters had been intensified to fever heat with regard to
Paganini by private letters from Vienna, immediately resolved
to take time by the forelock, and hastening with a friend to
the Hôtel de France, he succeeded in inducing the illustrious

Italian to prolong his stay for four or five days, in order that the opportunity for applauding his genius so earnestly desired by his would-be admirers in Leipzig might be arranged. Paganini, however, after announcing that he would give an orchestral concert in the hall of the Gewandhaus, left for Berlin on the morning of February 16th, the day on which it was to have taken place; and no little party spirit was evoked by the conflicting newspaper accounts of the reason of his abrupt departure, which was actually caused by a misunderstanding between his agent and the Gewandhaus committee. Wieck, determined not to miss a long-desired opportunity, went off to attend the concerts in Berlin, and returned with an overwhelming impression of the artist's powers. Paganini's dazzling treatment of his instrument; the extraordinary virtuosity of his bowing and manipulation of the fingerboard; the novelty of his style of staccato playing; the marvellous brilliancy of his presto; his double-stopping and unequalled command of harmonics and double harmonics; the great beauty of his renderings in widely contrasted styles of music; above all, the exquisite quality of his cantabile, soft and moving as the cantilena of an Italian singer, were dilated on to the circle at 36, Grimmaische Gasse, the Wiecks' dwelling-house at this date, with an enthusiasm that riveted the attention of the listeners, and awakened in Clara especially a lively desire to hear the extraordinary man who was the subject of her father's panegyrics. She had not to wait long for the fulfilment of her wish. Paganini, after informing himself through his manager later on in the year of the exact conditions attaching to the hire of the Gewandhaus concert-room, engaged the Leipzig theatre for a series of concerts, which were duly advertised for October 5th, 9th, 12th, and 16th.

Who so happy as Clara when, on the day before the first concert, she was taken by her father to call on the famous *maestro!* It did not even greatly matter that the hotel pianoforte on which she played him a polonaise of her own composition was old and worn, since he praised her musicality and said she had a genuine gift for art. That she was to be allowed to attend all his concerts had been

a matter of course ; but what a glorious privilege to be included
with her father, at two of them, amongst the invited guests
who occupied seats on the stage ! Perhaps of the many
delights of this festival week the greatest were those of
the rehearsals, at one and all of which she was welcome.
Who shall say whether father or daughter felt most pride
and satisfaction when the renowned artist, the observed of
all observers, on more than one occasion singled out his
incipient youthful colleague for special attention, presented
her to some critics from outside Leipzig, and allowed her
to introduce to him some of her own particular grown-up
musician friends? A second pianoforte performance on an
instrument sent from Wieck's warehouse to replace the old
one belonging to the hotel served to make Paganini acquainted
with a rondo based on some of his own themes by one of
Wieck's friends, and, at a farewell interview, the great man
again made Clara happy by contributing a graceful autograph
inscription to her album.

Paganini's performances made a deep impression on Clara,
who, at ten years of age, was sufficiently developed to enjoy
the beauties, and wonder at the strangeness, of his art. It is
probably not too much to say that the few days she passed in
the exciting atmosphere that is now and then produced by
the presence of a man or woman of magnetic personality, who
stands acclaimed before a crowd of fascinated admirers, first
brought to her some measure of real consciousness of the
possibilities of her own future. Long accustomed to play, at
her father's bidding, in the private circles of his intimate
friends, she had, on the evening of her one public appearance
a year ago, taken her place on the Gewandhaus platform at
Fräulein Reichold's side with a child's fearless pleasure in the
mere fact that she was prominently associated with her elders
in proceedings of importance. Henceforward the memory of
Paganini's genius and its victories helped her partially to
realise the meaning of the ambitious hopes which her father
had centred in her talent, and encouraged her to do her part
as a loving and confiding child by accepting the responsibilities
as well as the pleasures they brought her.

We close our incidental allusions to the illustrious violinist, whose individuality was sufficiently strong to have retained something of its personal interest during the lives of the three generations of musicians who have been born and have grown to maturity since his death in 1840, by quoting from an article on his Leipzig concerts of the *Allgemeine Musikalische Zeitung* of October 21, 1829. The extract, which records the immediate personal impressions of a prominent critic of the day, has some value as a supplement to the tradition that represents Paganini, with whose genius a touch of charlatanism was no doubt mingled, as a man of weird and ghostlike appearance, with hesitating gait and eccentric manners, whose personality gave colour to the extraordinary and absurd rumours that were circulated during his life : as that he had undergone a long term of imprisonment for crime, or had obtained his phenomenal successes by selling himself to the devil :—

" Paganini's outward appearance has, to our thinking, nothing repellent, but, on the contrary, something attractive about it. He certainly looks pale and sickly, but by no means gloomy, and it is only when he is intellectually in repose that there is any trace of this in his countenance or demeanour. His coal-black eye has an extremely benevolent expression ; in conversation, while maintaining a suitable dignity, he is very lively ; has polite manners without troubling himself much about outward formality. For the rest, his bearing is suggestive of a natural sincerity and modesty united with the earnestness and consciousness of solid achievement that belong essentially to a genuine man. His entry before the public here was by no means halting, as it has been described elsewhere, but firm and rapid, as though his arrival had been delayed."

CHAPTER IV

1830–1831 ·

Clara's performances before the court and private musical circles of Dresden —Schumann at Heidelberg—Law or music?—Decision referred to Wieck—Schumann returns to Leipzig—Clara's first appearances as a concert-giver in Leipzig and Dresden.

THE first two months of 1830 went by unmarked by any event of special importance in Clara's life. The days were passed in their usual busy regularity. The aspect of her home remained unchanged. Strangers and friends came and went as they were accustomed to do; the little brothers learned their lessons and played their games; the stepmother presided over domestic matters with quiet efficiency and conformed in all respects to her husband's ideas of wifely duty; the head of the house, confident in bearing, lithe of figure, arrogant of speech, directed his affairs at home and abroad with his wonted capacity for success, bright and happy in the exercise of authority that was rarely questioned, the consciousness of substantial achievement duly recognised, and the anticipation of a fast approaching time ripe for the accomplishment of still higher hopes. And Clara? Eager and affectionate, simple and natural, ardent at work and at play, stirred in a childlike manner by her own ambitious dreams, quietly self-possessed with strangers, easily moved to tears in matters of feeling, docile, yet cherishing in the unfolded depths of her nature the strong will that asserted itself now and then in refractory speech or perverse behaviour to the stepmother whom she nevertheless respected and loved, of keen intelligence and passionate heart—what prophet, perceiving the possibilities of her nature and comparing them with the circumstances of her child-life, would have hesitated

to foretell a conflict in store for her in the years to come,
or to declare, looking at her strangely pathetic eyes, that
neither ambition nor the instinct of filial obedience would
prove strongest within her to decide a coming struggle? Clara,
unconscious as yet of the very existence of the mysterious,
eternal force that was by and by to overwhelm her existence,
was to be brought into sight of the main issues of her destiny,
to be touched perceptibly by the influence that was to direct
her future to weal or to woe, before the year 1830 that opened
so quietly had run to the end of its course.

Early in March Wieck took his daughter for the second
time to Dresden, but not as before for the purpose of holiday
making. Provided with excellent introductions, he wished to
excite an interest in her talent that might avail him later on
amongst the private influential circles of the Saxon capital,
and at the same time to familiarise her gradually with the
responsibilities and excitements incidental to the career for
which he designed her. Writing his first impressions of the
visit to his wife, he says:—

"We are received here with unlooked-for favour and
have constant invitations. . . . Every one recognises Clara's
virtuosity and musicality, and people do not know which
to admire most, the child or the teacher. I am anxious
lest the honours and distinctions should have a bad effect
on Clara. If I should notice anything hurtful I shall leave
at once, so that she may get back to her ordinary life, for
I am too proud of her simplicity, and would not exchange it
for any honour in the world. People think her very amiable.
At present she is just as she was, simple and natural; often
shows deep understanding and rich imagination; is wild
withal, but very noble and reasonable. She is incredibly
fearless when performing, and the larger the party the better
she plays."

And a few days later :—

"It is impossible to describe the sensation your two monkeys
from the Leipzig menagerie are making here. No one would
believe that Clara could compose also, and all present went
into raptures when she extemporised on a given theme. We
are assured that your two monkeys are the general talk of

court and town. I will only tell you a few particulars about Clara. For instance : Yesterday Count Kospoth invites her to play duets next Monday with his wife, who is one of the first pianistes in Dresden. She replies, ' I will certainly come, but can your wife also play, then?' ' Yes, to be sure,' he answers. ' Indeed? then take me to her, I should like to make her acquaintance ! '

"How the girl has been kissed ! But it agrees with her; she looks better than ever. Yesterday we played duets at a large party. The piano was a very hard one, but she got through Herz's variations as well as was at all possible. At the end the whole audience applauded. She stood up, quiet and grave, and said, ' Now you are clapping, and I know I have played very badly'; she even cried, the only time she has yet done so. Every one insisted that I must publish my method."*

Few days went by during the visit, which was extended to a period of four weeks, without bringing to father and daughter gratifying tokens of the interest it excited among the musicians and amateurs of Dresden. Clara appeared before the Saxon court circle at two soirées given by the Princess Louise, consort of the Crown Prince, the first of which was honoured by the presence of the King and Queen ; and it was on the second of these occasions that the improvisation on a given theme took place alluded to in the letter from which we have quoted.

A year had now elapsed since Robert Schumann's departure from Leipzig, the greater part of which had been for him a time of comparatively unalloyed happiness. To the delights of the free student-life of Heidelberg, passed in the companion-ship of a few congenial friends, had been added those of a first journey in Switzerland and Italy, which are described with captivating freshness and drollery in his letters of the period.† That he had made perceptible progress in the study of law cannot be said. He attended a few lectures on jurisprudence, but more on account of his interest in Thibaut's personality and his relish of the philosophical tincture with which the professor was accustomed to flavour his discourses than from a desire to add to his information in a branch of

---

* First published by Kohut, p. 55.   † "Jugendbriefe."

study which he was still unable to reconcile either with his natural instincts or the intellectual habits and activities that he had cultivated from childhood.

"Pianoforte playing," says Dr. Gisbert Töpken, one of his fellow-students and intimate friends, "was the study that really occupied Schumann during the whole time of his residence at Heidelberg. The first thing I heard him perform was the opening movement of Hummel's A minor concerto, and I was at once struck by his aplomb and consciously artistic performance. I gladly seized the opportunity of meeting him for duet-playing and general musical intercourse. . . . To play with him was of instructive musical interest to me, on account of the hints he gave me on the conception and execution of every piece—hints that he was able to illustrate practically. When the duet-playing was over he generally extemporised on the pianoforte, capturing the hearts of all who heard him. I confess that these immediate musical outpourings of Schumann's invariably afforded me enjoyment of a kind that I have never since experienced when listening to the greatest artists. Out of a single idea each following one seemed to spring spontaneously, and in all dwelt a peculiar spirit, which clearly revealed the fundamental traits of both sides of his poetic nature : energetic and powerful on the one hand; fragrant, tender, dreamy, on the other." *

To the careful student of the authentic records of Schumann's early manhood, supplied by his own published letters and the reminiscences of his personal friends, it must be evident that almost simultaneously with his arrival in Heidelberg there was a subtle change in his frame of mind which cannot be altogether attributed to the direct operation of his new environment. His calmer and happier mood was probably induced in no small measure by a dawning consciousness that the painful and enervating mental struggle which had absorbed him during his residence in Leipzig had, at the time of his departure from that town, been practically determined. The uncertain attitude maintained by him throughout his university career did not proceed, as has too often been assumed, from an essential irresolution of will in the pursuit of an aim, but

* Wasielewski, "Robert Schumann," p. 55.

from the fact that the circumstances of his position prevented him for several years from definitely satisfying himself as to what his aim in life ought to be. Brought up in a provincial town that provided none of the musical advantages so frequently enjoyed by the public even of small German capitals, at a period when almost every reigning prince maintained a good orchestra in his service; without the constant incentive to progress that might have been afforded him by the intelligent sympathy of a musical home circle; denied the privilege of the special artistic training for which he expressly petitioned; the considerable, if defective, musical culture to which he had attained at the age of seventeen had resulted entirely from his own persevering enthusiasm for art. That he was not sufficiently sure of his powers to be capable, when he found himself confronted at the close of his school career by the immediate necessity of choosing a vocation, of at once opposing his own wishes to the determination of his mother and his guardian, followed necessarily from the course of his whole previous life, the effect of which was especially confirmed at this juncture by the loving relations that united him with his family.

Ten months' experience of the musical atmosphere of Leipzig, however; the ready appreciation of his gifts shown by Wieck, the first recognised authority to whom he had had the chance of submitting them; his awakening perception of the possibilities that might result from the training of his talent; all these things gave his mind a helpful impulse, which, encouraged, no doubt, by the beneficent influence of his Heidelberg surroundings, gradually brought it to the right solution of the problem that faced him. Nearly a year was to elapse after he had clearly recognised his dilemma (in the autumn of 1829 *) before he felt sufficient confidence in his chances of artistic success to reopen the question of the future with his mother; but that he practised enthusiastically during the whole of this interval, with a fixed purpose in view, is estab-

---

* Schumann has himself left it on record that this occurred on his return to Heidelberg after his Italian journey. By a passing slip of memory he has referred this return to Easter, 1830, instead of October, 1829. See " Briefe, Neue Folge," pp. 30–32 (Dr. Gustav Jansen).

lished by incontrovertible evidence, notwithstanding that a few passages in his letters may seem at first sight to point to another conclusion.   He devoted a considerable part of each day, often as much as six or seven hours, to hard work at the pianoforte, beginning at a very early hour of the morning with the methodical practice of finger exercises ; and, when starting on the pleasant driving excursions of a few hours or a few days that he frequently arranged with his friends, always took with him a dumb keyboard for the purpose of his mechanical finger-training.   He was by no means satisfied, however, with the rate of technical progress attainable by recognised methods, and frequently exchanged ideas with Töpken as to possible contrivances by which they might be supplemented. Appearing at a public concert given by the Heidelberg Musical Association, of which he was a member, that was honoured by the attendance of the Grand Duchess of Baden, and choosing for performance Moscheles' brilliant "Alexander" variations, a work that had been his favourite *cheval de bataille* at the Zwickau school concerts, he was so extraordinarily successful that in the course of the next few days he received offers of engagements for concerts at Mannheim and Mainz.   These he declined, and from this time was seldom to be prevailed on to play at private parties, as had formerly been his custom.   The obvious inference is that whilst his public success strengthened a secret resolution for the discharge of which his mind was becoming rapidly prepared, he was unwilling to run the risk of prejudicing a future artistic career by appearing for the present on the footing of an amateur.   His energy in making music with his intimate companions continued unflagging.

Whilst it is clear that the immediate object pursued by young Schumann at this period was that of developing his distinguished qualifications as an amateur pianist to the powers of a first-rate executive artist, it is, however, difficult to believe that he at any time seriously cherished the intention of devoting the best energies of his life to the career of the virtuoso, or even to that of the travelling pianist-composer whose special place in the history of art immediately precedes that of the virtuoso properly so called and of whose type Moscheles, the musical hero of Robert's childhood, was one of the latest eminent

representatives. Several passages in Schumann's letters to his
family, which refer to his feelings of shyness or diffidence before
the world, seem to show that when, a little later than our
present date, he actually found himself in sight of such a
career, he began to realise that it was hardly suited to his temperament. Other expressions again may be pointed to which
lead to the conclusion that a presentiment had at all times
dwelt within him, unrecognised as it may have been for
many years, of the fact that nature had primarily intended him
for a creative artist. It is true that he completed few compositions whilst at Heidelberg ; but he was beginning to realise a
truth impressed upon him not only by Wieck, but by the song-
writer Wiedebein, to whom he had submitted some of his lyrics,
namely, that he must not hope to be able to do justice to his
ideas until he was possessed of more exact technical knowledge
than was at his present command, and he added to his other
occupations the perhaps somewhat desultory study of the
theory and grammar of composition. * How constantly and
irresistibly he was possessed by his strong creative impulse is
evident in his correspondence with Wieck, whose letters are,
he says, his best substitute for the Leipzig concerts that he is
obliged to miss :—

   " You know that I have little affection for abstract *theory*, and
so I have quietly lived my own life here, have begun many
symphonies and finished none, have now and then slipped a
Schubert waltz in between. the Roman code and the Pandects ; dreamed often of the trio and the happy hour at
your house that made me acquainted with it—and have, as I
think, neither advanced nor gone back much—yet I feel that
my forte touch has become much richer and my piano gained
in freedom and impulse. . . . If you only knew what pressure
and impulse I feel within me, how I might by now have reached
Op. 100 with my symphonies if I had written them down. In

   * Schumann warmly thanks Wiedebein for his encouragement and advice
in a letter dated August 5, 1828, which contains the following passage : " I
forgot, apparently, to tell you in my former letter that I am neither
acquainted with the laws of harmony, thorough bass, &c., nor am I a
contrapuntist, but a pupil of nature pure and simple ; and have merely
followed a blind vain impulse that was content to remain unshackled."—
" Briefe," p. 7.

such a mood I was courageous enough to laugh, the other day, in the face of a critic who told me I had ' better not write since I *accomplish* nothing,' and to answer him that he did not understand the matter. Forgive my candour, which, however, is *not* really candour."

To his mother he says :—

" . . . Had I ever accomplished anything in the world it would have been in music. I have always been strongly attracted to music, and am conscious, not to overrate myself, of possessing creative power. . ." *

With all his engrossing artistic activity, he found time for the pursuit of his literary tastes. He wrote occasional poems, refreshed his mind by varied reading, took lessons in turn in Italian, English, French, and Spanish, and before his Italian journey in the autumn of 1829 was sufficiently proficient in the language to have produced translations of a number of Petrarch's sonnets which have been described by his companions as remarkable for their fidelity and ease.

By the summer of 1830 Robert's mind had become matured for action, and a letter to his mother, dated July 1st, conveys to her a note of preparation for what was to come :—

" . . . You may believe that I should like to become a great lawyer. . . . That I should never achieve more than average success, however, is not owing to myself but to circumstances and, perhaps, to my heart, which never willingly spoke in Latin. Only chance and, if it please Heaven, good fortune, can raise the dark curtain that hangs over my future. Thibaut does *not* recommend jurisprudence, ' since Heaven has *not* designed me for an official.' "

On the 30th of the month, a few weeks after reaching the age of twenty, he speaks out his entire thoughts :—

" My whole life has been a twenty years' struggle between poetry and prose, or call it music and law. . . . In Leipzig I lived for the moment, dreamed and trifled without troubling myself about a plan of life, and did nothing properly. Here I have worked more, but have been drawn, here as there, ever closer to art. Now I stand at the crossing of the ways and am alarmed at the question : whither ? If I follow my natural

* " Jugendbriefe," 79, 92.

instinct, it points to art, and, as I believe, to the right path. But—do not be offended with me, I speak gently and lovingly —it has always seemed to me as though you were standing in the way. For this you had your good mother's reasons that were understood by you and me, and called by us ' doubtful future' and ' uncertain bread '; but what then? A man can have no more torturing thought than that he has prepared for himself an unhappy, barren, and uncertain future. . . ." *

He proceeds to tell his mother of the conviction he has arrived at, that with industry, patience, and a good teacher, he would be able, in six years' time, to compete with any pianist, and says he feels the hour has come for a decision. Should he resolve to devote his life to music, he must return to Leipzig as soon as possible, put himself under Wieck again, and later on go for a year to Vienna, and if possible to Moscheles.

"One request only, my kind mother, which you may, perhaps, be willing to grant. Write yourself to Wieck and ask him openly what he thinks of me and my plan. . . . Enclose this letter in yours if you like. The question must, at all events, be settled by Michaelmas, and then to work briskly, vigorously, and without repining, for the attainment of the chosen object."

Few parents would have dared to incur the responsibility of refusing to consider such an appeal, which proceeded from no sudden caprice, no passing enthusiasm, but from the persistent instincts of nature itself, strengthened by the continuous activities of at least fourteen years of the lifetime of a youth of twenty. It came upon Robert's mother, however, who loved, but scarcely understood him, with the suddenness of a lightning stroke. For more than two years she had imagined him to be making steady progress in the study of jurisprudence, and had repeatedly sent, or persuaded his guardian to send, money for the payment of his debts or for the purposes of various indulgences, for which he pleaded as necessities, in the belief that, on the termination of his university career, enough would remain of the small capital left him by his father to enable him to live comfortably until

* " Jugendbriefe," 115–19.

he should have established himself in his profession. Now, when considerable inroads had been made upon his insignificant fortune, he asked for six years' education in an art highly precarious if regarded as a means of livelihood, and affording chances of distinction only to men of exceptional special talent, of Robert's possession of which she felt by no means convinced. The strong agitation of her mind is plainly reflected in the letter she wrote to Wieck, to whom she appealed as a husband, father, and the friend of her son, reminding him that Robert's whole future was to be decided by his answer, and imploring him to speak out his unbiassed opinion as to what might be hoped or feared should she, in opposition to the wishes of her three elder sons, bring herself to consent to Robert's desires.

Wieck's answer, candid and to the point, was, under the circumstances, hardly calculated to appease her fears, however flattering it may have been to her maternal pride. All, he said, depended on Robert's firmness of purpose, the steadiness of his resolution to submit his executive and creative talents to a long course of strict discipline. Granting his perseverance, Wieck would undertake to develop him within three years into a great pianist, who should excel both Hummel and Moscheles. As to his theoretical training, to which several hours of each day must be devoted, the help of Cantor Weinlich of the Thomas' School would probably suffice for a time.

That the mother, on receiving this communication, felt that the die was cast and that, whatever the opposition to be encountered, her boy must have his way, followed naturally from the circumstance that, with all her prejudices, she was a good, loving, self-sacrificing mother; and it is equally a foregone conclusion that Robert, on reading his master's judgment, was well-nigh intoxicated with delight and ready with any number of good resolves.

" The pathway to science " [i.e., law], he writes to Wieck, " lies over mountains, and very icy ones they are. The pathway to art leads over heights also ; but they are beautified with flowers, hopes, and dreams."

He is satisfied that whole pailfuls of theory cannot hurt him, and will stick to it without a murmur. He has attentively read the five "buts" suggested in Wieck's letter to his mother, and has asked himself repeatedly if he can fulfil the proposed conditions.   Reason and feeling unfalteringly answer in the affirmative.*

Thus had the hour come and gone which decided the destinies of two lives that were to become glorious, not only in the service of the art to which both were dedicated, but in that higher one in which it is granted to but comparatively few men and women to achieve success—the service of ideal human love.   By the middle of October, 1830, Robert was back again in Leipzig and settled as a student of music in his teacher's house.

The new and agreeable element introduced into the home life of the Wiecks by the admission of the gifted young ex-law student to its intimacies and privileges was quickly appreciated by the various members of the family party, from Friedrich himself, who was supremely gratified at being able to guide the daily progress of a pupil of whose genius he had long been convinced, down to the little boys who shared with Clara the delights of the stories of ghosts, hobgoblins, and robbers with which Robert often thrilled them in the twilight hours, and of the diverting charades and conundrums with which he dissipated the startling images conjured up in their minds by these wondrous tales.   That there were, as formerly, intervals of tension between Wieck and Schumann was the inevitable consequence of the individualities of the two men, each enthusiastic in the pursuit of his ideal and confident in his power of attaining it.   Schumann had become so thoroughly convinced of the necessity, to the executive artist, of complete command of his means that he was disposed to take it amiss when Wieck, who was now more than satisfied with his rapid progress in fundamental work, began to urge him in his lessons to the display of greater virtuosity and dramatic effect ; and it is characteristic of him at this period that he was surprised to find, on hinting to his master one day of his desire to place himself sooner or later under Hummel, that Wieck showed strong resentment at the idea.

* Schumann's letter, addressed to Wieck on August 21, 1830, is printed entire by Kohut, p. 84.

"I was alarmed at his outbreak of anger," he writes to his mother with reference to the incident, "but we are on good terms again and he treats me affectionately, as though I were his child. You can hardly form an idea of his fire, his judgment, and his understanding of art ; but when he speaks in his own or Clara's interest, he is as unmannerly as a peasant."

The course of Robert's daily life, his loving thoughts of his absent ones, his frequent changes of mood, his trifling personal needs, above all his chronic state of impecuniosity, are described to the anxious, indulgent mother with a mixture of simplicity and roguishness that make his home letters of this, as of the Heidelberg period, charming reading. His hair is an ell in length, but he has not a penny to spend on having it cut ; he has, for a fortnight past, been obliged to wear white neckties because his black one has worn in pieces : to-morrow they will be exhausted and he must go without any ; his piano is terribly out of tune, but he cannot afford a tuner ; he has not even money to buy a pistol to shoot himself with, and must bring his letter to an abrupt end as his only candle is going out. He has already borrowed twenty thalers (about three pounds) from Wieck and thirty from another friend. A few days after penning the recital of these trials he announces that he is having his portrait painted in miniature to send his mother as a birthday present !

Admirable as was the docility with which, on the whole, Schumann allowed himself to be guided in his pianoforte practice by Wieck's recommendations, he had not yet made up his mind to submit his theoretical studies to the direction of a teacher, notwithstanding the example set him by Clara, who, since her return from Dresden in the spring, had worked for several hours daily at harmony and counterpoint as Cantor Weinlich's pupil, and had now made sufficient progress to be able to write short four-part songs with correctness and some freedom. Robert's mind was filled with visions of a great opera on the subject of Hamlet, for the composition of which, in the absence of the usual technical training, his anticipations of success and fame were to fire him with the requisite power and imagination. The great event of the autumn for all the party was Clara's first appearance as a concert-giver, which took place in the Gewandhaus hall a few weeks after Robert had come among them. In the *Allgemeine Musikalische Zeitung* of November 17, 1830, we read :—

" On the 8th of the month an extra concert,* announced as a ' musical academy,' was given in the hall of the Gewandhaus by Clara Wieck, the eleven-year-old daughter of the resident pianoforte dealer and experienced teacher, in which convincing proof was afforded of the early satisfactory results attainable by talent, industry, and good teaching.   In the first part the concert-giver performed Kalkbrenner's ' Rondo Brillant,' Op. 23, and Herz's ' Variations Brillantes,' Op. 20, with a finished execution and the brilliant virtuosity of the day that ensured the approbation of the audience. . . . A performance of Czerny's ' Quartet Concertante,' Op. 230, for four piano-fortes with orchestra, by Music-director Dorn, Messrs. Knorr and Wendler, and the concert-giver, was rewarded with con-siderable applause.   The piece itself, arranged cleverly and with appreciation of the taste of the day, is pleasing. . . . We also heard some of the young virtuoso's own compositions: a song with pianoforte accompaniment, sung by H. Grabau, and variations on a theme for pianoforte solo performed by the concert-giver, and received with applause.   We have genuine reason to rejoice in the youthful talent and the diligence with which it has evidently been cultivated, and we sincerely desire for its future the success and prosperity so especially necessary to the career of an artist."

This first concert at home was followed by two given in January, 1831, at the Hôtel de Pologne, Dresden—at the earlier of which Clara was assisted by the court orchestra—and by several other public and private appearances in the same city.   The results were so satisfactory that Wieck could afford to be amused and even gratified by the circulation of some ill-natured reports that Clara was more than eleven years old ; that she was, indeed, well on in her " teens " ; that her surprising powers had been attained by twelve hours' daily practice, and so forth.   For the rest, it is enough to say that new friends vied with old in the heartiness of the welcome

* All concerts given in the Gewandhaus other than those of the subscrip-tion series arranged by the committee were described as " extra."

accorded to the youthful artist, and that all alike expressed, by the unmistakable ring of enthusiasm in their plaudits, the warm sympathy aroused by her personality and the cordial wishes for her future that accompanied the general assurance of her exceptional talent.

CHAPTER V

1831–1832

Clara's youthful compositions—Schumann and Musikdirektor Dorn—Schumann's "Abegg" variations—The "Papillons"—An "Opus 2"—Clara's first concert tour—Goethe—Spohr—Mendelssohn—Chopin—Wieck and Clara in Paris—Kalkbrenner—Clara's Paris concert.

THE spring and summer which succeeded Clara's return from Dresden were again spent by her in the varied artistic study that her father thought best adapted to promote the end he had kept steadily in view throughout the course of her development—the training of her powers, not merely to brilliant virtuosity, but to sound musicianship and, if it should please Heaven, to some measure of creative activity. While the prescribed three hours were regularly given to pianoforte work, she took violin lessons, practised score-reading, and even made a beginning with the first elements of instrumentation. Her Opus 1, a set of four polonaises for pianoforte solo, was issued by Hofmeister, of Leipzig, and mentioned in the *Iris* by the well-known critic Rellstab, of Berlin, who, however, perhaps justly, condemned their publication as immature. Written in the simple dance form of three sections, of which the third is a repetition of the first, they are evidently the work of a careful student, and though not giving special promise of future inventive power, are fresh and spontaneous. The trio of No. 3 gives unmistakable evidence of the composer's familiarity with the style of Hummel's music, and, judged from the standpoint of that school, may even be considered as remarkable writing for a child of eleven whose time was devoted in the first place to pianoforte practice. Each of the dances contains passages that are suggestive of the young artist's practical dexterity of finger and wrist.

Trio from Polonaise No. 3 (in D major).

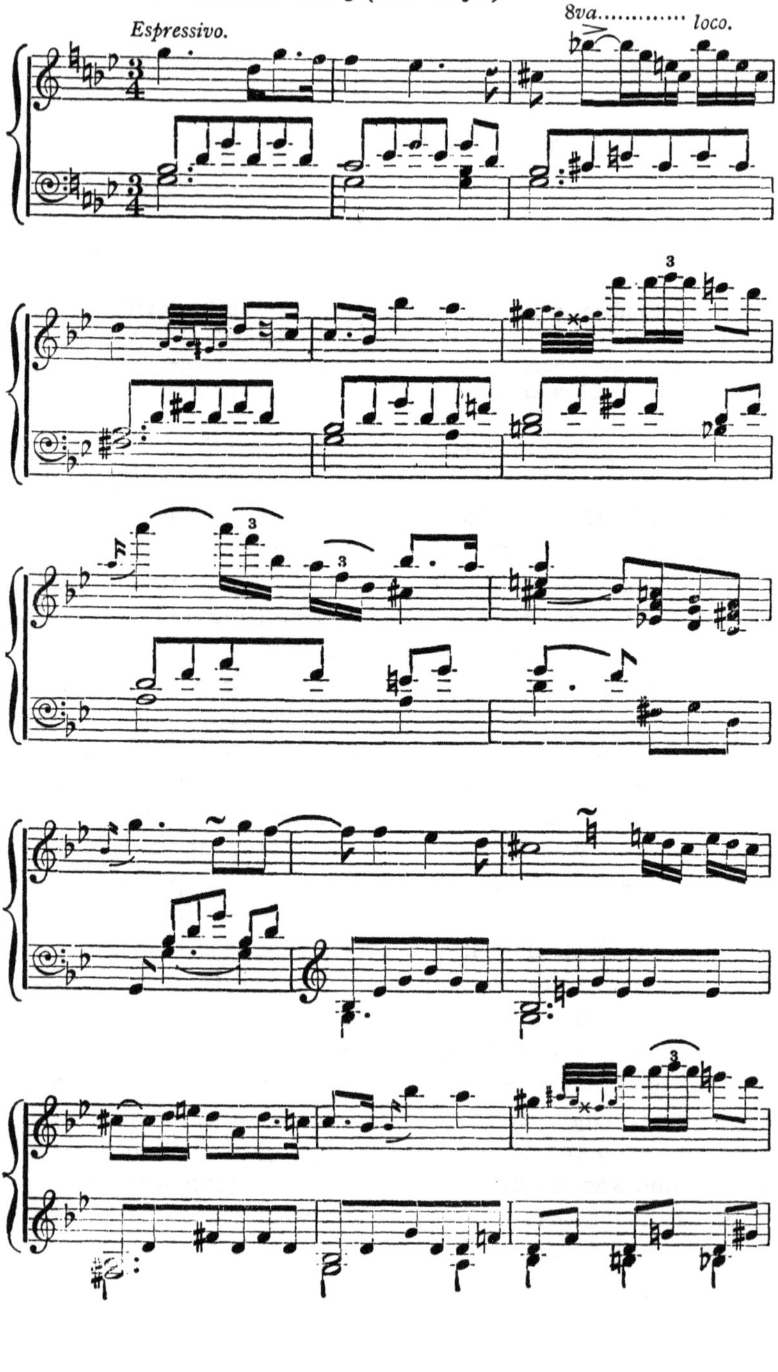

It may have been partly owing to his constant observation of the systematic diligence of his youthful colleague that Robert Schumann at length made up his mind to place himself under Music-director Dorn, of the Leipzig theatre, for a course of methodical instruction in harmony and counterpoint.* That he was, as yet, but half convinced of the wisdom of the step is evident from a note written by him to Dorn on July 5, 1831, in which, after requesting that a day may be fixed for the commencement of the long-talked-of lessons, he continues: " Though I doubt not that you will spread an Italian heaven above this strengthening ice-bath, I tremble and shiver a little in anticipation"; and an entry in his diary of July 12th contains the following :—

" I began thorough bass yesterday with the music-director. He had prepared himself and seemed nervous, but was kind. . . . I hardly wish to know more than I know already. It is in the mystery or unconsciousness of imagination that its poetry dwells."

When he had once taken the plunge, however, he became, in Dorn's words to Wasielewski, " an indefatigable pupil." " He was a very handsome young man at this time . . . generally giving the impression of being shy, though in his tête-a-tête intercourse with me he was sociable and communicative."

A fair measure of the progress to which Schumann had attained in the art of free composition at the time he became Dorn's pupil is afforded by his published works, Opp. 1 and 2,

---

* Wasielewski assigns the first lesson to the autumn of 1830, on the authority of Dorn, whose memory, however, obviously misled him here. See " Briefe, N. F.," 2nd edition, p. 492, note 14.

both of which were finished at this date. Op. 1, "Variations
on the name 'Abegg,' dedicated to the Countess Pauline von
Abegg," belongs entirely to his Heidelberg period and owes its
existence to the accident of his having danced at a ball with a
beautiful girl, the letters of whose name furnished him with a
musical figure from which he has constructed a theme of sixteen bars in waltz rhythm. The fact that the work is thus

outwardly stamped with the impress of the event out of which
it grew is of interest as showing, at the outset of Schumann's
career, a characteristic that proved a persistent part of his
artistic personality. The variations, written in the bravura
style of the day, prove, as a whole, that at the age of nineteen
Schumann had acquired considerable facility in writing
passages for the pianoforte, while they exhibit here and there,
notably the second, some foretokens of the individuality now
associated with his name. The fact that Meta Abegg was the
fiancée of one of his friends caused Robert to substitute for her
name, in the dedication of the work, that of an imaginary
Countess Pauline. The opus was published in the autumn
of 1831.

Op. 2, a set of twelve little pieces called "Papillons," of
which Nos. 1, 3, 4, 6, 8 were also composed at Heidelberg,
brings us into the immediate presence of Schumann the poet
and romanticist, who carries us in the few introductory bars of
his work to a dreamland of sparkling, tender, humorous fancy,
and keeps us enchanted there until, with the striking of the
clock at the close of the last number, the dainty vision is dispelled and we find ourselves again amid the prose of everyday
life. If, as has been demonstrated by some of the composer's
critics, the collection possesses but small artistic value, it has,
nevertheless, held its own amid the countless well-trained
artistic efforts which have struggled into accomplishment
during the eighty years that have gone by since its publication,
and will probably continue to live by virtue of the vivid freshness and originality, the imagination of genius, dwelling within

each and all of its numbers. Schumann's mind received the
impulse which resulted in the composition of the " Papillons "
from his reading of the scene of the masked ball in the last
chapter but one of Jean Paul's " Flegeljahre." *   That these
twelve charming trifles are not to be therefore regarded as
descriptive or imitative music is, however, established by
Schumann's frequent assurances to his friends that they were
not composed to the text, but that the text was found to suit
the music. The " Papillons " were published with a dedication to Robert's three sisters-in-law, Therese, Rosalie, and
Emilie, in April, 1832.

One of the most noteworthy events of the summer of 1831 to
the ardent musicians of Wieck's household was the discovery
of a new star in the firmament of art whose light, reaching
them towards the approach of autumn through the medium
of a certain Opus 2 already published by Haslinger of Vienna,
" Variations on Là ci darem," was acclaimed by them with
no little joy and exultation. It is pleasant to think of Wieck,
zealous from his youth in his appreciation of the dawning
musical romanticism that had fascinated the world in the
picturesque imagination of Weber, the delicate fancy of Field,
now at the age of forty-six eagerly recognising the genius
of young Frédéric Chopin, as yet almost unheard of outside
his own country ; pleasant to contemplate Robert's delight
on finding, at the very moment when he had become sufficiently aware of the artistic problem that confronted his
future to feel the necessity of seriously preparing himself
for its solution, that another was making progress on the
path to a goal which he perceived to be in some respects
similar to his own ; pleasant to picture Clara's satisfaction
in the thought that she would soon have the opportunity of
paying homage to the new composer. The variations had
made their appearance in Leipzig at an important hour of
her life. She was on the eve of starting with her father
on an extended concert journey that would take her for the
first time outside her native Saxony, and would extend, if
all should go well, as far as Paris. She immediately set to

---

* Not the "last" chapter, as Schumann inadvertently describes it in
some of his letters.

work on the variations and succeeded in mastering them during the week that remained before her departure; and the resolution that they should be included in the programme of her very next concert, wheresoever it might be given, was duly recorded in the diary that was kept punctually up to date by father and daughter in turn.

Some modification of Wieck's original plans for the tour was necessitated by the cholera scare of the year, and the travellers, who started from Leipzig on September 25th, instead of trying their fortune in Berlin, as had been intended, arrived on the 26th at Weimar, where their first impression, created by the indifference or hostility of members of the resident musical circle, was one of considerable disappointment. A visit paid by them, however, to Geheimrath Schmidt, an accomplished music-lover of the town, changed their prospects. Strongly interested in hearing the child artist perform Chopin's variations—which he immediately recognised as the work of a master with an art style of his own—not only with certainty and aplomb, but with unusual beauty of tone and phrasing, Schmidt took such energetic steps on her behalf that within a few days she had had the opportunity of making her powers known to many of those in Weimar whose friendship was best worth cultivating, and had been invited to call, with her father, on the great Goethe, now in his eighty-fourth year, but alert and interested as ever in modern development and genuine artistic faculty.

"I have to play to him [Goethe] for an hour every day from the great composers in chronological order, and tell him how they have developed things," Felix Mendelssohn, just turned twenty-one, had written to his parents some fifteen months earlier, when he, too, made Weimar the first station of a prolonged European journey; "and he sits listening in a corner like a Jupiter Tonans and flashes with his old eyes." *

Clara at twelve was hardly old enough to offer Goethe a historical recital, and the fact that the variations Op. 2 are written with orchestral accompaniment perhaps prevented her from introducing Chopin to his acquaintance. The old poet allowed himself to be interested, however, though it

* Mendelssohn's "Reisebriefe," p. 8.

would seem rather dubiously, in the compositions of Herz
and Hünten, which she played on the occasions of her first
visit and of a second, appointed by him for a week later,
and showed warm and unreserved appreciation of the powers
of his youthful guest:—

" A remarkable phenomenon was presented here yesterday,"
he wrote to Zelter; " a father brought me his pianoforte-
playing daughter, who, being on her way to Paris, played
me new Parisian compositions. The kind is new to me;
it requires great dexterity, but is always bright; one follows
it easily and is content to be pleased. As you are no doubt
acquainted with the sort of thing, pray explain it to me." *

The notice taken of her by Goethe sufficed to establish
Clara's position in Weimar, even though Hummel and other
leading musicians of the little capital elected to ignore her
presence within its walls. Hofmarschal von Spiegel called
especially on her father to invite her to play before the
Grand Duke and the court circle; the mayor placed the town
hall at her disposal for a public concert, which took place
on October 7th, and leading social notabilities vied with
each other in paying her attention and singing her praises.
Disappointment gave place to success and success became
triumph. One of the Weimar critics wrote, after giving the
programme of the public concert, which included Pixis'
concerto, Op. 130, and Chopin's variations, Op. 2, for pianoforte
and orchestra, Herz's variations for pianoforte alone, Op. 20,
songs composed by the concert-giver and a duet for pianoforte
and violin played by Clara with Herr Götze, of the court
orchestra :—

"The young virtuoso's first performance was rewarded
with very hearty applause, which became enthusiastic later
on. The great facility, certainty, and power with which
she executes the most difficult pieces, and, still more, the
intelligence and expression of her interpretation, which
scarcely leaves anything to be desired, are indeed remarkable. Demoiselle Wieck had played previously with great
success at court, and appeared, both before and after her
concert, in various private circles. When not seated at the

* " Briefwechsel," vol. 4.

instrument she shows herself to be a natural and attractive child."

Clara left Weimar with her father on October 12th, after a stay of rather more than a fortnight, carrying with her agreeable recollections, good wishes, and—treasured amongst memorials—a small bronze bust of Goethe, sent her by the poet with the written words :—

" In kind remembrance of October 9, 1831.
                                    " J. W. VON GOETHE.
    " Weimar."

whilst Wieck was complimented with a similar autograph :—

" Obliged by a masterly musical entertainment,
                                    " J. W. VON GOETHE.
    " Weimar, October 9." *

The fortunes of the travellers after their departure from Weimar were varied, and in the course of the next four months, during which they visited Erfurt, Gotha, Arnstadt, Cassel, Frankfurt-am-Main, and Darmstadt, not a few occasions arose when all the nerve, steadfastness, and resource at Wieck's command were needed to overcome obstacles little less than insuperable or to recognise impossibilities with sufficient fore-sight to preclude the chance of disaster. In the days when a journey could only be accomplished by means of some kind of horse-drawn carriage ; when communication by letter was slow and costly and the electric wire as yet undreamed of ; when comparatively few concert-rooms were available and little choice of good concert pianos was to be had even in the great centres of Europe, the business of a concert tour was involved in difficulties that can hardly be realised at the present day—difficulties that were accentuated by the increas-ing competition of the travelling artists who vied with each other and with the resident Konzertmeister or chamber musician of court and town in their efforts to attract the interest of the musical public. Wieck found it advisable to abandon the idea of arranging concerts at Erfurt and Gotha. At Arnstadt, a little town belonging to the princi-

* Litzmann i, 29,

pality of Schwarzburg-Sondershausen, the accident that the
reigning prince was in residence there with his family, and that
Clara's newly made friend, the Grand Duke of Saxe-Weimar,
was on a visit to him, opened the way for her appearance
immediately on her arrival. She gave a concert by command,
which went off with the brilliancy and success that the presence
of two reigning sovereigns and the attainments of the gifted
youthful executant might have been expected to ensure.

Among the most enjoyable weeks of the journey were those
passed at Cassel, where Hofkapellmeister Spohr, mightily
interested in Clara's personality, her playing, her compositions,
and the fact that she was able to make him acquainted with
a work by a composer hitherto unknown to him (Chopin),
which he recognised as being "extraordinarily imaginative
and original," could not do enough to promote her interests.
After giving her the opportunity of playing privately before
the musicians of Cassel, amongst whom was Moritz Hauptmann, later of Leipzig fame, he secured her engagement
for one of the court concerts, of which he was director, and
her achievements at this function produced the results that
seemed to follow her appearance before an audience of
cultivated amateurs almost as a matter of course. The
Elector of Hesse, who was present, offered Wieck the use
of the opera house for an orchestral concert ; and this was
succeeded by a musical "academy" given in the town hall.
The young artist was well supported and enthusiastically
received on both occasions.

The visit to Frankfurt was disappointing. Of the prominent
musicians of the city only Ferdinand Ries, with whom Wieck
had had relations earlier in his career, showed interest in
Clara's talent. Frankfurt was at this time one of the few
towns of Europe in which fine musical taste was encouraged
with commendable exclusiveness by the chief resident artists.
Here Bach, Handel, Haydn, Mozart, and Beethoven held
their own in the programmes of the best subscription concerts,
and no suitable opportunity was available for the introduction into any of them of either of the pieces that Clara had
prepared for her journey. Schelble, the founder and director
of the celebrated Cecilia Society, who made it his special

mission to prepare his fine choir for performances of unknown works by Bach, would not even allow the youthful virtuoso to be heard at one of his private meetings. "Wieck has written to Frau Malsburg from Frankfurt," remarks Hauptmann in a letter to Hauser dated Cassel, November 8. "He is satisfied with no one but Ries, and abuses Schelble because he has not allowed Clara to be heard at the choral union. Brother Herz would certainly have distinguished himself by the side of Sebastian!"

Wieck's undaunted perseverance enabled Clara to give a concert of her own in Frankfurt towards the end of January, but in this city, where there was no sympathetic court circle to help matters forward, the ring of enthusiasm, for which the father listened according to his wont, was absent from the applause that followed the performances, though she played her very best. Better luck was in store at Darmstadt, the last German town included in the tour, where she gave a successful concert a few days after her arrival.

Some indication of the impression which Clara made during the journey on those who were best qualified to judge of her gifts is furnished by a few words written by Spohr, at her father's request, before the close of the visit to Cassel. A reliable estimate of what her powers really were when she was twelve may be formed by comparing his expressions with the variations on "Là ci darem," which, though but the second published work of Chopin, are already distinguished to a very considerable extent by the original treatment of the pianoforte and the peculiar executive difficulties now associated with his name :—

" . . . If," says Spohr, " it is not now very unusual to find a child of Clara Wieck's years possessed of great mechanical dexterity on the pianoforte, she is probably the first who has united with it sound interpretation, correct accentuation, complete distinctness, and the finest tone shading. Her facility is such that she masters the greatest difficulties with a certainty and ease possessed only by the greatest virtuosi of the time. That, moreover, the distinctive qualities of her playing do not result merely from strict and admirable training, but also from natural endowment, is proved by her attempts

at composition, which belong, as does the young virtuoso
herself, to the remarkable phenomena of art.' *

Possibly the reader may be surprised to find that the name
of Herz occupies so prominent a place in the programmes
performed by Clara during the early years of her career, and
be tempted to draw from the fact an inference somewhat
prejudicial to her father's artistic memory. It may be well,
therefore, to point out before proceeding farther with the
narrative, that the cause is to be found in the history of
the development of more than one branch of musical art,
history of which the story of Clara's life forms a not
unimportant part.

At a time when the development of the pianoforte, to which
reference was made in our opening chapter, and the popularisation of musical art, together with the multiplication of concert-
goers and concert-givers to which that development led, were
rapidly proceeding; whilst the great literature bequeathed to
the pianist by Beethoven was still a sealed book to the mass
of amateurs and to not a few artists, a demand had arisen
for pieces written with a special view to the technique of
the favourite instrument and the requirements of the modern
concert-room. This demand was supplied, in the absence
of composers of genius, by Herz, Hünten, Döhler, and other
men of whom their names are representative. Benefit concerts were almost invariably given with the assistance of
an orchestra, and it was usual for the concert-giver to help
his audience through the fatigue of listening to a classical
concerto, if performed entire, by placing the minor items of
the programme between its several movements. No executant,
however famous, would have had the hardihood to invite
his patrons to sit through the performance of an unaccompanied solo of the length and quality of the sonatas or
larger variations of Beethoven, Weber, or Clementi. But
between such works, or others in the same forms having
a purely educational value on the one hand, and the bravura
variations, fantasias, and *pièces de salon* written for the market
on the other, the performer of 1830 and rather later who
wished to play without orchestra was obliged to choose, as

* Litzmann, i. 36.

6

very little else had been published—a few pieces by Weber and Field, some rondos by Hummel, some Schubert waltzes. Wieck did not commit what would have been the grave error of presenting Clara to the world as an executant of Weber's, or an interpreter of Beethoven's, sonatas whilst her physical and intellectual powers were immature, but he gradually prepared her—and with full consciousness of his aim—for the performance of Beethoven by training her in the art of fine tone production by means of the works of the best pianoforte writers of both the Clementi and Vienna schools. By generally choosing Herz's solos, which undoubtedly possessed educational value at the time of their publication, for the display of virtuosity which was required of Clara, as it was and is required of every public executant, he perhaps selected the best of what there was for choice, while he availed himself of a useful aid in developing the certainty and brilliancy of her executive powers.

It is interesting to remember that whilst Clara was introducing the "Don Juan" variations to the audiences of her concert journey, destiny, which had already linked her in friendship with one of the three young geniuses who were to develop and carry to maturity the romantic literature of the pianoforte, was drawing her within sight of the lives of the two others. Twenty short years later their work was accomplished. At the end of 1831 they were standing, imbued with the spirit of the time, arming themselves each with his peculiar weapons for coming struggle, at the beginning of the road that was to lead them to victorious warfare for the truth and beauty of their art: Felix Mendelssohn, approaching the age of twenty-three, not yet arrived at the end of the two years' holiday journey that had taken him in the first place to Weimar and Goethe; rich, happy, successful; just now a courted guest in the political, social, and artistic circles of brilliant Paris; Frédéric Chopin, but a month Mendelssohn's junior, an obscure stranger in the same city, depressed by the experiences of more than a year's absence from home, passed chiefly in Vienna, and now sad with the news of the Russian occupation of Warsaw; constrained to be grateful for the insolent patronage accorded him by the powerful Kalkbrenner, the great pianist who reigned supreme in the musical *salons* of the French capital, and who was now, at forty-three, at the height of his fame ; Robert Schumann, the youngest of the trio, yet only sixteen months younger than Mendelssohn, working away in distant Leipzig with generous thoughts in his heart of Mendelssohn and Chopin and Clara !

All musical readers are familiar with the first essay of Schumann's collected writings on music and musicians entitled " Ein Werk 2." It was written in September, 1831, immediately after the discovery of the work in question by the Wieck circle, and was published in the *Allegemeine Musikalische Zeitung* of December 7 of the same year :—

" Hats off, gentlemen : a genius ! " exclaims Eusebius, entering a room in which Florestan and Julius, the supposed writer of the article, are seated together at the piano, and laying before them an open piece of music, thereby introducing Chopin's variations to the readers of the periodical.

" We were not to look at the title-page," says Julius, " and as I absently turned over the leaves it was as though strange eyes were gazing on me—eyes of flowers, basilisks, peacocks, maidens.   Here and there things were clearer ; I seemed to see Mozart's 'Là ci darem' woven amid the chords ; Leporello actually leered at me, and Don Juan flew by in a white mantle.   ' Now play it,' said Florestan.   Eusebius consented, and we listened in a window corner.   Eusebius played as though inspired, and conjured up innumerable pictures of the most animated life. . . . When, however, Florestan turned to the title-page, and we cried, astonished, ' An Opus 2 ! ' and could only ejaculate, ' Yes, something worth listening to at last—Chopin—I have never heard the name—who may he be? —a genius at all events '—an indescribable scene ensued. Heated by wine, Chopin, and excited talk, we went off to Meister Raro, who laughed heartily and showed little curiosity, for, ' I know you and your new-fangled enthusiasms [in the original article, ' Your enthusiasms for Herz and Hünten '], but bring me the Chopin to look at.'"

Florestan contributes a fanciful discussion of the several variations, and Julius brings the article to a close with the words, "Your private notions are, perhaps, too subjective, Florestan, but I, too, bow my head before such genius, such endeavour, such mastery."*

Wieck, too, had found time when staying in Cassel to write a long review of the work, a copy of which he forwarded to the young Polish composer, and Chopin, on reading it, was considerably surprised, and not greatly edified, to find his composition described by his unknown admirer as " not so much a set of variations as a series of fantastic tone-pictures " referring to the dramatis personæ of Mozart's opera. Whimsical as the article is on the whole, however, it derives historical interest from the faculty of fine, independent judgment displayed in its opening passages, which deserve quotation here. It was published early in 1832 in the Hamburg *Cecilia.*

" Herr Chopin, a pianist of Warsaw," Wieck writes, " has published under the modest title of ' Variations ' a great bravura piece for pianoforte and orchestra which may be recommended confidently to the attention of all virtuosi who are acquainted with the great school of Field, and whose artistic aim is something higher than the mere display of mechanical dexterity, since it is easy to follow, is of importance harmonically, and is extremely interesting.

" I do not know whether Chopin is a direct pupil of Field, but that he is quite familiar with Field's expressive musical language and is a practical adept in his style of playing is shown by the whole tendency of the work, the imaginative character of which appeals to our sensibility ; by passages, often surprising and quite new, which, framed with logical coherence, afford in themselves artistic pleasure ; by the ornamentation, to which the composer gives bold and quite unusual variety ; and by the excellent marking for performance. The public must not, however, infer that my words are intended to suggest anything in the nature of an imitation of Field. No ; the work stands in every respect on its own merits. . . ."

Only a fortnight before the appearance of Schumann's article

---

* Schumann uses the names Eusebius, Florestan, and Julius throughout this article to give a particular shape to the expression of his own thoughts. Meister Raro stands here for Friedrich Wieck. Detail respecting Schumann's later employment of the pseudonyms will be found in Chapter VII.

poor Frédéric, just come to Paris and calling on Kalkbrenner with his unpublished E minor concerto, had had the satisfaction of seeing that great man read through his manuscript at a table, pencil in hand, and strike out such passages as did not commend themselves to his approbation !

Wieck and Clara arrived in Paris on February 15th after a fatiguing journey of four days and nights from Mainz, where they had taken a short rest on the termination of the German concerts.   Disappointment was in store for such expectation as Wieck may have formed respecting any great result of the visit upon Clara's immediate future.   Politics were in the air. Louis Philippe's reign was regarded with suspicion, and a feeling of unrest prevailed.   Resident musicians, anxious like other men for the future of position and pocket, regarded each other with mistrust or envy, and were alike in maintaining an attitude of reserve towards foreign colleagues.   Mendelssohn, indeed, possessing the advantages of wealth, position, and personal charm, lived in the daily intimacy of the notabilities of the city, but Chopin wrote : " One may be amused or dull in Paris, may laugh or weep, may, indeed, do as one will ; no one observes it, for thousands are doing the same." *

Wieck, who was fairly well provided with letters of introduction and who had an excellent adviser in his brother-in-law, Eduard Fechner,† received numerous invitations to private musical *salons*, where opportunity was now and then offered to the guests to admire Clara's talent, but these occasions were not always favourable for its display ; and the hopes which her father had built up on the presence in Paris of Paganini were dispelled by the *maestro's* illness and the consequent postponement of his concerts, at one of which the young pianiste was to have appeared.   It does not seem that she was heard at this period either by Mendelssohn or Chopin, though she and her father were often in their company and that of their friend, Ferdinand Hiller, at this time an habitué of Parisian circles.   Of Liszt, who was resident in Paris but was leading a very retired life, we hear nothing at precisely this date.   Poor Chopin had enough cares of his own to absorb his

* Karasowki's " Friedrich Chopin," p. 218, 2nd edition.
† See *ante*, p. 26.

attention. He succeeded by the help of Kalkbrenner and the violoncellist Norblin in arranging a concert, which took place after several postponements on February 26th in Pleyel's rooms, but it was attended only by Poles who had come to Paris to be out of the way of trouble at home, and did not pay its expenses. The programme is interesting as a curiosity of musical history :—

1. Beethoven.   String Quintet.
2. Vocal.
3. Chopin.   Allegro de Concert for pianoforte.
4. Vocal.
5. Chopin.   Romance and Rondo from pianoforte concerto in F minor.
6. Vocal.
7. Kalkbrenner.   Grand Polonaise, preceded by an Introduction and March for six pianofortes.
   (Messieurs Kalkbrenner, Mendelssohn Bartholdy, Hiller, Osborne, Sovinski, and Chopin.)
8. Solo for the oboe, performed by M. Brod.
9. Vocal.
10. Chopin.   Grandes Variations on a theme by Mozart (Là ci darem) for pianoforte.

" You should see me at the parties (most carefully got up beforehand by Fechner)," writes Wieck to his wife, " with lemon-coloured gloves and white necktie, hat always in hand, part German, part French, and part despair, moving about with pricked ears, that I may lose nothing, from ten o'clock till past two. Child, you would not know your Friedrich; you have never seen a more interesting-looking waiter ! Then my broad boots or shoes (which in shape resemble the ferry that used to ply over Mulde at Wurzen), a blue tailcoat with velvet collar and small brass buttons, and black close-fitting trousers. They give me the air of a young oak in the Rosenthal.

" We have heard Kalkbrenner; he is the greatest and comes nearest to my ideal. Here is some of our talk after Clara had played several of her own compositions on his hard piano, the keys of which are scarcely movable :—

" KALKBRENNER. ' C'est le plus grand talent ! ' He kisses her. Imagine a handsome, very vain man. His wife, a true Frenchwoman, young and very rich, sits by the fireplace fanning herself with a new French fan, and puts in :

" ' But what a pity; she will be ruined as a player in Germany ! '

" ' She will not be ruined, for I shall not let her go out of my hands.'

" KALKBRENNER. ' Excuse me, sir, but in Germany they all play in the same style; *i.e.*, the Hopp and Hummel scrambling style; Czerny, Ciblini, Pixis, Hiller, in short every one who comes here from Germany.'

" ' I must ask you to make me the first exception. I am much opposed to that manner. I am well acquainted with the school of Field, and have taught my daughter and my pupils on its principles only.'

" Thus we continued, and time will show who is right."

Unwilling to return to Leipzig without adding to Clara's reputation the prestige of a public success in Paris, at this time considered the sure road to German fame and the indispensable preliminary to English recognition, Wieck at length determined to risk giving a concert, which was announced to musical amateurs by a circular in the following terms :—

" M. ——, Mademoiselle Clara Wieck, jeune pianiste allemande, âgée de 12 ans, a l'honneur de vous inviter à assister au concert qu'elle donnera à l'Hôtel-de-Ville, salle Saint-Jean, le 9 avril à huit heures du soir.

" Elle vous remet ci-inclus quelques billets pour que vous ayez la bonté de les lui placer, vous priant de lui renvoyer, le 7 avril, ceux que vous n'auriez pas placés ou que vous ne seriez pas dans l'intention de garder.

" Le prix de chaque billet est six francs." *

Concert-giving is, however, an uncertain undertaking, and disappointment was again in store. The appearance of the cholera in Paris caused the rapid departure from the city of the most desirable of Clara's hoped-for patrons, and her father judged it prudent to change the locale of the concert, which took place, with the assistance of Madame Schrœder-Devrient, in the hall of the Franz Stöpel music-school. Anything in the nature of a sensational success was out of the question under such circumstances; but the concert is noteworthy in the story of Clara's career, inasmuch as she extemporised for

* Kohut, p. 59.

the first time in public on the occasion and followed the Paris custom, not as yet introduced into Germany, of performing an entire programme from memory.

A few days later father and daughter quitted Paris, and after a troublesome journey, lengthened, by unforeseen and vexatious causes of delay, to more than a fortnight's duration, arrived at home on May 1, after more than seven months' absence. Amongst the many warm greetings which awaited them, that of Robert Schumann was not the least heartfelt.

CHAPTER VI

1832-1833

The Wiecks' return to Leipzig—Schumann; his studies and compositions—
His injured finger—Clara's first appearance at the Gewandhaus subscription concerts—Her private performances of new works by Chopin
and Schumann—A happy summer—Autumn shadows.

IT would be difficult to say whether the returned travellers or
the family and friends who were so happy to have them
back in their midst were the more interested in all that had to
be related on either side during the few days that followed the
home-coming of Wieck and Clara. The boys were allowed to
celebrate the event by a week's holiday, and made much of
their sister in their own boisterous fashion, whilst the party of
lively children found a constant attendant on their walks and
excursions in Robert, who had a thousand topics to discuss with
his travelled youthful colleague. He had moved into independent lodgings—Neumarkt 641—on his teacher's departure
from Leipzig, but was a daily visitor at the Wiecks' house and
an indispensable guest at the sociable gatherings of its intimate
circle, which now took place nearly every evening. He had
been assiduously industrious during the winter and spring,
and was assured of receiving from Wieck, as from Clara, the
warm personal sympathy that was so helpful to his artistic
strivings. True that, not immune from the penalties to which
highly gifted, impressionable natures are especially liable, he
was subject to inexplicable changes of mood that quickly
reached extreme points of the psychical barometer; and there
had been times during the past months when, as he writes, he
had suffered from feelings of depression and lassitude which only
his strong innate dislike to intellectual inactivity had enabled
him to overcome. Perhaps it may have been owing to some

passing irritability or falling off of energy resulting from this cause that Dorn put an end, about Easter, to the lessons in theory and refused to take back his decision.   The last exercise prepared for him by Robert was a canonic movement in double counterpoint in the twelfth, " which I [Dorn] preserved for a long time among my papers as it was an interesting pianoforte study." *   The pupil had, however, by this time attained a point of progress that made him independent of further tuition.   He carried on his contrapuntal studies alone with the aid of Marpurg's treatise, testing and confirming the knowledge of principle thus acquired by daily search in the treasure of learning at hand in Bach's " Well-tempered Clavier." Robert had entertained a profound veneration and love for Bach from the time, towards the close of his school career, when he had first come across some of his works, though his admiration had, naturally enough, been attracted rather by the deep romantic feeling dwelling in the thoughts of the master of masters than by the inimitable artistic mastery of their expression.   For some years his admiration stopped short at the word " fugue," and as late as January, 1832, he wrote to Wieck: " I shall never be able to agree with Dorn; he wants to make me regard a fugue as music—heaven ! " †

Three weeks after his friends' return, however, he wrote in his diary: " Clara played me Bach's second fugue distinctly and intelligibly and with [illegible] tone shading. A fugue to which one may properly give the animation of colour is not merely mechanical, but a work of art." ‡

* Wasielewski, p. 83.   † " Jugendbriefe," p. 162.

‡ Litzmann, i. 49. This quotation is of peculiar value since it places Schumann in the ranks, to which Brahms also belonged later on, of those musicians who have considered that Bach's music should be interpreted with expression and colour. To the present author it is of extraordinary interest, as it recalls some words spoken to her in the year 1871 by Frau Schumann, whose pupil she had then become. That great artist, after hearing her play a work by Bach, whom she had been taught in England to interpret with colour and varying sentiment (as distinct from sentimentality), remarked : " I used to play Bach in that way when I was a young girl, but one must not do so. It chanced that one day when I was about sixteen, Mendelssohn overheard me practising Bach as my father had taught me, with colour and elastic tempo. He came to me and said : ' You must not play Bach in that way, it is not according

Not long afterwards he writes to his old friend Kuntsch :—

" I completed my theoretical course under Dorn a few months ago with canon, and have gone through the remainder with the help of Marpurg. Marpurg is an excellent theorist. For the rest, Sebastian Bach's ' Well-tempered Clavier ' is my grammar, and is anyway the best. I have analysed the fugues one after the other into their most minute parts. The process is very useful and has a morally strengthening effect on one's whole being, for Bach was a man—through and through—nothing half or sickly in him ; everything is written as though for eternity. . . . Now I must go on to score-reading and instrumentation.' "

It is characteristic both of Schumann and Dorn that their friendly relations remained undisturbed by the cessation of their regular artistic intercourse.

To the winter of 1831 belongs, by date of composition, the first movement of a sonata in B minor mentioned in a letter of the period, which was published three years later on as an " Allegro," Op. 8. The chief interest of the piece is that which attaches to it from its position as a landmark in the history of the composer's development. Written in what may be described as very free sonata form, it shows Schumann intent on acquiring the power of sustained musical thought, though he is evidently hampered by the difficulty of moulding his ideas into distinctness and by want of the technical resource necessary for their development. The rather important coda contains passages anticipatory of the so-called orchestral treatment of the pianoforte which Schumann originated, and here and there in the movement are to be found indications of rhythmical features that form part of his mature individuality as a composer.

The " Papillons " had been out a fortnight at the time of Wieck's return, and it was Clara's pleasure to apply herself without delay to the study of this second new " Opus 2," and

to tradition. His music must be performed in a *simply flowing* style.' " Frau Schumann generally spoke English with the author, and the words printed in italics are those actually used by her. The author has discussed Brahms' attitude towards this frequently debated question in another place. (See " Life of Johannes Brahms," i. 16.)

to gain for it the approval of her father and his private circle.

"Wieck takes the greatest interest in me," Robert tells his mother; "he is in love with the 'Papillons' and Clara plays them to perfection."

A week later he writes to Wieck :—

"Here are the titles of my new works. How much obliged I should be if you would speak to Hofmeister about them. I cannot do it well myself, and am too modest about terms. Four thalers a sheet would not, I think, be too much for the caprices [Studies after Paganini]. For the intermezzi and fandango, a louis d'or [about eighteen shillings]. . . . Every day that I cannot speak to you or Clara makes a blank in my Leipzig book of life." *

And again on June 8 :—

"Look favourably on the caprices; it was a divine task but rather herculean. Please—sit down by Clara with a pencil in your hand and mark anything that strikes you. . . ."

Clara had an Opus 2 of her own to show Robert, consisting of seven "Caprices en forme de Valses" which appeared simultaneously in Paris (Stöpel) and Leipzig (Hofmeister). The several numbers give evidence—and not only by their more developed form—that she had made considerable progress since the publication of the polonaises in the art of putting her thoughts into shape. No. 2, particularly, with its simple motif of two notes and its genuine slow-waltz rhythm, testifies to a quietly advancing power that contains promise of future ripeness.

Caprice No. 2.   First Part.

Allegro moderato.

Con grazia.

---

* The Fandango was accepted by Hofmeister, but was not published in its original form owing to the loss of part of the manuscript.

She worked steadily on for several hours daily at counterpoint and composition—now under Dorn's guidance—and
was happy enough in availing herself of the exceptional musical
advantages of her lot. Imperious or coaxing as the humour
took her, there was developing within her even at this early
age, side by side with the sensitive excitability of the artist's
temperament, a fund of practical understanding and good
common sense that were to do her brave service in years to
come. She gave two musical academies in the Gewandhaus
concert hall in July, with the assistance of the orchestra,
adding to the concert répertoire with which the reader is

familiar, Hummel's rondo " La Sentinella," the polonaise from Moscheles' E flat concerto, the first movement of Field's second concerto, and Herz's variations, Op. 48; and including in the first programme Chopin's " Don Juan " variations. All her selections were played from memory, and the applause, says the *Allgemeine Musikalische Zeitung*, was on both occasions " extraordinary."

What Schumann's feelings were for the child who afforded him an artistic companionship that reflected but little of the more than nine years' disparity of age existing between them may be judged to some extent from his words to his mother : " We are like brother and sister," though it is not difficult to perceive in some of his other expressions the foreshadow of a sentiment to come deeper than is here suggested. In his first letter to Clara, written during her stay at Frankfurt in January, 1832, he says: " You have a thinking head and understand your old moonstruck charade-proposer—so, dear Clara, I often think of you, not as a brother of his sister or a friend of his friend, but rather as a pilgrim of the distant altar image." " Clara will give you plenty to think about," he writes later to his mother.

Robert himself provided his family with matter for serious reflection in the course of the summer. He had news to tell which, reviving the old vexed question of his future, filled his mother with deep consternation. At some period after his return to Leipzig—probably during Wieck's long absence with Clara during the concert season of 1831–32, still dissatisfied with the rapid technical progress he was making as a pianist, his memory reverted to his discussions with Töpken at Heidelberg * and, working out an old idea, he contrived a mechanical appliance which was, as he fancied, to enable him to gain the desired flexibility of finger by means considerably shorter than any prescribed by recognised authority. He carried on his experiments in strict privacy, only confiding to his friend Julius Knorr that he had hit upon an infallible device for the speedy attainment of mechanical dexterity. No long time elapsed before he was obliged to confess to himself that he had injured the first finger of his right hand, but he

* See *ante*, p. 46.

did not speak of the matter for a while, trusting that nature and comparative rest might effect a speedy cure. Never was hope more completely disappointed. Possibly the irresistible temptation presented to him by Wieck's return to exercise his fingers as usual may have aggravated the mischief. Be this as it may, it became evident shortly afterwards that the hand had been rendered useless for pianistic purposes for the time being, and, as the event proved, neither nature nor art, rest nor remedies, ever availed entirely to restore the efficiency of the lamed finger.

It is small wonder that Robert's mother was brought near to despair when, under the first shock of his misfortune, he hinted that theology might supply him with an alternative profession if he should find himself obliged to abandon that of music, though it needs hardly to be said that the idea was a mere fleeting one born of natural perturbation. The very charm of young Schumann's letters to his mother is that they reflect his transient moods, his passing thoughts, his whimsical fancies, as faithfully as the graver passages of his mind. It was not long before he was able to face with complete equanimity, or perhaps with positive relief, the idea that he had cut himself off permanently from the virtuoso career, and in so far as the injury to his hand brought him the sooner to the full consciousness of his real destiny, it may be said to have been of advantage to him. The finger regained sufficient strength in the course of time to serve him for all private requirements, and no allusion either to the episode or its consequences is to be found in his published correspondence after the spring of 1834.

Clara, who had, as we have seen, appeared several times on the Gewandhaus platform in the course of the past four years in her own academies, or on other " extra " occasions, made her début on September 30, 1832, at the age of thirteen, at the great subscription concerts with Moscheles' G minor concerto and Herz's " Jägerchor " variations, and achieved brilliant success. Her position in the musical world was already becoming defined, not as that of a wonder-child, but as that of the youngest representative of the series of great players, headed by Clementi, whose names are inseparably associated with the history of the pianoforte.* Considered from the stand-point of to-day, this contemporary judgment is found to have been ratified by the course of events. Clara occupies a distinctive place in musical history—and with Clara the father who formed and directed her career—in virtue of a fact which is not generally recognised, but which will be seen constantly illustrated in the course of our story. From childhood her répertoire of concert pieces was steadily enriched as that of no other pianist of the same date by the addition to it of the very best music that offered itself for choice as her powers became sufficiently matured for its due performance, so that from the age of twelve, when she began to play Chopin, she must be considered as the pioneer *par excellence* of the highest developments of the pianoforte art of her time.†

A short journey in Saxony in the month of November made Wieck and his daughter acquainted with Robert's mother and other members of his family, and in Zwickau, as in Schnee-berg, where his brother Carl was in business as a bookseller, the impression made by Clara's personality in private circles was hardly less remarkable than the enthusiasm roused by her public performances. It is not wonderful that Robert's mother should have been conscious of a desire that she might one day know her son's career safe in the hands of the young girl whose rare qualities of character and heart she divined with the sure instinct of a mother's loving anxiety for her favourite child. The Zwickau subscription concert of November 18, to which Clara contributed solos, was made especially noteworthy by the fact that it presented Schumann's name for the first time to the concert-going public as a composer.

---

* See an article by Rellstab in the *Iris*, No. 41 of 1832.

† Dr. Gustav Jansen erroneously ascribes to Julius Knorr the honour of the first concert performance of Chopin's " Don Juan " variations, Op. 2, at a Leipzig concert of October 27, 1831 (" Die Davidsbündler," p. 217, note 15). The work was played for the first time in public from the MS. by the composer at his Vienna concert of August 11, 1829, and was performed in the same city by Mademoiselle Belleville, a distinguished young pianist of the day, remembered as Madame Oury, shortly after its publication by Has-linger at the end of the same year. It was first heard in Germany as per-formed by Clara on October 7, 1831, at her concert in Weimar, already recorded in this volume.

The programme included the first movement of a symphony in G minor with which he had been engrossed during the autumn, and on the Wiecks' departure from Zwickau, unable to hope for any immediate resumption of his pianoforte lessons, he settled at home for the winter to devote himself to the completion and revision of the work. Perhaps only his firm determination to succeed gave him courage to persevere with an undertaking for the satisfactory fulfilment of which his powers were not as yet ripe. " I am working industriously at the symphony," he writes to Hofmeister in December; " I often take blue for yellow in the instrumentation of the first movement, but this art seems to me so difficult that I think it must take years of study to master it with certainty. . . ." He received a reminder of his Leipzig friends a few days before Christmas in the shape of a delightful letter from Clara,* written during her convalescence from an attack of scarlet fever, to which, much to her father's annoyance, he returned no immediate answer : " In all haste an apology if I can find one," he writes to Wieck in January. " Great concert in Zwickau—Thierfelder wrote for the symphony—revision of the first movement—rewriting of parts and score—and you are still surprised and angry ? Seriously, it is an easy matter to write to you, but I have not yet felt equal to a letter to Clara. Do you believe this ? . . . I shall return to Leipzig in February for certain with the finished symphony under my arm. It would give me great encouragement if you could help to secure a performance." †

Clara made her reappearance after her illness with a selection from her standing répertoire at the Gewandhaus subscription concert of January 10, 1833. At that of February 28th she played Herz's variations on a theme from Rossini's " Joseph," and, with the principal soloists of the orchestra, Hummel's septet, both pieces being additions to her concert list. More characteristic, however, in the development of her career were her performances at a musical entertainment given at her father's house—now Reichsstrasse 579—on January 13th, to which admission was by invitation only, though the programmes were printed. On this occasion she introduced

* Published by Litzmann, i. 54.   † " Jugendbriefe," p. 199.

7

Chopin's first and second sets of mazurkas, Opp. 6 and 7, playing them entire; No. 2, in E flat, from the same composer's first set of nocturnes, Op. 9; and two numbers from Schumann's "Studies for Pianoforte after Paganini's Violin Caprices," Op. 3, all works scarcely dry from the printer's ink. Her own valses-caprices, Op. 2, added to the interest of a remarkable programme. Of the list of her achievements during the spring of the year two most noteworthy remain for mention—her own concerts in the Gewandhaus of April 29th and May 5th. To the first of these public attention was drawn by a paragraph in the *Leipziger Tageblatt* of April 28th, signed "O." (Ortlepp):—

" . . . Clara Wieck will, by general desire, perform Chopin's bravura variations. These will be followed by the first movement of a symphony by Robert Schumann, a young pianist and composer resident here, who has already made a favourable impression by several interesting and original compositions." The programme, which was headed by Mendelssohn's "Midsummer Night's Dream" overture, further contained two new works by Kalkbrenner and Pixis for pianoforte and orchestra. An article in the *Leipziger Tageblatt* of May 1st, entitled "Clara Wieck," by Dr. C. F. Pohl, contains honourable mention of Robert's work: "Who did not listen with pleasure to Mendelssohn's poetic and original overture and to Schumann's imaginative symphony movement?" Whilst of Clara we read:—

"What could we not say of the concert-giver? She has attained a degree of technical accomplishment which enables her to execute great difficulties with ease and certainty; a repose and presence of mind when performing which never desert her; a power which compels admiration."

At her concert of May 5th, the programme of which included Mendelssohn's overture to the "Hebrides," the extraordinary young artist introduced the finale from Chopin's lately published E minor concerto, two of the same composer's *études*, all for the first time in Germany, and a new manuscript movement of her own composition.*

* Litzmann does not mention Wieck's musical entertainment of January 13th. Of Clara's concerts he only says: "Clara gave a concert of her own

After its third performance at Clara's concert of April 29th in the Leipzig Gewandhaus, Schumann's symphony movement —given for the first time in Zwickau in November, 1832, and for the second time in Schneeberg in February, 1833—was not again brought to a hearing. It must be concluded, in the absence of evidence to the contrary, that the other portions of the work were never performed, though Schumann definitely states in a letter to Töpken of April 5, 1833, that he had finished writing them at that date.* Many years were to pass before he made a second attempt to accomplish the most onerous task that lies before the instrumental composer.

Robert had been able to rejoice his mother's heart, soon after his return to Leipzig, by sending her word of a very favourable review printed in the *Wiener Anzeiger* of his Opus 3; the studies after Paganini, lately published by Hofmeister and played in January, as we have seen, by Clara at her father's house. Not only the title chosen for this work, but the careful and interesting directions for practice placed before each of its six numbers, show that it was primarily intended to serve a purpose in the education of pianists. The idea of arranging Paganini's violin caprices as pianoforte studies was probably suggested to Schumann's mind by a paragraph contained in Kalkbrenner's "Pianoforte School," published simultaneously in Paris and Leipzig.† Its execution was, however, immediately useful to Schumann himself by giving him opportunity to apply and confirm his lately acquired knowledge of harmonic

in the Gewandhaus" (vol. i. 59). For the authentic records of these occasions see Alfred Dörfell's "Geschichte der Gewandhaus Konzerte," written for the Leipzig Society in 1884, and the *Leipziger Tageblatt*, May, 1833. Wasielewski mentions the performance of Schumann's symphony movement on April 29th, but speaks of it as though it had taken place at one of the regular subscription concerts ("Robert Schumann," p. 103, footnote 3).

* "Briefe," p. 40.

† "To complete this school it is necessary to play a great deal of music for other instruments, as the violin, flute, and violoncello, in order to acquire a mastery over passages difficult or almost impossible of execution. For instance, it is very useful to play Paganini's violin studies on the pianoforte when there is no longer danger of spoiling the position of the hands, and if one has a good method of fingering." Compare with this passage, quoted from Kalkbrenner's "School," the third paragraph of Schumann's preface to his own Op. 3.

laws; and, impressing him with certain of Paganini's distinctive rhythmic peculiarities which corresponded with tendencies of his own musical thought, it may be said to have been of permanent importance to his development. While the studies are arranged with fine tact and scrupulous care to preserve the individuality of the caprices, they are hardly less characteristic of Schumann than of Paganini. The significance of the work to the student of the pianoforte has been gradually diminished by the advance of virtuosity and the multiplication of pianoforte *études*; it possesses abiding value for the music-lover, however, by reason both of its intrinsic and historic interest.

The Intermezzi, Op. 4, completed about the same time as the studies, though not published until nearly a year later, show that Schumann's rich imagination was, at the time of their composition, becoming rapidly subject to the refining and formative influence of his advancing knowledge. He describes them in several letters of the period, in the terms of his favourite symbol, as "longer Papillons," but they stand on a higher artistic plane than the set of pieces originally so called, and are obviously the work of a musician; a youthful musician who has new and striking thoughts to give the world, the birth of which involves the realisation of a new method of expression. They are full of the glowing impulse that from first to last distinguishes Schumann's artistic personality, and if there is a want of cohesion in their texture, and some indistinctness in the presentment of their melodic fancy, they manifest a vigour of purpose that contains good promise of more perfect accomplishment to come.*

The spring and summer months of 1833 formed an idyllic period in the lives of Robert and Clara, bringing to them both an unconscious, unalloyed, youthful happiness such as they hardly again experienced. Robert had found almost a country

---

* The idea that Schumann intended to indicate by the title "Papillons," chosen for his Opus 2, the character of the pieces as "a mirror of butterfly nature, frolicsome, volatile, and coquettish," is expressly denied by the author in a letter to Töpken of April 5, 1833 ("Briefe," p. 43). The metaphorical meaning of his frequent use of the word with reference to his own music is partly suggested by a passage in one of his letters to Wieck: "I have assumed very much the state of a chrysalis, and am engaged quietly spinning."

lodging in "Riedel's garden," just outside the town ; "delightful, simple little rooms bathed in sunshine and moonshine,"
looking on to green fields, trees, and blooming flowers, where
he could study and muse in a quietude made luxurious by the
pleasant sounds of nature outside.   He not infrequently
relieved the solitude of his morning's work by despatching a
messenger to Leipzig on pressing business of the moment—
a request to Wieck or Clara for the loan of a piece of music,
a suggestion for an afternoon's excursion, or, it might be, for
the mere purpose of sociable greeting.   He had become the
centre of a circle of young men, chiefly musicians, who were
admitted with him to the intimacy of Wieck's house, and the
days were few in the course of which the lively group of artists
and students—Robert and his friends, Wieck and his pupils,
both youths and maidens—did not meet to walk, talk, or make
music.   Certain it is that neither of the young people was
more acutely interested in whatever might be the musical
topic of the hour than the middle-aged man, loved and
respected by them all, of whose struggles and victories they
were reaping the reward, and who felt himself at his happiest
when able to be in their midst.   Even when Robert was
confined to his room with a bad feverish chill, the result of
an all night carousal with some of his companions in the open
air, communication with the Wiecks' house was scarcely
interrupted, and the first act of his convalescence was to
make a spiritual appointment with Clara.   Both were to play
the adagio of Chopin's variations at a certain hour whilst
thinking intently each of the other, in order to bring about
a meeting of their familiars in the air, probably somewhere
above "the small Thomas gate."

"Clara is as faithful to me as ever," writes Robert to his
mother; "is just what she was—high-spirited and romantic—
runs and jumps and plays like a child, and, again, says the
most significant things.   It is delightful to see how quickly
her gifts of heart and mind are developing, and yet, as it were,
leaf by leaf.   As we were returning lately from Connewitz
(we walk for two or three hours nearly every day), I heard her
say to herself: 'Oh, how happy I am, how happy!'   Who
would not like to hear this!   There are some very unnecessary

stones on the footpath leading in that direction, and as it happens that I look up rather than down when I am talking, she always walks behind me and quietly pulls my coat at every stone, that I may not stumble. Sometimes in doing so she stumbles herself."

" One might take Clara at first sight," says a keen observer, writing about this time in the Hamburg *Cecilia*, " as she is at home—natural and childlike in manner to her father and friends—merely for an amiable girl of thirteen. Closer study, however, reveals something very different. The fine, pretty little face with the somewhat contradictory eyes ; the pleasant mouth with its trace of sentimentality which now and then —particularly when she *answers*—becomes scornful or sad ; the graceful carelessness of her movements, not studied, yet developed beyond her years—I confess that these things excited in me a quite peculiar feeling which I am unable better to describe than as ' an echo of Clara's scornful-sad smile.' The child looks as though she could tell a long tale of joy and grief, and yet—what does she know ? Music."

An enduring memorial of this happy summer-time exists in Schumann's Op. 5, "Impromptus on a theme by Clara Wieck," which possesses a double personal interest from the fact that Clara's melody, composed on a bass by Robert, had been used by herself as the theme for a set of bravura variations which she dedicated to her friend and that the two works appeared respectively in July and August. The impromptus, sent by Robert as a birthday surprise to Wieck, to whom they were originally dedicated, are written in free variation form, on a ground bass, and are modelled to a considerable extent on the set in E flat written by Beethoven for the pianoforte on the Eroica theme. The beautiful ideas with which they abound fail to produce an entirely satisfactory effect, owing to young Schumann's inexperience in the art of selection, but they stamp the work, which is rich also in new harmonic combinations and original rhythms, as that of a composer by the grace of Heaven, a born creative poet.

Autumn brought its dark clouds. Robert's nerves were completely shattered by the successive deaths of his sister-in-law Rosalie and his brother Julius ; and Clara suffered with

her friend, though her youth, her stronger nature, and the
ordered regularity of her everyday life, happily sufficed to
preserve her mind from morbid preoccupation with his
distress. The few public engagements she fulfilled during
the second half of 1833 brought no important addition to
her already large concert répertoire, though they derive a
general historical interest from the circumstance that they
again show her, at the age of fourteen, as the executive
representative on the pianoforte of the rapidly developing
romanticism that was soon to assert itself successfully as
the distinctive musical phenomenon of the nineteenth century.
Her father, true to his leading principle of working for the
permanent establishment of her career rather than for an
unbroken succession of youthful triumphs, ordained that the
next year should be chiefly devoted to the quiet study, not
only of her own special subjects, but also, and particularly,
of singing and foreign languages. It was one of Wieck's
favourite theories that training in the art of voice production
is useful to the pianoforte student, since it draws his attention
to an ideal standard of tone quality which it should be his
aim to approximate as far as possible in cantabile passages
for his instrument ; and every one having a clear remembrance
of the beautiful quality of Frau Schumann's tone, which
was one of the distinguishing characteristics of her art, will
allow that her father's opinion on this point is entitled to
respect. Clara was assiduous in her study of composition
during the period of comparative repose from the excitements
of public life which she enjoyed from the summer of 1833
to the autumn of 1834, and the hopes entertained by Wieck
as to a possible future for her productive talent are modestly
expressed in a letter addressed by him about this time to
Music-director Riem of Bremen :—

"I shall have much to say to you when we meet about
the new romantic school in which Chopin, Pixis, Liszt in
Paris and several of Robert Schumann's disciples here write
(and perhaps Clara promises to write). It forms, as I am
convinced, the bridge of return to the pianoforte music of
Mozart and Beethoven. Its [executive] difficulties are
certainly unprecedented, but this was successively the case

with the music of Mozart and Beethoven in their day. Those who have not been educated upon the works of these two giants and on Bach's 'Well-tempered Clavier,' who have not received a really *musical* education, must indeed let it alone. This will be a good thing, however, for there will be an end to the *jingling*." *

* Kohut, p. 69.

CHAPTER VII

1834

The *Neue Zeitschrift für Musik*—Progress of musical romanticism—
The Davidsbund—Florestan and Eusebius—Schumann as editor and
reviewer.

" TOWARDS the close of the year 1833," wrote Schumann
twenty years later than our present date, when preparing the first edition of his " Collected Writings " for the
press, " a number of, for the most part young, musicians
used to meet every evening as if by chance for social intercourse and for the interchange of ideas on the art which
was to them as the meat and drink of life—music. The
musical conditions of the time cannot be said to have been
satisfactory. Rossini still ruled the stage, Herz and Hünten
almost exclusively the pianoforte. Mendelssohn's star was,
indeed, in the ascendant, and wonderful things were reported
of a Pole, Chopin; but it was not until later that the influence
of these masters became effectively established. One day
the idea was suggested in the circle of young hotheads:
Let us not look on idly; let us bestir ourselves to improve
matters; let us bestir ourselves in the cause of the poetry
of art. From this thought resulted the first pages of a
new musical periodical."

That Schumann was himself the originator of this new
enterprise and that he had been considerably occupied
throughout the summer of 1833 with plans for its arrangement is shown by his published correspondence, and interesting
light is thrown on the story of his development, as well as
on the musical history of the time, by study of the circumstances under which the first number of the *Neue Zeitschrift
für Musik*, still in circulation in 1912, was issued in April,

1834, under the joint management of Schumann, Wieck, and two others, and with the support of nearly three hundred subscribers, by the bookseller Hartmann of Leipzig.

The young composer enumerates, in a letter to Wieck of August 6, 1833, the personal considerations that attracted him to the undertaking, and it is characteristic of him that the desire to make it remunerative was not the most prominent among them. He lays greater emphasis on his wish to acquire, by submission to the practical necessities of such a field of labour, the habit of working regularly and quickly; and on the certainty that conscientious literary activity, with music as its objective, cannot fail to correct and widen his special knowledge and help him to a clearer perception of his exact musical purposes. The artistic motives by which he was incited to the enterprise are stated in his editorial address of January, 1835 : * "Our design has been definite from the first. It is to dwell with insistence on the memory of the old time and its works, and to point out that new art inspirations can derive stability only at this pure source ; to oppose the tendencies of the immediate past, which has aimed at the development of mere outward virtuosity, as antagonistic to the spirit of true art ; finally, to prepare the way for, and help to hasten, the coming of a new poetic era."

These words have a remarkable interest for the student of musical history. As we look back across the three-quarters of a century that have elapsed since they were written, they seem to mark the very moment when the impulse that had stirred Weber and Field to their characteristic work—an impulse of the significance of which they were, perhaps, but half conscious—had become the chosen guide of the most gifted composers of a younger generation. Not Schumann only declared himself about this time ; Berlioz and Chopin had already made similar pronouncements, though neither knew that the other had spoken. German, Frenchman, and Pole each expressed himself in the language of romanticism ; but whilst there was a strong conservative element in Schumann's manifesto, that of Berlioz hinted at revolution.

* Reprinted in the " Collected Writings."

It may be well to explain at this point, for the benefit of the general reader, that the word " romantic," as applied to a certain group of composers of the nineteenth century, is not to be understood in its mere everyday sense.   It has acquired a special meaning in the nomenclature of musical history, which refers to a clearly-defined phase in the development of musical art—a phase resting on the principle of the suitability of music as a medium for the expression of ideas and mental images not immediately derived from the domain of tone.   This principle, though not unrecognised by the composers of earlier periods, had not hitherto been treated as an essential motive-power of creative activity.   It was now to be promoted from its comparatively subordinate position in the category of possible resource to become operative as a main influence of musical imagination.   Vindicated in its new relation to the art of the stage by the triumph, during the last quarter of the nineteenth century, of the life-work of Wagner, its application in the domain of purely instrumental music remains a subject of controversy in the second decade of the twentieth.

The so-called romantic phase of musical development shows itself as the complement of the famous schools of literature from which its designation has been borrowed ; of the German school, which was founded by a few thinkers and poets who rose to eminence at the dawn of the nineteenth century, older contemporaries, and some of them—as Tieck, Hoffmann, and Clemens Brentano—friends, of Weber; of the French school that flourished thirty years later, led to greatness by Victor Hugo and de Musset, of which Madame Dudevant was an apostle—the George Sand who exercised her fateful influence on Chopin's life.   Both literary schools were called into being, each in its day, by the longing of a youthful generation for more satisfying ideals than they found in the rationalism and modern classicism that had ruled the thought and taste of the eighteenth century ; the longing to penetrate with heart and soul into the warmth and colour and passion hidden beneath the surface of existence.   To the disciples of both, freedom, individualism, nationality, were watchwords ; and medievalism the subject of an enthusiastic cult.   But whereas the German writer, whatever his special branch of authorship, was primarily concerned about theories of life, the Frenchman occupied himself in the first place with its phenomena. The one was, before all things, a philosopher ; the other an artist.

The art of Weber, which, apart from its intrinsic value, has, as we know, a special interest as being generally representative of the distinctive musical tendencies of its time, was in intimate sympathy with certain sides of German literary romanticism. In it, as in an enchanted atmosphere, live the knights and dames, the elves and sprites, the sorcerers and hobgoblins, with whose shapes the fancy of the Middle Ages had peopled the forests and mountains and valleys of Germany, and whose half-forgotten appeal to the affections of the country had been renewed by the cultivation of medievalism encouraged by the romantic authors. The revival of Teutonic myth and legend, initiated by August and Friedrich Schlegel, Ludwig Tieck, and their friends, gave appreciable stimulus during the wars with France to the growing sentiment of German nationality which formed part of the essence of Weber's inspiration; and the three of the composer's works which especially indicate, by their picturesque characterisation, the strength of the current that was bearing dramatic and instrumental art towards the high-tide of musical romanticism, are precisely those that gave him his enduring place as the pre-eminent national singer among the poets and musicians of his time. "Der Freischütz," the "Concertstück," and the "Invitation to the Waltz," all produced after 1815, still seem instinct with the joyous stir of freedom that spread, after the fall of Napoleon, through the length and breadth of the Fatherland, and we may appropriately recall here the letter in which Weber has recorded that the movements of the "Concertstück" took shape, almost against his will, around "a kind of story" which obstinately thrust itself before his consciousness as he was occupied with the sketches of the work. When, later on, he played the finished composition to his wife and his pupil, Jules Benedict, he accompanied his performance with a running verbal commentary, fitting to the music, page by page, and almost bar by bar, the details of a typical love-tale of feudal times.*

* See "Carl Maria von Weber. Ein Lebensbild. Von Max Maria von Weber."

If, however, the attitude of literary romanticism may have
helped to determine that particular development of the tendency to musical characterisation which may be studied in the
brilliant, but not very profound, art of Weber and of those
whom he on the whole represents, its influence on the musical
imagination of a younger generation of tone poets was to be
much more radical.   To the young Schumann especially, with
his eager intellectual appetite, his ardent temperament and
speculative brain, the poetico-philosophic theories of life and
art embodied in the writings of the German romantic authors,
which are founded on the worship of genius, the mystic exaltation of the passion of love, and the sentiment of an intimate
emotional relationship between nature and man, could not
fail to be strongly attractive.   It is probable that the impression he had derived from them may have intensified the
mental struggle that seemed, for a time, to threaten the
promise of his youth.   The true explanation of his long-felt
unwillingness to apply himself to mastering the technique
either of pianoforte playing or composition, is certainly to
be found rather in his thoroughgoing acceptance of the
romanticist's faith in the self-sufficing, intuitive power of
genius—the belief that to subject the poetic imagination to
the restraint of law is to cripple its power of flight—than
in his repugnance to the patient study of detail, however
dry and tedious this may have seemed to him in anticipation.
It was a saying of his, in his early period, that he had learnt
more counterpoint from Jean Paul than from his music teacher.
Fortunately the vigour of his understanding, aided by growing
experience and the favourable circumstances of his second
residence in Leipzig, saved him from that unconditional
surrender to impulse which weakened the art and disfigured the
lives of some of the most illustrious of his literary predecessors.
The spirit of Schumann's music not only reflects, but enriches
and vitalises the vision of the romantic authors, while the
tale of his life is largely that of the realisation of aspirations,
the fulfilment of which they also had desired for themselves,
but knew not the way to attain.

The form devised by the young composer for the conduct of
the *Neue Zeitschrift für Musik* gives interesting evidence of his

predilection for romantic methods. Publishing his periodical as the supposed organ of a purely imaginary " Society of David " (Davidsbund), constituted for the purpose of waging deadly warfare against the platitudes of musical philistinism, he furnished his readers as time went on with a series of fanciful papers—purported records of the meetings and discussions of the mysterious association, notices of new compositions and passing musical events, varied by short paragraphs—all written by himself and a few of his friends, and generally signed by the associates (Davidsbündler) collectively, or with the names or numbers assigned to them severally as belonging to the inner circle of the brotherhood. The names Julius and Serpentinus, representing two of Schumann's responsible colleagues in the undertaking, Jonathan, Fritz-Friedrich, and others, appear occasionally under the articles ; whilst numerous allusions to the various members of the society, and especially to its one original lady associate, the young pianist Chiara, sometimes called Zilia, occur in the writings of Florestan and Eusebius, Schumann's own pseudonyms—already used by him in occasional articles written for other periodicals—whose frequent contributions, by carrying on the fictitious existence of the Davidsbund, give a certain loose unity to the scheme.

In his conception and treatment of these twin leading spirits of his association Schumann presents his readers with an original employment of the idea of the "Doppelgänger," "the man who walks double," which, originated and used under various forms by Jean Paul, appears in the works of several of the leading romantic writers, and is employed over and over again by, perhaps, the most fantastic of them all, E. T. A. Hoffmann. Schumann's Doppelgänger is conceived, not as a man and his wraith—i.e., personality and its reflection—but as a personality divided into two contrasting entities, to be reblended to completeness at the author's pleasure. "Florestan and Eusebius," Schumann writes to Dorn, " is my double nature (Doppelnatur), which I should gladly unite, as in Raro, to form a whole man."

The two phantoms, unlike the generality of their prototypes, are devoted friends and companions. They walk about arm

in arm, appear together at public and private assemblies,
share every interest, in short, confide in each other absolutely
and at all times. To Florestan, energetic, eager, vehement,
sometimes brusque, and, in his professional capacity, an
outspoken but generous critic, falls as by natural right the
position of senior in the alliance. His affectionate raillery
is received with invariable good-humour by the tender, dreamy
Eusebius, who is content to sit in a corner and follow his
comrade's movements with admiring attention, or to lean
over Zilia's chair whilst Florestan harangues the assembled
Davidsbündler from the top of a table; and who, when it
becomes his duty to judge the work of others, takes heed
of merits rather than defects. Any artistic question in dispute
between the pair is referred, as a matter of course, to Meister
Raro, whose decision is always accepted as final. Nor is it by
any means inconsistent with accepted romantic procedure that
this worthy, who in the early numbers of the *Neue Zeitschrift*
stands for Wieck, should gradually come to represent Schumann
himself in possession of his full personality; that Florestan or
Eusebius should not infrequently sign an original paper with
the name of a companion, or that Eusebius should write to
Chiara at Milan about Zilia at Firlenz—Milan standing for
Dresden, Firlenz for Leipzig, and both Chiara and Zilia for
Clara Wieck. The strategy of mystification, in which
Schumann took a youthful pleasure, fills a conspicuous place
throughout the art of the German romantic authors. It may
be remarked in passing, as illustrative of the honourable
position assigned by the Davidsbündlerschaft to their lady
member, that the only contributions to the *Neue Zeitschrift*
signed by Florestan and Eusebius jointly are a review of
Clara Wieck's " Soirées Musicales," Op. 6, and a poem written
on the occasion of one of her Leipzig concerts.

Whilst in the form of the *Neue Zeitschrift* as it was
originally published, and again in the style of its leading
contributor, the influence of German literary romanticism
is evident, the substance of its contents is interpretative of
those principles of what we may call German, as distinguished
from French, musical romanticism, which Schumann strove to
realise in his own manner, and which are suggested in the

passage we have quoted from his editorial address at the opening of 1835 : loving reverence for past achievement, active belief in possibilities to come. The young Davids-bündler live and labour as in the presence of the past gods and heroes of their art, but they are always on the look-out for those who may become its future prophets, and joyfully hail, in their periodical, all musical work in which they detect the germ of true creative activity. It not infrequently happened in later years, after Schumann had retired from connection with the *Zeitschrift*, that he was charged by adherents of either side of a bitter party warfare with having allowed himself, in the course of his editorship, to be too easily betrayed into mistaken enthusiasms. No doubt his judgment was at fault in the case of one or two now nearly forgotten musicians. No doubt, too, that a few years before his death, the joy he felt on recognising the genius of the young Brahms caused him, when writing the famous article, " Neue Bahnen," to overlook the value of literary restraint. On the other hand, the critical acumen and critical conscientiousness that distinguish the very numerous papers in which he stimulated and, in several notable cases, first awakened public interest in the work of Schubert, Mendelssohn, Chopin, Berlioz, Henselt, Sterndale Bennett, Stephen Heller, Niels Gade, Robert Franz, and others, must be evident to every competent reader who will take the trouble to refer to them. The earlier numbers of the *Zeitschrift* contain several more or less exhaustive reviews from his pen of new or important compositions, the most interesting being the well-known essay on Berlioz's " Symphonie Fantastique," a work which had become known to him through the medium of Liszt's pianoforte transcription. Later on, however, he avoided analysis and the discussion of minutiæ, preferring to dwell on the psychological aspect of the works he considered ; to reproduce in the mind of his reader something of the impression he had himself derived from their ideas and spirit by means of the language of poetic imagery, of which he had a facile command. Over small technical errors he passed lightly, only indicating them, as it were, *en parenthèse*. In his fund of kindly humour he possessed a resource which frequently enabled him to preserve his sincerity without too severely wounding the feelings of others. "To which of Shakespeare's plays are most of the overtures written?" Florestan asks Eusebius, who absently suggests "Romeo and Juliet." Florestan, however, opines that it is "Much Ado about Nothing"!

In order that the reader may be able to form his own opinion as to the happiness or infelicity of Schumann's remarks in certain cases in which his judgment has been particularly called in question, we give a very few sentences taken almost at random from some of his numerous reviews of compositions by Mendelssohn, Sterndale Bennett, and Berlioz. For ourselves, as, reading them, we recall the masterly and imaginative art of such works as Mendelssohn's concert overtures and violin concerto; the poetic sentiment and intellectual style of the young Bennett's fourth pianoforte concerto, "Naids" overture and short pianoforte pieces; Berlioz's whole startling artistic individuality, we can only conclude that the originators of the usual commonplace reflections on Schumann's critical style have not in the majority of cases informed themselves from the composer's own writings what his observations really were. It should be remarked that the comparative calm in the musical firmament welcomed by Schumann in his notice of Mendelssohn's D minor Trio, from which we quote, proved to be but the lull in a tempest that was to rage with unprecedented fury through the third quarter of the nineteenth century.

"It is the master trio of the present time. . . . The storm of the last years is beginning gradually to abate and, as we may confess, has already thrown many pearls on the shore. Mendelssohn, who has felt its grip less strongly than others, is nevertheless a son of the age. He too has had to wrestle; he too has had to hear from narrow-minded writers that the 'true flowering-time of art is behind us'; and, by wrestling, he has attained such a height that we may venture to say: he is the Mozart of the nineteenth century, the luminous master who sees through the contradictions of the times more clearly than others, and is the first to reconcile them. And he will not be the last. After Mozart came Beethoven; to the

8

new Mozart a new Beethoven will follow: yes, perhaps is already born."

Of Bennett Schumann writes:—

"After much meditation as to what offering may best induce the reader to reciprocate our good wishes at the beginning of the year 1837, it has occurred to me that I cannot do better than introduce to him a happy personality. Not a Beethoven who brings years of warfare in his train; not a Berlioz who, speaking with hero's voice, preaches revolution and spreads terror and destruction around him; but a still, harmonious spirit, who, working on alone like the stargazer on his height, heedless of the tumult beneath him, watches the course of phenomena; and, listening, possesses himself of nature's secrets. . . ." And later: "No one would call Bennett a great genius, but of genius he possesses a considerable share. In these days, which produce so much barren music, when brilliancy and mechanism are cultivated without limit or intelligence, let us rejoice doubly in the natural grace, the quiet intensiveness of his compositions. . . ."

Of Berlioz:

"As to whether the programme of Berlioz's symphony [fantastique] contains many poetical moments, we will say nothing. The important question is whether the music is of value apart from text and explanation, whether it has life. I think I have shown that it is not without the first attribute. No one will deny that it possesses the second, even in those parts where the composer is manifestly unsuccessful. . . . Should these lines serve so to encourage Berlioz as to induce him to moderate his inclination towards eccentricity; further: to make his symphony known, not as the work of a master, but as one distinguished by its originality from all others in existence; and lastly: to stimulate to fresher activity those German artists to whom he offers a strong hand in the union against talentless mediocrity, the object of their publication will have been accomplished."

That Schumann was fully and consciously fired with enthusiasm for the principle underlying musical romanticism —which we have described as that of the suitability of music as a medium for the expression of ideas and mental images not immediately derived from the domain of tone—and that to its development he looked for the realisation of a new efflorescence of instrumental art not less splendid than those evolutions of the seventeenth and eighteenth centuries which had culminated in the great creations of Bach and Beethoven, is directly shown by innumerable passages in his writings and letters. The precise means by which he believed that his desires might be accomplished are not so clearly indicated. A few of his very early sayings point in the direction of the extreme revolutionary tendencies of his time. Others, which are illustrated by features of his own creative activity, seem to indicate that he relied on the inherent energy of a new inspiration for the force of its appeal through extant forms and for the gradual adaptation of the latter to the needs of its future expansion. He declares repeatedly against the musical programme, which he regards as a concession to "materialism," and says that in his own case its effect is to disturb the enjoyment of listening to music by setting confines to his imagination. A title or motto placed at the beginning of a movement, by bringing the mind of the hearer into the right attitude for the reception of what is to follow, fulfils, he thinks, a legitimate purpose.

Schumann's anticipation that, by organising a musical party paper on the lines of modern thought, he would not only contribute to the advancement of the cause he had deeply at heart, but supply a public want, was justified by events. The *Neue Zeitschrift*, by its vigorous and ably pursued policy, its sincerity, and the fact that it represented ideas for the appreciation of which musical opinion had become ripe, soon took its place as a recognised power in the musical world. Sustained by an increasing subscription list in its unflinching opposition to the easygoing critical methods that had long been associated with the name of Fink, Rochlitz's successor to the editorship of the *Allgemeine Musikalische Zeitung*, while its range of influence was steadily widened by the additions made to its correspondence staff, there is no doubt that it bore its due share in the fulfilment of the main purposes of its origin. Nor may we question that Schu-

mann's editorial labours served an end in his artistic development that could not have been so easily reached by other
means. Circumstances, however, soon obliged him to assume
the sole management of the enterprise; and as time passed
on and he found himself unable, in the interest of the
paper, to withdraw from the exigencies of his position, he may
frequently have felt disturbed by the consciousness that he
was being prevented during the best years of his life from the full
exercise of his creative genius. His connection with the *Neue
Zeitschrift* outlasted the years of his youth, and as his fermentation period draws to its close the legend of the Davidsbund
gradually disappears from the pages of the periodical. The
distinctive qualities of Florestan and Eusebius may, however,
still frequently be traced in those anonymous contributions to
its later numbers which must be ascribed to the pen of Meister
Raro, whilst in the reprints from its volumes published, with
a few other papers, as Schumann's " Collected Writings," we
not only possess enduring memorials of an interesting period
in the development of musical romanticism, but are brought
into immediate contact with the sympathetic personality of
the great composer as it was during ten momentous years of
his life. Schumann's last contribution to the paper before
his retirement, at the close of 1843, from regular literary
activity, was an interesting essay on the composer Niels
Gade.

CHAPTER VIII

1834

Ernestine von Fricken—Clara in Dresden—Schumann and Ernestine—Carl
Banck—Schumann's " Carnaval "—" Études Symphoniques."

CLARA did not remain at home long to rejoice with her
friend in the initial promise of his new enterprise. Riper
in heart and mind than is usual at her age, she was at fourteen
and a half, with all her childlike naïveté of manner, rapidly
growing to womanhood, and this fact was marked, as the
summer of 1834 drew near, by an irritability of mood unusual
with her, which was rightly interpreted by Wieck as the
sign of some inward struggle. Not doubting that what he
probably regarded as a passing phase in her development
would yield to the influence of change of scene, he decided
that his daughter should pay a visit of some months to Dresden,
to pursue her studies in composition under Reissiger, Weber's
successor as Kapellmeister of the German opera of that city,
and that she should further utilise the period of her stay in
the Saxon capital by taking lessons in singing of a certain
Director Mieksch. Clara was, in fact, already beginning to be
conscious that she was even now not far from the determining
issue of her life, and the interval that sufficed to awaken
her to a clear perception of her feelings brought her, young
as she was, no slight suffering.

To the small circle of her girl friends, chief among whom
was Emilie List, the daughter of the American consul in
Leipzig and Clara's senior by about two years, had been
added in April of the year a new pupil of her father's,
between whom and herself an intimacy was quickly formed—
not so much as the result of a mutual sympathy of taste
or disposition as through the accident that the newcomer was

an inmate of the Wiecks' house during her stay in Leipzig, and that the two girls were thus brought into daily companionship. Born in September, 1816, Ernestine von Fricken was in her seventeenth year when she came to stay in Leipzig, and therefore of an age that entitled her to the position of the grown up "young lady" in the youthful society that frequented Wieck's house. She was a rather pretty blonde, goodnatured and not without musical aptitude; but, to judge from a few of her letters that have found their way into print, of inferior understanding, given to sentimentality, and inclined to see an admirer in every young man who paid her the ordinary civilities of social convention.

Under the circumstances of Schumann's close intimacy with the Wieck circle it was inevitable that Ernestine's meditations should, before long, be much occupied with the agreeable young composer, Clara's favourite friend and colleague, whose frequent visits to the house broke so pleasantly upon the pursuits of its inmates. Nor can it be considered in any way surprising that Robert, on his part, gradually becoming aware that Fräulein von Fricken was always summoned to attend his calls, that she looked at him sympathetically and was invariably interested in what he had to say, should fall into the habit of addressing his remarks especially to her, bestow on her the most bewitching of his "roguish smiles," and generally find his way to her side when he joined the family party—often made the merrier by the addition of friends—on their long daily walks. It happened, however, that, apart from the gratification naturally experienced by a young man of twenty-three on finding himself distinguished by the preference of a pretty girl who was, for the moment, a person of importance in his intimate circle, there dwelt within Robert at this time a consciousness which gave a peculiar significance to the pleasure he felt in Ernestine's society. He had as yet spoken of it to no one, but it inclined him, accustomed as he was to see events through the colours of his own enthusiastic temperament, to regard his acquaintance with Clara's friend as a special, mysterious indication of destiny.

Soon after his family bereavements of the autumn of 1833, he had written to his mother:—

" . . . I have been hardly more than a statue, feeling neither cold nor warm. Through forcing myself to work, life has gradually returned to me, but I am still so nervous and apprehensive that I cannot even sleep alone, and a good fellow is staying with me whose company comforts and gives me encouragement. [Carl Gunther, who had been Schumann's fellow-lodger in Riedel's garden.] Would you believe that I cannot make up my mind to travel to Zwickau *alone* in case of something happening to me ? Violent rushes of blood, unspeakable anxiety, momentary failure of the faculties, rapidly alternate. If you could form an idea of this complete spiritual apathy, the result of melancholy, I am sure you would forgive me for not having written. . . . One thing remains deep in my heart which I would not exchange for any price—the belief that there are still good men in existence—and a God. . . . "

Another letter followed two months later :—

"MY GOOD MOTHER,—I read your letter to-day for the first time. When I received it a week ago and divined its gloomy tone from the first few lines, I had not the courage to read it through. As the thought of other people's suffering so annihilates me at present as to destroy all my power of work, be careful not to mention anything that would cause me the slightest agitation—*or I must renounce your letters altogether.* I earnestly beg you in particular not to say or write anything that could remind me of Julius and Rosalie. . . . However, I have felt better and brighter the last few days than for a long time past ; perhaps cheerful thoughts may soon return. . . . You are mistaken if you imagine I give way to solitary brooding—a kind word makes me happy now ; I am grateful for every syllable spoken to me. For the rest, I live very simply, have given up all spirituous drinks, and walk a great deal every day, especially with my excellent friend Ludwig Schunke. . . ."*

Braced and strengthened by the companionship of this new friend, a young musician of extraordinary promise whose career was cut off by death a year later, and engrossed by the varied work necessary for the inauguration of his literary venture, Robert's mind gradually

* " Jugendbriefe," p. 227 and following.

recovered its tone with the approach of spring. But the impression of a night in October when, alone in his room, he had suddenly been assailed by the most appalling of all the terrors known to the morbid imagination—the fear of losing his reason—remained indelible in his memory; while the advice of the doctor whom he had consulted the next morning : " Choose a wife, she will soon cure you," had never since been absent from his thoughts. In this condition he had been prepared, from the day of his introduction to Ernestine, to find in her the being who could save him from himself, and his disposition to regard her as his providence, stirred as it was by her marked interest in him, was not lessened by the fact that her friends in Leipzig believed her to be the only child and heiress of a wealthy man. Probably after she had once engaged his attention she was, for the time being, magnetised by the immediate influence of his personality to a higher level of responsiveness than that of which she was usually capable, whilst Schumann, agitated by his remembrance of the past and his longing for the future, invested her with a thousand gifts and endowments that had no existence save in his own fancy. But a short time sufficed to establish a friendship between them that promised from the first to develop into a more intimate relation, and one of its earliest results was the disturbing effect it produced on Clara's daily life. For Clara, happy as she was, at first, to see Robert's merits so well appreciated by Ernestine, could not long reason herself into a satisfied acceptance of the light badinage which her old inseparable companion occasionally remembered to address to her, while his serious attention was increasingly engrossed by the new friend. Dissatisfied with herself and those about her, she acquiesced willingly in her father's suggestion that she should become Reissiger's pupil at Dresden, and, once relieved from the unavoidable contemplation of a possibility that could not but be distasteful to her, settled down to vigorous work, resolved to avail herself of every means of improvement and pleasure opened to her by the temporary change of residence. The whole proud courageous nature of the young girl speaks in a letter she sent Robert on his twenty-fourth birthday anniversary, June 8th : " the day when the good God dropped

such a musical spark from heaven, *i.e.*, when you were born."
Traces of the conflict that was passing within her are not
absent from it, and in more than one of its sentences may be
read a delicately playful reminder of her claims to the consideration of her friend :—

"... Is it really allowable, Herr Schumann, to take such
small heed of a friend as not once to write to her? I have
always been hoping at post-time to receive a letter from a certain
Mr. Enthusiast, but ah! I have been disappointed. I comforted myself with the thought that you were coming here, but
father has just written that you are not coming, as Knorr is ill.
Well, one must resign one's self to everything. . . .

"A card has been pasted on my door on which is written :
'Solemnly elected fellow-worker on the new musical paper,
Clarus Wieck.' You will receive six big sheets from me very
soon ; that will give you something to pay. . . .' "

Clara's attitude towards romanticism is indicated by the
style of signature adopted by her on this occasion :

" CLARA WIECK,

" CLARA WIECK,

" DOPPELGÄNGER." *

Robert's answer, when it did come, after an interval of
several weeks, was long and affectionate, "divided like a good
sonata into three parts: a laughing part, a chatting part, and a
talking part." "Your letter was *you*," he says. "You stood
before me talking, laughing, springing from earnest to jest, playing with veils like the diplomatists—in short, the letter was Clara,
the Doppelgängerin." † To Ernestine he alludes as " the bright
gem that can never be overvalued." There was not much consolation for Clara. Nor were matters improved by a short visit
she paid to her home about the middle of July to attend the
christening of a new little stepsister, Cecilia, for whom Robert
and Ernestine stood sponsors. The whole situation during her
stay is summed up, so far as she was concerned, in a single
laconic entry in her diary:—

"I made the acquaintance of Herrn Banck and Schlesier.

---

* The entire letter is given by Litzmann, i. 71.
† " Jugendbriefe," p. 246.

The former is an extremely cultivated musician and song-writer, who is making my visit very pleasant." She was soon back in Dresden, deeply plunged in work.

There can be little doubt that the rapidly growing affection between Ernestine and Schumann was noticed by Wieck with something more than equanimity. Probably he saw in it the cure of an incipient attachment in Clara, the development of which must, as it seemed to him, be inimical to the hopes that had been the inspiration of many laborious years of his life, at the very moment when time was becoming ripe for their fulfil-ment. He felt himself in duty bound, however, to warn Ernestine's guardian of what was going on, and, apparently in answer to a request from Captain von Fricken for more detailed information, wrote in a second letter :—

" Between Ernestine and Schumann there is—I will not say an intimate—but certainly a strong feeling. Of this I am con-vinced and need not go further into the matter. This inclina-tion, this constant preference for each other's society, this confidential relation between them is, however, of no unworthy kind. I could prove to you if we were together that no kiss, no caress, has passed between them; but they are greatly interested in one another. It would take me a long time to write you a detailed description of the rather capricious, head-strong, but noble, fascinating, enthusiastic, highly gifted, finely cultured composer and writer Robert Schumann. Now, my experienced friend, picture our Ernestine as rather restless —for a girl of that age is prescient—often somewhat absent— for she feels. It is hardly necessary for me to tell you, in short, that she watches in the window corner an hour beforehand in case Schumann should come to-day, as he did once before, an hour earlier than he arranged with her ! Are you not also aware that Ernestine changes her dress again in the evening, which is not at all necessary, before going for a walk with him and other friends ? That she jumps up from the piano after ten or twenty minutes, goes to another piano, happens to find herself by the window in the next room, goes to her own room, looks at me pleadingly, timidly (but without being tiresome, hasty, passionate, or determined), and asks if we are not going to drink our morning coffee in the Rosenthal to-morrow—and

one may read Schumann in her face. You ask what Ernestine
does when she is not playing. Never anything wrong! But
she often hangs about dreamily and she reads almost nothing,
for she reads and studies Schumann's face too much; and
what are dead letters to a living countenance?"*

It must be presumed that Captain von Fricken did not
altogether dislike the idea that Ernestine might make an early
marriage, since he only so far interfered in the progress of
events as to admonish her by letter to be discreet in her
behaviour :—

"Play duets with Schumann by all means, but be careful
to do nothing that could injure your peace or your credit. I
will not say more. I am glad that you have at all events sufficient respect for the opinion of the world not to appear in
public alone with Schumann." †

Matters took their natural course. Robert, who had by this
time become sure of his own feelings and could brook no uncertainty as to the exact nature of Ernestine's, availed himself
of the favourable opportunity of the joint sponsorship to
mention the word "love" for the first time. The same evening
he wrote her a letter which could only be interpreted as a
tentative declaration of his wishes, and to this a complete
understanding between the lovers almost immediately
followed.

"I was engaged to him quite definitely," Ernestine wrote
to Clara about two years later. "You cannot imagine how
it was possible that we should have been betrothed and often
have met without the knowledge of your good father! Yes,
my dear Clara, there were friends at the time who helped us.
Who and where and what they were are confidential matters
about which I can tell you nothing."

Early in September Ernestine quitted Leipzig in Captain
von Fricken's care, carrying with her as her "only comfort"
Schumann's ring and picture. The journey home to Asch was
broken for the night at Zwickau, and thither Robert, who had,
as usual, taken his mother into his confidence, hurried, without Captain von Fricken's knowledge, to bid his fiancée another
farewell. "My tears as I gave him the last kiss—oh, I could

* Kohut, p. 95.   † Wasielewsky, p. 141.

have died!" writes Ernestine in the later correspondence from which we quote.

There was a regular interchange of letters between Leipzig and Asch during the remainder of September and the greater part of October: "Ernestine writes every week," Robert informs his mother. "How she loves me! It is a supreme happiness. The foolish girl has persuaded herself that you do not like her." But though his own epistles were frequent and, as Ernestine records, "oh! so glorious," he was in a restless and miserable state of mind, which cannot be altogether explained by the cause to which he himself ascribes it—the revival, with the approach of autumn, of the sad memories of the preceding year. Nor can it have been due to a lover's anxiety as to how his suit was likely to be received by the family of his betrothed. Ernestine had already unbosomed herself unreservedly to her "mother," really her aunt; and there is every reason to believe that Captain von Fricken himself connived at his ward's correspondence with her friend. It is not difficult to understand Robert's resolution to quit Leipzig for a time and to pass the closing months of the year at home with his mother—the true mother who had always loved him and indulged him, even when his sanguine notions about life and its chances had tended most strongly to confirm her propensity to take gloomy views of things in general. Ominous for Ernestine's happiness was the letter he wrote on November 2nd, a few days after his arrival in Zwickau, to Frau Henriette Voigt, a gifted amateur pianist and the "Eleonore" of the *Neue Zeitschrift*, whose house in Leipzig had been the frequent meeting-place of the lovers:—

" . . . The condition of my mind is as it was—one that makes me shudder. I have a virtuosity in holding fast to wretched thoughts—it is the evil spirit which opposes and derides human happiness. I often pursue this habit of self-torture till it becomes a sin against my whole nature. At such times I am never satisfied with myself; I should like to transfer myself into another body, or to run away through eternities. Ernestine has written to me quite blissfully. She has inquired of her father through her mother, and he gives her to me—Henriette, he gives her to me—

feel what that means! And yet, this state of torment; as though I feared to take possession of this jewel because I should know it in unfortunate hands. If you ask what my trouble is, I cannot give it a name. I believe it is trouble itself—I cannot describe it more accurately. Ah! and perhaps it is love itself, and the longing for Ernestine! At all events, I cannot endure it any longer, and have written to ask her to try to arrange a meeting within the next few days." *

His overstrung nerves gave him no rest, however. He went off to Asch the next morning, to Ernestine's "indescribable joy," without waiting for her answer, and the actual presence of his fiancée, by reviving the influence of her tenderness for himself, seems to have relieved his mind for the moment from the apprehension which had tortured it. "Oh, he was irresistible and so fond of me," recalls poor Ernestine. Robert himself writes in a birthday letter of November 24th to Frau Voigt :—

"My mother ventures to add Bulwer's works to her congratulations; Ernestine and I, the Allegro—the latter with the assurance that the composer is worth more than his work and less than her to whom it is dedicated." †

The restored confidence indicated by the calmer tone of these lines, which were probably penned by Schumann with the intention of obliterating from Frau Voigt's mind any misgiving she might have felt on reading his former letter, seems to have been maintained for a few weeks, and he went to Asch again on December 4th, accompanied by his sister-in-law, Therese. This, however, was his last visit to the von Frickens. Nor, if it be permissible to draw an inference from the unintelligent style of Ernestine's later communications to Clara, can there be any difficulty in accounting for the circumstance, or in discovering the right "name" for his trouble, which Schumann himself had been unable to supply on November 2nd. It can hardly be doubted that the long weekly letters he received from Ernestine must have forced upon him a dawning

* " Jugendbriefe," p. 261.
† The Allegro in B minor, Op. 8. Dedicated to Ernestine, Baroness Fricken. See *ante*, p. 75.

consciousness that he would find in her, not the companion to whom he could look for help in the peculiar struggle imposed upon him by his hypersensitive nature, but the weak reflection of his own emotionalism, unredeemed by those leavening qualities of soul and spirit from which he derived his ideals of work and love.   That his distress should have been allayed by his first visit to Asch—particularly as this was the effect he desired from it—is intelligible enough.   Not less so, however, is the probability that when on, or soon after, the occasion of his second visit he was made aware that Ernestine was neither the daughter of Baron von Fricken nor a rich heiress, and that she had not the right to bear her own father's name, his fears may have returned with an aggravated force that prevented him from making the formal request to Baron von Fricken for Ernestine's hand which we may reasonably suppose him to have been meditating.   It is fairly certain that no direct communication passed between him and Ernestine's guardian on the subject of his suit, though the conclusion is obvious that the formal legitimation by Captain von Fricken of his wife's niece as his own adopted daughter, which was effected on December 13, 1834, immediately, therefore, after Robert's second visit to Asch, may have had some connection with the love affair.*   It is established that Schumann felt fettered by his promise to Ernestine, though her family did not press his sensitiveness on the point, and that he lacked the courage expressly to recall it for a very considerable time.   She was married in 1838 to the Count von Zedwitz, a man many years older than herself, was left a widow a few months later, and died from an attack of typhoid in 1844.

Two of Schumann's compositions, both of which, however opinions may differ as to their respective artistic value, must be included in the famous series which has placed him by Chopin's side as one of the two supreme creators of the romantic literature of the pianoforte, belong to this period of his youth.   The "Carnaval, Scènes mignonnes sur quatre notes," presents the fiction of the Davidsbund musically to our imagination, and, moreover, through the conception of a

* Compare Schumann's "Briefe," p. 495, note 64.

masked ball, which had previously served the composer's imagination in the charming fancies of the "Papillons." The idea is developed to greater length and varied by the introduction of several fantastic scenes in the later work, which is particularly associated by its principal title with the festival eve of Lent. The "Carnaval" is rich in vigorous as in graceful and humorous thoughts, and, if it does not tell much about Schumann's progress in the acquirement of sustained formative power, affords ample proof of his rapidly increasing ability to give compact, definite, and stirring expression to his fancies. Defying the attempts of imitators, it occupies a unique position in the literature of the pianoforte, and its inherent vitality is attested by the fact that for more than fifty years it has been a conspicuous item in the répertoire of nearly every pianist capable of executing it. Its artistic value was rated modestly—too modestly in our opinion—by Schumann himself. Essentially romantic in the widest sense of the word, it is found, when judged from the romantic standpoint, to possess both outward and inward unity, derived, on the one hand, from the rôle assigned throughout its pages to the four notes referred to in the second title, and on the other from the fact that its several numbers revolve round one central idea. Its origin, as the composer tells us, was due to accident :—

"The name of a little town [Asch] where I had a musical acquaintance was formed by those letters of the musical scale which are contained in my own name. This suggested a kind of pleasantry not unknown since Bach's time. One piece after another was completed—but in serious mood and with personal reference—about the carnival time of 1835. Later on I placed the titles above the pieces and named the collection 'Carnaval.' " *

The letters in question are easily recognisable in the rhythmical musical figures obtained from them, upon one or other of which the various numbers of the work are generally based ;

* "Collected Writings," iii. The original manuscript title, differing slightly from that to which we are accustomed in the published work, and probably altered in deference to the publisher's wish, was: "Fasching, Schwänke über vier Noten von Florestan" (Carnaval, Jests on four notes by Florestan).

or as they are used incidentally in the course of a few of the pieces. *

The first number of the composition, the "préambule," which, if we may be allowed the conjecture, was probably written after Schumann had formed the intention of binding his *jeux d'esprit* into a whole, introduces us to a scene of movement and gaiety at the moment when the vigorous strains of a band announce the commencement of a lively function.

Taking possession of a convenient vantage-ground, we look round in search of acquaintances and find that the Davids-bündler and their friends are present in force. The mask standing so quietly in the midst of the animated crowd is certainly Eusebius, and by his side Florestan is greeting old friends and new with his accustomed sprightly gestures. Not far from them Chiara and her friend Estrella (Ernestine) are talking with some one whose identity is uncertain. Florestan has whispered to Chiara that it is Chopin, just arrived from Paris, but we think Florestan is mistaken for once, or only jesting, and that the gait and manner of the unknown indicate the personality of young Robert Schumann. The band crashes out the last chords of the prelude, but the dancing is not yet to commence. The four traditional personages of the harlequinade are to take part in the diversions, and the clown steps forward with measured, fantastic tread to inaugurate the fun, followed by Harlequin, who performs extraordinary feats of agility. Now the band strikes up the "Valse Noble" and the guests sort themselves into couples for the dance. Whilst it is proceeding Eusebius and Florestan move towards a daïs. Florestan is to address the assemblage, and, springing up presently, he begins a discourse which is understood to refer to Jean Paul and butterflies. Seeming to hesitate after a few sentences, he becomes excited and vehement, and, ges-

The first form gives the order of the letters as they occur in Schumann's name.

(The German names of the notes E flat and A flat are "Es" and "As.")

ticulating wildly, is suddenly extinguished by the sensational entrance of the little dancer Coquette, who comes frisking into view on tiptoe and, without waiting for the musicians to get their instruments into position, pirouettes her greeting to the room. She is an established favourite, and almost before she has disappeared after her last twirl, is recalled by the band to take the inevitable encore.

Meanwhile some illuminated devices that have glimmered faintly on the walls throughout the evening have been growing brighter. Old medieval breves on modern five-line staves. Three patterns of them. What do they mean?

Enigmatic, sphinx-like, they shine on through the next number of the programme, a frolicsome butterfly ballet. As they reach their full lustre two groups of quaintly attired figures, animated symbols of certain musical letters, advance from opposite directions and, on meeting, form into order to dance surely the lightest, daintiest mazurka ever tripped. The tap of the little feet on the floor at the third beat of each measure excites the audience, and they perceive for the first time that all the costumes in the room, with a single exception, including those of the performers who have entertained the company or are about to do so, are decorated with one or other of the emblems displayed on the walls. The inference is obvious. The visitors spring forward to join in the mazurka; and the lights and colours, the movements and sounds, of the ball blend for a few instants as in the vision of a fairy dream. Chiara, however, does not dance. She comes forward as the mazurka is approaching its end, without glancing at the revolving figures on the stage, and is apparently expostulating, half in jest, half in earnest, with the unknown mask who, not wearing the badge of the evening, closely follows her. As he bends towards her to answer we distinguish the word "Chiarissima" in impassioned tones, but not those of Chopin's voice. Estrella has moved forward with her friends, but now remains behind them to gaze on at the retreating letters, and as the last one disappears she turns as if fascinated to the illuminated symbols on the walls. A mysterious wave of emotion vibrates through the room, but passes as it is felt, and the guests begin to stir freely, to exchange recognitions and chat with acquaintances. The order of the programme is resumed by Pantaloon and Columbine, whose nimble gyrations are succeeded by a most vivacious waltz danced by the company. It is soon arrested, however. Some one has discovered that Paganini is present, and the whole troup of Davidsbündler rush upon their great associate, honoured, though not formally elected, as such, and clamour for a violin solo. But Paganini is not to be persuaded. He prefers to watch the dancers, and the waltz is resumed. A pair of lovers sitting out come to an understanding in time to join the promenade that follows. Then there is a kind of pause, an unspoken question : What next? The musicians play a few bars from the prelude as a warning that the Fasching is drawing to its close. A sudden thought strikes the Davidsbündler : The Philistines! Out they all rush, helter-skelter, into the crisp night air, and, forming into procession, march away to challenge their adversaries to the accompaniment of a noble strain chosen, in defiance of all precedent, on account of its three-four measure. They become livelier with each step forward, and before long encounter the Philistines, who have advanced to meet them to the old tune of the "Grandfather's Clock." On they go, right through the enemy's ranks, sending peals of derisive laughter behind them, merrier and merrier, till a turn in the road leads them forward to a second combat. In the tumult that ensues, amid the warning figure of the prelude, the striking of clocks, the beating of drums, the frantic gambols of the Davidsbündler, the shriek of the tonic chord of A flat, loud, louder and louder still, the splendid Carnaval riots to its end.

In setting before the reader this slight expansion of its titles it is by no means our purpose to offer him a hard and fast "programme" of the Carnaval. To do so would be directly to contravene the purpose of its composer. Our desire is solely to afford him some guide to the appreciation of a work which, oy reason of its rapid changes, is not even at this date invariably understood by the general music-lover. Schumann did not, as we know, compose the pieces to the titles, but wrote the titles above the pieces. Nevertheless his own words above quoted,* together with other passages of his writings, induce the belief that here as elsewhere the titles do frequently indicate images which hovered more or less distinctly before him as he worked, and that in the Carnaval he speaks to us— reticently, indeed, through the medium of symbol and jest—of passages of his own life. Certain it is that diligent study of the composition in its various aspects reveals much that it behoves us to know about Schumann's individuality both as artist and man.

The Carnaval was published in 1837 as Op. 9, with a dedication to the violinist Lipinski, by Breitkopf and Härtel. It was performed for the first time in public by Liszt at his Leipzig concert of March 30, 1840, with but moderate success, and was gradually popularised in later years by the performances of Frau Schumann and Anton Rubinstein.

The second work that owes its origin to Fräulein von Fricken's visit to Leipzig was produced about the same time as the Carnaval, in the second half of 1834. The twelve Études Symphoniques are constructed on an expressive melody in C sharp minor by Baron von Fricken, which formed the theme of a set of variations composed by him for the flute, and are not only of extreme interest in the history of Schumann's career, but memorable in that of the great literature of the pianoforte. Written in the shape of variations, they stand chronologically, among the most famous independent examples of the form for pianoforte solo, as the successors of Beethoven's great set in C minor. They are not, however, moulded like these on the principle of "changes" on a constant theme which had guided the development of the form from obvious simplicity to highly wrought elaboration through the works of Handel and Bach, Haydn and Mozart, generally of Beethoven's first and second periods and sometimes of his third period, as in the stupendous second movement of the sonata in C minor, Op. 111. The conception of the variation form underlying the Études Symphoniques is

* "One piece after another was completed *in serious mood and with personal reference*," p. 111.

one which, if originated by Beethoven, is applied here in a new manner, and with a result that has a far-reaching effect on the later treatment of the form. It is that of the production from the theme of new musical ideas which, while they bear the direct impress of their descent, themselves become subordinate, but independent, texts for further treatment. Thus Étude No. 1 is built on a short subject derived from the first two notes of the original melody, the entire opening bar of which appears unaltered in the fifth and thirteenth bars of the variation.*

No. 1.

In No. 2 the first phrase of the theme, placed in the bass, supports the entrance of a new melody in the treble, the

No. 2.

second part of which is accompanied in the tenor by the opening phrase of the second part of the original melody.

No. 3.

Étude No. 3 is still freer in form. It contains no literal allusion to the theme, the general impression of which,

* It is assumed that the reader is familiar with the theme of the composition.

however, is preserved by a firmly moving bass which supports a new melody in the tenor, accompanied in the upper part by brilliantly scintillating figures of demi-semi-quavers.

New lights are thrown on the original theme by the progression of some of the harmonies in this and the preceding study through the subdominant side of the key of the work.

The relation to the theme of the next three studies is readily apparent to the music-lover. Nos. 4 and 5, both of animated character, the latter in twelve-eight measure, are constructed, the one in canonic, the other in free imitation at a half bar's and quarter bar's distance respectively.

The remarkably forcible effect of No. 6 is in great measure obtained by the characteristically Schumannesque device of anticipating the melody of the upper part with the left hand;

in this instance by a demi-semi-quaver and at the distance of an octave.

No. 6.

No. 7, in the key of the relative major, may be described as a brief fantasia, No. 8 as a meditation worked in free counterpoint, No. 9, in three-sixteen measure, as a scherzino, on the theme. In No. 7, as in No. 1, the first bar of the original

No. 7. *Allegro molto.*

No. 8.

No. 9.

melody enters twice upon the figure of which the study is composed—in No. 7, in transposed keys—and, here as there, has the effect of irradiating the variation while strengthening the unity of the work as a whole.

The tenth study is closely derived from the theme, but presents it in an aspect so new as to amount to fresh creation. The effect of this number is greatly assisted by the continuously moving semi-quavers of the left hand, developed from a motif of four consecutive notes.

No. 10.

No. 11, in the key of the dominant minor, plaintively melodious, is written in the form of an accompanied duet and may possibly have suggested to Mendelssohn the idea of the now familiar two-part song in the third book of " Lieder ohne Worte," which appeared after the publication of the Études Symphoniques.

No. 11.—Bar 2.

No. 11.—Bar 7.

No. 12, the finale, begins and ends in the key of the tonic major C sharp—in its enharmonic form of D flat.   It is a free fantasia, several pages in length, and brings the great composi-

tion to a brilliant close.   We may find in its principal subject
a remote reminiscence, by inversion, of the original melody of
the work, the opening bar of which is continually worked in
the middle section of the study.

No. 12.
Allegro brillante.

That we have ventured to direct the reader's attention in
the very cursory manner allowed by our limited space to
a few leading points of interest in so familiar and favourite
a composition as the Études Symphoniques, would require
some apology if it were not that Schumann's biographers
have, as it appears to us, devoted insufficient attention to
a work which, at the time of its production, constituted a
new departure in the literature of the pianoforte and remains
among the greatest solos of its class ever written for the
instrument.   The composer's advance during the eighteen
months from the summer of 1833 to the close of 1834 in the
power of selecting his ideas and concentrating them into
shape—as revealed by comparison of the Études Symphoniques with the Impromptus—approaches the marvellous,
and is hardly the less striking even in view of the circumstance, alluded to by Wasielewski, that he had devoted
particular attention to variation form meanwhile.*   It is,
indeed, not too much to affirm that Schumann, who saw
in Mendelssohn the Mozart of the new musical era of the
nineteenth century, himself, with the production of the
Études Symphoniques, takes a place amongst composers for
the pianoforte as its Beethoven.   To say this is in no wise

* Wasielewski mentions (p. 151) that Schumann composed variations on
Schubert's Sehnsuchtswalzer and on the allegretto from Beethoven's A
major symphony during the summer or autumn of 1833.   Both sets have
remained unpublished.

to raise the question as to how nearly at any subsequent period or in certain moments of his career the younger composer may have approached the sublime heights attained by the immortal master of Vienna. It means simply that whereas in Beethoven's works the most vehement artistic aspiration, the profoundest emotion, the loftiest sentiment of the age are found concentrated in a mighty stream of musical utterance ; so also the more purely lyrical tendencies, the growing freedom of thought and individuality of aim characteristic of the succeeding generation, nowhere obtain such glowing artistic expression as in the compositions of Schumann.

It is true that in the Études Symphoniques we find positive, as in the Carnaval negative, evidence that the young musician had not yet mastered the technical secret of success in the practice of the larger forms. The principle of development underlying the studies is, in the main, that of the employment in various transpositions of a figure or phrase derived from a given theme, with a view to the effective elucidation of some central idea, but without essential modification. This method, used by Schumann with brilliant result in short compositions and especially appropriate to variation form, is not flexible enough to become a successful substitute in a movement of any length for the art of thematic development which plays so prominent a part in the works of the Vienna masters. The art, that is to say, whereby the derived figures, themselves becoming pregnant with new form and new significance, provide an elastic material that may be moulded to larger or smaller dimensions. We learn therefore without surprise, from Schumann's own words, that the composition of the finale of the Études Symphoniques cost him some trouble.

Writing in November, 1834, to Captain von Fricken, he says :—

" I have not yet finished the finale of my variations. I should like to develop the mourning march to a grand triumphal procession and give it some kind of dramatic interest, but I do not get out of the minor, and to compose with an ' intention ' often causes one to go wrong and to become too material. If the right moment should come to me, however, I will give myself up to it like a child." *

We may further suppose, from the circumstance of his having made a considerable cut in the movement when he revised his work in 1852 for a new edition, that the composer was dissatisfied with the effect of the finale as it first appeared. Even in its later form, however, its coherence is marred not only by the disproportionate length of the episodes in A flat and G flat, of which the last is an exact transposed repetition of the first, but also by the too constant employment of the rhythmical figures—

one or other of which accompanies all transpositions of the episodical material throughout the movement. Complete explanation of these defects is furnished by the extract from Schumann's letter quoted above. It is evident that the episodes, with their march rhythm, were originally conceived as the continuation of the "mourning march" in the "minor," and that Schumann, unable to work out his first design to his own satisfaction, rewrote the movement for publication with its present principal theme in the major, which, brilliant and convincing in itself, is not of a sufficiently decided processional character to lend pertinence to what follows it and thus give unity to the finale as a whole.

The date of the rewriting and completion of the finale in the earlier of the two forms in which it is familiar to us—before the cut of the second edition—can be fixed with certainty as belonging to the first half of 1837. Wasielewski, who obtained great part of the material used in his Schumann biography direct from the composer, says:—

"A special significance attaches to the reminiscence, in the opening of the movement [finale], of Ivanhoe's melody 'Rejoice, proud England,' from Marschner's opera 'The

---

* "Briefe," p. 60. This extract indicates, incidentally, how greatly Schumann allowed himself to be hampered at this period by his old habit of composing at the pianoforte.

Templar and the Jewess.' It was intentional and meant as a compliment to the English composer, Schumann's friend William Sterndale Bennett, to whom the work [Études Symphoniques] is dedicated." *

Schumann made Bennett's acquaintance in the last month of 1836, and the publication of the work in question took place in June or July, 1837.

Many points of interest besides those we have mentioned urge themselves on the attention of the music-lover who desires fully to appreciate this noble work, the fruit of a genius nourished by the assiduous study of Bach and Beethoven, and now rapidly entering into confirmed possession of that faculty of idealised individual expression answering to the disposition of its time which is the peculiar inheritance of the creative poet. Our chapter is already too long, however, and we can only point out to the reader that Schumann's pianoforte style is that of free and broad part writing; a style marking a new development in the history of the pianoforte, which, as practised in the Études Symphoniques, establishes the composer as the originator of the so-called orchestral treatment of the instrument. This circumstance lends special interest to the title written on the original manuscript of the completed work : "Étuden im Orchesterkarakter von Florestan u. Eusebius." For the original published title, "Études Symphoniques par Robert Schumann," the words "Études Symphoniques en forme de Variations," &c., were substituted in the composer's revised edition of 1852, from which the studies Nos. 3 and 9 were omitted. These were restored in an edition of 1862. †

* Robert Schumann, p. 152.

† The first and second published versions of the finale (1837 and 1852 may be compared in Frau Schumann's edition of the Études Symphoniques. Five additional studies, set aside by Schumann, appeared in 1893, in the supplementary volume, prepared by Brahms, of Frau Schumann's complete edition of her husband's works.

CHAPTER IX

1834–1835

Schumann's Toccata performed by Clara at her concert in Leipzig—
Concert tour in North Germany—Mendelssohn comes to reside in
Leipzig—Summary of the musical development of Leipzig from 1489
—Progress of music in Vienna, London, and Paris.

THE autumn of 1834 and the winter that succeeded it,
marked in Robert's life by a series of occurrences and
activities of more than ordinary interest, may be said to have
constituted one of the turning-points of Clara's existence, for
it was during this period that the lingering traces of childhood
fell definitely away from her, leaving her to advance towards
an early, engaging womanhood with a heart tender to love,
a will strong to endure, and an achievement that was very soon
to place her amongst the foremost executive musicians of her
day. Henceforth her performances were to be judged not by
the measure of her years, but by the highest standard of
her art. She made her reappearance after about a year's
retirement from the public platform at a concert of her
own, given with the assistance of the Gewandhaus orchestra on September 11th, two days before her fifteenth
birthday anniversary, at the Hôtel de Pologne, Leipzig, for
the benefit of a charity. The programme included a concert
movement of her own on which she had worked in Dresden
during the summer, two of Chopin's latest publications—the
Fantasia on Polish airs, Op. 13, for pianoforte and orchestra,
and the Rondo in E flat, Op. 15, for pianoforte alone—and
was varied by some manuscript songs by Carl Banck, the
" extremely cultivated musician and song-writer " who
had made her visit to her home in the summer " very

pleasant.* It further remains distinctive among all others
of any period as having introduced Schumann's name for the
first time to the concert-going public as a composer for the
pianoforte. The work with which Clara inaugurated the
future triumph of her friend's genius in the domain it was
magnificently to enrich during the progress of the next years—
the Toccata in C major—was composed in its first form in
1830, when Schumann was a student at Heidelberg. Transposed from its original key, D major, and entirely remodelled
in 1833, it was published in final form in the summer of 1834
as Op. 7, and lives in the répertoire of the modern pianist as
a fluently written and effective study in double notes which
is sometimes heard in the concert-room. " You will recognise
an old friend in my Toccata ; he does not speak so wildly
now," Schumann wrote in August when sending a copy of the
newly published work to his former fellow-student, Töpken.

It would seem unlikely that Robert returned from Zwickau,
after his farewell interview with Ernestine on September 6th,
in time to hear Clara's performances at the Hôtel de Pologne,
as his paper merely gives the programme of her concert.†
He was, however, present at her birthday celebration on the
13th, and we may fancy that the day on which she completed
her fifteenth year must have contrasted sadly enough in her
mind with the recollection of former anniversaries. Her return
from her long visit to Dresden two days before the von
Frickens' departure from Leipzig had afforded her sufficient
opportunity to notice the advance in intimacy between the
joint sponsors that had followed the event of little Cecilia's
christening ; she had been duly informed by her stepmother
of the " beautiful letter " to Ernestine with which Schumann
had improved that occasion ; and, though Robert said nothing
about his hurried journey to Zwickau, the intuition of an
affection which, growing with her growth, had become part
of her very being, could not be mistaken. The rumour of
the engagement that reached her in the course of the next

* See *ante*, p. 106.

† The concert of September 11th is not mentioned by Litzmann. It is
recorded in the *Neue Zeitschrift* of September 15th and the *Allgemeine
Musikalische Zeitung* of September 24, 1834.

few weeks found her prepared to bear her ordeal with characteristic resolution, even though it seemed to her as if the light of life had been extinguished. We may safely conjecture that such intercourse as may have taken place at this time between herself and Robert must have been weighted to both by the consciousness that, try as they might, they could not return to the frankly confidential relation which had existed between them before Ernestine's visit to Leipzig. Probably Robert, filled for a little while with a lover's beatific visions and occupied by the varied and arduous duties of his double activity as musician and author, was less keenly aware of the change than Clara; yet the mere fact that he did not tell her of his betrothal seems to show him to have been sensible of some tension in their friendship. It was no doubt of advantage to both that, during the interval that elapsed between Ernestine's return to her home and Robert's departure from Leipzig on the long visit to his mother to which our last chapter refers in detail, he had been able more or less to substitute for his companionship with the Wiecks his newer intimacy with Herr and Frau Voigt, who were not only genuinely appreciative of his genius, but had been, as we have seen, his confidants and helpers throughout the progress of his love affair. Fortunately the natural course of events soon placed a considerable period of separation between the two old playmates. Wieck started with his daughter on November 11th on a tour through North Germany, and the fact that he invited Carl Banck to accompany them on its first stages seems to suggest that the father was quietly observant of his child's persistently restless mood, and still hoped to dissipate it by expedients in which many parents before and since his time have placed confidence under similar circumstances.

It must remain a matter of regret that but little authentic record is available of the programmes performed by Clara in the course of this journey, which extended to a period of five months. No mention of the tour is to be found in the *Allgemeine Zeitung*, and the *Neue Zeitschrift*, though giving the dates and whereabouts of some of the concerts, says nothing about the performances. Litzmann is equally reticent. By referring to Frau Schumann's progressive répertoire given at the end of his third volume we learn, indeed, that two of Beethoven's great works—the so-called sonata "Appassionata" for pianoforte alone and the "Kreutzer" sonata for pianoforte and violin—were, with three additional fugues from Bach's "Well-tempered Clavier," added about this time to the young artist's list, but some expressions used by her father in Hamburg, together with Litzmann's general observations on the tour, lead to the inference that the "Appassionata," at all events, was reserved at this date for special private performance. The names of Bach and Chopin, both of which we know to have been represented in the public concerts of the journey, suffice to give it historical interest. It included appearances in Magdeburg, Schöneburg, Halberstadt, Brunswick, Hanover, Bremen, and Hamburg, and, though making great demands upon the endurance of both father and daughter, was crowned with complete success. One of the many difficulties to which we have referred in an earlier chapter that confronted the travelling pianist in the first half of the nineteenth century, that of procuring a suitable instru·ment, is brought vividly before the imagination in an account of the second Magdeburg concert written to his wife by Wieck :—

"It is a wonder that I am alive to-day, after the anxiety and vexation of yesterday! Imagine: there were six hundred people again, and in the first part (Chopin's concerto) the keys of the pianoforte began to stick. It passed off, however, in spite of a thousand alarms. During the pause I am obliged to take the keyboard out in presence of the whole public and see to the keys. This succeeds. Now comes the second part. The pedal sticks; what am I to do? Clara plays, but dares not raise the damper because it does not fall again, and so I press it down a hundred times before the public during the performance." *

From Hamburg he writes on March 22, 1835 :—

" DEAR WIFE,—Yesterday brilliant appearance before a full house. Clara was received every time with loud applause. Hamburg is warm, and that is no trifle—ask those who know. Zollner, in the Hamburg *Abendzeitung*, calls Chopin's compo-

* Kohut, 124.

sitions unintelligible foppery and musical nonsense. You
ought to see the papers; no issue without the name of Clara
Wieck, who is the favourite and talk of the day. I pursue my
steadfast, iron course without noticing either chatter or good
advice. Every day we receive proposals for concerts, but be at
rest; we are longing for home, and only intend now to go to
Lübeck and Celle."

On the 26th he continues:—

"All the papers abuse Chopin dreadfully. How people
must wonder at Clara, who plays such crazy things by
preference! Next Saturday Clara appears for the fourth
time, and again in the theatre, and plays out of gratitude
to Moscheles the polonaise from his E flat concerto, and, by
desire, Herz's bravura variations.

"There is, however, a great deal of silly talk about Clara.
One person says that instead of the Bach fugue she should
have played something by Herz. Another asks why she has
played nothing by Moscheles or Kalkbrenner. They will
not hear of Beethoven. . . ." *

To the question frequently put to him in the course of
the tour: "Does your daughter play nothing by Hummel,
Kalkbrenner, Beethoven?" Wieck, as he records in the diary,
invariably answers: "Yes; but only in intimate circles and
from music. Not here, where she is to shine as the first
living German pianiste." †

But neither public triumphs, nor private successes, nor
even the experiences of a few particularly pleasant weeks
passed in Brunswick, where, as she jestingly wrote to her
stepmother, she had "fallen in love" with the resident
'cellist, Theodor Müller, could compensate Clara for the sense
of Robert's companionship that had accompanied her whether
at home or absent from Leipzig during so considerable a
part of her young existence and now seemed to her as a
vanished dream. Weary and indifferent, increasingly affected
by the worries of her unsettled life, she began to find it
difficult to summon her energies for the adequate fulfilment
of her artistic duties, and her father, whilst regretting her
"want of vanity," was himself sufficiently harassed by the

thousand and one business details and perplexities incidental to the journey to desire a rest. Giving up two or three projected final concerts of the tour, he wound up his arrangements in Hamburg, and returned with his daughter to Leipzig in the second week of April, 1835.

Schumann's impressions on his first meeting with Clara the day after her arrival are recorded in a letter of three years' later date :—

" I still remember how I first saw you at 12 o'clock midday," he writes in 1838 ; " you seemed to me taller, more distant. You were no longer a child with whom I could laugh and play. You talked so intelligently, and I saw in your eyes a secret deep gleam of love." *

But he gave no outward sign, and to the loyal, courageous maiden the brief interview brought only bitter pain.

" How distinctly I remember the first afternoon after our return from Hamburg," Clara wrote in 1839 ; " you entered the room and scarcely greeted me. I went to Augusta, who was with us then, and said, with tears :

" ' I prefer him to every one, and he has not even looked at me." †

Perhaps, however, the reader may be able to form a more accurate interpretation of Robert's apparent indifference than that of which the agitated Clara was capable. The summer found them reunited in an artistic companionship made the more heart-satisfying to both by their growing consciousness of the true nature of the bond that was drawing them every day nearer to each other. That Wieck remained contentedly passive for many months under such a condition of circumstances is to be explained partly by the accumulation of affairs that awaited his attention on his return after the long absence from Leipzig, partly by the generally accepted belief in Robert's engagement, and again by Clara's obviously revived interest in her art. And then Robert spoke no word of love. Soothed and happy when with Clara, he was subject at other moments to innumerable self-reproaches and self-questionings that ceaseless activity but partially enabled him to keep at bay. Fully recognising, at length, that his passing feeling

* Litzmann, i. 82.   † Ibid.

for Ernestine had been due to an accident of circumstances, penetrated by the conviction that he had possessed himself of the best affection of her life, appalled by the vision of the grinding struggle with poverty which a marriage with her would entail—a struggle that must either wear out his existence or wrest from him his high ideals of art—he shrank from writing the cruel decisive word that would seal her unhappiness and secure his own freedom. He temporised with his difficulties; told himself that his interest in Clara was solely that of an old friend, and wrote occasional letters to his betrothed which she opened with apprehension and read with dismay. Every hour that he could spare from his labours as sole editor of the *Neue Zeitschrift* was devoted to composition, and it is in the sense of his having achieved the final completion of the pianoforte sonata in F sharp minor —begun and put aside in 1833 and taken up again for a time in 1834—during these months of agitating suspense, that we must understand the later reference made by him to this characteristic work as "a heart cry for Clara." The manuscript, bearing the title "Sonate pour le pianoforte in Fis moll, Op. 11. An Clara zugeeignet von Florestan u. Eusebius," was in Clara's hands before the beginning of autumn. She immediately began to make propaganda for the composition among the friends and acquaintances of her father's house, and speaks in a letter to Robert of September 1st of having played it to "two gentlemen from Hanover." This letter answers one addressed to her by the composer during a brief visit to his mother, "which," she says, "greatly surprised me, as you did not give me much hope of one when you went away from here," and it adds force to the remarks made by us at the beginning of this chapter on Clara's rapid development at this period. In it may clearly be recognised the writer of the Dresden letter of 1834; in it still speaks the proud, loving, teasing Clara of a year ago, but her style has become matured, and it is with difficulty, as we read it through, that we realise the communication to be that of a girl who has not quite completed her sixteenth year.

"You have entrusted me with greetings to your chosen subjects" [the Davidsbündler], it concludes, "but as they have gone away with their lord to share his joy and sorrow, I cannot present the message. Offer many greetings to their lord, with whom you are probably acquainted, from me and from the Davidsbündlerschen Florestanschen sonata, which is anticipating with pleasure some further modification at the end of its enchanting tones : ' B minor instead of F sharp minor.' " *

The last words possibly contain some playful reference, intelligible to Schumann, to Clara's own Pièce caractéristique, Op. 5, No. 4 : " Le Ballet des Revenants," in B minor, which she mentions earlier in her letter as having been composed and completed at precisely this period. As, turning over the pages of the little work and glancing at its beginning and end, we recall the opening figure of the first allegro in Schumann's F sharp minor sonata, we seem to have Robert and Clara before our eyes, he just turned twenty-five, she on the verge of sixteen, as they lived through the summer of 1835 in all the delight of their newly recovered intimacy.

Robert—

Op. 11.

Clara—

Op. 5, No. 4.   CODA.

* The entire letter is printed by Litzmann, i. 87.

Clara had devoted all her available time to composition during the summers of 1834 and 1835, and besides having finished a set of concert variations and other pieces for her instrument, had so far profited by her studies in instrumentation under Reissiger as to be nearly ready with a concerto for pianoforte, with orchestral accompaniment in three movements, which she hoped to introduce to the public of her native town at an early opportunity.

The autumn of 1835 was a season of exceptional interest to musical Leipzig. Felix Mendelssohn had accepted the post of conductor of the Gewandhaus concerts made vacant by the retirement of C. A. Pohlenz and came, on the last day of August, to settle in the city that was to be his home during the greater part of his twelve remaining years of life, and to attain brilliant prestige under the stimulus of his genius as the musical metropolis of Europe. No happier combination could have been produced in the best interests of the art at this particular moment of its history than that of Mendelssohn and Leipzig. The three great creative musical periods severally represented at their culmination by the names of Palestrina (d. 1594), Sebastian Bach (d. 1750), and Beethoven (d. 1827), had developed and; passed. Their fruits, yielded in the first place in the service of the church, later in that of the prince or noble, and finally supplying a growing public demand, had as yet only in a limited sense come into the possession of the middle class burgher. The exquisite achievement of the early contrapuntists, the creators of the first period, was practically unknown; the tendency towards the appreciation of the significance of Bach's mighty performance had but been initiated. The orchestral, and to some extent the chamber, compositions of Beethoven were advancing year by year into a more general measure of acceptance; but for the rapid popularisation of the rich legacies bequeathed to the world by the genius of those who had been its greatest musical prophets, special circumstances and personality specially qualified to use them were needed to supplement the general progress of the age. The progress of events had produced both the one and the other. In Leipzig was the opportunity, Mendelssohn was the man.

We propose to present to the reader a very rapid summary of those conditions of its progress which had fitted the town of Leipzig for the exceptional position it was hereafter to hold as a musical centre, and to add a few words on the comparative musical development reached by some of the capitals of Europe during the transitional years that were to result in the vigorous artistic life familiar to the amateur of to-day. The inherent interest of these subjects and the fact that some acquaintance with them is necessary for the appreciation of the aim of our pages may, perhaps, constitute our apology for the interruption of the main narrative by what may seem to some extent episodical matter.

Though but little distinctively artistic material is to be found in the early history of Leipzig, the musical development of the town may be traced continuously in authentic records from the time of the first existence of anything that can be accepted as rudimentary musical art. Its supreme facts, reached in the first half of the eighteenth century, are, no doubt, that Sebastian Bach spent nearly twenty-seven years of his career as choirmaster, or cantor, of its ancient foundation school, that he was thereby responsible for the music of the principal Leipzig churches, and that he composed for their services the extraordinary series of sacred cantatas, oratorios, and settings of the Passion which, passing at his death from contemporary remembrance, were rediscovered three-quarters of a century later and are now numbered among the rare treasures of musical art. There are, however, other exceptional points of interest to be noted in the artistic development of the Saxon city, with one of which our pages are directly concerned. An emporium of industry and not the residence of a court, Leipzig was one of the very few towns of Europe that were independent of the liberality of a prince for their continued advance in culture, at the time when music was becoming finally emancipated from ecclesiastical direction. Its musical activity, originating with the choir of St. Thomas' School, of which in 1439 a certain Johann Urban was appointed cantor, spreading by natural processes to the body of university students, and finally establishing a centre in merchant circles, gradually created a nucleus of cultivated artistic taste in the ranks of the middle classes that enabled the town to attain its ultimate position as an influential agent in the musical education of Europe. The student society for private musical practice—the collegium musicorum—became, in the course of the seventeenth century, something of an institution in parts of North Germany, and the occasional introduction to the meetings of listeners led the way to the concert society in the modern sense. Two " weekly musical concerts or assemblies " [Zusammenkünfte] held in "Zimmermann's coffee-house" are mentioned in records of the time as having flourished through the first half of the eighteenth century, one of which, founded between 1701 and 1704 by G. P. Telemann, was directed for seven years by Sebastian Bach himself.

" The members forming these musical concerts are chiefly resident students, amongst whom there are always good musicians, so that, as is well known, celebrated virtuosi have often been gradually produced from them. Every musician is allowed the opportunity of a public hearing at these musical concerts, and listeners capable of appreciating the value of a skilled performer are frequently present." *

* Mitzler's "Neu eröffneten musikalischen Bibliothek zu Berlin." Annals of 1736.

A third collegium musicorum, founded by the bookseller
J. F. Gleditzsch, the furrier Zemisch and a few other prominent citizens of Leipzig, was inaugurated on March 11, 1743,
by sixteen performing members, and soon became prominent
as " the Grand Concert " (Dass grosse Konzert).   It is mentioned in Mitzler's annals of 1746 as holding its meetings
" under the direction of the merchants and other persons, at
the ' Three Swans ' in the Brühl, where the greatest masters
visiting Leipzig may be heard," and was " considerably frequented and admired with the greatest attention."

The Grand Concert had a really grand future before it.
After thirteen years of fairly prosperous existence its performances were suspended by the pressure of the Seven Years' War,
but they were resumed in 1763, when Johann Adam Hiller
was appointed musical director.   A man of mark in his calling,
Hiller promoted the special artistic activity of Leipzig in
many directions, and is to be considered the founder of its
modern musical reputation.   He is still remembered as a
composer by his operettas, written for the prosperous Leipzig
theatre of his day.   As artistic director of the merchants'
society his aims were eclectic, and he took pains to bring
before his audience the best available works of various schools.
His loyalty enabled the institution to survive the crises,
occasioned by lack of funds and the want of a locale suited
to the advancing needs of the time, that threatened its life
in the course of his leadership.   The primary requisite to its
prosperity was at length supplied, probably through the
energy of the then mayor of Leipzig, Geheimkriegsrath
Müller, by the purchase from the clothiers of the town of a
large warehouse which formed part of the building of the
ancient civic library, and the erection above it of a fine
concert-room, " which," says a contemporary account, " has
few equals for size and beauty."   Retaining its traditional
name, but placed on a sounder economic foundation under a
committee of twelve directors, the Grand Concert gave its
first performance in the hall of the Gewandhaus on November
25, 1781, with an orchestra of thirty members, and, progressing
from that date towards its ultimate position as the first
concert society of Europe, contributed not a little to the

advancing prestige of the town by which it was created and fostered.

Striking illustration is to be found in the programmes of the subscription and extra Gewandhaus concerts of the half-century following the season 1781–82 of the ground facts by which the general musical history of the period is characterised; the neglect by musicians and amateurs of what may be called the Protestant polyphonic art of North Germany that had culminated in the vocal and instrumental works of Sebastian Bach; the continuous progress of the homophonic style of the South that had, after Palestrina's death, extinguished the practice of the earlier polyphony originated and perfected in the service of the Roman Catholic Church; the increasing importance of instrumental art; the rapid growth and culmination of the school of Vienna; the rise of romanticism.*

Adam Hiller was, by education and preference, a disciple of the purely Italian style, and the list of works performed in the course of the four seasons during which he remained in charge of the Gewandhaus subscription concerts presents sufficient evidence of his inclination. But he was not the man to ignore the signs of his time. The era which was to fuse the influences of south and north, to temper the pliant Italian art with German strength, to shape it into closer symmetry by means of German musicianship, had already dawned. The pledge of its future was contained in the rapid

---

* Polyphony originally so called—the polyphony especially associated with the Roman Catholic Church—is that kind of unaccompanied vocal music in which each voice or part has an independent melody of its own, all being bound into a whole by the laws of strict counterpoint. The development of Protestant art around the instrumentally supported hymn or chorale of the Lutheran Church produced a polyphony for voices and instruments combined that was governed by a contrapuntal science gradually adapted to its requirements.

Homophonic art, formerly called music in the Italian style, and especially associated with the Italian Opera stage, assigns a melody to one, generally the upper part, and enriches it with massed harmonies or flowing accompaniments placed in other parts. Originating as simply accompanied tune, it has produced its peculiar methods: free part-writing and thematic development, the growth of which may be studied in the works of Haydn, Mozart, and Beethoven; and which are, to speak broadly, those of modern vocal and instrumental art respectively.

popularity attained by Haydn's symphonies and quartets, in even the earlier of which, slight as they may seem to the music-lover of to-day, the plan of the modern sonata or symphony movement, which was to revolutionise instrumental composition, is completely defined.   Before Hiller resigned his post —in which he was succeeded by J. G. Schicht—at the end of the season 1784–85, he had conducted thirty-seven performances of Haydn's symphonies, to say nothing of other classes of works by the genial master.   How many and which symphonies were played cannot be ascertained, as the programmes of the day gave no particulars, whether of key or movements, of the selections they announced.   The custom of appending the composer's name to the general title of certain kinds of works was in itself a recent concession to growing public interest in the subject, and was not extended even to concertos for solo instruments until 1795.

More indicative of the future, perhaps, than Haydn's great popularity with the Gewandhaus circle was the inclusion, at a concert of the first season (January 24, 1782), of a symphony " by the young Mozart," at that time nearly twenty-six (1756–91), the only appearance of his name during Hiller's Kapellmeistership.   Characteristic of the day was the representation of the Bach family genius by works of the great Sebastian's sons Emanuel and Johann Christian, musicians deeply imbued with the prevailing taste for the Italian style.   Emanuel's sacred choral compositions were given from time to time in Advent or Lent, and the name of Johann Christian, " the English Bach," as he has sometimes been called, a fertile and pleasing composer in various forms, appeared very frequently in the programmes.   No less than seventeen performances of his "sinfonies " were given by the Grand Concert during its first four years of Gewandhaus activity.   The mighty achievement of Sebastian himself, entirely ignored, so far as is known, at the performances of the " Three Swans' " celebrity, was recognised in the Gewandhaus hall on one occasion only during its first fifty years of existence, and then in a singularly unfortunate way.   A Mass for double chorus and double orchestra, part of an extant score of which is copied in Sebastian Bach's handwriting, was included in one of the programmes of 1805 as the master's work. Later authoritative criticism, however, refused it a place in the catalogue of his compositions.

A second performance of a Mozart symphony in 1786 was received with indifference no less discouraging than that which had followed the first in 1782, and the composer's works were not again drawn upon in the eighties. The education afforded in the course of nine seasons, however, by good and regular production of the average music of the day, and of very numerous examples of Haydn's art, no doubt bore its fruit; and it was supplemented, in the spring of 1789, by a visit paid to Leipzig by Mozart, who, arriving in the company of his pupil, Prince Carl Lichnowsky, is described as a "young, fashionably dressed man of middle height." He gave a concert of his own compositions in the Gewandhaus, played the "fortepiano" in several friendly houses, and extemporised one morning for an hour on the organ of St. Thomas' Church. The two aged musicians, Gorner, who had been organist of the church in Bach's time, and Cantor Doles, of the Thomas' School, sat near him and managed the stops, and it is pleasant to know that to Doles it seemed as though his "teacher, the old Sebastian Bach, had risen again."

From 1790, the year following this visit and preceding that of the composer's death, Mozart's symphonies appear regularly in the programmes, and by 1794 the society had advanced to a decided Mozart cult. This was stimulated by the appointment, at the end of the year, to some of the prominent musical posts in Leipzig of the organist, flutist, and composer August Eberhardt Müller. Madame Müller, a gifted pianist, described in Gerber's lexicon as "the ornament of the Leipzig concert," was especially admired for her performance of Mozart, and frequently played his concertos, and occasionally his chamber works for pianoforte and other instruments, in the Gewandhaus with immense success. Nevertheless, at a period when musical art was regarded by the average amateur rather as an elegant pastime than a subject for serious pursuit, no concert director could venture to subject public endurance to severe strain, and important works were not always given without a break. In a Gewandhaus programme of 1804, to give but one of similar

instances, the possible tedium of Mozart's Requiem was provided against by the interpolation between the Offertorium
and Sanctus of a concerto for bassoon and an opera overture
by Bierey. Sixteen years later Rochlitz was able to write
with legitimate pride: "With us symphonies are performed
not only entire, but consecutively. Unfortunately this is
rarely the case elsewhere."

Directors and patrons of the Grand Concert rose to the
height of their opportunity and won special, enduring fame
for the society by their immediate appreciation of Beethoven's
transcendent powers. His symphonies, overtures, and pianoforte concertos, all produced in the Gewandhaus immediately
on publication, and often repeated, were received from the
first with a reverent interest that progressed with cultivation
to profound sympathy. Three days after the first Leipzig
performance of the ninth symphony, on March 23, 1826, the
Tageblatt published the following paragraph :—

"The honourable Direction of the Grand Concert is
earnestly requested to arrange another performance of Beethoven's new symphony at the Palm Sunday concert for the
benefit of the poor, as the entire depth of this sublime poem
can only be revealed by its repetition.

"In the name of several friends of art."

The pianoforte concertos Nos. 1-4 were first played in
Leipzig by Madame Müller. Her place as the special Beethoven pianist of the Grand Concert was taken after 1810,
when the Müllers left Leipzig, by Friedrich Schneider, of
whom passing mention was made in the opening chapter of this
volume.* His performance of the E flat concerto on February
29, 1816, the first outside Vienna, excited the audience to "an
enthusiasm that could not be satisfied with ordinary expressions of acknowledgment and delight."

The instrumental art of rising romanticism was represented
from an early date by works of Weber and Spohr, conducted
or performed on some occasions by the composers ; by Field's
concertos, played by Wieck's pupils ; and by other less impor-

* *Ante*, p. 13.

tant names; that of the younger generation of romantic composers, from 1827, when Mendelssohn's C minor (Reformation) symphony, Op. 11, was performed from the MS. at one of the subscription concerts. The first Gewandhaus performances of works by Chopin (" Don Juan " Variations at Julius Knorr's concert of 1831) and Schumann (G minor MS. symphony at Clara Wieck's academy of 1833) have already been recorded. It is an interesting circumstance that, whilst minor societies were successively formed during the half century we are considering which supplemented the activity of the central concert institution of Leipzig, the academic bodies by which the musical life of the town had been originated and first assisted remained factors in its matured artistic activity. Among the official obligations of the cantor of St. Thomas' School was, and still is, the holding of Saturday afternoon performances of sacred choral music, at which, year in, year out, visitors are welcome; and from 1820 it became the privilege of the singing scholars, officially granted them by the mayor, to assist at certain of the Gewandhaus concerts. The university musical society continued to be an attractive feature of student life, and the organists' and other musical posts of Leipzig were frequently filled from its ranks.

An increasingly influential position was held in the town from an early period of its musical development by the printing, publishing, and bookselling house founded in 1719, four years before Bach was called to be cantor of the Thomas' School and twenty-four before the inauguration of the Grand Concert at the "Three Swans" coffee-house, by Bernhard Christoph Breitkopf. His son and successor, Johann Gottlob Immanuel Breitkopf, included music in the scope of his affairs, publishing many works by Emanuel Bach, Graun, Adam Hiller, &c., and, a man of great inventive talent and commercial enterprise, may be described as the founder of the modern German music trade. Passing near the end of the century into the hands of Gottfried Christoph Härtel, the business, known thenceforth as that of Breitkopf and Härtel, was extended in many directions, literary as well as musical, and gained special reputation by the issue of collected editions of the works of famous composers, as of Haydn and Mozart, Clementi and Dussek. When, in 1835, Gottfried's son, Dr. Raymund Härtel, became head of the renowned firm, the house stood ready to co-operate as one of the special influences converging remarkably in the Leipzig of the day, that were to result in the wide and rapid expansion of cultivated musicianship witnessed by the succeeding decades of the century.

The *Allgemeine Musikalische Zeitung*, often referred to in these pages, founded in 1798 by Gottfried Härtel and edited by Rochlitz, exercised considerable educational influence in Germany for many years as the recognised best periodical of its kind. Its value became impaired after 1827, when the editorship passed to G. W. Fink. A certain dubious interest attaches, nevertheless, to Fink's name as that of one of the Philistines-in-chief against whose banalities Schumann and his Davidites began, some little time later, to wage musical and literary warfare.

It has sometimes been assumed that the prevalent unsatisfactory musical conditions repeatedly referred to in Schumann's early correspondence and collected writings had resulted from a decline of the general musical taste of Europe from a higher to a lower standard; but consideration shows that this was not the case. Public musical taste had spread and improved continuously in North Germany from the middle of the eighteenth century, but neither there nor elsewhere did it pass from its evolution stage until after the first quarter of the nineteenth, and, at the beginning of the thirties, neither the average music-lover nor the average musician was sufficiently educated to be able to discriminate with certainty at all points between art of the first and of the second order. Most of the German capitals of the period enjoyed the educational advantages afforded by the activity of a court orchestra, which, engaged more especially in the performance of opera, gave a certain number of annual subscription concerts; and in some towns not the residence of a court, similar opportunities were provided by the municipal orchestra and choral society, presided over by a musician of standing. Though the ordinary concert performance of instrumental music may not have been immaculate as compared with that of a later date, yet, whilst Haydn's symphonies were already becoming superseded, the orchestral works of Mozart were at this time established, and those of Beethoven had made considerable way, in the affection of the concert-going German public. Of the larger capitals, Munich under Bärmann, of the smaller, Cassel under Spohr, were, perhaps, the most musically important. The public taste of Vienna was at a comparatively low ebb, but it should be described rather as unformed than decadent. The great early musical reputation of Vienna, as of Prague, so far as it applied to instrumental music, with which alone we are concerned, was the result of conditions that had directly associated the genius of the three creators of the modern symphony and sonata with the private circles of the music-loving, music-practising Austrian aristocracy. As those conditions became modified by the exigencies of political events and at length entirely passed away, neither city was possessed of a sufficiently developed concert society, or a large enough paying public, to support its fame as an artistic centre, which, in the case of Vienna, rested for a considerable period chiefly on tradition, and in that of Prague was soon practically extinguished. The slow musical advance of the middle classes of the imperial city may be recognised in the fact that the now celebrated "Gesellschaft der Musikfreunde" performed the first movement and scherzo, only, of the ninth symphony at one of their annual subscription concerts of 1827, placing between them a vocal aria by Pacini and a set of variations by Mayseder. After the death of Schuppanzigh, the leader of the Rasoumoffsky quartet, in 1830, no public quartet concerts were given in Vienna till about the middle of the century.

In the two world cities, London and Paris, where the institution of the public concert had been fairly secure since the first and second decades of the eighteenth century, general appreciation of Mozart rather preceded that of Leipzig, and London was only second to the Saxon town in its early recognition of Beethoven, with whom, indeed, it repeatedly held direct communication. The master sold three of his overtures to the Philharmonic Society, for which, moreover, according to his autograph statement, he composed the ninth symphony, and which gave the first (manuscript) performance of the immortal work (May 21, 1825), after those of Beethoven's own concerts in Vienna in the spring of 1824.* Paris, gradually made

* See *ante*, p. 16. Czerny's letter to Wieck.

acquainted from 1821 onwards by the Baillot Quartet with
certain of the composer's works for strings, waxed enthusiastic
over his symphonies at the Concerts du Conservatoire, founded
by Habeneck in 1828.

In the domain of the instrumental soloist's, and particularly
of the pianist's activity, the first thirty-five years of the nineteenth century formed a period of transition, in the course of
which, in the first place, the executant *par excellence* gradually
became differentiated from the composer-performer; and, in
the second place, both the larger public and the executive artist
were led, by the general advance in musical perception, the
continued improvement of the pianoforte, and the progress of
a technique that became increasingly certain, elegant, and
astounding, sometimes even poetical, through and beyond the
contemplation of mere virtuosity towards the conception of the
higher ideals of the great art of interpretation. During this
period the distinction between concert and chamber music,
very generally accepted when Mozart composed his symphonies
and concertos for public performance, and his sonatas, trios, and
quartets for private use and enjoyment, was still practically
accepted as valid in its application to pianoforte music, though
public performances of chamber works for strings had become
frequent. The executant, on whatever instrument, gave his
benefit concert with the assistance of an orchestra, and was
expected to bring forward one or more, if possible original,
compositions with orchestral accompaniment especially adapted
for the display of his technical skill; to vary his programme
with shorter, possibly vocal, numbers; and, if a pianist and of
high rank, to supplement his prepared performances with a
free improvisation. Beethoven's great pianoforte works for
the chamber, both solo and concerted, were cherished in the
best private musical circles of Europe from the date of their
publication, but two only of his pianoforte solos seem to have
been heard in public during his life, and the performer was in
both cases an amateur. The thirty-two variations in C minor
were played in Vienna at a public concert of 1808 by Madame
Bigot, the wife of Count Rasoumoffsky's librarian; the sonata
Op. 101 by Stainer von Felsburg at a Schuppanzigh quartet
concert of 1816, held shortly after the destruction of the

Rasoumoffsky palace by fire. One or another work of Beethoven's concerted pianoforte music was occasionally heard in Vienna during the master's life at a charity benefit, at the "academy" of a travelling virtuoso, or at one of the orchestral or quartet concerts held by Schuppanzigh during the early years of the century in the concert-room of the Augarten, a public pleasure-ground situated in a suburb of the city. Here, for instance, in May, 1814, Beethoven himself appeared for the last time in public as a pianist, repeating the B flat trio, Op. 37, which he had played for the first time on April 11th, at the Hôtel Romischer Kaiser with Schuppanzigh and Lincke. At the public quartet concerts arranged by Schuppanzigh between the years 1824 and 1830, a work for pianoforte and strings by Beethoven, or, during the last two seasons sometimes Schubert, was frequently heard between two string quartets. This form of programme, however, which appealed especially to the aristocratic music-lovers who supported the undertaking, was not imitated by other quartet associations of the period. Nor is the reason far to seek. The pianoforte chamber music of Beethoven and Schubert, as later that of Mendelssohn, Schumann, and even Brahms, was written in the first place with a view to the capabilities of the instrument, on which each and all of these composers excelled as performers, and with which they were in peculiar sympathy. It was regarded as the especial property of the pianist, on whom, excepting in the case of four of Brahms' works of the class, devolves the execution of the leading part and the responsibility for the ensemble. A work of chamber music by Beethoven or Mozart for pianoforte and what were in their days regarded as "accompanying instruments" was sometimes included in the programme of a great orchestral concert, but particular personal considerations were accountable for the later frequent recognition accorded to the art of the pianoforte in the concerts of string quartet parties.

The tradition consistently observed until five years after Beethoven's death, if never expressly formulated, of the unsuitability of the pianoforte sonata for concert performance was at length broken by Felix Mendelssohn. At his orchestral concerts given in Berlin, November 9 and December 1, 1832, for charitable purposes, he played respectively Beethoven's sonatas in C major, Op. 53, and in C sharp minor, Op. 27, No. 1, so far as can be ascertained for the first time in public. His programme of December 1st included, moreover, Bach's D minor concerto for clavier with orchestral accompaniment. It was probably the influence of this example that moved the composer and pianist, Wilhelm Taubert, of Berlin, to introduce the C sharp minor sonata to a Leipzig audience at his orchestral concert in the Gewandhaus of April 11, 1833, and thereby to associate his name with the first public performance of a Beethoven sonata for pianoforte solo in the Saxon city.

Mendelssohn's programmes of 1832 were not his first distinctive pronouncement of the faith and purpose by which an important part of his career, that of the reproductive musician, was to be guided. Two or three years earlier, on March 11, 1829, holding a public concert in the Berlin Singakademie, the twenty-year-old musician had conducted the first performance of Bach's Matthew Passion given since the great cantor's death, seventy-nine years before, and with such splendid success that a repetition was arranged for March 21st. One other act and his declaration of the belief that was in him—the more significant from its unconscious spontaneousness—was rendered complete. Arriving in the autumn of 1833 in Düsseldorf to take up the duties of his first official appointment as municipal music director, and finding that the répertoire of the town did not contain "a single tolerable solemn Mass," but only "modern rubbish," he started at once on a voyage of discovery, and, after hunting through the libraries of Elberfeld, Bonn, and Cologne, returned with an immense packet of Masses, occasional services, and motets, by Palestrina, Orlando di Lasso, and other masters of the great medieval schools. Lasso's motet "Populus meus" was put immediately into rehearsal and sung publicly in church on the last Friday of October, and the study of other works of the same class followed.

These dates, taken together with that of Mendelssohn's installation as director of the Gewandhaus concerts, mark the beginning of an epoch that was to awaken general musical intelligence to the perception of the purist's art standard and

11

to witness a quickly widening acceptance of the greatest works produced by the musical genius of the ages. It would be too remote from our immediate subject to examine how far these results were assisted by the steady development of the national sentiment of Germany, to which we briefly referred in our remarks on the rise of musical romanticism.* We may point out, however, that the fulfilment of the German aspiration for a national opera, which had found its first satisfaction in the success of " Der Freischütz," and was sustained after Weber's death by the works of Spohr and Marschner, became assured at precisely the moment which secured the triumph of the fatherland as the recognised home of classical art. Wagner's first and last symphony was performed in Prague in 1832 and Leipzig in 1833; his early opera, " Die Feen," composed in 1833. Henceforward his attention was to be absorbed by the study of dramatic art.

No happier combination of advantages can be imagined than those brought by Mendelssohn to the pursuit of the object which inspired his career—" to help the progress of art along the path which seemed to him the right one." His brilliant genius, its early maturity, the clear and pure quality of his imagination both as creator and interpreter, the extent and thoroughness of his special acquirement, ensured him the respect of his colleagues, while his sincerity of nature, his eminent social qualities and fascinating personality, attracted to him the affection even of casual acquaintances. Absolved by his private circumstances from the necessity of engaging in either of the two branches of professional labour that would have been distasteful to him—concert-giving for his own benefit and private teaching—he yet willingly accepted his parents' dictum that he must earn his living by the profession of his choice, and entered on his musical career prepared to devote himself ungrudgingly to practical artistic work. The experiences of his two years' activity at Düsseldorf did not altogether answer to his hopes, and he had the more readily responded to the advances of the Leipzig committee since, having been present in 1834 at one of their rehearsals, he was able to foresee some of the musical possibilities that might

* *Ante*, p. 92.

follow his acceptance of the conductorship of the subscription concerts. The Gewandhaus directors, on the other hand, doubtless felt they had reason to congratulate themselves on having secured for the work of their society the co-operation of one in whom the best opinion of Europe was beginning to recognise the first rising musician of the day. Perhaps, however, they hardly realised that by associating the gifted individuality of the young Mendelssohn—now twenty-six years of age—with their institution, fitted by a unique past to respond readily to its stimulus, they were, so to speak, bringing to a focus the many scattered forces that had long been working unobtrusively for the benefit of art, and were supplying the final impulse that was sooner or later to crown the musical striving of the centuries by placing its results at the service of mankind.

CHAPTER X

1835–1836

Mendelssohn and Schumann—Chopin in Leipzig—Moscheles—Mendelssohn as conductor of the Gewandhaus concerts—Konzertmeister Matthäi—Ferdinand David—Music at Wieck's house—First performance in the Gewandhaus of a work by Sebastian Bach—Robert and Clara—Clara's concert in Zwickau—Blissful meetings—Clara in Dresden—A farewell —Clara in Breslau.

"MENDELSSOHN is a splendid fellow, a diamond direct from heaven; we like each other, I think. Besides, we have a great deal to talk about."

So wrote Schumann in his generous, impulsive way to a friend at Halle on September 25th, about three weeks after he had made Mendelssohn's acquaintance. The precise circumstances of the first meeting between the two young musicians who were to be remembered as the masters of their time in their own domain are not given in any published work bearing on the period. They may very likely have been introduced to each other at Wieck's house, where Mendelssohn became intimate immediately on his arrival in Leipzig, and we may infer from fragments of authentic information to be gleaned from occasional sources that Schumann's favourable impression was reciprocated. It is much to be regretted, however, that all mention of Schumann's name should have been withheld from the well-known collection of Mendelssohn's letters published many years ago by his family. It is difficult to suppose that he never alluded, in the course of his constant intimate correspondence, to the gifted colleague whom, from the time of his coming to Leipzig, he was accustomed to meet almost daily during the remaining year and a half of his bachelorhood, and with whom he remained on terms of friendship to the end of his life.

This month of September, 1835, has great interest for us. We may, if we please, picture Mendelssohn, Schumann, and Chopin assembled on the evening of the 30th in ·Mendelssohn's music-room; two of them, who were almost old friends, taking their places at the piano, the other come to make the personal acquaintance of his Polish colleague, and listen to his own interpretation of sundry new *études* and other compositions.

"Chopin would only stay one day," wrote Mendelssohn to his family, "so we passed the whole of it together, making music. . . . The evening was really rather curious. I had to play him my oratorio [the lately completed St. Paul] and he dashed out his new *études* and a new concerto between the parts, while inquisitive Leipzigers stole in to listen and to have seen Chopin. . . . He solemnly promised to come again in the course of the winter if I would compose a new symphony and perform it in his honour. We agreed to this on oath before three witnesses, and it remains to be seen whether we shall keep our word."

What more likely than that Schumann should have been one of these witnesses, and Clara and her father the other two? Mendelssohn had taken Chopin to Wieck's house earlier in the day, and, not finding Clara at home, had left him there to await her return. There was a double pianoforte recital when she came, for, of course, she and Chopin played to each other. Clara, besides giving a short selection from Chopin's works, performed for him her friend Robert's manuscript sonata, which she had already made peculiarly her own. Schumann was certainly not allowed to remain in ignorance of Chopin's arrival, which the members of the Wieck circle had been impatiently expecting for some days past. "Chopin has been here," Eusebius observes in an October number of the *Neue Zeitschrift*; "Florestan rushed at him. I saw them gliding, rather than walking, along together, arm-in-arm."

It is interesting to compare the opinions of Chopin's playing left on record by the three famous musicians who had followed his creative activity with strong interest since the year 1831— the year which had produced Schumann's enthusiastic literary welcome of the Opus 2, and found Mendelssohn, Chopin, and the child Clara assembled in Paris. In the four short intervening years between then and now, Mendelssohn's career as a creative and reproductive artist had been distinctly established, and the appearance of a new composition by Chopin become something of a musical event ; whilst Chopin himself, accepted as the favourite pianist of Parisian *salons*, had attained a position as a teacher that allowed him to consent or refuse to give final lessons to Kalkbrenner's best pupils. Schumann had not only made himself a musician of resource, but had produced works that were to achieve enduring fame ; and Clara, the youngest of the group by nine or ten years, had been steadily growing ripe for the interpretation of Beethoven's sonatas and of Robert's great works to come.

" Chopin is now one of the very first pianists," Mendelssohn had written in the spring of 1834, after a chance meeting of the two musicians and their mutual friend Ferdinand Hiller at Aix-la-Chapelle. " He does extraordinary things which one would never have thought possible, like Paganini on his violin. Both he and Hiller rather overdo the Parisian sensibility and despair, and often take too little heed of time, repose, and sound musicality ; I, perhaps, too much ; so we supplemented and learned from each other, I feeling rather like a schoolmaster and they like *mirliflors* or *incroyables*."

" There is something fundamentally original in Chopin's playing," he now declares ; " and it is so masterly that he may be called a perfect virtuoso." *

Clara, as Litzmann relates, whilst doing full justice to the marvellous delicacy of Chopin's touch in pianissimo passages, found his style, on the whole, too capricious for her entire approval. Schumann wrote in the *Neue Zeitschrift* of October 6th :—

" Chopin was here, but only for a few hours, which he passed in private circles. His playing is exactly like his compositions —unique."

Clara had played Robert's " Davidsbündlerschen " sonata to Mendelssohn a few days after his arrival in Leipzig. What he thought of it can only be partly surmised from the fact that he asked for a repetition of the scherzo at her birthday party of September 13th, in the festivities of which, musical and

* " Briefe," ii. 41 and 99.

otherwise, he took a prominent part. Wieck, proud and radiant throughout the evening, must have felt, as he looked round on the merry, distinguished circle over which he was presiding, that he had begun in very truth to reap the full reward of his laborious life. For Clara, the day on which she completed her sixteenth year was probably the happiest, as it was to be the last happy birthday passed under her father's roof.

Another eminent visitor gives us glimpses of the intimate doings of the party early in October. Moscheles, arriving in Leipzig on the September evening just described, was at Mendelssohn's house in time to shake hands with Chopin before his departure. Of the following day, October 1st, he records in his diary :—

"I was at Wieck's also and made Clara play to me a great deal; a manuscript sonata by Schumann, amongst other things. Though very laboured, difficult, and rather confused, it is interesting. I went again in the evening at nine o'clock to meet Schumann, who is a quiet but interesting young man. Clara again played a number of things to me ; excellently, as I have already said. I also gave them a little specimen of my improvisation."

On October 3rd :—

"Felix came to dine at the table d'hôte. Then we were invited to Wieck's with Schumann, Banck, Hofrath Wendt, and others. Clara Wieck played Beethoven's great trio beautifully ; then I mine, which gave great satisfaction." *

On October 4th Mendelssohn made his first public appearance on the Gewandhaus platform, and at once introduced what was then the innovation of conducting with a stick.

"A hundred hearts flew to him in the first moment," reports Eusebius in the *Neue Zeitung*, though he frankly owns to having been disturbed during the performance of Beethoven's B flat symphony and the new Kapellmeister's "Meeres stille" overture by the movement of the bâton. "But it was a delight to notice how every turn of the compositions was anticipated in the countenance of Felix Meritis [Mendelssohn], who floated onwards, drawing musicians and audience with him, himself the most blissful of them all." Certain passing

* "Aus Moscheles' Leben von seiner Frau."

criticisms, modestly and sympathetically expressed, are not withheld from the article.

Mendelssohn, sending an account of the concert for family reading, says :—

" I cannot tell you how satisfied I am with this beginning and with the entire aspect of my new appointment. It is a quiet, regular, business post. One perceives that the institution has been in existence fifty-six [read fifty-four] years, and then the people seem genuinely well-disposed towards me and my music. The orchestra is very good, thoroughly musical ; and I think it will be still better in six months' time, for the kindness and attention with which these people receive and instantly follow my remarks have quite touched me at the two rehearsals we have already had. . . .

" After the concert I received and offered a number of congratulations on the platform. First the orchestra, then the Thomaners [the singing scholars], who are capital lads and arrive and depart so punctually that I have promised them an order ; then came Moscheles with a train of amateurs, then the two musical papers, and so forth. . . ."

It happened, owing to the illness of Konzertmeister August Matthäi, whose place was occupied by a substitute during the ante-Christmas half of the season 1835–36, that the moment of Mendelssohn's appointment was favourable for the transfer to his own responsibility as Kapellmeister of those important functions for which the leading violinist, or Konzertmeister, had in accordance with custom in Leipzig, as elsewhere, been previously responsible. The traditional duties of the Konzertmeister were to hold all rehearsals of purely instrumental music and to guide its concert performance, for the efficiency of which he alone was answerable, from his place as first violinist, while the director sat at a pianoforte closely following the progress of the symphony, overture, or concerto in a score placed on the desk of his instrument, and gave such assistance as might occasionally be needed to keep the performers together by striking a few notes or chords. Matthäi had filled the requirements of his post with devotion and success for more than thirty years, and it was greatly owing to the talent and enthusiasm with which he had carried on the good work of his predecessor Campagnoli that the Gewandhaus orchestra attained the excellence and musicality so strongly commended by Mendelssohn. A pupil—like Böhm, of Vienna, now remembered as Joachim's teacher—of the famous Rode of Paris, the leading representative in his day of the great violin school of Viotti, Matthäi rendered good service to his art. He was a fine soloist and quartet player, and established a special claim to remembrance in the season 1808–09 by instituting a series of quartet evenings in association with some of his colleagues, which were held in the ante-room of the Gewandhaus concert hall, and which, becoming an annual feature of. Gewandhaus activity, gradually familiarised the music-lovers of Leipzig with the string chamber music of Haydn and Mozart and of Beethoven's first and second periods. Matthäi had been officially connected with the Gewandhaus since 1806, and after a few years' activity as assistant Konzertmeister, had succeeded the veteran Campagnoli as leader of the orchestra. He never played under Mendelssohn, and his memory has been somewhat unjustly obscured owing to the fact that Ferdinand David, who followed him, was a leading figure in Leipzig throughout the most brilliant period of its musical fame.

David had passed much of his childhood in the house of his guardian, Abraham Mendelssohn, father of the composer, in close intimacy with Felix, who was his senior by a year ; and, having achieved early distinction as a violinist, was invited by his old comrade to appear at one of the December subscription concerts of 1835. Matthäi's death took place the same month, and David, following up his Gewandhaus success as a soloist by giving three quartet concerts, was at once appointed to the post of Konzertmeister, in which he officiated for the first time on February 25, 1836. He continued to fulfil some of the established duties of the position by conducting preliminary rehearsals, especially of new works, and, though, perhaps, somewhat more of a martinet than was necessary or desirable, made himself respected as a thorough and energetic musician. He carried on the quartet evenings led for twenty-six years by Matthäi, and, moved by the consideration of Mendelssohn's residence in Leipzig, added to their attractiveness by sometimes introducing as the middle number of the programme some work of pianoforte chamber music in the performance of which he was assisted by his old friend. It was in this way that the tradition was finally broken by which the chamber works of the great masters for pianoforte and strings had been reserved for private hearing. No wonder that the Gewandhaus ante-room no longer sufficed for the accommodation of the subscribers to the quartet evenings, which were removed in the course of David's first season to the concert hall, where they were held until Mendelssohn's death.

Two days after the event of Mendelssohn's first appearance, Wieck gave a private musical afternoon at his residence in honour of the celebrities present in Leipzig. It was a great occasion in Clara's life, for after playing one of Schubert's trios with two of the resident musicians, she had the delight of performing Bach's concerto in D minor for three claviers with Mendelssohn and Moscheles. Had it ever been played before in Leipzig, even privately? We may be sure that her father stood his most erect as he turned over the pages for her, and that Robert's heart, full of still unspoken love, beat, as he looked at her, in tender sympathy with her joy. "Clara grows more charming inwardly and outwardly every day, every hour," he had written to a friend a few days before.

"The concerto is very interesting," remarks Moscheles to his wife; "I am having it copied for London. There were about thirty people present to listen." Of Clara's playing of his own G minor concerto he says: "No better interpretation or execution of the work is possible. I myself could not give it more effect. She plays it just as though it were her own composition."

One important musical event quickly succeeded another during this momentous autumn season. Clara's concert, given on November 9th in the Gewandhaus, was and remains scarcely second in historical interest to that of October 4th, signalised by Mendelssohn's installation. Her programme included her own lately finished concerto and Mendelssohn's caprice in B minor, Op. 22, both with orchestral accompaniment; and—the Bach concerto in D minor for three claviers with quartet accompaniment, in the performance of which Mendelssohn and Rakemann a pianist of Bremen distinguished as a Davidsbündler by the name "Walt," were her colleagues. The high distinctive significance of the occasion is not to be found in its having been marked by certainly the first public performance of this particular work, but in the fact that while more than two thousand concerts had been given in the hall of the Leipzig Gewandhaus since its inauguration on November 25, 1781, the building now resounded for the first time with the tones of the marvellous master who, eighty-five years previously, had been borne to his rest from his home within the city walls, leaving the majority of his works to the chances of life or death; to a lengthened slumber in public libraries, private collections, or forgotten cupboards, and happily to a final glorious resurrection. The programme of this academy of Clara's was the legitimate outcome of her father's devoted training of her powers. She had been brought up from her childhood in the veneration of Bach's great name. At twelve she had, as we have seen, converted Schumann from his disbelief in the possibility of finding music in a fugue by playing him one of the two in C sharp minor contained in the "Well-tempered Clavier";* at fifteen, or possibly earlier, she had introduced Bach's fugues to the audiences of her public concerts, an experiment previously undreamed of by pianist or impresario; now at sixteen it was her privilege to invite Mendelssohn to assist her in the execution of one of the most characteristic of the great cantor's extended instrumental works. The day of the concert was a day which in itself had made her life worth living. Of the performance of Mendelssohn's work the composer wrote to his sister: "Imagine, Fanny; I listened to my B minor Caprice for the first time at Wieck's concert (Clara played it like a little witch), and it pleased me very much!"†

Clara's own concerto in three movements, published a

* *Ante*, p. 74.
† Hensel's "Die Familie Mendelssohn."

little later as Op. 7, which might, perhaps, have been more appropriately entitled " Concert-stück," was coldly received by her Leipzig audience. She achieved considerable success with it, however, in the course of some of her concert *tournées* of the following two or three seasons. It retains some interest, so far as it still survives in a few private collections, as attesting the musicianship to which Clara had attained at the age of sixteen and as a relic of the performer-composer period, which, as we have already explained, required that an executant hoping to attain first rank as an artist should bring forward an original work of extended dimensions at his or her benefit concert.*

It is clear, from all we know of Schumann's vehement temperament, that there could be no indefinite prolongation of the peculiar relation between himself and Clara, in which both had found the happiness of the summer. That he constrained himself to silence on the subject of his attachment to her for the greater part of a year sufficiently indicates how deeply his confidence in his own stedfastness had been shaken by the circumstances of his entanglement with Ernestine. But as the summer declined and the autumn wore on and Clara's instinctive understanding of his nature began gradually to restore him to faith in himself, he began to perceive that his feeling for her was not of sudden growth, but that he had loved her always. Even when he had become fully aware, however, that she was his very life and felt almost sure he might win her, with her true heart and all the attractiveness of her youth and art and dawning fame, to be his, he could not find words to tell her of his hopes. So Dame Nature had to make the matter her own, and help him with one of her characteristic promptings; and it happened that Clara, lighting him downstairs after an evening spent at her father's house towards the end of November, suddenly, without word or warning, felt Robert's first kiss.†

* The Bach concerto introduced by Clara on this occasion was first printed in 1846 in the Czerny and Griepenkerl edition of the master's instrumental works.

† Litzmann, i. 92.

The artistic circumstances of the short concert journey on which Wieck and Clara started the very next day, if Litzmann be right in his conjecture, after this important occurrence, need not detain our attention. We may be sure that, however gratifying they may have proved to Wieck, they occupied an entirely subordinate place in the meditations of his daughter. For Clara the interest of the tour will certainly have been concentrated in the concert she gave early in December in Zwickau, where Robert was present to meet and admire her and delight in her success, and to express his congratulations afterwards in a manner of his own to which he now seemed to consider himself privileged by established right. "I shall never forget that kissing; you were too sweet that evening. And then you could not see me during the concert, you, Clara, in your blue dress."*

There was much to be discussed between the lovers, Clara being concerned above all to learn the exact state of Schumann's present relations with Ernestine. No doubt the young composer had unburdened himself on the subject to his mother; no doubt she had given him the best advice. Unfortunately, however, the want of resolution to face unpleasant facts, which had already been the means of prolonging poor Ernestine's unhappiness and had caused himself months of miserable suspense, had involved him in a very difficult situation, from which he again sought refuge in procrastination. He allowed several more weeks to pass before putting the matter on a right footing, leaving Clara under the erroneous impression, meanwhile, not only that his engagement had been definitely broken off, but that his former fiancée was again betrothed.

For Clara, therefore, the year closed blissfully, and if Robert was at times troubled by thoughts of the still unwritten letter to Ernestine or of the communication of his relation with Clara that must shortly be made to Wieck, he forgot his perplexities in the rapturous joy of the frequent *tête-à-tête* interviews with his beloved allowed him by his old habit of intimacy at her father's house. Constitutionally subject to extremes of mood, he had at this time persuaded

* Litzmann, i. 92.

himself that Wieck's openly expressed enthusiastic admiration of his genius pointed in a direction favourable to his desire to become that autocratic gentleman's son-in-law. In this hope he was to be undeceived in the near future. The nervous dread which had caused his long delay in writing the last necessary letter to Ernestine proved, however, to have been needless. On at length receiving it, she restored him his freedom without question or remark, and for so doing deserves to be remembered kindly by all lovers of Schumann's art.* As the Frau Gräfin von Zedwitz she stood, later on, in friendly relations with the composer and his wife, and Schumann paid her the tribute of dedicating to her his Opus 31, the set of songs which includes his impressive setting of Chamisso's ballad, "The Lion's Bride."

It could not but be that the profound emotion which thrilled Clara's being at this period, that the exquisite consciousness of Robert's love which made each hour of the day and each business of every hour sacred to her, should find reflection in her outward manner and bearing. For many months she had kept her intense nature under strong repression; had proudly disdained to acknowledge to herself how bitter a thing life had become when it seemed as though her old friend had gone from her not to return. Now he had come back, and had come, not as to his child playmate, but as to the woman who held his fate in her hand, and had imperiously demanded her love; now she might confess to herself and to him that she loved him infinitely, and desired nothing better than to pass through life at his side and to remain his throughout eternity. The entire personality of the young girl seemed irradiated. A new, tender light beamed from her dark eyes, she grew daily more gentle, seeming to move as in a dream. "Clara Wieck loves and is loved," wrote Schumann a little later to Dr. A. Kahlert in Breslau; "you will easily discover it by her gentle, rapt air and demeanour." Tokens such as these could not altogether escape the notice of the home circle. If Wieck himself, preoccupied with his numerous affairs, did not immediately perceive them, Frau

* Kohut, 104.

Clementine had both leisure and opportunity for closer observation, and it is probable that she by and by whispered a word of warning to her husband. Clara, who had accepted the invitation of the Gewandhaus committee to play the pianoforte solo of Beethoven's Choral Fantasia under Mendelssohn at the subscription concert of December 15th, was allowed to remain at home for some weeks yet; but Robert was gradually made aware that his visits to the Wiecks' house were too frequent and too long, and, by the beginning of the New Year, felt that it would be prudent to discontinue them almost entirely for a while. About the middle of January, 1836, Wieck accompanied Clara to Dresden, to give her a few weeks' change in the society of intimate friends before starting with her on the first concert journey of the year. Her musical preparations for the tour were relieved, and her days enlivened, by walking or sleighing excursions in the keen, crisp winter air of the beautiful neighbourhood, by frequent visits to the theatre, by private festivities of which she was the centre; by the various distractions, in short, on which her father relied for the final extinction of such smouldering embers of what he still regarded as a mere child's romance as might, he feared, be stirred into dangerous flame by the continuance of her renewed intimacy with Schumann. But his precautions were taken too late. On one of the last days of January the first of two concerts took place that had been arranged in Dresden as the opening appearances of the tour. It was as successful as usual. The room was crowded with a distinguished audience; the applause was overwhelming; but—Clara had been nervous before making her entrance for the first time in her career, and had, as Wieck wrote to his wife, "even shed a few musical tears!" Litzmann surmises that before this date Wieck, warning her that her friendship with Robert must not exceed the bounds of artistic companionship, had prohibited the exchange of confidential letters between the pair; and quotes in support of this conjecture a few words written in the diary by Clara at the end of January:—

"Schumann sent me his new Paganini studies with a

few lines, which I received on the 21st. His attention gave me great pleasure."

What, however, could paternal prohibition avail to arrest the force of an overmastering attraction that had insensibly drawn two passionate young souls towards each other during years of mutual understanding and intimate sympathy, and had been recognised at length by both and avowed by each to the other? Robert and Clara were already standing together as professed votaries within the gates of the sacred temple of love, and during the years of trial that lay immediately before them, neither the threats of father, nor the watchfulness of stepmother; neither the sorrow of separation, nor the absorbing interest of artistic success, nor even the passing mists of doubt in the other's constancy by which each was occasionally oppressed, could tempt them to retrace their footsteps. Stricken as their future was to be by cruel and manifold suffering, yet it was also to be infinitely blessed, since destiny itself had chosen them to become pledges before the world, through life unto death, of the supreme possibilities of love's perfect fulfilment.

Apprised of an opportunity that awaited him in the second week of February, Robert hastened to Dresden in Wieck's absence, and, with the help of some of Clara's intimate friends, contrived to arrange more than one lengthy interview with his beloved. The joy of their meeting was chequered by sadness of a more special kind than that necessarily involved in the occasional conferences of parted lovers. Robert had lost his mother but a few days earlier, and that he put off going to Zwickau till after the funeral may be interpreted at once as a sign of his acute distress and a new indication of his constitutional dread of facing trouble. It is not difficult to imagine the purport of the forbidden interviews between the lovers; the transport of meeting, the renewed vows of constancy registered on both sides. "Be faithful," said Robert, as they parted, and Clara, looking after him with tearful eyes, sorrowfully inclined her head. The situation is fairly summed up in a letter written by Robert just before starting on his return journey to Leipzig after two days spent in Zwickau.

" At the Zwickau Posthouse, after 10 o'clock.

". . . I have been waiting for the express post for two hours. The roads are so bad that perhaps I may not get away before 2 o'clock. You are always present before me, my loved, loved Clara; ah, so near, it seems to me as though I could touch you. When I loved formerly I was able to express what I felt in suitable language, now I cannot do it. I could not tell you if you did not already know. Only love me entirely —I demand much, for I give much.

" My day has been agitated by many things—my mother's will, the accounts of her death. Your fresh image stands behind all shadows, however, and helps me to endure.

" I may venture to tell you that my future is now much more secure. I cannot, indeed, fold my hands in idleness, and shall have to work hard in order to win what you recognise when you happen to pass the mirror—but you also will desire to remain an artist . . . you will contribute, co-operate, share joy and sorrow with me. Write to me about this.

" My first business in Leipzig will be to put my affairs in order. Inwardly I am at peace. Perhaps your father may not withhold his hand when I ask for his blessing. On this subject there is, indeed, much to consider and weigh. Meanwhile I trust in our good angel. Fate has destined us for each other. I knew this long ago, but had not the courage to speak and come to an understanding with you. . . .

" The room is dark. Passengers are asleep near me. Outside it drizzles and snows. I will bury myself deep in a corner, my head on a cushion, and think only of you. . . .

" YOUR ROBERT." *

Wieck was back in Dresden by February 14th, and was immediately informed by some one unknown of the visit received by his daughter during his absence. Who shall describe his anger? The torrent of indignation, accusation, menace hurled by him at the defenceless Clara was varied by violent denunciation of her lover, still more painful to her to hear. But she had her amulet secure in her heart: the

* " Jugendbriefe," 267,

assurance of Robert's love; and so long as this remained to her, what could she not bear with patience? It may even be allowed that her father's was the worse predicament, since it was, from the first, hopeless. Circumstances, helped, perhaps, at an earlier stage of the matter by his own shortsightedness, had already decided against him. No little obloquy was incurred by Wieck, and still attaches to his memory so far as this yet survives, on account of the inflexible opposition offered by him from first to last to Clara's attachment. It is, however, no less easy to be wise about other people's affairs than to see clearly after the event. We, looking back upon Schumann's high and generous character, his essential stedfastness of purpose, his noble artistic aims, the splendid fulfilment of his genius—attained, in spite of many obstacles, through sheer and unremitting devotion to art; remembering his unswerving fidelity to the young girl who loved and believed in him, his unconditional surrender to her inspiration, his passionate strn *gles to win her; we, to whom the story of Robert and Clara _ s come as a realised spiritual inheritance, who may contemplate its various stages of hope and despair, of struggle and of victory, may easily be so carried away by its fascination as to forget that there was another side to it while it was still in the making which could not but engross the attention of Friedrich Wieck. Whilst no word can be said in defence of the methods at last employed by him to force Clara to acquiesce in his absolute rejection of Schumann's wishes, neither is it possible to contest the reasonableness of his views at this comparatively early period of the development of the attachment. What father of normal sensibility could have regarded without dismay the entanglement of his child—as it must have seemed to Wieck—with a man of inconsiderable private means, not given to prudent regulation of his expenses, apt to take impulse as his guide in the affairs of life, of uncertain health and liable to extremes of mood; who, as it appeared at the time, had wasted years of youth in aimless trifling and repeated change of purpose, and was now at twenty-five only at the threshold of a composer's career—a career demanding unremitting toil and offering but little prospect of certain income

—a man generally believed, moreover, to be engaged to another girl? And the natural consternation felt by the father on suddenly realising with completeness that his scarcely grown-up daughter was bent on hazarding the happiness of her life on the chances of an indefinitely prolonged engagement or an early and imprudent marriage was aggravated in Wieck's case by his perception not only of the disastrous consequences which either of these catastrophes might entail, but of the brilliant possibilities it might prevent. Wieck, as we have seen, well understood the meaning of the word " privation." He had worked his way upward by the exercise of certain great qualities, with the possession of which it would scarcely have been possible for him to credit Robert; and he had already achieved one of the constant purposes of his mature manhood: he had practically secured Clara from the miseries of an uncertain future. Whilst exercising his right as her father, her sole teacher, her sagacious business manager, to reserve for his own benefit a definite proportion of her earnings, her own appointed share was punctually allotted and invested for her use, and he might confidently expect that the continued employment of her powers, the growing recognition of her name, would, by the time she should reach maturity, have placed her in a position of artistic independence. Then, over and above these prudential considerations, there were his feelings of delighted pride in the gifts and successes of his child, his pupil, the supreme object of his affection and his life. Who shall blame him for the apprehension that the artistic fruit which had grown and bloomed under his watchfulness with such rare promise of perfection might, if snatched from his care before it had ripened to fullness, be bruised or even crushed by adverse influences from which he would have protected it? It was part of Wieck's nature to recognise an obstacle only as something to be overcome by determination, and it was in this spirit, his love for Clara notwithstanding, that, now the lovers had directly contravened his will, he unhesitatingly joined issue with them. His first measure was to post a letter to Schumann, written in such harsh and insulting terms as to bar all immediate possibility of further intercourse between the young musician and himself.

The experiences of the past year, during which she had been a constant prey to agitation alternating between the extremes of happiness and pain, had not been calculated to fortify Clara's mind with that tranquil habit in regard to outward affairs which is so valuable an asset in enabling the executive artist to withstand the nervous strain of personal publicity. She gave a second concert in Dresden about the middle of February, and started soon afterwards for Breslau; but both she and her father seem to have been sensible during the tour rather of the inconveniences than the rewards attaching to the career of the travelling virtuoso. Success left Clara indifferent and apathetic, and Wieck, infected, probably, by her depression, made no attempt to conceal his impatience of the drudgery entailed upon himself by his rôle of impresario. Meanwhile Schumann, in Leipzig, was left to divine their movements as best he might. No communication seems to have passed between him and Clara at this time, and the attempts made by him to obtain indirect tidings of her were only so far successful as to procure him occasional information of her whereabouts. "Clara is in Breslau," he wrote on March 2nd to his sister-in-law Therese. "My stars are strangely disturbed. God grant a favourable issue!"

Schumann's correspondence clearly shows, however, that his mind derived solace during these few weeks from his engrossing work as author and composer, his consciousness that he was making rapid progress in his art, and his intimacy with those of the foremost musicians of the day with whom he felt in warm sympathy. It may even be said that he was for the time fairly at peace; probably because he cherished the conviction that the growth of his artistic power, which was, as he could perceive, attended by some slow advance of his recognised artistic position, must eventually break down the barrier of paternal opposition that withheld from him his beloved. It was not wonderful that, having frequently heard himself described by Wieck as "the younger Bach," "the second Beethoven," "the German Chopin," he should have built hopes for the future of his attachment upon such enthusiastic recognition of his genius.

"You would approve of my way of life," he writes to

Therese on April 1st. " I was always partial to extremes, and so, as I was formerly one of the most inveterate, I have become one of the most moderate of smokers and Bavarians. Four cigars a day at most, and for the last two months *no beer at all.* Everything is mending now, and I am becoming very vain. Do not praise me, therefore ; I do this sufficiently for myself."

The society of Mendelssohn, with whom and with David he dined regularly in the middle of the day at the Hôtel de Bavière, afforded him constant delight and stimulus. Any letter of special musical interest received by him was brought to share with this friend, whose name is mentioned constantly in his own correspondence.

" I look up to Mendelssohn as to a lofty mountain ; he is really a god ! " he exclaims to Therese. " I am often with David, also with a Dr. Schlemmer, tutor to young Roth-schild, and with the latter himself. We will talk about Wieck and Clara when we meet. My position there is critical, and I do not as yet see the way out of it. As matters stand, however, either I shall never be able to speak to her again or she will be entirely my own." *

The dinner-party at the Hôtel de Bavière was frequently enlarged by the addition of one or more friends of distinction who might be staying in Leipzig, and the names of the poet Chamisso, of our English composer Sterndale Bennett, and of Walter von Goethe, the great man's grandson, are associated, amongst others, with the meetings of this and the following year. Late in the evening Schumann was accustomed to join a circle of friends at the " Kaffeebaum," a sort of club-restaurant in Meat Street (Fleischergasse).

" A cheerful informality prevailed at these meetings, from which the spirit of the clique and the habit of dissipation were alike absent. Schumann, on entering, would take his place in a favourite dark corner, sitting sideways at the table always reserved for the party, supporting his head with his arm, his eyes half closed, absorbed in meditation and frequently pushing away the hair that fell over his forehead. Awakened to participation in any interesting exchange of

* " Briefe," p. 72.

ideas going on around him, one could observe that his spirit had returned to the outer world by the animation that replaced the usually absent and dreamy expression of his eyes." *

At the Voigts' house, which rivalled Wieck's as a private musical centre of Leipzig, he was always sure of sympathy, and was equally welcome as an invited guest at their musical gatherings—when he would sit characteristically in the darkest and farthest corner he could find, to enjoy the performances of Mendelssohn, David, and others—or as an unexpected visitor who might drop in at any hour of the day. Voigt has left on record the story of a particular occasion when, as he was sitting in the drawing-room alone with his wife, Schumann entered unannounced. Smiling a silent greeting, he crossed the room to the closed piano, opened and took his seat before it, and played softly for about fifteen minutes. Then, rising and shutting the instrument, with a farewell glance at his friends, he departed as he had come, without having uttered a word !

The return to Leipzig, early in April, of Wieck and his daughter could not fail to disturb the unusually equable mood that had been preserved by Schumann for several previous weeks. To pay his accustomed visit of welcome on their home-coming was impossible; endeavours to meet Clara as if by accident proved futile, and the double consciousness of his nearness to his beloved and his entire separation from her, in itself sufficiently agitating, was rendered the more painful by Clara's unexpected and enigmatical behaviour on the two or three occasions when chance brought them together in the presence of others. Not by a single special glance or word, or even by return of his hand-pressure, did she seek to convey the assurance, for which Robert was passionately longing, that she had kept her promise to be faithful to him. Nor was a protracted interval of suspense the worst he had to bear. To it was added before long the torture of a not well-founded, but certainly very natural jealousy. Something of the state of his mind during the ordeal may be learned by study of the sonata in F minor, Op. 14, on which he was engaged during the weeks immediately succeeding the Wiecks'

* " Die Davidsbündler," by Dr. Gustav Jansen, p. 53.

return, and which we shall consider in our next chapter. That
Schumann worked vehemently during the period to which its
production is to be referred, the sonata itself tells us. Not for
nearly two months did he find opportunity of putting to the
test the fears that consumed him and such hope as he may
have retained in the matter of his love. Towards the end of
May, however, the publication by Kistner of the F sharp
minor sonata as Op. 11 made it possible for him to send
a greeting which, as he fancied, must procure for him some
sign from the young girl who remained the centre of his
thoughts. He wrote no word, but forwarded her a copy of
the newly printed work, which had been issued with a fantastic title-page designed by the artist Genelli, and the original
manuscript dedication by Florestan and Eusebius to " Clara."

CHAPTER XI

1836

WITH the completion and publication of the two works
for pianoforte solo—six Concert studies after Paganini,
Op. 10, and Sonata in F sharp minor, Op. 11, published
respectively in September, 1835, and June, 1836, Schumann
may be said to have fulfilled some of the strivings of the
earlier years of his career. He has himself explained in
the preface to Op. 10 that the purpose pursued by him in
the arrangement of his second book of Paganini *études* was
of a more ambitious kind than that which he had set himself
to accomplish in the Opus 3 :—

"Instead of copying the original almost note for note,
perhaps to its prejudice, as in an earlier set of Paganini studies,
and merely supplying the harmonies, I have this time rejected
the pedantry of a literal transcription, and have endeavoured
to give the work the character of an independent composition
for the pianoforte from which the traces of its origin as a
violin solo have been effaced without sacrifice of its poetic
thought. It is manifest that, for the attainment of this
object, it has been necessary, whilst observing the caution due
to the revered genius of Paganini, not only to make certain
alterations in the manner of his expression, but to add or
take away something here and there. I leave it to the
sympathetic friends of art to decide, by a comparison—not
in itself uninteresting—of the original with the pianoforte
arrangement, as to whether I have accomplished my task
with discretion."

That Schumann could not fail to profit by the insight acquired by him through the exercise of his talent in any special field of labour is a foregone conclusion. The concert studies give evidence, however, not alone that the experience gained during the preparation of his Opus 3 had taught him the only method by which the transcriber can impart permanent artistic value to his work, but that every new effort of his genius was giving him more facility in the control of his powers. Each of the six numbers of Opus 10, whilst clearly presenting the essential ideas of its parent caprice for the violin, justifies its existence as a pianoforte study, and, in the hands of a competent virtuoso, remains an effective concert solo even in the present era of what would have been considered in Schumann's day phenomenal pianoforte technique.

The sonata in F sharp minor, filled with gems of glowing musical imagination, derives value for the lover of Schumann's music not only from the passionate beauty of its ideas, but as a memorial of the composer's early artistic aspirations and conflicts and partial victories. It is from first to last, to use Clara's words, a "Davidsbündlerschen Florestanschen" composition, and even carries us back to the first months of Robert's career as a university student, supposed by those who loved him best to be devoting his energies to the dry details of the law studies to which they had condemned him whilst his spirit had taken irrepressible flight to a dreamland of romance filled with visions and tones of beauty.

"Life in Leipzig continues its old, dreary, humdrum round, and I would rather be in pepperland than in Leipzig," he wrote on July 29, 1828. Two days later he had composed the enchanting melody to Kerner's song "An Anna":

Hei - math beim Ge - mur - mel der Sil - ber - quel - le.

which we have learned to love in its adaptation as the
second movement of the F sharp minor sonata, and which
lives in its original form in Brahms' supplement to Frau
Schumann's complete edition of Schumann's works.

The first of the four movements which constitute the
sonata must be referred to the period when the circumstance
of Robert's injured finger, spreading consternation among
his relations, had given definiteness to the conviction which,
as we have shown, had probably been long latent in his
mind, that his future was to be that of the creative and not
the executive musician. There is no room for doubt that
it originated as the "Fandango" of which Robert speaks
in a letter of 1832, soon after the Wiecks' return from
Paris.* A second mention of this piece, which had been
accepted by Hofmeister, occurs in a letter written the
following January from Schneeberg, in which the young
composer tells his publisher that he has lost a sheet of the
fandango and cannot recall the thread of the composition
to memory. Nothing more was heard of it until after
Schumann's death, when an incomplete manuscript entitled
"Fandango" was found among his papers. Of this, which
passed into the hands of Brahms and is now preserved in
the library of the Gesellschaft der Musikfreunde in Vienna,
the first movement of the sonata is an enlarged and developed
version.

In the history of the sonata, therefore, may be found
the explanation of those of its defects on which Schumann's
critics have most constantly insisted; the defects, in a word,

* See *ante*, p. 76.

of immaturity. It is the work of ardently pulsating genius not as yet subdued to disciplined musicianship. Yet it displays musicianship in the making. Who that brings imagination and sympathy to the study of the first allegro will fail to find an element of attraction in the very laboriousness of its development, so faithfully does it represent the determined effort of the eager, impulsive Robert to obtain control of his thoughts, to expand and mould his fandango to legitimate sonata form ! The beautiful introduction, " un poco adagio," which precedes this movement was probably, if we may judge by internal evidence and especially by the sustained breadth of its phrases, one of the composer's latest contributions to the work; while the scherzo is only less satisfactory than it might be in consequence of the introduction of a second trio—an intermezzo " alla burla ma pomposo," based on a trivial motif, which is succeeded by a recitative for the left hand leading to the final reprise. It must be conjectured that this brief episode had its antecedent in some set of events, real or imaginary, associated with his work in the composer's mind—something, in fact, in the nature of a " programme." Musically it cannot be justified, since it weakens the impression derived from the striking principal theme and bold rhythms of the scherzo itself, as well as from the soft, romantic charm of the first trio. The last movement with its fine principal subject and powerful climax is, nevertheless, too deficient in coherence and in balance of its parts to be of any considerable value from the standpoint of musical art. Yet, what then ?

" I send you my F sharp minor sonata," wrote Schumann in 1837 to Pastor G. A. Keferstein; " receive it kindly, and it will answer you. Much heart's blood adheres to it."

The music-lover of 1912 does not, any more than did the critics of 1836 and 1837, find in the composition a finished work of art, yet it rests securely in his affection, for its tones answer to certain sympathetic strings of his own being, and stir to quicker vibration within him the eternal human longing for the beauty and fullness of life.

" L'aria des pages 14 et 15," wrote Liszt of the sonata, in

a remarkable review of three of Schumann's works which appeared in the *Gazette Musicale* of November 13, 1837, " est une des choses les plus achevées que nous connaissons. Bien que l'auteur ait écrit en marge : ' Senza passione,' l'abandon le plus passionné en est le caractère. La passion, à la vérité s'y manifeste d'une manière indirecte et voilée ; elle s'y trahit plutôt qu'elle n'y éclate ; mais elle y est vraie, profonde, et vous prend aux entrailles. Remarquons nous ici, la musique de M. Schumann s'adresse plus spécialement aux âmes méditatives, aux esprits sérieux qui ne s'arrêtent point aux surfaces et savent plonger au fond des eaux pour y chercher la perle cachée. Plus on pénètre avant dans sa pensée, plus on y découvre de force et de vie ; plus on l'étudie, plus on est frappé de la richesse et de la fécondité qui avaient échappé d'abord."

Moscheles, who reviewed the sonata, by Schumann's request, in the *Neue Zeitschrift,* wrote :—

"The composition is a genuine product of the wide-spreading romanticism of the day. It is certainly the work of one mind, though the title ascribes its authorship to two names. Just as in their writings Florestan and Eusebius often oppose each other in argument in order to obtain a wider field for the exposition of their views and the play of their humour, so also this double brotherhood seems to have been adopted here as a basis for the contrasting elements of the sonata. The accomplishment of a task so elevated as that which the composer has here set himself can be attained only by means of a series of works in which his important creative activity cannot fail to become developed to greater clearness."

In a private letter of the time Moscheles remarks :—

" For finger gymnastics I play through Thalberg's things, for the mind I have Schumann. His romanticism strikes me as so new, his creative gift is so great, that I intend to devote myself more and more to the study of his things, in order to be able to form an unbiassed judgment of the merits and weaknesses of this new school. He has sent me his just published sonata, Florestan and Eusebius, and requested me to review it for the *Neue Zeitschrift,* saying I am the only person who can do this properly."

Whatever favourable expectation Robert may have formed as to the result of the message he had designed to convey to Clara by sending her the published sonata was to be mercilessly disappointed. The only communication he received from her throughout the summer was a packet of his own letters to her, with a formally written request for the return of hers to him.

The lovers had exchanged neither word nor letter since the snowy winter evening in February when Robert, after writing to Clara in the dreary waiting-room at Zwickau of his desires and resolutions for the future, had buried himself "deep in a corner" to think only of her. His hopes had, as we have seen, evidently been encouraged during the early part of the year, in spite of the blow dealt them by Wieck's letter from Dresden, by the rapid progress he felt himself to be making in his art. Possibly they had retained more vitality during the two months of suspense that followed Clara's return to Leipzig than he himself was aware of. Whether or not this be so, however, the final collapse of the illusion by which he had lived and worked shattered his self-control and brought him to the brink of a precipice from which, conceivably, he might not have been saved. Fortunately a timely voice gave him warning of his danger. He lodged at this time in the house of a certain Frau Devrient, an elderly widow lady who had been formerly resident in Zwickau. She was capable of appreciating his character and genius, and strove tenderly to play the part of a true friend to him in his hour of necessity. How dire that necessity was may be conjectured from the contents of a letter which he addressed to her soon after receiving the only acknowledgment granted him of the copy of the sonata he had sent Clara:—

"MOST HONOURED LADY,—Your valued letter has refreshed my heart. . . . Why should I trouble you with complaints of frustrated plans, deserved and undeserved troubles, such as fall, probably, to the lot of every one? I still have my glorious hours; hours passed at the pianoforte, in the companionship of excellent men, in the consciousness of an honourable sphere of activity and the hope of continued and greater achievement. This very exaltation of the faculties, however, often degenerates into extravagance, when it seems to me as though I could take the whole world by storm. The reaction follows, and then the artificial means to restore one's self. I am well aware of the cure that could avail to reconcile such dangerous extremes ; a loving wife could do it. Here, however, let me be alone with my sorrow, and keep silence about the strange complications for the solution of which, though I do not expect it at present, I daily implore my good angel. . . ."

At the end of June a second letter follows :—

"Your hand comes from the clouds. It is impossible for me to remain after what you have written to me, and the sooner I go the better. Everything causes me deep regret, especially as I have a real affection for you (though you do not know this). The dismal weather and constantly increasing troubles of which I can speak to no one had made me reckless. You are so very right. Only do not think too badly of me, and excuse me from saying more to-day."

But Schumann did not leave Frau Devrient. On the contrary, he lived in her house whenever he was in Leipzig until the date of his marriage. On July 1st, probably the very day after sending the last quoted letter, he wrote :—

"A kind good-morning to Frau Devrient, and nothing but force shall move me from my room. . . . I thank the star that brought me to this house, and am above all grateful for your solicitous care."*

If, indeed, there had been moments when Robert, in the agony of his disappointed love, feeling that he was forsaken of God and man, was tempted to yield to the devil's bait by which not a few young men of impressionable genius have been ensnared to their ruin ; if he, on one or two occasions, tried to forget his pain in noisy excess, yet, as we saw when we contemplated the struggle of his adolescence, his was a nature that base allurements could not long hold in thrall. Intellectual, spiritual activity was a necessity to him. From childhood he had instinctively sought refuge at the pianoforte from the attacks of terror to which his hypersensitive nervous organisation rendered him occasionally liable. To it he had been able to confide his nameless alarms ; through

* "Briefe," pp. 73, 74.

it he had found their alleviation. It was from his beloved
instrument that he was to now derive the solace which
saved him from despair.

"I have finished a fantasia in three movements that I
sketched in detail in June, 1836," wrote Robert to Clara
two years later. "The first movement is, I think, the most
passionate thing I have composed—a deep lament for you."

What music-lover will need to be reminded of the mag-
nificent Fantasia in C major known now as Schumann's Opus
17; of the surging, tumultuous sorrow of the first movement,
its noble plaint, its infinite tenderness, the courageous,
resigned spirit of its middle episode? If ever musician was
led through suffering to victory, then was Schumann here.
If ever pain has been translated into elevated artistic
achievement, then do we possess its result in this, one of
the greatest compositions ever written for its instrument, and,
in the author's opinion, one of the very few works of musical
art whose grandeur is enhanced by a certain obscurity of
outline. The first movement seems to give expression to the
very elemental sorrow of the human soul which, desiring the
supreme felicities of earth, perceives them to be unattainable;
which, resigned, is not yet reconciled, to fate. We have
devoted a few lines to the fantasia in this place because,
like the Carnaval and the Études Symphoniques, it must
be considered, historically, in close association with those
particular circumstances of the composer's life that called
it into being and developed it to advanced form. All three
compositions remained, however, for several years in manuscript, and their place as works of art in the list of Schumann's
publications properly belongs to that later date when he
revised them finally for the engraver. This fact is indicated
in the fantasia by its opus number, and we shall return to its
more detailed consideration.

In the sonata in F minor, Op. 14, known to us as the third
of Schumann's works in this form, we have, as the composer
writes, a remembrance of the October days of 1835 in which he
made the personal acquaintance of Moscheles, to whom the
sonata is dedicated.* The first movement was sketched

* "Briefe," p. 69.

in the late autumn of that year; and is therefore to be referred to the time of mental stress, which we have already discussed at length, when Schumann, having become fully cognisant of the true nature of his feeling for Clara, had not as yet had courage to free himself formally from his engagement to Ernestine; and the date, June 5, 1836, written on the MS. at the end of the last movement, assigns the composition of the entire work to the period which covers the composer's avowal of his attachment to Clara, the weeks of their intimacy as confessed lovers, his hurried visit to Dresden in Wieck's absence and the cessation of all communication between himself and his beloved until the publication of his first sonata. The composition was not only finished and revised in the summer, but published in the autumn, of 1836.

As a work of art the sonata, Op. 14, is disappointing in spite of the testimony it affords as to Schumann's advancing aims. If both the first and last movements contain moments —of which the opening of the first movement is the most striking—that are hardly surpassed in their passionate intensity of feeling in any instrumental work from the master's hand, yet in neither is the inspiration sufficiently sustained so to override its defects of craftsmanship as to compel the music-lover's acceptance of the whole work as a successful composition in the highest form of art for the pianoforte.

The first movement is based on a design inadequate to the requirements of the most important portion of a great sonata; a design from which the free fantasia, almost to be regarded as the keynote of the form, is absent. This is not the place for detailed analysis, but the reader interested in the subject may ascertain for himself that the movement consists of two only of the three fundamental parts of sonata form—the exposition and recapitulation. The departure from regular design, which would not in itself be necessarily objectionable, is, in this instance, open to criticism from the fact that the method adopted to extend the movement—the multiplication of the sections of the second part of the exposition, sometimes called collectively the second subject—has failed to secure its unity.

In the last movement, written in toccata style, unity of a

certain kind has been attained by the continuous employment of a figure of semi-quavers in triplets; but its satisfactory effect is injured by the harshness of many of the harmonies from which the passages are derived. Logically, perhaps, justifiable, they are frequently unacceptable to the ear even when played up to the "presto possibile" marked by the composer. The second movement, a scherzo with trio, has a broad opening theme, but lacks spontaneity. The third, a set of four variations on an andantino by Clara Wieck, is of attractive clearness.

The chief permanent interest—and it has its deep fascination—attaching to the sonata in F minor is, in fact, that which it possesses psychologically, as a reflection of the tumultuous agitation that possessed Schumann's mind during many months of a critical phase in his career. Essentially a product of romanticism, it gives musical embodiment in a quite special way to the darker of the ruling spirits of the cult, the spirit of mystical emotionalism which, with its attendant demons, lured some of the most gifted of the German romantic poets along the downward path from enlightenment to despair; which hastened the premature death of Novalis, led Kleist to madness and suicide, and, at times, seemed to threaten the vitality of Schumann's high powers. In Schumann's case, strength was, as we know, to prevail over weakness, intellectual energy over ungoverned feeling. Even with the completion of the sonata the demon within him would appear to have been partially subdued, and some words written by him to Therese in November of the year seem to express his own consciousness that in the gathering together of his best strength of mind and soul for the accomplishment of the fantasia in C major he had already practically secured the victory over himself and come forth from the fight sound and almost healed. " Clara loves me as warmly as ever," he writes, impelled, so far as can be ascertained, solely by the conviction of his own calmer mood; " nevertheless I have resigned all hope. Thus do events move in circles. Life is a strange thing."

The sonata Opus 14 was published in November, 1836, by Haslinger, of Vienna. Completed as a work of five movements, it first appeared as one of three only, the two scherzi which formed part of the original manuscript having been set aside by Haslinger's desire. For the title " Grande Sonate " chosen by Schumann, the unsuitable one " Concert sans orchestre " was substituted on the same initiative. In the second edition of the work, which was issued in 1853, the original MS. title and the second of the two scherzi were restored. The original first scherzo may be studied in the supplementary volume, to which we have referred more than once, of Frau Schumann's complete edition, published by Breitkopf and Härtel.

Some little effort of imagination is needed for the right understanding of Clara's attitude during the period that followed her return to Leipzig in the spring of 1836; the persevering attitude that made it possible to her to leave Robert to the anxiety of more than a year's suspense as to her exact feelings towards himself; possible to send him the cruel packet of his letters; to ask for the return of her own; worse than all, possible to receive the sonata which he had completed, so to speak, before her eyes during the summer of the previous year in the new, unspoken consciousness of their mutual understanding, to receive it without even an acknowledgment; Robert's first published great work, on which he had written her name.

We may be well aware now, just as Robert was well aware at the time, that, had Clara been minded to communicate with him, neither prohibition nor watchfulness at home would have prevented her from letting him know by word or sign that these things had not come to pass by her desire, but had been forced upon her. But we may also realise with clear comprehension what Schumann, under the pangs of his disappointment, could not have been expected to perceive: that Clara, being, as we have seen her, brave and proud as well as loving and true, acted as, by her extreme youth and by the loyalty and strength of her nature, she was bound to act, and that she could have done no otherwise.

What had been the supreme realities of her short sixteen years of life? Her father, Robert, and the art and artistic life with which both were inseparably associated in her consciousness. But of the two personal influences by which her outward existence was guided, that of her father was necessarily and rightly by far the strongest at this period. The tie that bound her to him was of a more intimate kind than that by which parent and child are commonly united. If she had at times felt impatient under his autocratic rule, she had never as yet seriously disputed it and had been almost insensibly aware of the security she enjoyed under its protection. She saw her father esteemed, honoured, consulted at home and abroad by those who were eminent in the circle in which she moved; she knew herself to be the object of his dearest affection; she identified her ambition entirely with his, of which she was, indeed, the centre; she loved him, and what is more to the present purpose, she absolutely respected him. Her very feeling for Schumann had been, as it were, part of her father's gift to her. She had come to know Robert in the first instance, far away back in her childhood, as Wieck's favourite pupil, rescued by his arbitration from a dreaded future, for their beloved, beautiful music. She had heard her father's frequent outbursts of anger at Robert's selfwill, impatience of discipline, habit of acting on impulse; but she had noticed, also, his unwonted leniency in the forgiveness of such sins when this gifted pupil was the culprit. Together they had tried and admired and criticised Schumann's early compositions, together noted his rapid artistic progress, together looked forward to his future triumphs. And then, before Clara, child as she was, had known that she had come to love him with other than a child's love, everything was suddenly changed. Robert was lost to her, seemed almost to forget her presence when they were in the same room, was happy only at the side of another girl older than herself, the acquaintance of a few weeks. But her father had remained to her; and we know how Clara had borne herself during many months of disappointment and suspense which drew from her no word of complaint. Then had come the reunion, the gradual awakening, the vision of paradise; and all was again lost. Yet not all, for Robert had said he loved her, and Clara believed and continued to believe him in the depth of her soul, though in the brief instants of their one or two accidental meetings she was incapable of retaining the presence of mind which might have enabled her to show him this. She knew, however, that she was her father's child, bound to him alike by duty and affection, and though she had promised to remain faithful to Schumann, there can be little doubt that she had referred the question of a formal betrothal to her father's decision. Though she must have been conscious of violating his wish when she had bidden or permitted her lover to visit her at Dresden, it is not clear that Wieck had at the time laid her under the obligation of any positive commands as to the future of the old friendship. Now, however, no mistake on that score was possible, and Clara must not, could not, would not, set herself in systematic opposition to her father's will. Not, at any rate, as yet.

Wieck was far too wise, and, let it be added, too kind-hearted a man to leave his daughter, who was at no time in her life entirely free from the tendency to melancholy that had been noticeable in her early childhood, alone with a despondency which must certainly have injured her health had she been altogether deprived of the artistic comradeship to which the friendship with Schumann had accustomed her. Carl Banck, whose musical sympathy had certainly helped her through the difficult period of Robert's preoccupation with Ernestine, was now welcomed more warmly than ever by the ruling powers of the Wieck household as an intimate of the family, and Wieck took pains to establish his visits on a satisfactory footing by engaging him to give Clara singing lessons. He was allowed much the same freedom of the house that had been accorded to Robert, and with him Clara was able to discuss her studies in composition, her father's plans for her next *tournée*, the latest additions to her concert répertoire; the various topics, in short, that made the interests of her daily life. Possibly she lived in the hope that he would some day bring her the tidings of Robert for which she was secretly longing, but if this were so she was doomed to disappointment. Banck, understanding what was expected of him by the elders, told her nothing that she wanted to hear, and even seems to have bragged to Schumann of his friendship with her.

The exaggerated reports current concerning Robert's unsettled condition could not fail to reach the ear of Wieck, whom they provided with additional matter for the indignant disapproval of Schumann to which he not infrequently gave expression in Clara's presence. But he had a still sharper weapon at his command, which he used the more mercilessly in his efforts to cure his child's inclination, from his entire belief in its integrity, and with which he struck deep wounds in the love and pride of her heart. It was the weapon of Robert's entanglement with Ernestine, the exact course of which had remained a mystery to Robert's friends ; and as the summer wore on and Clara, who searched each new issue of the *Neue Zeitschrift* for news of Robert, could find in it nothing to tell her how he fared or what he did, or any sign that she could interpret as a message to herself, she resolved on action. She opened a correspondence with Ernestine, begged for an exact account of her past and present relations with Schumann, asked if these had amounted to a definite engagement, whether it had been broken off, if so, when and why; and above all if Ernestine were now, as Robert had informed Clara, again betrothed. We have referred in a former chapter to the letters, printed by Kohut, in which Ernestine replied to these questions, and which carry with them the entire conviction of the writer's sincerity.* They cannot have afforded Clara much edification, or armed her with any defensive reply to her father's condemnation of Robert's conduct, though they must have satisfied her that all relations between Schumann and his former fiancée had come to an end. She had no resource but to endure. It is, indeed, possible that from about this time or a little later, the activity of her life, the interests of her art, and the force of everyday habit may have sufficiently modified her feelings as in some measure to deaden her sense of Robert's absence from her life. But she did not forget, nor for a moment cease to love ; she only waited.

"Never, I think, was a young girl so unhappy as I during the four years of my life between the ages of sixteen and twenty, when I was torn between the claims of my father and my lover," said Frau Schumann many, many years afterwards

* See *ante*, pp. 107, 108.

to a very interested listener—her pupil, the present writer—as she recalled the romantic experiences of her youth and love that remained as an ever-abiding present in her consciousness till the end of life.

Towards the middle of September, Chopin, who had been staying for a few weeks in Marienbad and Dresden, arrived for the second time in Leipzig to spend a day with Schumann. Exactly a year had passed since his first visit, and he had meanwhile reached the summit of a happiness that was to be only too short-lived. He had just become engaged to Marie Wodsińska, a beautiful young Polish girl, and was on his return journey to Paris to dream for a few months of a home in his own country, a beloved wife by his side, and a life passed in retirement and devoted to art. Chopin, at twenty-seven, had entered into the fullness of his creative powers. No work now written by him was less than a perfect example of his own peculiar art, whether in regard to the quality of its poetic ideas, the inseparable unity of its thought and expression, or the refined clearness of its form. His compositions were not as yet by any means generally accepted outside the exclusive private circles of Paris before which he was accustomed to produce them in the first instance, but his name was growing constantly more familiar to the musicians and amateurs both of Germany and England. His strong love of country and family had, if possible, grown stronger during the six years of expatriation to which circumstances had already doomed him, and in manner he had retained much of the simplicity of his early youth. The meeting with Schumann gave pleasure to both composers. Of Chopin's playing Schumann wrote in the *Neue Zeitschift* a little later :—

"Imagine an æolian harp possessed of all the scales and these made to vibrate altogether by an artist's hand, with every kind of fantastic embellishment, but in such a manner that a fundamental bass note and a softly singing upper part were always audible, and one has a fairly good idea of his [Chopin's] playing. No wonder that one prefers those of his pieces heard from himself, and therefore let us mention in the first place the A flat Étude—more a poem than a study. It would be a mistake to imagine that he allows all the small notes to be distinctly heard ; one was aware, rather, of the undulation of the A flat major chord, strengthened afresh here and there by the use of the pedal ; but one was always sensible through the harmonies of the wonderful melody of the big notes, and, about the middle of the piece, a tenor part was heard distinctly from the chords. When the piece terminated one felt as though, but half awake, one would like to seize a beautiful picture seen in a dream. It was impossible to say much, and praise was unutterable. He went on to the second in the book, in F minor, another which leaves an unforgettable impression of his originality—so seductive, so dreamy, so soft—something like the singing of a child in its sleep."

In an account of the visit sent two days later to Dorn, Schumann says :—

" Chopin played me a new ballade [No. 2 in G minor]. It seemed to me the finest of his works, and I told him I liked it the best of all. After a long pause of reflection he said with great energy : ' I am glad of that ; it is my own favourite also.' He also played me a number of new *études*, nocturnes, mazurkas, all incomparably. It is touching to see him at the piano." *

Chopin called also on the Voigts and Wiecks, played a number of his new works at both houses, and listened to Clara's performance of her own latest publications, Op. 5 and Op. 6, and of Robert's sonata, Op. 11. It would have been deeply interesting to learn his impression of the sonata—which, as the reader is aware, he now heard from Clara for the second time—and generally of Schumann's art and personality. Unhappily, none of the home letters of his Paris period, in which he sent his family regular and detailed accounts of the events and impressions of his daily life, are in existence. Carefully preserved for many years by his mother and after her death by his sister, Madame Isabella Barcińska, of Warsaw, they were burnt, during one of the street riots that preceded the Polish uprising of 1863, in a bonfire built by the Russian soldiery with the valuable effects of two neighbouring houses situated in one of the best quarters of the town, in one of which the family Barciński inhabited a flat on the second floor.

* " Briefe," p. 78,

Chopin did not find Mendelssohn at home this year. He had been away part of the summer officiating for his old friend Schelble as conductor of the famous Cecilia choir, of which passing mention has been made in these pages,* and had meanwhile formed an attachment to Cécile Charlotte Sophie Jeanrenaud, second daughter of a former clergyman of the French reformed church of the city, a girl of seventeen, of great personal attraction. Her father had been dead some years but her mother remained a well-known and favourite member of the prominent social circles of Frankfurt. Mendelssohn became engaged to Cécile on September 9th, about three weeks after the betrothal of Chopin and Marie Wodzińska had taken place in Marienbad and three days before Chopin and Schumann met for the second time in Leipzig. It is improbable that the happiness of either of his two friends was known to Schumann at this early date, but his letters of the later autumn contain several pleasant allusions to Mendelssohn's engagement as well as to that of Konzertmeister David, who at precisely this period announced his impending marriage with a rich Russian lady.

It is not without interest to music-lovers, whose world has been enriched by the genius of the three tone-romanticists of the nineteenth century, that the choice of their best affection was decided at about the same period of their lives and that the three girls loved by them were, like themselves, within a year of each other's age. The first felicity of successful courtship was, as we know, not to be followed in Chopin's case by its natural result. His hopes for the future were shattered by the communication, made to him a little less than a year after his betrothal, that his affianced bride had forsaken him to become the wife of a man of title. Her faithlessness was, in its ultimate effect, fatal not only to his happiness but his life. Sad and discouraged, far from home and country, the gentle, affectionate Frédéric, at a moment when his overwhelming disappointment had wrought his nerves to a condition of morbid sensibility, came across the experienced George Sand, who was suffering from the loneliness caused by her final break with the poet

* P. 68.

de Musset. The connection into which Chopin allowed himself to be drawn with the famous French authoress resulted, in the first instance, so far as he was concerned, from his gratitude for the affection she quickly developed for him, though he gradually learned to reciprocate her attachment. The friendship absorbed most of the remaining years of his life, and his second visit to Germany was his final one. Neither Schumann nor Clara ever met him again, whilst Mendelssohn had seen him for the last time on that October evening of 1835 when the two composers played to each other in Mendelssohn's rooms, and "inquisitive Leipzigers stole in to hear the music and to have seen Chopin."

CHAPTER XII

1836–1837

The Gewandhaus concerts—Mendelssohn and David—Clara in Berlin—Her concert programmes—Beethoven's sonata, Op. 57—Thalberg—Henselt —Clara's concerto and the *Neue Zeitschrift*—Return of Clara and her father—Carl Banck's departure from Leipzig—Clara's visit to Frau Majorin Serre in Dresden—Ernst Adolf Becker—Clara's concert in the Leipzig Börsenhalle—The Day of Aurora.

MENDELSSOHN'S anticipations as to the musical receptivity of the Gewandhaus orchestra, expressed in a letter to his parents after his *début* as its conductor at the first concert of the season 1835–36, had been more than justified by succeeding performances, and he returned to take up his work in Leipzig in the autumn of 1836 with the agreeable consciousness that he was to preside over a body of executants not only familiarised with his manner of conducting, but eager to respond to the slightest indication of his wishes.

"Mendelssohn devoted so much care to the technical study of the works selected for performance," says Dörffel, "and brought so much vital power to their interpretation . . . that it soon became a point of artistic honour with each and all of the instrumentalists to earn the entire approval of their inspired leader. Their confidence in his guidance was unlimited and now and then even caused the windplayers, especially, to become over-excited in their anxiety to attain perfection. The majority of the audience, to whom the previous achievements of the band had seemed almost unsurpassable, were amazed at the increase of excellence effected by Mendelssohn from the very beginning of his conductorship. The life of the orchestra was quickened by an entirely new pulsation, animated by a spirit of which the listeners had formed no previous conception. . . . Mendelssohn knew the masterpieces of art through and through as, perhaps, none of his contemporaries knew them; and could certainly have conducted them all without score, although one cannot recollect any instance of his doing so. Frequently, however, when the performance was in full swing, he would lay the bâton on the desk and let it rest there for some time as though the orchestra needed no further guidance, and he seemed in this way to express his entire satisfaction with the players."

The mysterious influence of magnetic personality had, in a word, begun to make itself felt on the Gewandhaus platform, and it was to spread and develop in many directions both within and beyond Leipzig in the course of the next decade, with a result to the highest interests of musical art the beneficence of which can hardly be exaggerated.

Not the least important development of the time, under the then prevailing conditions of concert-giving, was that briefly alluded to in the last chapter, of Mendelssohn's occasional co-operation in David's quartet concerts:

" When playing with Mendelssohn," Dörffel continues, " David often rose to the full height of his revered colleague. The performances of the two masters of executive art, and particularly their performances of the ' Kreutzer,' can never be forgotten by those who heard them. They used to make their entrance alertly, take their places, without intervening music desks, in full view of the audience, begin the glorious work and, as it were, set it through its progress with the highest and completely unanimous spontaneity of interpretation, giving the impression of its having just been created by genius itself. There was something incomparable in the whole atmosphere on such occasions which cannot be described in words."

We almost seem to be present in the inner circle of the musical Leipzig of the day as we read these accounts, the meaning of which many of us are enabled to a certain extent to realise by memories of our own in which the very Clara of this volume and a younger musician, who, in 1836 a child of five, was to come later on to Leipzig and Mendelssohn—the great Joachim—are the principal figures.

"We shall have a rich life here again this winter," Schumann remarks in a letter of September; "Mendelssohn, David (brilliant intellect), Liszt, Clara. Two standing concerts. Two musical papers. Twelve quartet performances. Better church music. Stegmayer, Banck (good song composer). Much besides that does not occur to me at the moment."

Except for two concert journeys, each of a few days only, on the first of which she started with her father on her seventeenth birthday anniversary, Clara remained quietly at home for the rest of the year 1836, busied with preparations for her next important tour and greatly encouraged in her work as a composer by the unstinted praise bestowed on her latest productions by her old friend Spohr, who visited Leipzig early in the season. She was to pass in the coming year into a new phase of her artistic existence; to enter veritably upon the career for which her father had prepared her through twelve long years with the careful insight of a born teacher and the enthusiasm of an ardent musician. At seventeen she had become ripe for the fulfilment of his dearest hopes. She was now not only to astonish and delight her audiences—that she had done from early childhood—but to begin effectively to lead them; to lead them towards the appreciation of the masterpieces in the literature of her instrument, and thereby to help hasten the radical revolution imminent in the life of the concertgoer as well as the concert-giver. She was to appear not only as the interpreter of Bach, but also of Beethoven, taking her position in so doing, so far as concerned her own branch of art, by the side of Mendelssohn, and, for the time being, alone by his side.

With his customary sagacity, Wieck arranged that Clara's first public appearance with part of one of Beethoven's great sonatas for pianoforte alone should be made in Berlin, where, as he probably hoped, the precedent set by Mendelssohn's concerts of 1832 * and the permanent influence exercised by the Mendelssohn family culture on certain of the literary

* See *ante*, p. 144.

and artistic circles of the city, might have prepared the way for the innovation. That her visit to the Prussian capital, where she had not yet played, was welcomed with interested expectation, is shown by the names of acquaintances made by her on her arrival. We may mention those of Count von Redern, musical intendant of the Prussian court; of the composer Spontini, manager-general and chief conductor of the Royal Opera; and of Bettina von Arnim, the Bettina Brentano of Goethe's " Correspondence with a Child." This lady is described in the diary as " exceedingly clever, animated, and overflowing with humour"; but as holding "utterly perverted " musical opinions.*

Clara appeared for the first time before her new audience on February 16, 1837, at the Royal opera house. The programme of the occasion, as advertised in the *Preussische Staatszeitung* of the 14th, is of some interest as recording a custom of the day by which the travelling musician not infrequently obtained opportunity to submit his virtuosity to the favour of an untried public, or to advertise to former patrons his arrival in their town.

" ROYAL PERFORMANCES.

" Thursday, February 16. In the opera house :

" 1. Concerto for the pianoforte composed and executed by Clara Wieck.

" 2. Variations brillantes by H. Herz, Op. 76, performed by Clara Wieck.

" To be followed by : Robinson, a pantomimic ballet in three acts."

The young artist seems to have met with her usual success. One of the critics speaks of her concerto as being full of " character and originality," and adds that her performances were rewarded with " unanimous applause."

Her own first concert was given on February 25th, at the Hôtel de Russie. The programme, which is printed in a report contained in the *Allgemeine Musikalische Zeitung* of March 22nd, constituted an entirely new departure in artistic annals. Clara was, herself, solely responsible for each instrumental item,

* Litzmann, i. 106.

and that it placed her, as an executive artist, alone in the front
of her time is best shown by the list of pieces played by her
and by comparison of it with the form of programme customary
in the benefit concert of the day, of which we have already
given some account :—

First Part.

Mendelssohn...	... Caprice in A minor, Op. 33, No. 1.
J. S. Bach ...	... Fugue in C sharp minor. (" Well-tempered Clavier.")
Beethoven ...	... Andante and finale from sonata in F minor, Op. 57, for pianoforte alone.
Chopin ...	... Nocturne in F sharp major and Étude in G flat major No. 5. (Black keys.)

Second Part.

Clara Wieck...	... Bolero and Mazurka.
Henselt ...	... Andante and Allegro (" Wenn ich ein Vöglein war "). MS.
Herz	... Variations.

Vocal contributions by Herrn Bade and Ziesche.

That Clara herself was, on the whole, satisfied with her
performances, and greatly delighted with her reception, appears
from a letter of the time to Carl Banck : " Beethoven's sonata
created a *furore*. Father says he would have given me credit
for much, but not that I could have played the andante so
finely." On February 27th the following notice appeared in
the *Preussische Staatszeitung* :—

" A considerable reputation had preceded the arrival of the
pianoforte virtuoso, Dlle. Clara Wieck, and it was most
brilliantly justified by the young artist's performances on the
occasion of her recent concert. In her case it was not mere
technical facility that we were called on to admire, but playing
of irresistible musical charm, which so captivates the attention
that one almost forgets to notice the triumphant skill by which
the greatest mechanical difficulties are vanquished. The artist
has become so completely one with her art that it informs her
whole being. We cannot better describe her than by calling
her the Schechner of the pianoforte.* As each tone of the

---

* Nanette Schechner-Waagen, a famous singer who retired from the
stage in 1836. Mendelssohn, hearing her after her gifts had become impaired through illness, wrote that though he found her voice much gone off,
her power of expression was still so great as to move him to tears.

singer seemed to well forth from her inmost soul, so here each
tone of her instrument seems to breathe forth the spirit of the
pianiste. In the outward style of her playing she reminds us
most of Felix Mendelssohn, only the latter controls his performance to greater repose; his rival allows herself to be more
carried away by her enthusiasm, without, however, exceeding
the limits of feminine grace. An interesting comparison presents itself as we recall the performance of another pianoforte
virtuoso of first rank, Herr Döhler. As, in the masculine
temperament of the one artist, feminine ingredients are combined, so also the femininity of the other is penetrated by
masculine power and imagination. From this it probably
follows that they are especially admired for different qualities :
the one for the graceful facility and soft elasticity of his
execution, the other for the powerful impulse, the passionate
expression of her playing. We understand that Dlle. Wieck
has, from childhood, been strictly trained by her father, who
teaches music in Leipzig, and, indeed, it would be scarcely
conceivable, her genius notwithstanding, that she should have
reached her high attainment in art at so early an age without
unremitting study. It is, however, precisely because he devotes
his life to his calling that the position of the true artist is so
great. This was appreciated by the assemblage before which
the pianiste displayed her talent yesterday, and her successive
appearances were greeted with increasing and genuine enthusiasm. With a rare power of endurance Dlle. Wieck played
nine different works on this one evening, all without accompaniment, resting only during the performance of four vocal
pieces. To notice her renderings in detail would be out of
place here, but we cannot refrain from alluding particularly to
the thoroughly musical interpretation of a Mendelssohn caprice
and of two movements of Beethoven's F minor sonata; to the
brilliant execution of a very difficult study by Chopin, and an
excessively fatiguing allegro by Henselt, or from mentioning
that the young artist played her entire programme from
memory. In Boleros and Mazurkas of her own composition
she showed not only that she is no stranger to the theoretical
side of her art, but also that she has studied it with intelligence. We hope we may frequently have the pleasure of
listening to her admirable playing."

At a second concert of her own given on the last day of the month in the same hall, Clara's programme included :—

Beethoven	...	Sonata in F minor, Op. 57, for pianoforte alone. (The whole work by desire.)
Bach ...	...	Prelude and Fugue in E major.
Mendelssohn	...	Lied ohne Worte.
Chopin ...	...	Mazurka, in F sharp minor.
„ ...	...	Arpeggio Étude in E flat, No. 11.
Clara Wieck	...	Bravura Variations on a theme from Bellini's "Il Pirato."

And at a third, advertised as her last, she played :—

Beethoven	...	Sonata in A major for pianoforte and violin, Op. 47 (Kreutzer).
Chopin ...	...	Nocturne in B major, Op. 82, No. 1.
„ ...	...	Study in C minor, No. 12.
Henselt...	...	Andante and Allegro (repeated by desire).
Clara Wieck	...	Bravura Variations (repeated by desire).

Of the success of the second concert we hear incidentally in the notice of an entertainment given in the opera house on March 4th by the brothers Ganz, which contains the following paragraph :—

"Dlle. Clara Wieck was unfortunately prevented by indisposition from contributing to the programme as announced ; a circumstance which was more regretted by music-lovers since opportunity had again lately been afforded them at a second soirée of her own to admire her talent."

Of the third concert, given on March 11th, the same critic writes (*Preussische Staatszeitung*, March 13th):—

" Fräulein Clara Wieck again delighted us in the hall of the Hôtel de Russie by her pre-eminent pianoforte playing ; unfortunately—according to the announcement—for the last time, though her concerts have been received with such growing sympathy that she might certainly reckon upon a constantly increasing attendance, and therefore choose a larger room for her performances, should she resolve to continue them. The virtuoso displayed her talent the day before yesterday in the most diverse lights. In Beethoven's great sonata in A major, in which Herr Kapellmeister [Hubert] Ries accompanied her very beautifully on the violin, her passionate impetuosity and expressive touch were particularly manifest, though here, and especially in the andante with variations, a somewhat more moderate tempo may have been desirable. In the artist's own variations on a theme from 'Il Pirato,' all imaginable difficulties were piled up with almost too manifest design, and therefore the impression produced was chiefly that of astonishment at the masterly fashion in which they had been attacked and conquered. The same may be said of the Chopin *étude*, which occasioned admiration of the extraordinary strength and dexterity of the pianist's left hand. If Dlle. Clara Wieck really intends to leave Berlin already, we at least hope soon to welcome her return here, where she will be held in cherished remembrance."

. Wieck accordingly arranged a fourth concert in the "large Jäger hall," capable of holding five hundred people, where, on March 20th, Clara played before a crowded audience. Her selection included :—

Mendelssohn	...	Caprice in F sharp minor, Op. 33, No. 3.
Chopin ...	...	Variations, Op. 2.
Thalberg	...	Caprice, Op. 15.
Herz ...	...	Variations on a theme from "Joseph."

The Berlin correspondent of the *Allgemeine Musikalische Zeitung*, giving a résumé of the series of concerts, remarks that the programmes, being made up almost entirely of pianoforte solos and songs, were somewhat monotonous, but that the performances of the concert-giver were, throughout, masterly.

It may surprise the reader to learn that when, at the first of her Berlin concerts of 1837, Clara played two movements, and, at her second concert, the whole, of Beethoven's sonata in F minor, commonly known as the "Appassionata," the great work was almost certainly heard for the first time in public, whether in part or entire. "The constant severity of style proper to the sonata," to quote some words of Liszt written this very year, had, as we have shown, been deemed incompatible with the expectation of refined but not too serious entertainment, which, accounted natural in the patrons of a benefit concert, had hitherto regulated the programmes of the virtuoso, and the desire of Clara's audience

for the performance at the second soirée of the whole
of Beethoven's long and unfamiliar composition implies
a power in the artist and a recognition of such power in her
hearers which we of to-day, with our intimate acquaintance
with the great masters, can with difficulty estimate at its
true value.* Nor must the significance of the—so far as can
be ascertained—first concert performance of Beethoven's
F minor sonata nearly thirty years after its publication cause
us to overlook other features of exceptional interest in these
programmes. That Clara associated her name with the tone
poems of Chopin and Mendelssohn as they appeared, we
have abundantly shown. The addition to her concert répertoire
of pieces by Thalberg and Henselt affords further proof, if such
were needed, of her father's alert and progressive interest in
the distinctive developments of his time. Thalberg and Liszt
were, in 1837, beginning to be accepted by the musical public
of Europe as the rival exponents of a new and higher virtuosity,
the one in its most perfect, the other in its most forceful
form; while Henselt, a youth of twenty-two, who had as
yet published but one work, was favourably known to a few
circles as a pupil of Hummel and a composer for the pianoforte
with strong leanings to the romantic school.

"A new element was introduced into the superficial musical
life of the thirties, which had hitherto occupied itself with mere
agreeable entertainment," says Hanslick in his "Geschichte des
Concertwesens in Wien." "The father of this new pianoforte
style was Thalberg, who, though known rather earlier, took
his place as a personality and a complete master of technique
about the middle of the thirties. His pieces, refined, elegant,
brilliant, extremely playable in spite of their difficulties, without force and depth, yet not without a glimmer of mind and
spirit, were received with enormous approval. They modified

---

* It is possible that parts of the sonata may have been included in
one or other of Clara's provincial concerts of the autumn of 1836, of which
no mention is to be found in the available press notices of the period. But
even if this were the case, such an occasion must be considered in connection
with, and as a rehearsal for, the important Berlin performances. All
possibility of her having performed any portion of the work in public before
the year 1836 is excluded by the extracts from Wieck's correspondence
and diary quoted by us on p. 128.

the concert programmes of the day far more than Listz's, though Liszt's lasted longer."

With some of Henselt's MS. compositions Clara and her father had become acquainted, in the first place, through the young musician's enthusiastic pupil and Clara's intimate Dresden friend Sophie Kaskel, the "Sara" of the *Neue Zeitschrift*, and Wieck wrote in the autumn of 1836 to invite him to send two or three new works for the purposes of Clara's projected tour in North Germany. The terms of Henselt's reply seem to suggest that Wieck had sent his letter, as a mere business document, for Schumann's perusal and signature, and that his proposal included suggestions for publication and held out the prospect of a review in the *Neue Zeitschrift*. That Henselt speaks of Clara by her Christian name is to be explained by the circumstance that Wieck preferred her to be so known and so called :—

"WEIMAR, *October* 11, 1836.

"MOST ESTEEMED SIRS,—In haste I beg to send my thanks for your kind and friendly letter and my apologies for not having replied to it sooner. I wished to copy some things for Clara and send them at the same time. . . . I have quite determined to take your advice and publish two things this winter, and have selected for the purpose six *études* and a set of variations, but I shall make no arrangements without your approval and am truly happy to have found such kind friends. I really need them, for I have no experience in such matters. . . . I am engaged for my first work, the variations, to Haslinger, of Vienna; with my second I can do as I please, and shall be guided by your kind advice. I will send you some *études*, more than six, that you may select those best worth reviewing. Again a thousand thanks for your letter; it is long since I have been so agreeably surprised.

"With kindest regards,

"Yours,

"HENSELT.

"You will receive the music for Clara, whom I cordially greet, on Sunday evening or Monday morning."*

* Kohut, p. 248 fol.

" Henselt owed a good part of his rapidly acquired fame to Clara Wieck, through whom he first became known and appreciated as an original and poetic composer for the pianoforte," remarks Hanslick.

We have probably said enough to satisfy the reader that Clara's success in the Prussian capital, whilst brilliant in itself, was strikingly prophetic of the triumphs of her mature career. Nevertheless, partly, perhaps, owing to the fact that it was genuine and exceptional, it had its detractors. That the novel programmes prepared by his daughter would be readily accepted by either of the jealous cliques into which the professional world of Berlin was divided in 1837, especially as introduced by a newcomer, a young girl of seventeen who stood outside them all, ought hardly to have been anticipated by so practised an impresario as Wieck. He seems, however, to have given vent in the diary in no measured terms to the chagrin he experienced on finding that most of the resident musicians, to whom he sent complimentary tickets for one or more of the concerts, were represented at the performances only by the vacant seats that had been allotted to them. Nor is it even certain that unreserved satisfaction was felt in distinguished amateur circles at Clara's triumphant achievement in a field of art which Felix Mendelssohn alone amongst pianists had hitherto ventured to tread in Berlin—at her successful interpretation of a great Beethoven sonata. A certain historical interest attaches, however, to Frau von Arnim's indictment of the young pianist as " the most insufferable artist she had ever come across," who had the " audacity " to play the whole of her programmes by heart. It was the accepted opinion of the period, which Mendelssohn's example in the first place, and after his, Clara's, helped gradually to dissipate, that to perform the work of a great master without book, even in a private circle, was to show disrespect to his art. Analogous explanation may be accepted of the complaint of the programmes as " monotonous " made by that portion of the press led by Rellstab, the influential critic of the *Iris*. It points to the absence from the list of works performed of those purely orchestral items that had been hitherto included in the programme of the benefit concert. Wieck had, indeed, intended to vary the pianoforte soirées with an orchestral concert of the traditional kind, and it was not the least of his disappointments as entrepreneur that the difficulties of arranging the preliminaries did not allow him sufficient time to carry out this purpose.

Clara made seven or eight public appearances during her two to three weeks' stay in Berlin. We have dwelt at length on the particulars of her own four concerts not only or chiefly because they indicate an important departure in her own career, but because they mark the exact moment of the birth of that era in pianistic art in the course of which the highest ideals of the virtuoso and his hearers have become those of interpretation. The programme performed by the young pianist at the Hôtel de Russie on February 25, 1837, was absolutely the first of its kind, representing, as it did, the greatest achievements for the keyboard of the composers of all ages from Bach to Beethoven and from Mendelssohn to Henselt. Nor should it be forgotten that the name of Schumann, though he had not yet reached the maturity of his career, had before this date been recognised in her concert répertoire.* When she quitted Berlin to fulfil the remaining engagements of her tour, which included appearances in Hamburg and Bremen, only an appropriate confirmation of the great step forward taken in the Prussian capital was needed to carry her secure above the criticisms of envy to a recognised place in the front rank of her profession. This was to follow before another year had passed over her head.

There can be no question that Clara, from whose mind the remembrance of Robert never was and never could be absent, associated as he had been with her every interest and effort from childhood onwards, had, nevertheless, by the beginning of 1837 become sufficiently accustomed to a life which he no longer shared, to take a healthy pleasure in the excitements and successes of her brilliant career, and that her father now seldom found cause to deplore her indifference to the indications of sympathy and appreciation that were called forth by her appearance whether in public or private circles. It happened, however, that an incident of February brought

* *Ante*, p. 125.

the image of her old friend with special prominence to her thoughts, and in a manner that could not but be very painful to her, conscious as she was of needing every encouragement that could help her to bear the strain of her public life. About the time she was leaving home, her concerto had been published by Hofmeister as her Opus 7, and had been sent by him to the papers for review in the ordinary course of business. Schumann, as editor of the *Neue Zeitschrift*, received a copy, but felt, and naturally felt, that under the circumstances of the moment he could not himself write about Clara's work. His attitude towards the Wiecks had been manly and consistent from the hour he had received Friedrich's violently written interdiction of all communication between Clara and himself. Convinced at length that Clara had determined to acquiesce for the present in her father's will, Robert, suffer as he might, would not attempt to persuade her to change her resolution. Like her, he could only work and wait. And even when, as sole acknowledgment of the copy of the sonata sent her, he had received the packet of his own letters with a request for the return of hers, he bore his disappointment as became him, without sending her word or sign of remonstrance. In the matter of whether she would take him or forsake him, after the confessions and promises that had passed between them, her will was his law. But Robert had not ceased to love; and to write and publish a review of the work of her he loved, to know his printed words about her in the hands of a hundred indifferent readers! No. In his present state of uncertainty, at any rate, this was impossible to him. He resolved on a course which, though not, perhaps, readily comprehensible to the girl herself, was natural enough to a man in his position, and wrote the following letter to one of the regular contributors to his periodical, C. F. Becker by name :—

" MY DEAR SIR,—Herewith I send you Clara's concerto and shall be glad to hear if you can let me have a notice of it, which it certainly merits in the *Zeitung*, by Monday morning. You are aware, perhaps, that my relations with her father are such as to prevent me, to make it seem to me unsuitable, to write about the concerto myself. Perhaps you may accept this as an additional reason for fulfilling my request. Half a page will suffice, but I wish for your signature, C. F. B. The review would follow one of a concerto by Herz and the entire series conclude with a few words on Bennett's concertos. Perhaps this may suggest the idea to you. . . ." *

The request was fulfilled by Becker with strange tactlessness. Instead of paying Clara—at this time, it must be remembered, an artist of widespread German reputation—the respect of candidly dealing with the shortcomings of the work, or even expressing the opinion that she had attempted a form of composition beyond her powers, he assumed a style of patronising badinage, disclaimed the intention of criticising the concerto on the score of its having been produced by a lady, and filled up his short contribution with idle chatter and complimentary phrases that could scarcely be regarded by the composer of the piece in question otherwise than as a badly disguised form of contempt.

It is unnecessary to insist upon the disappointment which the article, published in the *Neue Zeitschrift* of February 17th, caused the young artist, who, having just introduced her work with success to an untried Prussian audience, had looked forward with confidence—though, it may be, somewhat unreasonably under the circumstances—to reading in her old friend's paper the words of encouragement which she would have welcomed as the best reward of her artistic striving. The publication a week later of a review of the third concerto of Sterndale Bennett, with whose art neither she nor her father was in sympathy, written by Schumann himself, with the delicate insight and suggestiveness that were so readily at his command when he treated a congenial subject, pointed a most painful contrast to her view.

" What do you think of the review of my concerto? " she writes to Banck, with whom she maintained a regular and frequent correspondence during her absence from home ; and a little later :—

" Schumann's paper lies before me. I do not know what to say. Is this really Schumann? Could he be so biassed?

* " Briefe," p. 85.

I cannot, and yet I must, believe it. . . . He could write in such terms of Bennett's concerto and had no words for mine? I know, however, if I had left the first movement as it was and the finale also it would have caused surprise that a girl of sixteen could have written such a concerto. I shall not worry myself about it any more, for masculine caprices are not worth a moment's vexation." *

This extract is not only of interest in our pages as exhibiting Clara's character in a somewhat new light. It shows that at this date a certain change had taken place in her feeling for Schumann, whether it had been effected by her long continued separation from him, her correspondence with Ernestine, her intimacy with Banck, or a combination of these and other causes. That her words betray some injustice in her judgment of Schumann is of little importance. Clara knew what she herself had gone through during the past year, but perhaps hardly realised the suffering she had caused Robert by obeying her father's desire a little too literally when she asked for the return of her letters without adding a word on her own account that could soften the harshness of the demand. She could hardly be expected to weigh the difficulties of a busy editor, who, having bespoken an article for which he had reserved a special place in his periodical, had to choose between insertion of what Becker had sent him and an indefinite delay in the notice of the concerto. It is, however, not inconceivable that Robert, to whom it must at length have seemed that Clara had deliberately decided to follow the path in life for which her father had designed her and from which he was himself to be excluded except under impossible conditions, and who was increasingly irritated by the rumours which reached him of the much-talked-of intimacy with Banck, may have felt that Clara must take the chances of the artist's position for which she had apparently abandoned him, and that, until time should enable him to think of her with greater tranquillity, the only thing left for him was to stand aloof from all personal participation in her affairs. We may confess that this view would not have been unnatural.

* Wasielewski, 175 and 176.

" You think I judged Schumann unjustly ? " writes Clara
again to Banck. " I am not of your opinion ; but it is
very nice of you to see the matter in its best light and
you have given me a warning that one must consider things
carefully and not express one's self about them rashly.*

Banck accompanied Frau Clementine when she went on
May 3rd to meet her husband and stepdaughter on their
return to Leipzig, and his intimacy with Clara was re-estab-
lished on a sufficiently pronounced footing to alarm Wieck
as to its possible consequences. Taking an opportunity of
speaking to his protégé, he warned him that his manner
to Clara must be more reserved, and added that it was
especially important her attention should not be distracted
from her work since he was arranging a concert journey to
Austria for the autumn and winter season, on the preparations
for which it would be necessary for her to concentrate her
best energies. With what feelings Banck received this broad
hint it is impossible to say. He was wise enough to act
upon it at once and in such manner as to preclude all future
misunderstanding of his intentions. He came no more to
the Wiecks' house, but, after devoting a few days to the
arrangement of his affairs, left Leipzig for good, finally
settling down in Jena.

It is obvious that this affair must have prepared a second
extreme mortification for Clara, who, greatly perplexed as
to the reason why Banck did not appear as usual to make
music and chat with her, was partly informed by her father
of what had occurred even before the young song-writer
had quitted Leipzig. It may possibly have helped, however,
to hasten the reunion with Schumann for which the girl
was secretly longing, even though her displeasure was
roused anew within a day of Banck's departure by a second
article in the *Zeitschrift*, on this occasion from Schumann's
own pen. †

* Wasielewski.

† The satirical article " Bericht an Jeanquirit aus Augsburg " in which
Banck was ridiculed by the angry Robert under the transparent pseudonym
of De Knapp, appeared in the *Zeitschrift* of May 19th, and is reprinted
in Book II. of the " Collected Writings." It gave great offence to Clara
not only on her friend's account, but because she formed the quite mistaken

" We must have become estranged from each other at that time," Robert wrote to Clara a year later as he told her how, after hoping against hope, he had, in the winter of 1836–37 and right up to the spring, almost come to give up his faith in her constancy and had tried to force himself to forget her, to marry some one else ; how, indeed, another woman had, at one time, nearly caught him in her toils ; how he had dreaded taking up a newspaper, fearing to see in it the announcement of Clara's betrothal, the thought of which had caused him to wring his hands in agony and cry aloud to heaven to be permitted to preserve his reason if this thing were indeed to befall him. Yet these imaginings on either side were, after all, but the misunderstandings of true lovers and with Banck's departure from Leipzig Robert and Clara had nearly reached the end of their first great trial, the trial of their faith in one another. Who does not rejoice that they were brought at length, by the operation of a mysterious mutual affinity, through the haze of such misapprehensions to a true knowledge of each other ?

Towards the middle of June Clara accompanied her father and stepmother to Dresden, and, on the return of the parents after a fortnight's holiday, remained behind on a visit to the Serres, a musical family living on their estate near the capital, to enjoy further recreation in the youthful society of their intimate circle. The entries made in the diary during these days " breathe for the first time a spirit of constant cheerfulness," says Litzmann. Nor is the explanation difficult. It is to be found, in the first place, in the relief from the conflict of mind which the late rapid increase of her intimacy with Banck and the rumours to which it gave rise must have occasioned the young artist, who, after recovering from the annoyance entailed

---

notion, and, according to Litzmann, persisted in it for some time, that the absurd pianist Ambrosia, who figures in the paper, was intended for herself. No one who reads the article with knowledge of the circumstances under which it appeared can fail to see that the Davidsbündlerin Clara, the Zilia of the *Zeitschrift*, figures in it as Ambrosia's younger sister Beda, though Schumann, partly out of regard for propriety, partly from the delight in mystification which he had inherited from his favourite romantic authors, has mingled his characters and their qualities in an uncertain medium and endowed Beda not with musical talent, but with a special gift for drawing fancy portraits.

on her by the circumstances under which the friendship had
terminated, certainly felt the happier from being quit of an
affair liable to misconstruction, but in which her heart had
never been involved. Then again she had lived for a year and
a half under the constraint of an atmosphere heavy with the
disapproval of Robert. How must her spirit have been
lightened when she found herself surrounded by those who
talked freely and admiringly, without doubt or reservation, of
her old friend and his music ! Especially favourable for her
escape from the cloud of uncertainty that had so long
burdened her mind was the frequent presence at Major
Serre's house of a friend of her family, Ernst Adolf Becker,
a man old enough to be her father and a warm admirer of
Schumann and his work.* To the tale of Becker's
enthusiasms Clara listened with delight, and to his interest in
Schumann's advancing art she most readily responded on the
pianoforte, even playing him the "Études Symphoniques,"
which were published in July. No wonder she grew bright
and joyous. She was beginning to understand that at nearly
eighteen she had acquired the right to a voice in the selection
of her own path in life and was every day gaining confidence in
herself and her love. The intelligence that her father had
announced a concert for August 13th occasioned her rather
unwilling return home on one of the opening days of the
month, but her reluctance soon gave place to eager interest.
She was to find at length the opportunity she had been await-
ing. Clara had not appeared before her Leipzig audience since
the momentous occasion of November 9, 1835, when she had
brought Johann Sebastian Bach and the Gewandhaus public
together. Her programme of August 13th, 1837, was to include
her own bravura variations, Liszt's *Divertissement* on Pacini's
cavatina, " I tuoi palpiti " ; Henselt's successful Andante and
Allegro, Chopin's B major nocturne, and to be especially
signalised by the first performance of a work which has had
few rivals among compositions of its class in the esteem of
music-lovers since it became really well known in the course of
the second half of the nineteenth century. She was to play a

* Not to be confounded with Carl Ferdinand Becker, organist of St. Nicholas
Church, Leipzig, and contributor to the *Neue Zeitschrift*.

selection from the Études Symphoniques of Robert Schumann. How would he take it? What would he think of her? Could she get through her task without faltering? Yes; for the occasion had come when she could tell him by token of his own tones of her love and longing. Yes, again; for the growing recognition of his art would be placed for the moment in her hands to promote or to hinder.

It would be a mistake to suppose that Wieck, when he selected, or allowed Clara to select, Schumann's lately published work for her programme was moved by any other than artistic considerations. Neither now nor later did he swerve by a hair's-breadth from his objection to Robert as his daughter's suitor; but neither now, nor, perhaps, until a period when Clara's constancy to her attachment would almost seem to have temporarily deprived him of his reason, did he falter in his opinion of the significance of Schumann's genius. All available evidence indicates that he would gladly have renewed the old intimacy and welcomed the young composer again to his house if he could have been certain that Clara's romance had ceased to be more to her than a memory of her childhood. Probably only extreme circumstances would have caused him to neglect a favourable opportunity for the recognition in her programmes of Schumann's art. Nevertheless it is not unlikely that he had at the present time allowed himself to be reassured as to the condition of his child's affections by the general recovery that had taken place in her spirits for some time past, as well as by her severe and undisguised censure of Robert's action on two recent occasions.

Among the friends who came to Leipzig to attend the concert was Ernst Adolf Becker, from Freiberg, who rejoiced Clara's heart by his arrival at her father's house two or three days beforehand. Perhaps he took an opportunity, as Schumann's confidant, to show her that not she alone, or chiefly, had had cause for mistrust and complaint during the past year and a half. He certainly told her of her old friend's unhappiness, his perplexity, and the constancy of his love; and when he called at a quarter to eleven on the 13th, to ask Schumann to accompany him to the "Morning Entertainment" at the Börsenhalle, he gave him a message—the message for which Robert had hoped and prayed, and of which he had at last despaired. It was Clara's petition for the return of the packet of his letters which she had sent him by her father's command.

And this is what Robert thought of Clara's performance, as he wrote to her six months afterwards:—

"I shall never forget your playing of my Études. As you interpreted them they were all masterpieces. The public cannot appreciate this, but one sat there who, though his heart throbbed with other feelings, did homage to you as an artist with his whole being." *

The *Allgemeine Musikalische Zeitung* of September 4th gives the programme of the concert, which was diversified by several vocal contributions, and adds:—

"We do not ourselves attend matinées, but we hear that the entire selection was played with extreme brilliancy and was warmly applauded, and that the Études Symphoniques were given with particular predilection." †

"We went for a walk later in the day," wrote Clara to Robert when recalling events at a later period, "but I saw neither the trees, the flowers, nor the meadows. I saw only you—and yet did not, might not, see you."

And on the next day, August 14th, Becker, handing her a bouquet and a letter addressed in well-known handwriting, told her Robert's answer to her petition. She could have— not the old letters back, but new ones. Clara, opening the first new one, read the following words:—

---

* Litzmann, i. 181.

† Litzmann, i. 116, says that Clara played Schumann's F sharp minor sonata at this matinée, but does not mention the performance of the Études Symphoniques, or any other item of the programme. The programme, as given in the *Neue Zeitschrift* of September 1st, which contains a notice of the concert contributed by E. A. Becker, agrees in every detail with that printed in the *Allgemeine Musikalische Zeitung*, and is the version quoted in the text (compare also Jansen, "Briefe," p. 498, note 101). Careful search among the printed and dated records of the time does not show that Clara played the F sharp minor sonata at any public concert, whether of this or the two following years. It is, however, certain that she performed it at some of the private invitation concerts given at her father's residence, whether in Leipzig or elsewhere, for which printed programmes were generally provided.

" August 13, 1837.

"Are you still faithful and true? Firmly as I believe in you, yet the strongest courage may be disconcerted if one hears nothing at all of that which one holds dearest in the world. And this you are to me. A thousand times have I considered everything, and everything tells me: It must be if we resolve and persevere. Write me the simple word 'Yes,' if you will yourself give your father a letter from me on your birthday (September 13). He is well disposed towards me now, and will not reject me if you beg for me. I write this on the day of Aurora. If it were to be that we were parted now by a single sunrise only? . . .

"I mean this with my whole soul as it stands written and subscribe it with my name. . . ."*

The following day Schumann wrote to Wieck:—

"Allow me, most esteemed Herr Wieck, to offer you my best thanks for the honour shown to my compositions last Saturday. It was too remarkable for me to be able to keep silence about it to you—especially Liszt (the slip was the best part of the performance), then Henselt, and chiefly everything. . . .

"Accept my best endeavours for your kind favour. . . ."†

Clara wrote her answer to Robert the day after receiving his letter through Becker:—

"You ask only for a simple 'Yes'? Such a little word—so weighty! Yet—shall not a heart so full as mine of unspeakable love be able to utter this little word with the whole soul? I do so, and my inmost spirit whispers it to you unceasingly. . . . Nothing shall make me falter, and I

---

* Litzman, i. 118. Schumann's allusion to the "day of Aurora" is to be explained by the closing words of his "Schwärmbrief an Chiara," published in an October number of the *Neue Zeitschrift* of 1835 and signed Euse-bius: "Do not forget to look out August 13th in the Calendar, where an Aurora unites your name with mine." August 12th, 13th, and 14th are called in the Saxon calendar by the names Clara, Aurora, and Eusebius.

† "Briefe," p. 89. Clara's memory failed her for an instant in the course of Liszt's *Divertissement*, but the mishap did not cause her to lose her presence of mind or to break off her performance.

will show father that a youthful heart can also be sted-
fast. . . ."*

So the day of Aurora did in very truth unite Clara and
Eusebius, and the day of Eusebius remained sacred henceforth
to Schumann and his bride as that of their betrothal.

* For the entire letter see Litzmann, i. 119.

CHAPTER XIII

1837

Suspense—Clara's eighteenth birthday anniversary—Schumann's letter of petition to her father for Clara's hand—Wieck's anger—Clara's "Soirées musicales pour le pianoforte"—Stolen interviews—Schumann's "Phantasiestücke," Op. 12—"Die Davidsbündler"—Publication of the "Carnaval"—Moscheles' appreciation.

WITH his present knowledge of the impetuosity of Schumann's temperament, the reader will hardly be surprised to learn that the letter he designed to send Wieck was thought out and put on paper almost immediately on his receiving Clara's consent to his plan. The agitation of his mind during the three weeks that were to intervene between its completion and despatch found some vent in a letter to Becker, written on August 26th, in which he enclosed the important document for his friend's approval :—

"Here, my dear friend and guardian spirit—if this does not touch your heart I do not know what more to do. You can imagine my state of mind, but I am tranquil and happy in the firm belief in Clara's stedfastness. What bliss it is to be able to believe in, to depend upon, some one! The old man treats me kindly and on the whole gives me courage. For the rest, everything remains as we arranged. Cl[ara] wishes to see me, but it is better that we should not meet yet. . . ."*

Becker, too well acquainted with Wieck's idiosyncrasies to reply to this letter with rash assurances of his confidence in the success of the impending appeal, sent Robert such a

* "Briefe," p. 93. It seems probable from this and other letters that Wieck and Schumann had occasionally met during the period of the latter's separation from Clara.

cautious answer as almost induced him to abandon his plan;
but Clara, to whose judgment the letter was now submitted
through the services of her faithful maid Nanny, urged that
while it could not but make a good impression on her father,
the approaching birthday would afford the best chance for
its favourable consideration.

"I did not wish to discourage you, my good Schumann,"
wrote Becker on receiving a second communication from
Robert; "I earnestly beg that you will let nothing prevent
you from carrying out the arrangement, especially as Clara
must know best how the chances stand. I do not know to
whom I would rather promise my daughter than to a man
who is as sound as yourself under the left buttonhole and
who can write such *études*."

To Clara's anxiety it was due not only that one or two
more verbal or written messages passed between the lovers
during this interval of suspense, but that they actually did
meet by appointment one bright moonlight evening in the
beginning of September as Clara was returning from her
friends' the Lists' house in Nanny's charge. It was happiness
to find themselves together again, and the strong emotion
of the moment prevented them from much speech. Both
were building hopes on the renewal of pleasant relations
between Wieck and Schumann which seems to have followed
the concert in the Börsenhalle. Whether in connection
with the *Zeitschrift*, in which Wieck had never lost interest,
or on other musical business, it is clear that Clara's father
and lover were now meeting frequently: "The old man
treats me with great tenderness and cordiality," Robert
tells Becker on September 8th, and on the same day Clara
writes to Robert: "I count on his [father's] love for you
and me."

We may be sure that Clara's rest was not a prolonged
one on the morning which completed her eighteenth year,
and may imagine with what peculiar force the memories
and emotions belonging to the day stirred within her when
the first vague awakening sense, with which we are all
familiar, of something important being about to happen had
been succeeded by definite consciousness of the new signifi-

cance that this particular anniversary was to give to her life. The family congratulations were offered and accepted at the appropriate hour, and the morning brought the usual complement of birthday letters and birthday visits, but Clara, longing only for one letter, one message; knowing, too, that it had been duly sent and delivered, heard no mention of Robert's name either from father or stepmother as the hours passed. When at length they shut themselves into a room apart with a lady friend to discuss, as she divined, her affairs, her Robert's letter, written by him with hopes and fears and prayers, and a heart filled with love, not for her alone, but for her father also; this indignity, this cruelty was too much for her to bear with even an appearance of tranquillity. The day, changed to bitterness, was passed by her in tears. Nor could she regain her composure as the week wore on and still no word was spoken to her of the matters that filled her heart. She turned to Robert's portrait as her only consolation, and when at last her father took the letter from a locked drawer of his writing-table and placed it before her, reproaching her with her folly, she could not even look at it. Did she not know every word of it by heart already? Clara, as we have seen, clearly recognised the just obligations of filial duty, and was keenly sensitive to the influence of affection as well as that of love, but she had inherited Wieck's pertinacity of will, and if means had still been wanting to weld the heart-bond between herself and Robert to indissoluble union, it might possibly have been supplied by her father's action on her eighteenth birthday.

The reply to Robert's letter had meanwhile been promptly conveyed in a personal interview.

"Wieck's answer was so ambiguous," Schumann wrote to Becker on September 14th, "so unintelligibly repellent and compliant, that I do not know what to do. *Nothing at all.* If only you had been here, or were here now for a few minutes, that he might have spoken to some one who could have moved him in regard to certain points attributable, as it seems to me, to vanity; and then from his idea of letting Clara live and die a concert-giver! He could not bring forward any essential objection, but, as I have said, it was impossible

to make out what he meant.   I have not yet spoken to Clara;
my only hope is in her firmness. . . ." *

"The interview with your father was terrible," he writes
a few days later to Clara. "The coldness, the bad will, the
inconsistency, the contradictions. . . .

"Not to be allowed to see you once! We could, he said,
but in the presence of others, a spectacle for every one. . . .
We might also write to each other when you are travelling!
He would not consent to anything more! . . .

"It is in vain that I seek a worthy, well-grounded reason
for your father's refusal; as that you would be injured as
an artist by an early betrothal, that you are too young, or
the like. Nothing of the kind—believe me he will throw you
to the first man who has sufficient money and title. His
highest object is travelling and concert giving. For this he
leaves you to your suffering, disturbs my energy in the
impulse to achieve something worth doing in the world,
laughs at your tears. . . .

"But attention to our aim. You must compass everything
by your goodness, and if this does not succeed, by your firmness. I can do almost nothing except keep silence. . . . Ah,
how distracted I feel! I could laugh for agony. . . .

"Comfort me, pray God to keep me from despair. . . ." †

Schumann's letter to Wieck had been couched in straight-
forward language, without attempt to overstate his means
or prospects. Secure, he said, as far as human foresight could
predict, from want; with good intentions, a youthful heart
filled with enthusiasm for everything noble, hands to work,
the consciousness of a glorious sphere of activity, the hope
of accomplishing all that could be expected of his powers,
respected and loved; yet what could all these things weigh
against the sorrow of being parted from the very being to
whom all his endeavour was dedicated and who truly and
fervently returned his love? He referred to his already
proved perseverance in essential matters, entreated that he
might be tested further, declared that his love for Clara was
grounded in the profound conviction that a union between
them would be attended by a favourable combination of

* "Briefe," p. 98.   † Litzmann, i. 126, fol.

circumstances seldom attainable in marriage, and asked for the assurance that nothing should be decided as to Clara's future for the time being, offering in return his promise not to see her without Wieck's consent. He begged only for one concession—the permission to correspond with her when she travelled :—

"I place my future trustfully in your hands," the letter concluded; "a considerate and explicit answer is due from you to my position, my talent, and my character. . . .

"I implore you with the most profound expression of which an anxious and loving heart is capable: be a benevolent friend again to one of your oldest friends, and the best of fathers to the best of children!"*

A short note to Frau Clementine and two or three lines to Clara were enclosed, together with a detailed statement of his means.

It is certain that from Robert's point of view the letter was perfectly legitimate and perfectly justified. Every word it contained was true to the letter. But what of the father's standpoint? Did Schumann's eloquent representations go, in effect, much beyond Becker's pithily expressed summary of his qualifications as a bridegroom: "I know not to whom I would rather promise my daughter than to a man so sound under the left buttonhole as yourself and one who can write such *études*"? Were they such as, at the time, warranted his aspirations to Clara's hand? Very apposite to the present moment of our narrative is the poetic, but at the same time literally accurate, summary of Clara's artistic position and prospects contained in Schumann's article: "Soirées pour le pianoforte par Clara Wieck," which appeared in the *Neue Zeitschrift* of September 12, 1837, the day before the longed-for, yet dreaded birthday :—

". . . . The 'soirées' certainly give evidence of a tender, overflowing life that seems stirred by the slightest breath. They show, also, unusual resource . . . such as one is accustomed to find only in experienced artists, in men. We can make no mistake as to the composer's youth. To appreciate her resource one must be aware that she stands as a

* First published by Kohut, p. 110.

virtuoso at the summit of her time, whence nothing is hidden from her. She has penetrated the depths in which Sebastian Bach has intrenched himself and the heights whence Beethoven stretches his giant fist; is acquainted with the modern musical endeavour that would bridge the space between these depths and heights, and imparts her wisdom to us with girlish charm. But even by so doing she has raised such expectations of her future as might well occasion solicitude for their result. I may not venture any anticipations on this point. The future of such talent is concealed by curtain behind curtain and each withdrawal creates fresh surprise. That the progress of her musical powers should, however, be watched with interest step by step is to be expected from all who see in the developments of our time, not the random incidents of chance, but the natural, intimate union of the kindred spirits of the past and present."

That Wieck should have viewed Schumann's suit with an intolerant anger almost amounting to disgust can scarcely cause astonishment to those able to realise the details of the situation; yet the deliberate obedience yielded by the lovers to the strange force of mutual attraction which enabled them to offer successful resistance to the opposing energy of the father's will was, as we know, to be justified by future events. "I cling fast to you; if you give way I am undone," exclaims Robert in an agony of apprehension a few days before Clara's departure on her autumn concert journey of this year. That he was fortified for his struggle with life and his achievement in art by Clara's strength; that through her unshakable constancy he was enabled to do the things "worth doing in the world" which he had set himself to accomplish, is not more true, however, than that when the last "curtain behind curtain" concealing her future had been withdrawn, it was seen that she, too, had reached the highest glory of her achievement through the inspiration and suffering of her love. Of these things, however, Friedrich Wieck had, and could have, no prescience. And through all Clara's difficulties in the coming years one sweet trait in her character is especially apparent: her tender loyalty to the father to whom she had been, from her birth, the centre of existence.

Many letters passed, and a few stolen interviews took place, between the lovers during the month that intervened between Clara's birthday and her departure from Leipzig, in which solemn pledges of constancy and of unshakable faith in each other under all conceivable circumstances were given and taken and repeatedly renewed. Robert was to remain quiescent for a reasonable time, but he already whispered to Clara, who did not say him nay, of the possibility of an ultimate appeal to the law of their country, which, though not accepting as valid a marriage entered into without the consent of the parents or guardians of the contracting parties, itself intervenes and assumes guardianship under certain conditions. " Heaven forbid that it should ever come to that !" he adds.

Meanwhile a sort of compromise was arrived at between Wieck and Clara, who frankly persisted that she considered and should consider herself bound by her engagement to Schumann. She promised to be cheerful and to live for a few years longer for art. In return she was to be allowed to write openly to Robert and to receive his letters, addressed to her under cover to her father, during her absence on artistic journeys :—

" DEAR ROBERT,—I have read your letter. . . . But now an answer which is difficult to me. I cannot write secretly to you. Should I find a perfectly safe opportunity I shall certainly use it, but it is impossible to promise anything. Tears fill my eyes at being obliged to write this. But write quite freely (and very often) to father and me as a friend. Friend? ah, what a cold word ! We are, however, something more to each other and that is enough ! . . ."

Clara performed her own, a minor, concerto at the second Gewandhaus concert of the season on October 8th, which was received, says the *Allgemeine Musikalische Zeitung*, " with but moderate applause." * In the second part, Henselt's Introduction and variations for pianoforte and orchestra, played to perfection, were followed by such loud and prolonged demonstrations that she " acceded to the desire of the

---

* The work, though described by the A. M. Z. as a " concertino," was no doubt the concerto Op. 7.

audience and repeated the last variation, for which she received tumultuous thanks."

A swift look of recognition exchanged between herself and Schumann, who had stationed himself at the entrance door of the Gewandhaus to watch for her arrival, perhaps gave Clara additional élan for her work this evening. Her greeting, delivered to him after the concert was over by her cousin Pfund, the famous drummer of the orchestra, no doubt sweetened the remaining hours of Robert's day. They managed to secure a last interview on Tuesday, October 14th, the eve of a long separation, when the agitation of the hour wrought one or both of them to a mood that added the shadow of a passing misapprehension, one of the transitory clouds incidental to all true love-making, to the pain of their farewell. The young artist started on October 15th with her father and the faithful Nanny on a concert journey to Austria. This was, as we shall see, to prove epoch-making in the musical life of Vienna and must have opened a new and brilliant chapter in Clara's career as a virtuoso had it continued to develop on the old lines under her father's management. This, however, was not to be. "I am greatly moved," she writes, in the first of the "secret" letters that she found means, after all, to send Robert during her absence, "to see how unhappy father looks when he is thinking that he will have to lose me some day. I feel my duty towards him and yet I cannot help loving you so boundlessly!"

No sympathetic student of Schumann's career can fail to be struck by the rapid growth of the power of continuous concentrated intellectual activity that marked his development from the day he had been enabled to make his final choice between the poetry and prose of life—to exchange the hated study of law, openly and conscientiously, for the congenial pursuit of art. Even if his first impatience of the long, straight paths leading to pre-eminent musical achievement may be traced in the imperfect cohesion of his early productions in extended form, it is not improbable that he may, with his peculiar and original genius, have been right in choosing his own methods in his endeavour to make good his insufficient youthful training in the groundwork of his art.

"I think of you almost daily," he wrote in the autumn of
1836 to his old teacher, Dorn; "sometimes regretfully because
I worked so irregularly, always gratefully because I learned
more than you imagine." Irresistibly impelled to deliver himself of the musical thoughts that welled constantly within
him, the world is, perhaps, the richer that he did not, at
twenty, attempt to dam the fount of his inspiration until he
had painfully acquired sufficient technical mastery to express
himself to the best possible advantage, but found his own
means for giving utterance to his imagination while it was
still young and fresh. There is no manner of doubt that he
worked long and ardently and in many directions to obtain
the command that at last came to him, and it is not impossible
that he was conscious of a direct, as well as indirect, progressive gain to his creative power through his continued labours
for the success of the *Neue Zeitschrift*. Its management
had gradually involved him in a round of onerous business
duties—correspondence, original contribution, editing the contributions of others, receiving visits, to say nothing of his
careful study of new music for review—that might well have
been deemed incompatible with the necessities of musical
composition. Nevertheless the year 1837, when we find him
intent on plans for improving the form of his paper, for
widening its scope, for strengthening its beneficial influence
on the causes he had deeply at heart—the spread of true musical
culture and the encouragement of original talent—has its own
special interest among the ten during which he composed
exclusively for the pianoforte. To it belong, in the first place,
the favourite Op. 12, Phantasiestücke, in two books, a collection of tone poems each complete in itself, without essential
connection with that which precedes or follows it. The first
of Schumann's publications for pianoforte solo to be received
into wide favour, several of its numbers have retained a
peculiar place in the affection of the musical public. While
all are highly imaginative and absolutely original, the most
musically perfect are, perhaps, the romantic "Des Abends"
and the delicate "Warum?" of the first book, and the passionate "In der Nacht" of the second. In these, especially,
unity of thought and expression is complete. The several

titles, added, as usual, after the works were finished, were intended as little more than the suggestions of a mood, an atmosphere. The composer, however, after copying " In der Nacht," discovered in it a musical resemblance to the legend of Hero and Leander, which it certainly fits in surprising detail. Of the "Ende vom Lied" he wrote in 1838 to Clara :—

"Towards the end everything gives place to a gay wedding, but then the sorrow about you returned, and one hears the marriage bells and death knell sounding together."

The reader should, however, be careful not to understand such fanciful minutiæ too literally, or to feel it his duty to find them realised in all cases in the music to which the composer refers them. Schumann not infrequently gave more than one interpretation of the same work or part of a work ; and in so doing intended merely to indicate the general currents and undercurrents of thought that may have possessed him while in the act of composition. To label line and period of his pianoforte lyrics would frequently be to run the risk of missing the poetic significance of his tone-imagery.

The Opus 12 was finished in the spring or early summer of 1837, and published by Breitkopf and Härtel in February, 1838. Wasielewski surmises that the manuscript work may originally have contained the little piece " Leid ohne Ende," which bears the date 1837 and was published many years later as part of Op. 124. Miss Anna Robena Laidlaw, to whom the opus is dedicated, was an accomplished English pianist resident for some time in Germany. She gave a concert in the Gewandhaus on July 2, 1837, and was on friendly terms with Schumann during her fortnight's stay in Leipzig.

The second work of 1837, now known under the title " Die Davidsbündler (Davidsbündlertänze), 18 Charakterstücke für das Pianoforte, Walther von Göthe zugeeignet," as Opus 6, was originally published as " Davidsbündlertänze von Florestan u. Eusebius," and was the last of Schumann's compositions inscribed with these symbolic names. Opening with a " motto " taken from the fifth number of Clara Wieck's " Soirées Musicales," it is to be associated with the revulsion of feeling caused in Robert by Clara's petition for the return of his letters conveyed to him on the morning of August 13th, and fascinates us not only by its original and spontaneous charm, but on account of the insight it affords into the connection existing between Schumann's musical productivity and the events and emotions of his inner life. If we read into the word "dances" the signification "gambols" indubitably intended by the composer, the intention and suitability of its employment here becomes evident. The Davidsbündlertänze are expressions of the gay delight, the tender rapture, the saucy pride, the impatient longing, that alternated in the soul of Florestan-Eusebius during the days which immediately followed the re-establishment of his heart relationship with Zilia. The mad antics of his shadowy disciples in the "death dances, Vitus dances, dances of the graces, hobgoblin dances," of which Schumann writes in a letter to Carl Montag, are reflections of the quickly changing phases of mood of a spirit that has abandoned itself for the time being to the very ecstasy of joy. Begun towards the end of August, they were completed before the middle of September. "They will please you, I hope," says the composer, writing to young Goethe on September 11th, about the dedication. "I am in excellent humour now and fly a great deal."

Sterndale Bennett, lately returned to London, who describes Schumann in his diary as "one of the finest-hearted fellows I ever knew," writes to him on August 26th:—

"MY DEAR FRIEND,—You really were most kind to send me such a charming letter. You show yourself, my dear fellow, in so happy a mood and I trust that your joy springs from the heart. Yes! as you say, your style is no longer that of an *editor* but of a maiden of eighteen. . . ." *

To Clara, Schumann wrote on the publication of the Davidsbündlertänze: "My Clara will find out for me what is in the dances; they are more her own than anything else of mine—they tell the story of an entire 'Polterabend,' the beginning and end of which you may imagine for yourself. If ever I was happy at the pianoforte it was whilst I was composing them." †

* "Life of Sir W. Sterndale Bennett," by James Robert Bennett.
† "Jugendbriefe," p. 274. The term "Polterabend," which, in German-English dictionaries, is generally translated "nuptial eve," has no real

Musically the Davidsbündlertänze are interesting from the particular evidence they afford of the attention which the composer continued to devote to the craftsmanship of his art. Though they are not connected the one with the other as parts of a symmetrical architectural design, they derive an inner unity, like the *scènes mignonnes* of the Carnaval, from the idea around which they centre, and to the earnest student they reveal in a remarkable degree Schumann's rapid advance in the technique of composition. His natural facility in the invention of novel effects of rhythm and in the discovery of new harmonic combinations has here attained entire clearness, whilst his increased command of the various details of resource frequently tells us that he was so indefatigable a student of Bach as to have acquired considerable power of applying the lessons to be learned in the pages of the great cantor to purposes prompted by his own creative genius. No wonder that through the long years of her later career Frau Schumann was frequently invited to select for public performance these attractive memorials of perhaps the most profoundly touching moment of her romantic youthful history. To those who, like the author, have enjoyed frequent opportunity of hearing her play them, her powerful, tender, humorous renderings of the various numbers must remain among the most vivid memories of her interpretative art.

The publication of the Carnaval in August or September gave Moscheles, to whom Schumann sent a copy, opportunity to express his growing sense of the importance of the musical tendencies of the time by a few kindly words to the young composer in whose works he found them so strikingly represented. Schumann's acknowledgment is interesting as belonging to the early days of the period that witnessed the publication of his largest and most representative works for pianoforte alone, but when "there was little foresight that he [Schumann] would become a celebrated musician."

equivalent in the English language. Literally rendered it signifies "evening of noise" or "racket." It alludes to the merriment of the hobgoblins and sprites who are supposed by German tradition to haunt the bride's dwelling on the eve of a wedding and to testify their interest in the occasion by noisy fun in which practical jokes are prominent.

"LEIPZIG, *September* 22, 1837.

"MY DEAR, HONOURED SIR,—. . . . May the consciousness that you have inspired a young artist, who often feels solitary in his difficult path, with courage for new work, reward you for accepting me so kindly. Your letter contains three words especially about the character of my compositions which give me the more satisfaction as coming from you. . . ."

Even more gratifying because so entirely unexpected must have been the warmly appreciative expressions used by Liszt in the article on three of Schumann's compositions which appeared in November, 1837, in the *Gazette Musicale* from which we have already quoted.* Its value was enhanced by the circumstances under which it was written.

"On playing these works through," says Liszt, "I at once perceived what musical pith they contained, and, without having previously heard of Schumann, or knowing how or where he lived (as I had not at the time been in Germany and his name was quite unknown in France and Italy), I wrote the review which appeared at the end of 1837, and became known to the composer."

All the more disappointing by contrast with the frank acceptance of Schumann's art by two of the great musicians of the day is the complete reserve perseveringly maintained towards it, so far as can be discovered, by a third and greater one. It is in vain that we search the entire published correspondence of the period in the hope of finding one single expression from Mendelssohn, favourable or otherwise, respecting the endeavour and advancing achievement of the man of genius who had sat daily at his side for many months at the dinner-table of the Hôtel de Bavière and of whose almost unqualified admiration of his own art he was well aware. We, for our part, have been led to the conclusion that during the first few years of his residence in Leipzig Mendelssohn regarded Schumann chiefly in his capacity as an editor and that he did not feel in sympathy with, or perhaps entirely apprehend, the tendencies of his literary activity. That, at a later period, he had appreciation to bestow on Schumann

* *Ante*, p. 172.

the composer, the author was frequently and emphatically assured both by Joseph Joachim and Otto Goldschmidt.

Among the notable musical visitors to Leipzig during the autumn of 1837 were the French violinist, Henri Vieuxtemps, and the English singer, Clara Novello, who, at eighteen, in all the freshness of her clear ringing soprano and charming simplicity of manner, created a *furore:* " The public is quite beside itself when she sings with such perfect intonation, such ease and reliable musicianship," reports Mendelssohn; "half Leipzig is in love with her."

Schumann describes his life during the autumn to his sister-in-law Therese in a few quiet words which, however, seem to tell us much : " Little Walter Goethe frequently speaks of you and with the greatest enthusiasm. We often see each other. Otherwise I live quiet and retired, my thoughts with Clara and the future."

CHAPTER XIV

1837–1838

The "Carnaval" in Dresden—Clara's Austrian journey—Concerts in Prague and Vienna—Schubert's Grand Duet for pianoforte—First public performance in Vienna of Beethoven's sonata, Op. 57—Clara honoured by the Emperor—Expected arrival of Liszt.

ACCUSTOMED as the reader has become to associate some special artistic achievement, whether in public or private performance, with each new season of Clara's activity, he will not be surprised to learn that a fortnight's stay with her father amid their large circle of friends in Dresden, by which she was refreshed for the coming exertions of the later stages of her journey, was marked by a private production of high importance. On Friday, October 27th, she played Robert's Carnaval in her father's rooms to about twenty acquaintances who had been expressly invited to hear the newly published work. We may imagine the enthusiasm to which Clara abandoned herself on the occasion, conscious as she was of being surrounded by Robert's admirers, and may sympathise, even at this distance of time, with her feeling of elation as she recorded the initial brilliant success of the work in her diary. Again, too, does the incident afford evidence of her father's constant admiration of Schumann's genius. Wieck, however, remained consistent with himself in other respects also. Without mentioning the matter to Clara, he took the opportunity of the stay in Dresden to send Robert a written answer to the birthday letter of courtship, probably imagining there would be less opportunity during his daughter's absence from Leipzig for her mind to be disturbed by the receipt of secret intelligence of his action from her lover. According to Schumann's account of the matter in a letter of later date, the communication was expressed in unmistakable language. The writer acknowledged Robert to be an excellent man, though not the best of his acquaintance. He did not know his intentions for Clara's future, nor was he as yet concerned about them; but before he would see two such artists unhappy together in cramped condition and with limited means he would sacrifice his daughter singly, and only Schumann would be to blame if he should find it necessary to arrange another marriage for her.*

The travellers, journeying by coach, for the first line of German railway was not opened till the end of 1836, reached Prague on October 30th, to feel the depressing effect of a first arrival in a strange city; and Clara was sensible that the impressions she formed during the next few days of the musical atmosphere of the Bohemian capital compared unfavourably with those of her visits to some of the important German cities. The time had been when Prague was possessed of a musical life of its own, similar to that of the traditional Vienna and rivalling it in brilliancy; when the palace of the patrician or wealthy burgher was not complete without its private band, formed partly from the family, partly from the servants of the household. In those days the master might be seen playing second violin, maybe, to his butler's first; his son or his friend performing on the flute near the footman responsible for the oboe, the whole troupe kept together by the huntsman or steward presiding at the harpsichord. The necessities of such a band had called forth the symphonies of Haydn and, as time passed on and the nobles had less time and opportunity for music, the demand created by the private quartet or quintet that replaced the orchestras produced the chamber music of the Vienna school. But as in Vienna, so in Prague, these conditions passed away about the beginning of the nineteenth century and had not been effectively succeeded. The best centre of musical life in Prague during the thirties was, perhaps, the Konservatorium; but what could the civilities of an entire body of director and professors avail a young artist

* "Briefe." Schumann's letter of June 30, 1839, to Advocate Einert; and Litzmann, i. 141, 142.

who, in her daily home life, breathed the atmosphere created by Mendelssohn and Schumann, who could claim Chopin and Spohr and Moscheles as friends, and was now introducing Henselt to the world as the youngest rising tone poet? Yet Clara was soon to learn that no people in Europe are more capable of showing their appreciation of such music as appeals to them than the Bohemians.

Wieck, not deeming it prudent to attempt the usual subscription list for the Prague concerts, had arranged with Director Dionysius Weber that Clara should introduce herself in the first place to a small but intelligent public by giving a matinee in the Konservatorium; and on November 12th she performed the following programme before an audience that consisted chiefly of musicians and pianoforte students:—

Henselt ...	... Variations, Op. 1.
Thomaschek	... Rhapsodie.
Chopin ...	... Arpeggio Étude in E flat.
Clara Wieck	... Concert-variations on a theme from "Il Pirato."

She had thirteen recalls, and wrote the same evening to Robert: "Heavens, I have never known such enthusiasm! You may imagine I really did not know what to do. I was obliged to come out of my hiding corner over and over again; and then the curtsies which I make so badly! The thought of you so inspired my playing that the public became inspired too. I have already received letters and visits of congratulation—the people here seem almost crazy." *

A concert followed on November 18th in the Konvikt Hall, which, with seating accommodation for six hundred, was well filled. The pianist again played unaccompanied solos only; a Bach fugue, Henselt's variations, Liszt's Pacini *divertissement*, and her own concert variations, which, having been received with particular favour by the Konservatorium audience, were now repeated by desire. She was overwhelmed with applause, bouquets, and congratulations, and during the next few days letters, visits and floral tributes were poured upon her. She made a third appearance on the 23rd, at the

* Litzmann, i. 145.

theatre, when she played her own concerto and, by desire,
Henselt's variations in the interval between two short
comedies, and, contrary to all the prescribed laws of etiquette,
was recalled four times after each performance by the packed
and delighted house.

It is impossible, as we reach this stage of our narrative,
to help feeling a passing regret that the happiness of the
young artist should have been disturbed, at this hour of a
brilliant triumph that had been purchased by the assiduous
effort of many years, by such a struggle between passionate
love and filial duty as was passing day by day and week
by week within Clara's breast. Nor may we withhold our
sympathy from Friedrich Wieck in his difficult situation.
Strongly as he might suspect, he could not prove, the fact
of his daughter's secret correspondence with Schumann, for,
with Nanny's help, she was able to post and receive her
letters under precautions that baffled even his acute vigilance.
If he could have looked over her shoulder and read what
she wrote on the last evening of the visit to Prague, he would
have found that there were moments even now when the
pleasure of her varied life and its progressive artistic success
struggled within her for the mastery of her being. Yet any
hope he might have derived from the knowledge of such
conflicts must have proved delusive. Clara had, as we have
seen, passed from the first stages of her ordeal. Love had
set his seal upon her and claimed her as his own; and,
whatever her loyalty to her father and her art, whatever
her enjoyment of her friendships and her popularity, it was
no longer hers to choose her path in life. Henceforth to
the very end she must follow love's call.

Leaving Prague and their many newly made acquaintances
behind them on November 25th, the Wiecks found themselves
involved, almost immediately on their arrival in Vienna, in
a round of visits, parties, and business engagements fatiguing
enough to Clara, conscious of being on her trial before professional critics apt to take limited views of art, and fastidious
patronesses inclined to accept personal prepossession or
prejudice as the ultimate arbiter of judgment. Musical
life in Vienna, as we have more than once hinted, was not

in the vigorous condition of maturity that might have been expected in the city famed as having been the home of Haydn, Mozart, and Beethoven, to say nothing of the then little known Schubert. Containing elements of rich vitality, the leader to combine them in a centre from which they might obtain effectual energy was lacking. The Gesellschaft der Musikfreunde, with an archduke at its head, had been in existence a quarter of a century, but its four annual performances of oratorio were conducted by its best musical members in turn, and its weekly soirées of miscellaneous chamber music were not of considerable artistic value. It had as yet established neither orchestral nor choral union, while its Konservatorium, founded in 1817, was animated by a spirit the reverse of progressive. There were no philharmonic concerts and the Singakademie was as yet undreamed of.

" They ought to have Mendelssohn here—good heavens, how an energetic musician is needed ! " exclaims Wieck in the diary a week after his arrival.

With regard to the soloist's art, the general standard here, as elsewhere, was that of virtuosity, of which, no doubt, Vienna possessed great traditions. The greatest and best of these were, however, cherished only in a few aristocratic and other scarcely less exclusive circles, and the amateurs of either would have found it hard to realise that their city had fallen behind the times in its cultivation of artistic activity, or to believe that the musical leadership of Europe, which had passed in the course of the ages from Flanders to Italy and from Italy to Austria, and had seemed for a time to be about to devolve on Paris, had again been transferred to the North. Yet, as we know, more than a century of continuous and progressive opportunity created and used by a population of middle-class burghers, an aristocracy of merchants, publishers, and booksellers, had brought it about that commercial Leipzig, whose theatres and concert-rooms remained unadorned by the presence of duchess or princess, was, under the stimulus of a man of genius and enthusiasm, already leading to its rapid consummation that democratisation of the highest musical art which has had its share in revolutionising the conditions of the modern world.

At the time of Clara's visit to Vienna the era of the composer-pianist, of men of the stamp of Dussek and Ferdinand Ries, of whom, perhaps, Moscheles was the last very distinguished representative — men who, though not possessed of pre-eminent creative power, united in their musicianship the acquirements of the trained composer and the trained executant—had almost passed away. The composer and the performer of the highest distinction had become to a great extent differentiated. Mendelssohn, it is true, sometimes played his own works, or those of Bach or Beethoven, at the Gewandhaus concerts, but he did not, on these occasions, come forward as a professional pianist. He played because it delighted him to do so and because his performances gave delight to his hearers. Chopin scarcely appeared in public after his early youth; Schumann, never as an executant after his amateur student days. The most renowned of the pianoforte virtuosi, on the other hand, still composed for their instrument, but more and more with the exclusive object of creating a medium for the display of their peculiar excellencies as executants. The possibilities of the pianoforte had been marvellously increased by the patenting, in 1821, by the house of Erard, of a perfected repetition action, the merits of which, but little recognised for some years, ultimately placed the house at the head of the pianoforte makers of Europe, a position it maintained for several decades. The advantages of the action were first clearly realised in 1830 by Hummel's pupil, the young Viennese pianist Sigismund Thalberg, in the course of his first extended concert journey. Thalberg associated his talents with Erard's instruments from this date, and, by the middle of the decade, had succeeded in working out that new phase of virtuosity to which we referred in our last chapter, and which, with the first few performances of his " Huguenot " fantasia, gave him his place as a phenomenal executant.

"How completely he [Thalberg] is master of his language and idea, and how properly he behaves," ironically remarks Schumann, who seldom found a good word for this inventor of new keyboard marvels; but he continues: " The enthusiasm which the Huguenot fantasia is creating in Paris and elsewhere is quite intelligible. . . . It would be difficult to give those who have not heard and seen him for themselves an idea of Thalberg's way of handling the instrument, to describe his new method of placing accompaniments above the melody, his remarkable pedal effects, his power of giving prominence to single tones amid his arpeggio masses. Let our younger pianoforte composers form thus, each one for himself, his own style of instrumentation. They will find their satisfaction in many possibilities of the instrument which, so poor in the sustained singing power of single notes, is, nevertheless, so astonishingly rich in the means of combination."

From this date the traditional concert programme of the travelling pianist was doomed. The extraordinary sensation excited by Thalberg's performances wherever he appeared made him independent of the orchestra, and the triumph of the pianoforte and the pianoforte virtuoso was complete when, about the year 1835, he began to give public performances, generally of his own compositions only, alone with his instrument. In Vienna, where the fame of the once favourite Döhler had been considerably eclipsed by the successes of his somewhat older rival, and where Liszt had not been heard since his boyhood, Thalberg, at the close of 1837, had been established for two years in the esteem of the concert-goer as the reigning pianoforte marvel of the day. His new developments in technique, his dazzling trills, his cascades of arpeggios that played around, but never obscured, the melodies selected for treatment, his octave passages, above all the ease and perfect purity with which he performed his fantasias, caprices, and *études*, produced their intended effect—that of delighted astonishment—with a certainty that could hardly have been reached had his aims been less mechanical.

"Thalberg with his composure and within his more restricted sphere is more perfect as a virtuoso," writes Mendelssohn in a letter of 1840, comparing him with Liszt. " A fantasia by Thalberg is a piling up of the most well-chosen and delicate effects, a continued succession of difficulties and embellishments that amaze one. Everything is so calculated and subtly contrived and with such certainty, knowledge, and refined taste. Then, too, the fellow has such a trained and incredible lightness of finger as no one else possesses."

Two social engagements stand out especially in the list of private engagements fulfilled by Clara during the first fortnight of her stay in Vienna, as having served to give her father and herself the encouragement they both needed for the ordeal of her first public appearance, fixed for December 14th. At a soirée given by the Baroness Pereira-Arnstein, one of the gifted amateur pianists of Beethoven's circle, she enchanted her private audience of connoisseurs by giving numerous selections from her Chopin and Henselt répertoire; and at a large party arranged by Fischhof, a musician with whom Schumann had been in occasional correspondence for some years, and, apparently, the one resident professor possessing any knowledge of the late developments of the romantic school, after taking part in a performance of Schubert's trio in B flat, she created a sensation by playing a Bach fugue for which she gained a double encore. Probably the famous contrapuntist, Court-organist Sechter, was present, who, an enthusiastic student of Bach, was supposed to write a fugue every day, and, later in his career as professor of composition at the Konservatorium, numbered Nottebohm, Bibl, Anto Brückner, and C. F. Pohl among his pupils. Clara did not play anything of Chopin's this evening; perhaps because his works were already well known in Vienna, where he had given concerts early in his career. She rather chose to introduce her favourite Henselt, who had been living, little known, in the imperial city for three years past, with the " Vogel " étude that she was making so popular.

" Mendelssohn is almost unknown here," she writes to Robert; " I should have liked to play something of his at my concert, but dare not until I have the public on my side. Your compositions have a great protector in Professor Fischhof, especially since he has heard some of them from me—all the others are your enemies; one scarcely dares mention your name, it makes them so angry; and why? Because of Döhler and Thalberg." *

The evening arrived at length on which Vienna was to

* Litzmann, i. 157.

decide, in the words of Bäuerle, of the Vienna *Theaterzeitung*, whether " the modest young artist who is placed in Germany by the side of Chopin and Liszt can hold her ground near Thalberg." The programme had been carefully chosen. It was not too severe to be enjoyed by the fellow-citizens of Lanner and Strauss—neither Bach nor Beethoven could be ventured upon as yet—not too insignificant musically to lower the performances as a whole to the level of mere mechanical display; yet not too sparing of virtuosity. It was, taken altogether, refined, pleasurable, and individual; but also, and indispensably, wonder-making. A concert rondo by Pixis served as the opening piece; then came several Chopin numbers, Henselt, and Clara's bravura variations, written, it will be remembered, for the express purpose of exhibiting the latest technical resources of the pianoforte and the command of the performer.

In estimating the effect which Clara was to produce on her susceptible Vienna audience, the influence of her personality must not be left out of account; the impression of her youth, her tall—but not too tall—slight, figure; of her big dark eyes with their pathetic look; the black, glossy hair that framed her face; the appealing, almost timid air with which she made her first curtsey to the audience, her simplicity of manner, her absolute self-forgetfulness when once she had fairly entered upon her work. Nor should it be forgotten that her whole life had been, as it were, one preparation for this great moment of her career. Never, surely, was a young artist formed by method so admirable, circumstances so favourable. Bathed in the best music from her earliest years, taught the inevitable drudgery of her art by easy stages almost from babyhood, by a father as fond, with all his strictness, as the father of Mozart, the results of her tasks became so entirely a second nature to her that she ceased to realise them as having been acquired. Kept to a natural, healthy round of work and recreation by which her slight inclination to despondency had been as far as possible counteracted, she had grown up a natural, lively girl, who, as she herself writes, had never known a care. In judgment and maturity of thought she was, in many respects, beyond her years, and this fact, together

with the circumstance that she had always been in contact not
only with the best musical, but the best social circles of her
time, had given her a confidence in herself and her status as
an artist which, insensibly felt by her audiences, contributed
to the success of her public, as of her private life.

The concert was held in the hall of the Musikverein.

" My triumph," says the diary. " The public consisted of
the élite of the most distinguished and most musical people in
Vienna. . . . I satisfied connoisseurs and amateurs and was
recalled twelve times in all."

The second concert took place on December 21st. The programme was selected from the same composers with one
notable exception. The name of Bach was substituted for
that of Pixis. Clara's concerto took the place of the concert
variations.

" Again a triumph," writes Clara to Robert; " you should
have heard the storm of applause. I was obliged to repeat
Bach's fugue and the Henselt variations. No more delightful
feeling than to have satisfied an entire public." *

Wieck writes the next day :—

" VIENNA, *December* 22, 1837.

" DEAR WIFE,—Clara is the theme of all Vienna. She has
won all hearts even at court. The papers no longer write
notices; they have become enthusiastic and emotional and
weave laurel wreaths. ' It is touching and costs me many a
tear,' I can tell you. Yesterday we dined with Rettich [a
leading actress]. To-day we are to dine with the Emperor's
musical intendant [Count Amade] to talk over the pieces Clara
is to play before the Empress. Yesterday a copy *de luxe* of
Schubert's great duet that has just been published with a
dedication to Clara Wieck was presented to Clara by Diabelli.
It has already been advertised in the papers with the words:
' Dedicated to the greatest pianist, Clara Wieck.' Clara is
very much pleased about it. We received the copy through
Haslinger and will send it you by the next opportunity. Send
a copy to Henselt, to whom you might write word of Clara's
success in Vienna, especially with his things, and say that she

* Litzmann, i. 158, 160,

always excites enormous enthusiasm, play what she may. She even plays fugues of Bach in public and has to repeat them, a thing unheard of in Vienna."

Wieck continues on the 26th :—

"This evening at eight o'clock to the Empress. Clara will enjoy a distinction never before accorded to an artist. It is not to be a concert with orchestra in which she would play at a distance. Clara is to improvise and to play several times at intervals in the imperial apartments surrounded by the whole imperial family. Amongst other things, she is to perform a duet with Blagrove, who has a letter from the Queen. She is going to practise it to-day.

"It is not certain how many concerts we may give. Beethoven's and Schubert's trios and Beethoven's sonata Op. 47 [Kreutzer] will certainly be included in the programme, and Clara will be the first virtuoso who has dared to venture on such a thing." *

* Kohut, 315 and fol. More than passing interest attaches to the mention in this communication of Schubert's great "duet" for pianoforte.

Schumann, answering a letter of Clara's from Vienna, writes about seven weeks later : " I have been raving over the Schubert duet, but I cannot believe it was intended for the pianoforte, though I have borrowed your original manuscript from your mother." The *copie de luxe* (" Pracht-ausgabe ") presented to Clara by Diabelli was, therefore, the original Schubert manuscript, and was sent home to surprise, and be kept in safe custody by Frau Clementine.

Schumann retained his opinion that the work had not been intended for publication as a pianoforte duet, and about fifteen years later, Joachim, who was a child of six at the date now reached by our narrative, scored it for full orchestra on the master's recommendation. Twenty years later still, the work returned in this form to the land of its birth, and was heard as a symphony at the concert of the Gesellschaft der Musikfreunde of November 10, 1872, the first to be conducted by Brahms, who held the post of artistic director to the society for three seasons. (See the author's " Life of Brahms," ii. 116). Thus Diabelli's present to Clara became, in after years, a link that directly associated Schumann's two favourite young musicians with Clara's early successes and with the romantic years of Robert's and Clara's youth. In England the work was heard as a symphony at one of the Crystal Palace concerts of the mid-seventies under August Manns. It was performed in Queen's Hall, London, on December 9, 1908, at an orchestral concert given by the Classical Concert Society under the direction of Dr. H. P. Allen.

For the third concert, of January 7, 1838, the house was sold out immediately on the announcement of the date, and Wieck, now sure of the temper of his audience, placed Beethoven's sonata Op. 57 (Appassionata) in the programme. Clara played it to a packed audience of eight hundred people, amongst whom was seated the Baroness von Ertmann.

"Complete triumph over Thalberg," writes Wieck in the diary; and to his wife: "The Baroness Ertmann and Cibbini declared after the concert was over that the sonata had never before been played in Vienna with such fine understanding and expression." *

The fourth concert was devoted "by desire" to Thalberg and Liszt; "the antipodes," as Wieck calls them; "in order to silence those," writes Clara, "who persisted in thinking I should not be able to play Thalberg." It brought thirteen recalls.

"You will not be able to understand this enthusiasm, for you do not really know what I can and what I can not do, you know too little of me as an artist," says Clara in her next report to her lover; "but do not think that I am piqued with you on this account. On the contrary, I am glad of it, as I know you do not love me for the sake of my art, but, as you once wrote me in a little note, 'I do not love you because you are a great artist; no, I love you because you are so good.' That pleased me immensely and I have never forgotten it."

The fifth concert, of February 11th, brought forward Mendelssohn's name, as represented by one of his pianoforte caprices. A selection from the Études Symphoniques, talked of for the same occasion, was rejected for reasons explained by Clara in a letter to Robert of March 4th. Nor does it

---

* Kohut, 131. The Baroness Dorothea von Ertmann, to whom Beethoven's sonata in A major, Op. 101, is dedicated, was one of the most gifted pianists of the private Beethoven circle. Mendelssohn made her acquaintance at Milan in 1831, when her husband was commandant of the city, and gives a graphic account of his visits to her house in a letter of July 14th of that year. ("Briefe," i. 208–211. Lady Wallace's translation, i. 202–204.) The allusion in the text to the previous performances of the sonata Op. 57 is to those of distinguished amateurs before private audiences. Madame Cibbini was one of the ladies of the imperial court and an accomplished musician.

seem that any portion of the great work was heard at the sixth and last concert of February 18th. Clara probably played some of the variations, however, at one or other of the private musical receptions given by her father in the course of the long stay in Vienna. A fugue by Sechter was heard at one—probably the third—of the concerts. The programmes of the last three included works of chamber music for pianoforte and strings; those of the first three were probably varied by vocal numbers.

The Vienna correspondent of the *Allgemeine Musikalische Zeitung* says, in a general notice of all the concerts published on March 7, 1838 :—

" Her [Clara Wieck's] performances created a sensation on each occasion only to be compared with the enthusiasm roused by a Paganini, a Lipinski ; and which was excited, not only by her technical bravura, but, in an incomparably greater degree, by her invariably individual, sympathetic conception and interpretation of the music she played. An original feature in her programmes, the inclusion of several short pieces played in succession, sufficiently shows the standpoint from which she must be judged, her aim to present clearly the individuality of each master, to reproduce his inmost being with understanding, feeling, and enthusiasm. The instrument itself becomes, under such treatment, the means to an end, deriving a warmly pulsating life from the intellectual conception breathed into it. The interest of a public which is accustomed as a rule to mere firework effects—rondos, fantasias, caprices and the like—was secured even for a work of Bach, and desire was expressed for a second hearing, not only of some bagatelles by Chopin and Henselt, but also of the difficult fugue movement. To this wish the illustrious artist readily acceded, and by so doing increased the tribute of admiration due to such mastery." *

* The violinist Karl Joseph Lipinski, of Lemburg (1790–1861), was, in his lifetime, regarded as almost a rival to Paganini, though he founded his style on the school of Viotti, and was essentially a performer of classical music. He had an enthusiastic preference for the works of Bach and Beethoven, was a good composer for his instrument, and was greatly esteemed by his friends and acquaintances. His name is mentioned with great cordiality in Clara's correspondence.

It is to be remembered that Clara's performance of the
F minor sonata at her concert of January 7th was the first
public production of the work in Vienna and probably the
second in that city of any of Beethoven's sonatas for pianoforte alone.*

"Clara Wieck gave her first concert," says Hanslick, "on
December 11 [read 14], 1837. A half-opened rose, with all
the charm of the bud and the fragrance of the developed
flower! No wonder-child, yet still a child and already a
wonder. It was another new, unforeseen aspect of virtuosity,
which, having presented itself in Thalberg in the guise of an
amiable Pelham, now appeared in Clara Wieck as girlish
innocence and poetry. With all the spell exercised by this
poetry in Clara's personality and performance, yet the foundation and measure of the admiration lavished upon her
were, nevertheless, those of virtuosity. If, in the year 1837,
Clara Wieck had, as in later years, devoted her art solely to
the profound intellectual compositions of Bach, Beethoven,
and Schumann, she would not, could not, have excited such
enthusiasm. 'She stands by the side of Thalberg, at the
height of accomplishment,' wrote the *Sammler* after Clara's
first concert, and with this everything was certainly spoken.
The poetic and romantic charm of virtuosity was represented
in her programmes chiefly by Chopin and Henselt. Besides
her solid, serious programme numbers which included fugues
of Bach, Clara in the thirties always played one and another
mere glittering bravura piece, most frequently the C major
rondo of Pixis, her own variations on 'Il Pirato,' and
things of Thalberg and Liszt. Of Beethoven's sonatas
she occasionally played the F minor, Op. 57, the D minor,
Op. 31, and the C sharp minor, Op. 27, and with this
modest beginning, performed a deed for which the warmest
acknowledgment is due to her, for, so far as I am aware, to it
belongs the priority. Beethoven's sonatas found their place
in the programme of the virtuoso in the first instance through
Clara's example, and soon afterwards through that of Liszt,
and it was only by slow degrees that they became acceptable
to the public even then. . . . The youthful, poetic Clara

* See *ante*, p. 143.

excited an enthusiasm in the public for Beethoven's sonatas (though it may not have been very lasting at the time) and had reason to be proud of the warm poetic tribute to which she inspired Grillparzer." *

Clara's public appearances did not terminate with the last of her series of six concerts. She played twice at the Kärthnerthor court theatre, and on both occasions large numbers of people were turned away from the doors.

" I do not understand it," she writes; " I know that I play well, but I do not know why I excite such enthusiasm."

The enthusiasm, however it may have been awakened, could not fail to cause bitter envy in some of the professional circles, and if Clara's admirers were only induced by considerations of prudence to abandon their design of crowning her with a laurel wreath at one of her concerts, her enemies threatened to hiss her off the stage on her second appearance at the theatre.

" But I am a well-armed girl, as you yourself said," she declares the day before the expected hostile demonstration, as she stands at a table in her bedroom, paper before her, pen in hand, running into the adjoining sitting-room for each fresh dip of ink, afraid of removing the inkstand lest her father should come in from his walk and find her in the act of writing a confidential letter to Robert !

The climax of success was reached on March 15th :—

" She is a great virtuoso ; I have never heard such playing," the Empress had remarked after Clara's appearance at court, " but I am still more pleased with her personality."

A few more weeks of public and private successes which justified the impression created by the young girl, the great artist, in the most august circle of the land worked a

---

* Grillparzer's charming verses " Clara Wieck und Beethoven. F moll Sonate" appeared in the Vienna Zeitung für Kunst, Literatur, &c., on January 9, 1838. They are printed by Litzmann (i. 170).

Hanslick is probably mistaken in saying that Clara Wieck performed Beethoven's sonatas, Op. 27 and Op. 31. They are not mentioned either in the programmes or reviews of her Vienna concerts of 1837-38 as given in the available newspapers of the time ; and they appear for the first time in the catalogue given by Litzmann (iii. 615-624) of Frau Schumann's entire répertoire, in the list of 1842, two years after her marriage.

miracle. On March 7th, Wieck received the personal communication of the minister, Count Kollowrat, that Clara
had been appointed chamber musician (K.k. Kammervir-
tuosin) to her Imperial Majesty; a title of distinction to
which neither salary nor fixed duty attached, but which
carried with it at the time considerable indirect advantage
to an artist's career. It was an honour, reserved until now
for Austrian subjects, which she shared with Paganini,
Thalberg, Pasta, and a few other musicians of the highest
celebrity, and which had never hitherto been conferred on a
Protestant or on any quite youthful artist.

" Well then, if Clara really wishes it and it will please her,
I will make an exception," the Emperor is reported to have
said when the matter was laid before him.

" Four florins for the stamp and a new Austrian ducat,"
records Wieck on March 15th, the day on which he received the
official document that secured the appointment to Clara. " I
have never felt such pleasure in spending money." And who
will not sympathise with his elation ? Was not the seal that
entitled Clara to add the mystic " K.k." to her signature, and
conferred on her the full freedom of the imperial city for life,
the outward sign that stamped her father's career—his early
painful struggles and later successes, his ideal ambition and
his practical devotion to duty—with the mark of complete
victory; the sign that the world had already recognised his
child as one of the bright stars of the artistic heaven; his
Clara, of whom, even before her birth, he had dreamed
dreams ?

The honour brought with it many trying necessities, however. Appeals that could not well be refused reached the
newly made court pianist for her co-operation at public and
private functions, large charity concerts, and the like, the
granting of which involved some expense and considerable
additional fatigue. Visits innumerable had to be received and
paid, and both Clara and her father had already been sufficiently occupied. The morning's practice could not be
neglected ; the pianist Fischhof would look in to play duets ;
violinists and other musicians followed suit; attention to the
toilette was imperative; and then Clara had private engrossing

occupations known only to herself and Nanny. Robert's hand-writing had not become more easily decipherable with the increase of his business correspondence, and Clara, who would have liked to spend consecutive hours over his letters, had to study them at chance moments during the day, or on her return late at night from her engagements, when she ought to have gone at once to rest. The exchange of confidential letters between the lovers was, no doubt, an open secret which the father shared, though he was baffled in his endeavours to bring it to open proof. " If Clara marries Schumann I will say on my deathbed that she is not worthy to be my daughter," he declared to Nanny. The loud imprecations with which he coupled Robert's name after Clara had retired for the night awoke her from her sleep in the next chamber, but he never allowed his distracting, ever-present consciousness of his daughter's favoured suitor to disturb his appreciation of Schumann the composer of genius.

" I must relieve you of a great error," Clara tells her lover. " You do father great injustice when you say that he always speaks badly of you to me and tells me of all your faults. He does not do this. On the contrary, he speaks of you to every one with the greatest enthusiasm, and allows me to play your compositions to people. He lately invited a large party (Vienna's greatest poet [Grillparzer] among others) expressly to hear the Carnaval. . . ."* Nor was this done merely to satisfy Clara. Sending his wife an account of this first of his private assemblies in Vienna, Wieck says :—

" His [Schumann's] Carnaval was played in our rooms lately before great connoisseurs and made a *furore* ; and as people talk, gossip, relate, listen, visit a good deal here, his name has become quickly known as a composer. Clara has played the sonata [F sharp minor] also, but of course it was not so generally understood. . . . Up to now Clara has played every time—it is seven times—quite wonderfully ; everything by heart, of course. . . ." †

By the end of March Clara was tired out, and in order to relieve her of the unceasing obligations that had followed her rapidly acquired fame, her father took her for a few days to

<hr>

* Litzmann, i. 172.   † Kohut, 181.

Pressburg. Here, however, matters were but little better.
Many undertakings were in progress for the relief of the
suffering caused by great floods in Hungary, and the young
artist found herself obliged to appear twice at the theatre
during her four days' stay.   On her return to Vienna she was
summoned by express command of the Emperor himself to
play again at the Burg.*   The true artistic inspiration never
failed her, however, in the presence of her Austrian and
Hungarian audiences.   She forgot her fatigue as she took her
place at her instrument, and, whether in concert-room, in
theatre, or at court, held and fired her hearers up to the last.

Clara's professional duties in Vienna were now at an end.
No more artistic engagements, whether public or private, were
to be accepted ; but the incidence of Holy Week and the
approach of Easter offered opportunities for a fortnight's holiday freedom which could nowhere be more agreeably spent
than in the imperial capital.   There was, moreover, a very
special artistic reason to induce Wieck and his daughter to
stay on for a short time longer.

This was neither more nor less than the long-expected and
now imminent arrival of Liszt.

* The imperial palace in the capital.

CHAPTER XV

1838

FRANZ, the son of Adam Liszt, a steward in the service of
Prince Esterhazy, was born on October 22, 1811, at Raid-
ing, near Ödenburg, in Hungary. His musical gifts attracted
notice from his early childhood, and before he reached the age
of ten he was sent to Vienna, by the liberality of some nobles
of his native country, to study the pianoforte under Czerny
and theory and composition under Salieri and his pupil,
Benedict Randhartinger, the intimate friend of Schubert.
That his talent was regarded favourably in the Austrian capital
is perhaps indicated by the fact that he wrote one of the
fifty variations on a waltz by Diabelli (*Der vaterländische
Künstlerverein*) contributed by well-known musicians of the
day and published in Vienna in June, 1823, in aid ·of a charity
when little Franz was not quite twelve.*

His progress in pianoforte playing was astonishing, and
towards the close of 1823, after he had made several strikingly
successful public appearances in Vienna, his patrons sent him
to Paris in the hope that his talents would procure him
admission to the famous Conservatoire. Cherubini, the great
director of the institution, refused, however, to set aside the
rule that excluded young Liszt, as a foreigner, from the

* The anecdote which associates with the production of these fifty
variations the origin of Beethoven's thirty-three variations on a waltz by
Diabelli is too well known to need repetition here.

benefits of its education, and the boy pursued his studies in counterpoint and free composition privately under Reicha and Päer. He took no more pianoforte lessons; and mention of his precocious powers as an executant at this period occurs, as the reader may remember, in Czerny's letter to Wieck, from which we gave quotations in an early chapter of this volume.* *Don Sanché*, an operetta in one act, composed during these Parisian student days, was produced without much success in October, 1825, at the Académie royale. To the same early period belong Liszt's first published pianoforte pieces—some *études*, an allegra di bravura, &c.—but his theoretical studies were neither persevering nor particularly sound, and his productions deserve mention only as having served for the display of his great executive powers. His successes as a pianist throughout several concert journeys of the years 1824 to 1827 were enormous, but the experiences he derived from these tours of the life of the travelling virtuoso made the thought of adopting it permanently repugnant to him. Of an emotional and enthusiastic temperament, he had from childhood felt aspirations for a religious life, and at sixteen was seriously attracted towards the priesthood. The death of his father in 1827, however, imposed upon him new obligations. He sent for his mother and settled down in Paris to support her and himself as a pianoforte teacher.

There is but little to relate of the young musician during the next three or four years. He went through the various phases common to youths of genius: religious doubt, desire of knowledge, love, world-weariness. He practised regularly and played occasionally at private parties or concerts, giving, in 1828, the first Paris performance of Beethoven's E flat concerto, but retained his aversion to public life, and at nineteen was more strongly inclined than ever to the priesthood. In 1831 came a turning-point in his life.

On March 9th of that year Liszt was present in the opera house to hear the first Paris performance of Paganini, whose German tours of the last two or three years had been exciting northern as well as southern audiences to fever heat. We remember the profound impression which the Leipzig

* P. 18.

appearances of this extraordinary man had produced upon the ten-year-old Clara Wieck, adding a new perception, a dim anticipation, a vague ambition to her life. Liszt, brought at twenty under the same influence, was able to realise its meaning more fully. The French romantic movement was gathering force. Hugo's "Hernani" had been produced in 1830 and a group of young men were striving to express, each in his own art language, the motives and enthusiasms that had called the work into being and from which all alike derived their favourite aspirations and dreams: dreams of a picturesque, intense passionate life, with freedom to think and to feel, aspirations to perform great deeds, to work revolutions. Poets and novelists, painters and musicians were alike to be found in it. Gautier had published his first volume of lyrics; Dumas was engaged on "Antony"; Balzac was writing novels in his garret. Delacroix was already known to fame; Berlioz had completed his "Symphonie Fantastique," on the hearing of which, in 1833, Paganini himself, as the story goes, kneeled before him and kissed his hands. Liszt was essentially a child of his time. He was keenly sensitive to the influences of the new romanticism, though he had not as yet become prominently associated with its circles. His own proper medium of expression he was still seeking. He was not satisfied with the results of his superficial studies in composition, and his command of pianoforte technique acquired under the schooling of Czerny meant little to him. Paganini's performance and the feeling of demonic power conveyed by the whole artistic personality of this wizard of the violin took hold of him as nothing had ever done before. It brought to him the revelation of his own appointed means, and he resolved that what Paganini was and did by and through his Stradivarius, that he would become and effect by and through the pianoforte. From this hour dates the interval of his life, still spent in retirement, during which he qualified himself for the full exercise of his extraordinary powers. For some years he devoted many hours daily to the acquirement of a phenomenal mastery of the keyboard, not only as an end in itself, but for the more special purpose of forging a means for the expression of his distinctive temperament, and it was at this period that he succeeded in individualising his fingers to such an astounding degree as to make each one, as it were, a special messenger of the brain, imbued to the very tip with musical intelligence. The moment that brought him within the great awakening influence which determined the main direction of the earlier part of his mature career has its memorial in his transcriptions of Paganini's caprices for violin, of which the first numbers were completed in 1831.

Musical events of scarcely less importance in Liszt's life than the performances of Paganini were Chopin's arrival in Paris in the autumn of 1831 and the return thither of Berlioz in 1833, after three years' study in Rome. The French composer was eight years, the young Polish master less than three years, his senior, and Liszt's rare susceptibility to the manifestation of distinctive artistic genius enabled him to appreciate the startling musical personality, the intellectual vigour, the sensational imagination of the one, no less than the deeply original poetic endowment, the perfected musicianship and mastery of style, of the other. He assimilated into his own artistic nature much of the individuality of both musicians, whose influence is clearly to be traced in the development of some of his characteristics as an executant. Continually attracted by the philosophico-religious and social speculations and experiments of his time, and alternating between varying ideals of life, his literary activity dates from this period, though it was not until a little later that attention was attracted to his articles in the *Gazette Musicale*. He began to be known in Parisian *salons* as the friend of Chopin and a pianist of exceptional qualifications; assisted rather more frequently at the concerts of other artists, taking part in the fantasias for two hands on three, six, or even eight pianofortes that were the fashion of the day, and sometimes played a solo at one of the Habeneck Conservatoire concerts. It was not, however, until the winter of 1834–35 that his career as a virtuoso of phenomenal power may be said to have really commenced.

During this season he gave concerts of his own for the first time for many years, and arranged others in association with Berlioz, achieving success with concertos of Beethoven and works of Chopin and Moscheles, and making an extraordinary sensation by his performance—the first in Paris—of Weber's Concertstück, a composition that remained his favourite *cheval de bataille* for several years.

"Nothing seemed wanting to ensure him a foremost position among the celebrated pianists of his time," says Fétis, alluding to this period. "And yet, in spite of the astonishment caused by his marvellous performances Liszt did not achieve this. Perhaps because he allowed his passionate temperament to lead him into all sorts of exaggerations. . . . Charged with attaching too much importance to mechanism, he tried to show that he was under the influence of fervent inspiration, and one found him treating the works of the most famous composers as mere themes to be altered at will and according to his fancy, whether in respect to character, time, or even the melodic and harmonic construction of their phrases; whilst the public, by applauding his extravagances, probably encouraged them. These youthful errors were frankly acknowledged by Liszt later on. Another cause that for some time helped to limit the acceptance of his talent was his long hesitation as to the ultimate path into which it should be directed, the fact that he relied on his splendid faculty in the execution of the music of others instead of creating works of his own suitable for the display of his peculiar individuality as a performer. It would seem that the young artist at length perceived this to be the case. He retired from Paris and wrote, within a comparatively short space of time, several fantasias and capriccios which may be accepted as representative of his matured natural gifts."

In the autumn of 1835 Thalberg, who had been quietly employed for several years in developing and perfecting his distinctive style, again undertook an extended concert tour, and, appearing in Paris in the course of the ante-Christmas concert season, took its musical public by storm, exciting, on his first appearance at the Conservatoire, immense enthusiasm that increased with each of his subsequent performances. Liszt, who was staying in Geneva at the time, returned to Paris in order to hear him, but only to find that Thalberg had just left. He reimbursed himself for the fatigue and expenses of his journey by giving a soirée in the Salle Erard, which was attended by most of the distinguished amateurs and musicians of the city. The result was, however, disappointing. It was conceded by those who went to listen and compare that perhaps Liszt might be the more powerful of the two virtuosi, and that he alone was worthy to compete with Thalberg. Further than this, however, the *grandes dames* of the fashionable *salons* would not go, and Liszt returned to Geneva to work out his salvation in retirement and the companionship of the Countess d'Agoult (the " Daniel Stern " of romanticist circles), who, penetrated by the ideals of her set, took possession of him whether he would or no, as George Sand took possession a little later of Frédéric Chopin, and insisted on sharing his voluntary exile. Liszt remained in Geneva for a year, busily and variously occupied. The central aim of his activity would seem to have been to provide himself with such an equipment of original fantasias and other productions suitable for the display of his salient characteristics as a virtuoso as might enable him to compete with Thalberg on equal ground, but his diligence was not limited to these efforts. He wrote occasional articles for the press, and it was at this time that he constituted himself the literary champion of the principles of musical art embodied in Berlioz's works, thus laying the foundation of his leadership of what came to be known later on as the revolutionary school, or the Music of the Future.

In December, 1836, Liszt went to Paris to assist at a concert announced by Berlioz for the middle of the month, and, appearing in public for the first time since his soirée in the Salle Erard, played a " Symphonic Fantasia " of his own for pianoforte and orchestra on themes by Berlioz, his *Divertissement*, to which we have referred in our account of Clara's concerts, on Pacini's cavatina, and fragments from his transcription of Berlioz's Symphonie Fantastique—" le Bal," and the " March au Supplice." His triumph was instantaneous and complete. It was, perhaps, the first important public occasion on which he had felt able to assert his full personality, but from this date onwards, given a receptive audience, he exercised the same kind of influence on his hearers as that which, perhaps, Paganini alone of living virtuosi had hitherto had at his command. Instead of returning to Geneva as he had intended, he remained through the winter 1836–37 in Paris, playing frequently to crowded rooms, and the beginning of the year is historically memorable in the musical life of the city, on account of the four concerts given by him in the course of January and February in association with the violinist Urhan, known as a Beethoven worshipper, and the violoncellist Batta. They were arranged with the special object of introducing Beethoven's chamber music for pianoforte and strings, hitherto reserved for private per-formance, to the concert-going public, and the ensemble playing of the three artists was varied with pianoforte solos selected from the works of Weber, Chopin, Moscheles, and Liszt himself. Thus Clara in Berlin and Liszt in Paris were working on different lines in the same month of the same year to a similar end.

A depreciatory article on Thalberg's fantasias which he contributed to the *Gazette Musicale* towards the close of the season drew on Liszt the pronounced hostility of the musical world of Paris, and was discussed in terms of reprobation in German circles, where it was condemned as having been dictated by envy of a favoured rival. Such an interpretation is by no means borne out, however, by perusal of the article, and is contradicted by all that is known either of the public or private life of Liszt. If the desire of competing fairly with Thalberg was strong within him, the unworthy feeling of professional jealousy was foreign to his character, and the worst that can justly be said of him in this matter is that he was unwise to commit himself to any expression of opinion on Thalberg and his productions. The man whose soul had responded to the tones of Paganini and the music of Berlioz, to the writings of Victor Hugo and George Sand, the poems of Byron and the lyrics of Heine and de Musset, could hardly have found much sympathy to bestow on the glittering trills and arpeggios, the scales and octaves of a Thalberg. Nor is it by any means certain that Liszt, in the secret recesses of his mind, appraised his own fantasias and caprices, written as they were for concert production, as mediums for special display, at a much higher value than those of his rival. It is not difficult to perceive from the whole course of his career that what Fétis, writing from the standpoint of the day, regretfully describes as Liszt's early "hesitation as to the ultimate path into which his gifts should be directed," resulted from his perception of an ideal of executive art higher than that to which he had grown up; from a more or less deliberate endeavour to compromise between his instincts as a musician who sympathised intensely with the thoughts of others and his ambition as a virtuoso desirous of attaining unrivalled celebrity. His consciousness of the limit of his creative gifts is indicated to some extent by the fact that his concert répertoire largely consisted of pianoforte transcriptions of the orchestral and vocal works of others, in the making of which he was, and has remained, unrivalled.

In the spring of 1837 Liszt, who was accompanied by the Countess d'Agoult, paid a lengthened visit to George Sand at her country estate, Nohant; the autumn and winter months were passed in Italy in the continued pursuit of his activity as a composer, transcriber, and writer on musical subjects. It was, according to his own account, while staying in the autumn on Lake Como that he received from Schlesinger the packet of music which, making him acquainted with Schumann's genius, impelled him to write the article on the impromptus, and the sonatas Op. 11 and Op. 14, from which we have given a short extract.* The "Dante" fantasia and the "Études d'exécution transcendentales," together with various miscellaneous pianoforte pieces, were

---

* *Ante*, p. 172. Though Liszt writes to Wasielewski ("Robert Schumann," Appendix E) that he had never heard of Schumann before this date, it is established by Jansen ("Die Davidsbündler," p. 224, note 41) that Pixis had shown him the "Abegg" variations in Paris in 1834—a circumstance evidently forgotten by Liszt meanwhile—that Liszt had played them through at sight inimitably, and had expressed himself as being much pleased with them.

composed during this Italian sojourn, to which belong also
many transcriptions, notably the Rossini " Soirées musicales."

By the end of 1837 Liszt was ready to re-enter the arena of
public life and to challenge all competitors for its triumphs.
Not as yet, however, as an interpreter. He had not been
educated, like Clara, to the ideals of a Friedrich Wieck; he had
not passed his youth, as did Joachim later, under the aegis of
Mendelssohn. He had, as we have seen, been taught the
pianoforte by Czerny, had found his inspiration in Paganini,
and, though he had drunk deeply at the pure fount of Chopin's
art, had drawn his breath through the greater part of his life
in the atmosphere created by Victor Hugo. He had taken his
place in Paris as Thalberg's rival and was now to present himself in Italy as the emulator of Paganini, and—as we at this
distance of time may clearly perceive, though perhaps unconsciously to himself—as the representative, in the domain of
executive musical art, of the more sensational aspects of
French romanticism. He announced an " academy " at Milan
in the Scala theatre for December 10th and has described his
feelings when he found himself for the first time in his career
" alone " before the public with his piano, his " faithful
Erard." It was a public which, though not filling the spaces
of the vast building, outnumbered any before which he had
hitherto appeared; a public sensitive to the *bel canto* of the
great singers of the country, to the trivial melodies of Italian
opera, to noisy effects of instrumentation; before which very
few of the great pianists of the day, not Kalkbrenner, nor
Thalberg, nor Moscheles, had cared to test their powers.
Liszt chose for his programme three of his lately composed
fantasias, and records the effect produced in one laconic
sentence : " They were applauded." At a second concert given
in the same building in February, and a third in a more suitable locale in March, he was assisted by other artists. For
these his selections included Hummel's septet; a set of six
concert variations on a march from " Puritani " severally composed for a charity in Paris by Liszt, Thalberg, Pixis, Herz,
Chopin, and again Liszt, and known as the " Hexaméron "; and
an arrangement for four hands on three pianofortes of the
overture to the " Zauberflöte," in the performance of which he

was assisted by his old Paris friends J. P. Pixis and Ferdinand Hiller, the Viennese musician Schoberlechner, now settled in Italy, and two Italian pianists, Arrigi and Pedroni by name. Amongst the concerted performances were interspersed pianoforte solos, but they were little to the taste of the audience. As, at his second concert, the great virtuoso was about to begin one of his lately composed "transcendental" studies, a voice from the stalls called to him, "Vengo al teatro per divertirmi e non per studiare!" "I accepted the forbearance with which they heard me to the end as a proof of their goodwill," adds Liszt, who, however, succeeded in exciting a *furore* at the third concert by improvising on themes chosen by his audience.

In March, 1838, moved by the accounts of the distress in Hungary, he determined that after fulfilling some public engagements in Venice he would go to Vienna, and wrote to Haslinger to arrange two concerts for him there, one for the relief of his suffering compatriots, the other for the defrayment of his expenses. That the presence in the Austrian capital of Clara Wieck, of whose successes he had read, and of whose talent he had heard from Chopin and other artists, may have added weight to the principal motives of his resolve, is to be surmised from a few lines written by Liszt at the beginning of the year to the Leipzig publisher, Haslinger, in which her name is cordially mentioned.*

Liszt left his card on the Wiecks the very day of his arrival in Vienna, April 11th, and his intercourse with them during the remainder of their stay was of the most intimate kind.

"We have heard Liszt," records the diary on the 12th. "He can be compared with no other player, is unique. He startles and astonishes and is a very amiable artist. His appearance at the piano is indescribable—he is original— forgets himself at the instrument. . . . He sets no limits to his passion and not infrequently does violence to one's sense of beauty by torturing the melodies and by too frequent use of the pedal, which must make his compositions still more unintelligible to the laity, though not to connoisseurs. He has a great mind, and one may say of him : 'His art is his life.'

* Printed by Litzmann, i. 198.

" On the 13th Weber's Concertstück played by Liszt. (He began by breaking three copper strings of the Conrad Graf.) Who can describe it? The absence of the bass note did not seem to disturb him; he must be used to it. His movements belong to his playing and suit him well. He attracts one—one forgets one's self also."

" The 14th. Galop for four hands with him. He plays Clara's soirées at sight; and how? If he could restrain his force and his fire, who could come up to him? . . . And where are the pianos that can render the half of what he wishes? " *

Liszt gave his first concert on April 18th with a miscellaneous programme that included orchestral as well as vocal numbers. For his own performance he had selected Weber's Concertstück, which he played on an Erard pianoforte that had been sent to Vienna for Thalberg's use; the " Hexaméron " concert variations (Graf pianoforte); his own " Teufelswalzer " and " Grande Étude " (second instrument by Graf), and he accompanied Beethoven's " Adelaide." The two shorter solos were encored. All three pianofortes were left with broken strings.

" Yesterday we heard Liszt at his concert," writes Wieck to Frau Clementine. " For a pianist it was something never to be forgotten. Although the public only half understood his Puritan Fantasia [the Hexaméron variations], his ' Teufelswalzer " only a quarter, and the so-called " Grande Étude " still less, he achieved the purpose of the concert with Weber's work, which he performed excellently, rather too fast, perhaps, but with extraordinary understanding, originality, and creative energy; and his artistic personality, combined with the highest, most incredible mastery of all possible mechanism, excited tumultuous applause. It was the most remarkable concert of our lives, and will not be without influence on Clara, and that Clara does not copy his many follies and eccentricities, of that an old schoolmaster will take care." †

Schumann, his compositions, and his art tendencies were

---

* Litzmann, i. 199. These records relate to private performances.

† Kohut, 131. Wieck frequently signed his contributions to musical journals or other literary productions with the letters D.A.S. (der alte Schulmeister).

eagerly discussed by Liszt with Clara and her father. His first impression of Robert's genius had been deepened by more intimate acquaintance with the three works reviewed in the *Gazette Musicale*, and he gladly listened to others introduced to him by Clara on the occasions when they made music together informally. He was especially impressed by the Carnaval and the Fantasiestücke, Op. 12, and it is probably to his immediate appreciation of the character and temperament of these compositions that Wieck particularly refers in another paragraph of the letter to his wife from which we have quoted above : —

"Liszt gives another concert on Monday for himself, and wished to give it with Clara, she to play *à quatre mains*, and for two pianofortes with him, *but* we are leaving. We must go, and are satisfied to have become acquainted with this courteous artist. You may imagine how much we have been with him ! He is composing a concertstück for Clara, and is going to dedicate it to her. *The power of musical apprehension of this Liszt really approaches the incredible.*"*

All those, indeed, who were so fortunate as to come in contact with Liszt describe him as having possessed in marvellous measure that gift of sympathetic imagination which is the indispensable attribute of the really great reproductive artist. His ready receptivity for the manifestations of true creative genius is shown remarkably by his early admiration for the works of three such different artistic individualities as Berlioz, Chopin, and Schumann; and though he was ready to court the taste of his time by his choice of solos, and by his whimsicalities of manner, his discrimination was, at bottom, entirely sound. A letter of acknowledgment written at this time to Schumann, who sent him a manuscript (the first novelette) with a few words of thanks for the *Gazette* article, is too interesting and apposite to our subject to be altogether passed over here : —

"... Le Carnaval et les Phantasiestücke m'ont extraordinairement intéressés. Je les joues vraiment avec délices et Dieu sait que je ne puis pas en dire autant de beaucoup de choses. Pour parler franc et net, il n'y a absolument que les

* Kohut, 131.

compositions de Chopin et les vôtres qui soient d'un puissant intérêt pour moi. . . . Vous avouerai-je que je n'ai pas été très emerveillé des études de Henselt et que je les ai trouvé au-dessous de leur réputation ? Je ne sais pas si vous partagez mon opinion, mais cela me paraît très *insouciant* somme tout. C'est joli à entendre, c'est fort joli à regarder, l'effet en est excellent, l'impression (grâce à notre ami Hofmeister) est très soignée ; mais au total je doute que Henselt soit autre chose qu'une médiocrité distinguée. Du reste, il est fort jeune et sans doubte il se développera. Esperons du moins. . . ."*

"He [Liszt] is an artist whom one must hear and see for one's self," writes Clara to Robert. " I am sorry you do not know him, for you would get on well together, you are such a favourite of his. He praises your compositions extraordinarily ; far above Henselt, above everything he knows of the present time. I played him your Carnaval, which quite enchanted him. 'There is a mind,' he said ; 'that is one of the greatest works I know.' You may imagine my delight." †

At his second Vienna concert Liszt performed two movements of his favourite Hummel septet ; his own " Niobe " fantasia (on themes by Pacini), and his lately written transcriptions of Schubert's " Ständchen " and "Lob der Trä-nen." The two transcriptions brought him an ovation, and were constantly called for in the course of the series of concerts, given at 12 o'clock noon, with which he followed up his first successes. The programmes of these performances were selected very much on Liszt's usual lines. For one or two of the earlier ones an orchestra was engaged to provide " Zwischennümmern " or " Ausfullungsnümmern " (*i.e.*, intermediate numbers), but this was dispensed with later on and the pianoforte solos were relieved only by Schubert's songs, accompanied by the concert-giver, or by other vocal contributions.

Among the works played by Liszt were : a Weber concerto, the "Invitation," short solos by Handel and Scarlatti, Moscheles and Chopin ; Czerny's A flat sonata, in compliment to his old master, and several of his own transcriptions : Rossini —Tell Overture, Li Marinari, La Tarantella, La Serenata ;

* " Liszt's Briefe," edited b La Mara.   * Litzmann, i. 198.

Berlioz—Le Ball and the Marche au Supplice from the Symphonie Fantastique.

Of his own fantasias and other pieces his programmes included: "Reminiscences des Huguenots," "Reminiscences de la Juive," "Fantaisie sur une mélodie suisse," "Rondeau fantastique," "Galop chromatique." To these selections, however, were added two works which, incongruous as their inclusion in such lists may appear, give historical value to the programmes apart from such as they may possess as records of the development of virtuosity. Profiting by Clara's example, and by the "enthusiasm for Beethoven's sonatas which she had created," again to quote Hanslick, Liszt now played two or three of these great works—the A flat, Op. 26, and the C sharp minor, Op. 27. From this date the sonatas found their way gradually into the concert répertoire of the virtuoso, whose highest distinction it has become to be accepted as a fine Beethoven player by a public well acquainted with the lofty achievements of musical art.*

Wieck and his daughter left Vienna on April 20th, Clara having received a command the day before to a farewell audience of the Empress. Another extraordinary distinction conferred on the young girl before her departure was that of her unanimous election by the committee of the Gesellschaft der Musikfreunde as an honorary member of the society. She shared the distinction with one other lady, the Grand Duchess of Weimar, and with a few famous musicians of the time.

Wieck had planned concerts in Graz and Munich, but changed his intentions on receiving unfavourable reports from Munich of the prospect of concert-giving at so advanced a period of the year. A week was spent in Graz, where Clara made a successful appearance at the theatre; and a couple of days' break at Vienna of the homeward journey enabled the travellers to hear and make the personal acquaintance of Thalberg, of whom they received a very favourable impression both as artist and colleague.

"The influence of Clara Wieck is already apparent in the domain of pianoforte playing in Vienna," wrote Fischhof to Schumann shortly after their final departure. "She has been

* See *ante*, p. 235.

the first to make the public acquainted with works of the romantic school, the first to include fugues and *études* in her concert programmes, and has even performed a great work of Beethoven, an undertaking scarcely ventured upon hitherto except by the managers of the Concerts spirituels."

(Fischhof is here alluding to the orchestral and choral concerts arranged annually by the Gesellschaft der Musik-freunde and referred to in a previous chapter.*)

" I had the pleasure of becoming acquainted with the young and very interesting pianist Clara Wieck, who made a sensation here [in Vienna] during the past winter," Liszt records in the *Gazette Musicale*. " Her talent delighted me. Complete technical mastery, depth and sincerity of feeling, and unalloyed nobility of aim are her distinguishing characteristics. Her remarkable and very fine rendering of Beethoven's celebrated F minor sonata inspired the famous dramatic poet Grillparzer with a poem in which he celebrates the praises of the charming artist."

So, on May 13th, after a short rest in Dresden, Friedrich Wieck brought back his child, his pupil, his triumph, to her home in Leipzig. Together they had, more than two years ago, presented to Leipzig its Sebastian Bach; together they had now, in one important domain of art, restored to Vienna its Beethoven. What of the future?

* See p. 142.

CHAPTER XVI

1838–1839

Schumann's activity as a composer—" Noveletten "—" Kreisleriana "—
" Kinderscenen "—Clara's homecoming—Schumann in Vienna—Clara
starts for Paris—Difficulties and disappointments.

WE have accompanied Schumann's progress through eight
years of artistic striving—years marked by the production of several of the larger and smaller works that have
made his name famous as a composer for the pianoforte, and
it is not difficult to perceive from his own words that about
the date we have now reached he was himself conscious of
having attained a definite stage in his artistic development.

" I write much more easily, clearly, and I think attractively
now," he says in a letter of February 11, 1838, to Clara in
Vienna. " Altogether I have felt during the last year and a
half as though I had become possessed of the secret. This
may sound strange. There is still much within me. If you
continue true to me it will come out ; if not, it will remain
buried." *

Nor was the composer unconscious of the moral and
spiritual, as distinct from the artistic, development that had
marked his passage from youth to manhood.

" Your father calls me phlegmatic? " he exclaims a few
weeks later—" Carnaval and phlegmatic ! F sharp minor
sonata and phlegmatic ! Love of such a girl and phlegmatic !
And you hear this quietly ? He says I have written nothing
in the *Zeitung* for six weeks. In the first place this is not
true ; secondly, if it were so, he knows how I have worked
in other ways ; and lastly, where am I always to find material?
Up to now I have published about 80 printer's sheets of my

* " Jugendbriefe," p. 274.

own thoughts, to say nothing of editor's labours; have completed ten large compositions in two years—heart's blood has gone to them; have spent several hours daily in severe study of Bach and Beethoven, and made many studies of my own; have attended punctually to a large correspondence which is often difficult and detailed; am a young man of twenty-eight, a hot-blooded artist, and yet have been sitting still in Saxony for nearly eight years; have been careful of my money; spend nothing on entertaining or horses, but continue to take my quiet walk to Goblis; and your father has no acknowledgment for this industry, this simple life, this achievement?

" One would like to preserve one's modesty, but one is really not allowed to do so. I have, therefore, praised myself for once. You know now what you have to expect, and where you are. . . ." *

It is impossible to say that Schumann appraised his own worth, or the value of his growth in the power of self-control, too highly, as we remember what those eight years of un-remitting labour had given to the world. The works which, as he says, had cost him his heart's blood, have become so familiar a possession to us that we can scarcely realise a musical life of which they do not form part, but it is good for us occasionally to call to mind the self-discipline, the power of enthusiastic application, the will to persevere and to hope to the end, which made their ·production possible. The first fruits of the year 1838 are mentioned to Clara in a letter of February 6th :—

" I have composed a shocking amount for you the last three weeks—jests, Egmont stories, family scenes with fathers, a wedding—and called the whole 'Noveletten.' "

It is clear from these words that, as the Davidsbündlertänze resulted immediately from the almost frantic joy experienced by Robert on being restored to certainty of the faithful-ness of his maiden, so in these "longer romantic tales," as he calls the " Noveletten," he has continued the tale of the inexhaustible imaginings suggested to him by his love. His narrative has not fallen on deaf ears. Rich in musical ideas and changing moods, some of the Noveletten—notably the first

* " Jugendbriefe," pp. 287, 288.

in F major and the finely sustained second in D major—have attained a place in the affection of the amateur only second to that occupied by the Phantasiestücke, Op. 12, though their form is less concise than that of these fanciful and popular little tone-poems. They were published in July, 1839, in four books, each of two numbers, with a dedication to Henselt.

"This music within me, and always such fine melodies," Schumann writes again, on April 13th, about two months after completing the Noveletten; "only think, I have finished another entire book of new things since my last letter. . . . I mean to call it 'Kreisleriana,' in which you and the thought of you play the chief rôle. . . . My music strikes me as so coherent now with all its simplicity. It seems to speak to the heart, and it affects those to whom I play it—as I often do now—in the same way." *

Of the "Kreisleriana," the title of which was chosen in remembrance of one of Hoffmann's tales, Wasielewski says: "As in Hoffmann's literary production the sufferings of Kapellmeister Kreisler, behind whom the poet conceals his own personality, are described in words, so here Schumann gives voice in glorious tone language to the various emotions of love that vibrated within his soul. . . . And he does it with the full power of his genius. In no other pianoforte work does he reveal such a rich world of feeling, such intense poetic concentration and refined penetration; nowhere is he more truly a tone poet in the literal meaning of the word than here." †

"Play my Kreisleriana often. A positively wild love is in some of the movements and your life and mine, and many of your looks," writes Robert to Clara.

To the same fruitful period—the first four months of 1838—belong the exquisitely finished "Kinderscenen," described by the composer as reflections on the past by an adult for adults. Contrasting in mood with all Schumann's previous works, these beautiful miniatures are, nevertheless, to be associated in a certain sense with the source from which so many of his previous inspirations had been derived. They owe their existence, as their several titles—"Am Kamin," "Fürchten-

* "Jugendbriefe," p. 280.   † Wasielewski, 220, 221.

machen," "Haschemann," "Kuriose Geschichte," &c.—would suggest, to Schumann's memories of the year 1830, when, as a youth of twenty and a member of the Wieck household, he had been accustomed to amuse himself in the twilight hours with Clara and her brothers, frightening and delighting them alternately with ghost stories, games, and conundrums. The Kinderscenen were published by Breitkopf and Härtel early in 1839 as Op. 15.

We cannot be surprised to learn that Clara's homecoming after her seven months' Austrian tour acted unfavourably on Schumann's work as a composer. Wieck gave his daughter free permission to meet her old friend on terms of artistic companionship and even took the trouble to call on Schumann to invite him to his house. But while he discussed every other imaginable topic of mutual interest with the young musician, he carefully avoided all reference to the subject of Robert's suit ; and this pretence of disposing of the real question at issue by the simple process of ignoring it could not be accepted by the lovers, who found no immediate opportunity for a private interview. As the days passed on, indeed, the combined sense of nearness to Clara and of separation from her which had caused Schumann acute distress in the spring of 1836 again pressed upon him so absorbingly as almost to paralyse his creative energy, and Clara suffered with him. Some measure had to be adopted as speedily as possible to restore partial tranquillity of mind to both, and the only means available to procure it seemed to be that of actual bodily distance. There had been times during her long absence in Vienna when Clara had fancied she perceived signs that her father, once convinced of the soundness of Robert's prospects, would yield to her wishes and intentions in the matter of her future marriage :—

". . . . I talked about you to father a long while to-day," she had written in March; "and he told me he intended to be quite friendly with you on our return ; you should be on the old, intimate footing in our house. . . . He had written to you secretly from Dresden that he would *never* give his consent in *Leipzig*, but he would certainly do so if we would move to another large town, and I have promised him *never* to remain in Leipzig, though I have also said I could never love any one but you. He gave his consent and wrote it in my diary. . . .

"Remember, dear Robert, I can earn nothing in Leipzig by my art and you would have to work yourself to death to gain what we require. And for my sake? This I could not endure. No, let us arrange as I will tell you. We will move here, or you shall go first, give your paper to Diabelli, Haslinger (a very good house), or Mechetti, a young man of vigour and enterprise. In the first place, your work will be twice as well remunerated here; in the second, you will be much more widely recognised and esteemed than in Leipzig, and thirdly, living is pleasant and inexpensive here; of course considering the size of the town and what beautiful surroundings! Then I, too, am thought of much more here than in Leipzig. . . . I could give a concert every winter which, with the high prices usual here, would bring me in a thousand thalers. Then I can and will give a lesson every day that would bring me in, through the year, another thousand thalers and you have a thousand; what more do we want? . . . Do not imagine I have exaggerated. Father expounded to me all that I have written for an hour to-day. He even said : 'If Schumann does not care to be long without you in Vienna I will do this for him; I will go to Vienna with you.' You see by this that father is kind, so do not be cold to him; he wishes us well.

"He probably sees that I can never give my heart to another, and to bestow my hand without my heart—a father like mine does not do that." *

Robert had greeted the proposal with rapture :—

---

* Litzmann, 187 and 188. Litzmann adds that Wieck based his objection to Leipzig on the ground that his daughter would find it unendurable to live there as Schumann's wife in the intimacy of Mendelssohn and David, each of whom was in a position to maintain a large establishment. His entry in the diary of which Clara tells Robert was as follows: "March 3. Morning. Talked to Clara about Schu. : that I will *never* give my consent for Leipzig, and Clara entirely agrees with me and will *never* change her views. Schumann may manœuvre, philosophise, rave, idealise, as he likes; it is settled that Clara can never live in poverty and obscurity—but must have over two thousand thalers a year to spend."

" How can I even attempt to tell you what you are making of me, you love, you glorious girl ! Your letter has raised me from joy to joy. What a life, what prospects you hold before me ! As I read your letter again and again I feel as the first man must have felt when his angel led him from height to height through the fresh young creation and, as each beautiful region disappeared behind another still more lovely, said : ' All this shall be yours. . . .'

" Your hand then ; it is decided. I have considered it well. My most ardent wish, our object—Vienna. We shall leave something behind. . . . Evening and morning bells will unite their sounds when we go away together, but the morning bells will be the finest—and then you will be resting on my most happy heart—*it is decided, we go !* . . ." *

It is difficult to judge as to how far Wieck had been sincere in allowing Clara to build hopes on what he probably regarded as the remote contingency that Robert would be persuaded to think of leaving the town in which he had, by sheer intellectual energy and determined perseverance, made himself the acknowledged centre of a sphere of activity not as yet, perhaps, very prominent, but steadily advancing into recognition. He understood far better than Clara could be expected to do what such an uprooting must mean for the composer, who attached great value to his independent and growing position in Leipzig, and to the distinguished friend-ships and connections afforded him by his residence there ; and for whom, for the successful prosecution of his creative genius, peace of mind and possession of his time were primary essentials. It seems on the whole probable that whilst her father was easily able to convince Clara of the fallaciousness of Robert's visions of love in a Leipzig cottage, intensified by sympathetic artistic fellowship and facilitated by occasional treasure-gathering journeys to Paris and London, he merely hoped to gain time by suggesting for her contemplation the favourable results that might follow Schumann's permanent removal to Vienna ; and time in his view and that of his wife could not fail to bring him victory.

Certain primary convictions of Schumann's mind, which

* Litzmann, i. 192.

ultimately ruled his action in this as in other matters, stand out clearly, however, through the facts of his life and the details of his correspondence. He was aware of the impulses within himself of an original genius striving for expression, for the full fructification of which his absolute communion with, his possession of, another soul was essential. He had found this other soul, this second self, in Clara, and would strive to accomplish any present sacrifice that might be demanded of him in order to gain his own, to fulfil his nature, to become an entire man. He had received Clara's solemn pledge that she would not delay her coming to him indefinitely. For three years from the date of their betrothal in August, 1837, she would keep her word to live yet a while for the world and for art. But she had promised to become Schumann's wife in 1840, when she would reach the age of twenty-one, with or without her father's consent; and Robert, moved now by the misery of his present relations with her family to take prompt and energetic steps for his journey to Vienna, was, no doubt, strengthened in his resolve by his confidence in Wieck's judgment in business matters and his hope that when the longed-for time should have arrived he might have arranged a home and a future for his bride that would compel the father's blessing on the union. For he had not forgotten what he owed to Wieck :—

"If it were only possible," he writes, "to gain the affection and confidence of your father, to whom I am indebted for so many of the pleasures of my life ; for teaching—and also for suffering—and whom I would gladly make happy in his old age, so that he should say : They are good children. If he knew me better he would have spared me many a pang, would never have written me a letter which has aged me by two years. Well, it is forgiven ; he is *your* father, has brought you up to the noblest ideals, wishes to weigh well the happiness of your future, to know you sure of the same happiness and security that you have enjoyed under his protection—I cannot reckon with him—he desires the best on earth for you. . . ." *

In spite of the vigilance with which Frau Clementine

* " Jugendbriefe," p. 275.

guarded her stepdaughter's footsteps the lovers found numerous opportunities during the weeks of early summer of discussing their plans by word of mouth. Immediate departure, however strongly he might desire it, was out of the question for Robert. He was bound before risking his future on so serious an undertaking as that of changing the locale of his paper to satisfy himself as to the chances of support likely to be extended to him in the Austrian capital, and, on the other hand, to make efficient arrangements for the conduct and continued prosperity of the *Neue Zeitschrift* during his absence. These necessities involved detailed correspondence and a considerable period of painful uncertainty that might have tried the fortitude of a more practical business man and one less engrossed in the pursuit of ideal ends than the imaginative and sensitive composer. The long interval of waiting till a decision could be formed was lightened to Clara by her acquisition of a new and congenial girl-friendship. Pauline Garcia came to Leipzig with her mother and brother-in-law, the violinist de Bériot, towards the end of May, in the course of her first professional tour, and an intimacy was formed between the two young artists, the pianist and the singer, who, nearly of the same age, were animated by similar serious ideals of art, that remained a source of satisfaction to both till the end of Clara's life. In Pauline's society Clara found some relief from the irritation to which her feelings were constantly exposed, not only at home in Leipzig, but during a few weeks passed by both girls in Dresden during July and August of the year. Wieck was becoming seriously alarmed at this time by the practical energy of resolution displayed by Robert, and was awakening to the possible consequences of his own opposition to his daughter's choice. His growing apprehension that his will might be impotent to decide the final issue of the matter in question was, however, very far from moving him to yield an inch of ground to the lovers. From about this date, indeed, the very nature of Friedrich Wieck seems to have undergone a change for the worse. The element of hardness in his nature began to crystallise into cruelty; his stubborn refusal to perceive any desirable possibilities in Schumann's suit to become tinged with the desire of revenging himself on the man who had possessed himself so firmly of Clara's love; his fondness for his child to merge in the desire to make good his claim to be the tyrannous arbiter of her destiny.

"Already," says Clara in a letter from Dresden of July 8th, "I sometimes have the terrible thought that I no longer love father as I ought, but must it not arouse bitter feelings, must it not be most deeply wounding, to hear one's dearest, to hear my Robert (is it possible?) spoken of slightingly, misjudged, laughed at? Dear Robert, I have received a letter from father, the first here, that has hurt me so; it has preyed on me for days and I cannot forget it. Think how much worse it would be if father knew everything. But when the time comes rely on me! *I shall follow you to Vienna.* The parting with father will be hard. I shall encounter many difficulties, *but love will give me strength for everything.* . . . God in heaven will pardon me—it is only love! . . .

"Father believes and hopes that Ernestine will intervene. Father will use his best persuasion to induce her to do so. This worries me fearfully, the thought almost turns my brain. Pray write to me about it *openly.* . . ."

"*You have a strong girl in me!* . . ." she writes a few weeks later. "May this thought accompany you to Vienna. . . . Whether I am in Holland, or Paris, or London, believe always that your girl is near you. No triumphs will make me forget you for an instant. If all the lords in London and all the cavaliers in Paris were at my feet I would leave them and hasten to the simple artist, the dear, glorious man, to lay my heart at his feet. . . ." *

The question of the objective of Clara's annual concert tour had been left open longer than usual this year. Wieck proposed Munich and Holland for the season 1838–39, but Clara's experiences in Berlin and Vienna had given her a taste for the triumphs of larger centres. For years accustomed to travelling, she looked forward with pleasure to the change and excitements of her winter campaigns, in spite of their fatigues and anxieties, and longing with the eagerness of youth to try her powers in the two great cities of the world, she laid stress on

* Litzmann, i. 218, 222.

her desire to go to Paris and London.   Clara, dreaming, in the fresh springtide of her powers, of many events to come, little dreamed of the circumstances under which, eighteen years later, her first victories were to be won in the vast, thronged capital of Britain, the London in which, at a still more distant period, she was to become a familiar and beloved personality.

Clara opened her season on September 8th by giving a concert in the Gewandhaus, and included in her programme three of Liszt's recently published Schubert transcriptions: "Ave Maria," "Lob der Tränen," and "Erlkönig." That the applause was tumultuous and the demand for a repetition of the "Erlkönig" irresistible signifies more than is implied in the mere record of these facts.   The Gewandhaus public, educated as no other in the world to the appreciation of musical art, accustomed to almost perfect performances of the greatest works, pluming itself on the possession of Mendelssohn and David, had become spoilt and critical.   It seldom greeted the appearance of an artist on the platform with any sign of recognition, and was accustomed to reserve special tokens of approval of an accomplished performance for illustrious strangers visiting Leipzig on tour.   The fact that Clara was a Leipziger born and bred had not contributed to the recognition she had gained in her native town after the interest excited by her child appearances had been forgotten, and the warmth of the reception on this as on the last occasion of her Gewandhaus performances must be accepted as a tribute not only to her maturing musical powers, but also to her rapidly advancing position as an eminent personage in the world of art.   Whether Robert, who placed himself in a dark corner to gaze at her unobserved and undisturbed, and who wrote to her the next day that she had played "gloriously," felt undivided satisfaction in her triumph is not quite clear.   Being a mere man, it is to be feared that he allowed himself to be discomposed by the consciousness that others beside himself were there who were also privileged to gaze at and admire her!

"I thought: It is certainly a great happiness to call such a girl one's own, but Heaven grant that we may not be dependent on those who only listen to you in order to *be obliged* to praise you.   In a word, you are too dear, too high, for the life which your father regards as the goal, the greatest happiness. What pains, what labour, what days, for a couple of hours! And you are to endure it indefinitely and to accept it as the object of your existence. No; my Clara shall be a happy wife, a contented, beloved wife. I hold your art as something great and sacred—I hardly dare think of the joy you will give me by its means. . . . You will not misunderstand me, will you? You regard me as an artist who hopes to be able to preserve you for art without the necessity of making great concert journeys? Yes, you will find in me a true music-man to whom it is all one whether you play a little too fast or too slow, or a few shades more delicately if it only streams forth from within, and with you this is so. . . ." *

The performances were characterised in the *Neue Zeitschrift* of September 18th as " the most subtly and fragrantly romantic that we have heard for a long time, and, in virtuosity, faultlessly perfect "; and the occasion was commemorated in the issue of the 21st by a charming poem signed "A. L.," but in reality, like the review, from Robert's pen.

The farewell interview between the lovers was over. Robert's leap into the mystery of the future, carefully planned, had been resolutely taken, and the first two stages of his journey accomplished. What wonder that the young composer, after passing eight of the best years of his life in the confinement of Leipzig lodgings, felt as he wandered on the last day of September through the streets of ancient Prague with its hundred towers and mountain distances, its old memories, its unfamiliar faces, as though the very stars of heaven shone with a new light and the flowers of earth breathed with a fresh fragrance for him! If only he could have had his beloved, his bride, at his side, he might for the moment veritably have imagined himself a soul new-born in Paradise. And yet, in spite of the courage and resolution and sense of relief animating his letter to Clara of October 1st, there is in it an undertone which tells us that he had not exaggerated the truth in declaring that Wieck's hostility had aged him by two years— a tone which tells that something of his youth had, indeed, gone from him.

* Litzmann, i. 230.

For the devoted maiden left behind with her grief matters were rapidly approaching a final crisis. A "terrible" letter from her father, absent on business in Dresden, was answered in a spirit of courageous forbearance astonishing in a high-spirited girl who had just completed her nineteenth year. Clara frankly informed Wieck of her plans for the future and expressed her conviction that she should find strength to carry them into effect. Her communication was accepted as a challenge to open warfare, and the first act of the angry father after receiving it was to send Fräulein von Fricken his own request for a formal document of release for Schumann from his engagement to her. That Wieck, who had never been definitely informed of the end of Robert's former love-affair, addressed himself to Ernestine in the hope that she would claim the fulfilment of what he imagined to be an unretracted promise is certain, and his disappointment was unquestionably great when he received the prompt reply in which Ernestine disclaimed all right to interference in Schumann's affairs and added that she was herself shortly to be married.

"How is my good Clara?" continues the letter. "I have read a great deal about her in the newspapers, which, as you may be sure, has given me and my parents much pleasure. Clara will never be happy without Schumann. She told me so, for she loves him unspeakably." *

Foiled by Ernestine's unexpected indifference as by Robert's unwelcome energy, Wieck, finding himself without other vent for his wrath, began to concentrate his ingenuity on devising means for the petty persecution of his child which might, as he hoped, by wearing out her patience, bring her at length to accept his reasoning as to the matter in dispute between them. Her health, her feelings, her self-respect, were alike unconsidered by him. Clara at nineteen, the glory of her father's house, the recognised colleague of the great artists of the day, the favourite of the imperial court, was made to empty out her pockets before her stepmother after a visit paid to the Wiecks by a certain Dr. Reuter, who was suspected—rightly indeed—

---

* Ernestine's letter is printed in full by Kohut, but with the erroneous date 1836 (pp. 104, 105).

of being the intermediary of a secret correspondence between herself and Robert. No journeys were to be undertaken, no concerts given, during the season ; she was to dismiss her old attendant Nanny ; to engage to hand over to her own mother in Berlin from the day of her marriage the whole of the small interest derived from the savings of her artistic labour—she who had hitherto been prevented from the exercise of occasional generosity to Frau Bargiel by her father's express commands. Roseate prospects of life were held out before her on the other hand if she would consent to renounce her love. But : " To leave you, to live without you—I have no power to do that. My hand is trembling so that I can scarcely hold the pen." Her most welcome distraction was found in the Sunday evening music that took place this autumn at Mendelssohn's, David's, and her father's house alternately. It was only to be expected, however, that her troubles should affect her art, and we find her regretting that she is playing with less mastery and certainty than usual : " I know it, and yet cannot help it." The resolution was at this time forming within her to get away from the intolerable conditions of her present life at home and to venture on what might have seemed the impossible : to undertake her concert journey, though somewhat later than usual, if not under her father's protection, then without it. There was, however, some one besides Clara who felt, and perhaps as strongly as she, the deprivation of the accustomed round of excitements and successes—Friedrich Wieck himself. Apart from the loss of such small income as he had for some years derived from his appointed share of the profits of the annual tour, he severely missed the gratification he had been used to experience on seeing his child the centre of a crowd of enthusiastic admirers, on being able to note the beauty of her performances and to read her praises in the newspapers. He suddenly resolved that she should appear in Dresden in the course of November, give a concert later on in Munich, possibly proceed thence to Paris, and finally to London, the goal of Clara's wishes.

Meanwhile Schumann's experiences in Vienna were bringing him no nearer to the fulfilment of his dreams. The feasibility of transferring from North to South Germany a literary activity such as his, which was not official, but depended for its success upon his personal exertions and connections, would have been questionable under any circumstances. In the conditions which prevailed in Austria in the thirties, however, the strictness of the censorship, the difficulties surrounding the conduct of newspapers, the prevailing jealousy of the outsider, the undertaking would seem to have been, from the first, hopeless. Yet Schumann did not immediately give up all hope. Whilst he tried to come to terms with one publisher after another, he submitted with all the patience he could summon to the endless delays occasioned by the necessary interchange of communications with the bureaucracy of the official-ridden city. Quietly observant of the conditions which might make for or against the choice of Vienna as a suitable home for Clara and himself, he was struck, as Wieck had been, by the absence of an influential centre of musical life such as had been provided in Leipzig for more than half a century by the annually recurring subscription performances of the "Grand Concert." He saw clearly the opportunity that might be open to a leader of genius with sufficient practical energy to override the prejudices of côteries and weld the scattered artistic force of the imperial capital into an organisation effectual for public advancement, but he knew his own gifts did not qualify him for success in that direction, and avoided the mistake towards which many men in his position might have been tempted, of imagining that he in Vienna might one day be able to emulate the activity of Mendelssohn in Leipzig. He was attracted by the natural musicality of the Austrians, liked, if he somewhat mistrusted, their agreeable manners, enjoyed the beautiful surroundings of their ancient capital, but, as the weeks went by, became increasingly sensible of the superficiality, the provincialism, of their views of art, and missed more and more sensibly the vigorous pulsation, the freer atmosphere, the higher culture, of the musical life of Leipzig. Of the numerous musicians with whom he came in contact he seems to have preferred the society of Lipinski and Thalberg, for both of whom he conceived a feeling of hearty esteem.

In his letters from Clara, Schumann found a source of mingled joy and disquiet. His sense of bliss in the certainty of her love and the assurance of her spiritual strength ; his intense sympathy with her trials ; his impatient longing to call her his own, alternated and combined within him till his feelings sometimes seemed almost beyond his power of endurance. Tender, indeed, were the letters of counsel and appeal that he wrote to her at this period. His advice to her was to take her life into her own hands, to follow her own counsel in her emergency, and he would gladly have known her settled for a time under the protection of his sister-in-law Therese. When he heard, however, at the beginning of the New Year that Wieck had again suddenly changed his plans and that Clara was about to start on the distant journey to Paris without her father's protection, without the solace of Nanny's attendance, alone in the company of a stranger, a Frenchwoman, then, indeed, his heart was shaken with foreboding and worship, for he knew that his fearless maiden was about to enter a pathway strewn with thorns and that she had chosen to enter it for his sake. " I have packed up your compositions, Toccata, Phantasiestücke, &c.," wrote Clara on January 7, 1839, the evening before her start ; " it cost me some battle, but I said, ' *I will!* ' "

There is no doubt that, apart from the natural desire of a lively and ambitious young artist, whose career had hitherto been one of constantly advancing success, to see the great cities of the world, and to test her powers against those of her contemporaries in one after the other of the most formidable arenas of competition, the main considerations which induced Clara's persistent desire to visit Paris and London during the season 1838–39 are to be found in her expectation of being able to return with a sum of money that should contribute substantially towards the expenses of the first year of marriage, and her hope that she might found an artistic reputation in the two most wealthy European centres that would provide a valuable pecuniary resource for her future life as Schumann's wife. Nor can there be any question that Wieck, who alleged business obligations as his excuse for not accompanying her, was really kept behind by his jealous divination of her purposes and his desire to frustrate them as completely as possible. No one could have been more thoroughly aware than he of the fatiguing details, little consonant with the concentrated mental energy necessary to ensure artistic success, in which his daughter would find herself plunged at the very outset of her undertaking ; the visits to be made and received, the business to be arranged to ensure the prosperous issue of each concert she might announce, to say nothing of the exhaustion and vexations inseparable from a long carriage journey of several stages with a stranger and a foreigner as her sole protector. That her difficulties would prove too great to be overcome even by her resolute spirit, and that they would bring her to the abandonment of her tour or to a temporary surrender to his will, was, certainly, not less hoped than anticipated by him. But Clara was, as we know, "a well-armed girl."

Trials of various kinds awaited the young artist at Nüremberg, Stuttgart, and Carlsruhe, where she gave concerts of her own or played at court. Her courage was painfully tried by the fact that she received no tidings either from Leipzig or Vienna for some little time after her departure. Robert's letters were sent direct to Paris, where they were detained in the post-office for several weeks, whilst Wieck let his daughter severely alone for a fortnight and wrote at length only to reproach and complain, and to withdraw the hope he had held out that he might join her in Paris. Clara was provided with safeguards, however, in her artistic eminence, her force of character, and her candid, unsuspicious nature. After overcoming such difficulties as she had been prepared to encounter, and passing unharmed through others of which she was not at the time even aware, she reached Paris on February 6th, with her French companion and a young girl, Henriette Reichmann, whom she had accepted in Stuttgart as a pupil. The profits of her German concerts had furnished her with the wherewithal to meet the first expenses of her sojourn in the great city and she hoped that no long time would elapse before she should be able actively to pursue the main object of her visit and turn her gifts to advantageous account. Some of her particular friends were fortunately resident in

Paris at this time, and she was able, two days after her arrival, to send Robert the reassuring tidings that she was moving into private lodgings in a house where Pauline Garcia was staying with her mother.   We find her immediately confronted with the difficult professional question which has presented itself through more than a hundred years to every pianist proposing to appear before the public of a strange capital—the question of the choice of an instrument.   It has an intimate connection with the artistic individuality of the performer, and yet cannot be solved on purely artistic or personal grounds, complicated as it is by prudential considerations.

"I have an Erard in my room, the keys of which are scarcely movable," she writes on February 14th.   "I had lost all courage; but yesterday I played on a Pleyel, and these are not so hard.   I shall have to practise for three weeks longer before I can play a note to any one.   I have already had three great instruments offered me for my room.   Each maker is anxious that I should use his.   If I only knew how it were possible to use Pleyel without offending Erard, who shows me every imaginable attention. . . ." *

How sorely Clara missed her father's counsel and experience when faced by this and other difficulties of her position needs not to be insisted on.   "I have written to ask Frau von Berg † if she cannot come, for it is impossible for me to go to any parties without being chaperoned by a lady of position.   Probst and Fechner [two of Wieck's friends] angered me on two following days by trying to persuade me to go back.   Am I to have come to Paris for nothing?   Father would give something to have me back again, but I shall not go.   Perhaps I shall remain here all the summer and give lessons, and go and live with the Lists."

And this, the best solution of her difficulties that could have been thought of, was the one she ultimately adopted.   The father of her friend Emilie had, not long before this date, been promoted from his consular appointment in Leipzig to a position in Paris, and by the end of March Clara had dis-

* Litzmann, i. 286.
† A Dresden friend, whom Clara was in the habit of playfully addressin as "mama."

missed the obnoxious French lady, and come to an arrangement by which she and her pupil Henriette took up their abode with her American friends for the remainder of the season.

The subject of her *début* before the public of Paris cost her much anxious thought. It was late in the season to find a favourable opportunity for her appearance, and she was now and then not far from experiencing something of the feeling with which Chopin had written in the late autumn of 1831 : "One may be amused or dull in Paris, may laugh or weep, may, indeed, do as one will. No one observes it, for thousands are doing the same."* She attended many concerts, but heard little that attracted her sympathy, while she was not invariably treated by her French colleagues with the respect due to her position as a German artist. A meeting with Berlioz, whom she describes as a quiet man with very thick hair and eyes continually cast down, who talked much of Robert, was naturally of interest to her ; and it may be taken as a marked indication of the advancing reputation of Robert's art that Kalkbrenner requested her to play him a selection of Schumann's compositions, adding that he had heard no one could do them so much justice as herself. The two musicians who would have greeted her with especial warmth as a friend and colleague were absent from Paris. Liszt was still in Italy with the Countess d'Agoult, delivering himself of innumerable concert pieces wherewith to astonish the world, and making occasional concert journeys. Chopin was lying ill at Marseilles, scarcely yet secure from the menace of death to which his winter sojourn at Majorca under the guardianship of George Sand had exposed him. The twenty-four "Preludes" costly memorial of the baleful visit, had just been published, and of them Schumann wrote a little later in his periodical : "I had expected to find them developed in large form like his studies, but the contrary is the case. They are sketches, commencements of studies, or, if one may say so, ruins ; some of them eagle-flights, all variegated and wild and placed together without arrangement. But in every one of the pieces may be read in his diamond type : 'Frédéric Chopin wrote it.'

* See *ante*, p. 69.

He is, and remains, the boldest, proudest poet spirit of the time. . . ."

Perhaps the thought may not have been far from Schumann's mind, as he penned these words, that life, which had prepared for him many a bitter struggle, had, after all, been kinder to him than to his Polish colleague. What if he had risked his happiness on a Marie Wodzińska? Is it not conceivable that a George Sand might have waited on the hour of his desolation to lure his spirit to its destruction? What though Schumann was haunted by the fear that Clara's irrepressible pangs of tenderness for her father might at last delay her promised coming to him at Easter, 1840? What though, as the longed-for time drew nearer, whilst he was penetrating ever further and deeper and with increasing confidence and joy into the secrets of his art, he began to realise the possibilities of friction that might lie in the home-life of two impulsive, strong-willed natures each worshipping the other? to foresee the difficulties that might confront the composer of genius requiring quietude above all other essentials, and the pianist of genius faced by the alternatives of practising or losing her art, who should live together as man and wife? What if Schumann would have desired in his heart of hearts that Clara should lay down the glory of her career at the hour of its morning brightness, exchange the laurel wreath for the metaphorical "housewife's cap," * and live, at all events for a time, only as his adored wife and companion and the mistress of his modest establishment? The passing storms that occasionally disturbed the happiness derived by the lovers from their constant correspondence were the inevitable outcome of the absolute confidence existing between them. They told each other all their hopes and fears, and Robert was conscious with every nerve of his being that his love and life and art were safe in Clara's keeping; that she would guard them securely, even, if need be, at the sacrifice of claims only less sacred to her than that of her plighted troth.

* The German expression " Unter die Haube kommen " (" to assume the cap ") to which Schumann playfully alludes in his letters to Clara signifies : to be married.

Was it the presentiment of such dangers to his daughter's future tranquillity and of others that might reasonably be feared that hardened Wieck's heart to implacability in his hostility to Clara's choice? that inflamed him to a furious hatred of her lover which seemed at length to border on insanity? The idea of her marriage was not, as it would seem, absolutely repugnant to him. Clara had had numerous admirers, and more than one suitor—not in every case of particularly brilliant position in the world—had been encouraged by her father to perseverance since Carl Banck's flight from Leipzig.

CHAPTER XVII

1839

Works composed by Schumann during his residence in Vienna—His brother
Edward's death—His return to Leipzig—Clara in Paris—A stormcloud
and its dispersal—The final turning-point of Clara's girlhood—Publication of Schumann's Fantasia, Op. 17—Clara leaves Paris.

THAT the serious interruption of his accustomed routine
of life, the excitement of his new experiences, the
harassing uncertainties that attended his efforts to arrange
for the transfer of the *Neue Zeitschrift*, to say nothing of
his anxiety on Clara's behalf, should have had the effect
of temporarily crippling Schumann's creative activity was
inevitable. Yet it was not entirely suspended even during
the first two months of his stay in Vienna. He devoted spare
half-hours to dreaming and improvising at the piano, producing some of the short works which appeared later on
in the "Bunte Blätter," Op. 99, the Albumblätter, Op. 124,
and other collections of short pieces. The last movement
of the G minor sonata, Op. 22, to which we shall return later,
belongs to this period; and in the course of December and
beginning of January, 1839, he wrote the Scherzo, Gigue, and
Romanze of Op. 32, the romance being one of his finest
inspirations for the pianoforte in song form, to which the
Fughette was afterwards added. The bright melodious
"Arabesque," Op. 18, and the Blumenstück, Op. 19, the
latter described by the composer as "variations, but not on
any theme," and dedicated to the Majorin von Serre, were
completed in January.*

---

* A glance at the two works, Opp. 18 and 19, is sufficient to show that
Wasielewski has made a slip in applying Schumann's above quoted words,
which occur in a letter of January 24, 1839, to the Arabesque. The com-

With the completion of these slighter pieces, the tide of Schumann's inspiration was set swiftly flowing again, and on March 11th he was able to tell Clara :—

"I have been sitting at the piano the whole week, composing and writing, laughing and weeping, all at once. You will find this pictured in my Opus 20, the great Humoresque, which is already being engraved. See how quickly things go on now. Imagined, copied, and printed. That is what I like. Twelve pages written out in eight days." *

There can be little doubt that in choosing the title of this work, which he describes later on as "rather melancholy than otherwise," Schumann used the word "humour," not in its ordinary narrow sense, as meaning a particular form of wit, but in that larger signification in which it may be applied to the romances of his favourite authors, Jean Paul and E. T. A. Hoffmann—as the expression of his sense of the combined irony and earnestness of life, of its mingled laughter and tears. His own mind was peculiarly liable, under the stress of the circumstances in which he was placed, to be swayed by "humour" of this kind, and, as usual, sought and found its relief in music. Nevertheless the Opus 20, which is interesting from its changing emotional characteristics—its bright, concise moments and its subtle Schumannesque pathos, suggestive at once of heaven and earth, of delight and pain—bears, in its looseness of construction, especial traces of the method of its composition—improvisation at the pianoforte—and cannot be placed as a work of art by the side of the composer's best previous productions. Probably Schumann was not himself entirely satisfied with it after the first fever heat of composition had passed away. Writing on March 15th to Simonin de Sire, to whom the Humoresque is dedicated, he says :—

"I have met with little sympathy here. An artist cannot fail, however, to derive stimulus and benefit from the city

poser's description of the originally so-called "Guirlande" as "variations" unquestionably indicates the Blumenstück, for which the first-chosen title would perhaps have been more appropriate than that under which it was published.
* "Jugendbriefe," p. 299.

of Vienna, and I have written a good deal, though not of my best."

The overstrain to which the young musician's nerves were at this time subjected is more definitely felt in the " Nacht-stücke," Opus 23, the composition which immediately followed the "Humoresque." His imagination was haunted, as he wrote it, by the grimmest of visions : processions of corpses, coffins, despairing human souls; and its general character, or at all events that of its first two numbers, is not inadequately suggested by the weird title "Leichenphantasie" ("Corpse fantasia") which originally suggested itself to him as appropriate for the work. It consists of a series of tone-pictures kept in low, sombre colour, the first of which, though unillumined by the faintest gleam of passion, makes distinct appeal to the performer—though hardly, perhaps, to the listener—by its sad, intimate, fatalistic vein; whilst the second seems inspired solely by a spirit of grim mockery. From these morbid conceptions the third number offers some relief, and in the fourth, a short movement in march rhythm with a fine opening subject, Schumann is almost himself again. Superscriptions which the composer had some idea of adding to the several numbers were as follows :   Funeral procession ; Strange company ; Night banquet ; Round with solo voices.*

It happened strangely enough that before he had completed this work Schumann was shattered by tidings, which reached him on March 30th, of the sudden and hopeless illness of his brother Edward, to whom he was bound by ties of the warmest affection, and we can hardly be surprised that he should have seen, in the disturbed imagination to which he had been a prey, the premonition of the calamity that was about to befall him.   Having at this time relinquished all hope of being able to carry out the purpose that had brought him to Vienna, he now started on his homeward journey, filled with forebodings as to the news that might await his arrival in Leipzig.   His trouble was aggravated by anxiety as to what might prove to be the condition of his brother's bookselling business, in which, as it would seem, part of the capital he had inherited

* Trauerzug; Kuriose Gesellschaft; Nächtliches Gelage; Rundgesang mit Solostimmen.

under his father's will had remained invested. The apprehension that a fresh obstacle might intervene to delay the fulfilment of his ardent desire for union with his beloved was too overwhelming to be kept within his own breast, and the letters that reached Clara in Paris were well calculated to shake her belief in the wisdom of adhering, under every conceivable circumstance, to the date agreed upon for the marriage. These things led to an important turning-point in the history of the lovers.

On April 16, the very day on which her long-delayed Paris concert at last took place, Clara received the announcement of Edward Schumann's death in a letter despatched to her by Robert on his arrival in Leipzig; and though the groundlessness of his fears as to the security of his small independence immediately became clear, she was soon afterwards induced to take a step which roused Schumann's passionate anger. Her first two appearances in Paris since the child concert of 1832 had taken place on one day, March 21st, at a matinée arranged by the publisher Schlesinger in the Salon Erard, and at one of the annual soirées given by Zimmermann, professor of the pianoforte at the Conservatoire. Her programmes were chosen from her répertoire of virtuoso pieces, and contained only the names Henselt, Schubert-Liszt, Clara Wieck and Thalberg. They suited her audiences and no more classical selections would have been advisable or allowed. Clara was in every respect successful; was greatly applauded and, indeed, hailed as a second Liszt. It became possible to announce a concert of her own in the Salon Erard, and meanwhile she had gained sufficient reputation to venture on performing the greater part of the Carnaval, as well as pieces by Scarlatti, before an audience of amateurs at a private house. Her concert of April 16th was brilliantly attended, and her playing created, as she writes, a " veritable *furore*," but concert-giving in Paris is an expensive undertaking, and she had to content herself with the consciousness of her artistic success. The costs of the experiment were, indeed, covered, but no profits remained.

"I expected nothing else; my reputation is made and that satisfies me," she writes to Robert.

"I hope you are tranquil, my dear one," she continues, passing quickly from her own immediate concerns to answer the letter she had received in the morning. "I cannot realise Edward's death, and it troubles me that he was not to see us united; but do not lose courage, my Robert! Remember there is one who remains with you till death—if you should lose everything. One who clings to you with the most boundless love! . . ." *

Perhaps there may be a few amongst our readers who are able to realise something of the nervous strain endured by the actor, or musician, or orator whose duties bring him constantly before the public; something of the nature of the indemnity with which he has to pay for the attainment of success in his calling. Almost necessarily of a temperament sensitive to slight disturbing influences that might leave the man of affairs unruffled, he is bound to acquire a control over himself and circumstances which many a business man might envy. He has to learn to bear the fierce gaze of the public eye with outward and inward calm, to maintain a philosophical attitude towards the ignorance of friend and foe, to accept success with self-restraint and failure with dignity; to set aside indisposition, care, bereavement, in order to serve the audiences who admire him so generously, criticise him so mercilessly, envy him so naïvely, and never count the cost at which their favour has been gained or their disapproval encountered. Such readers may have found food for reflection in our story of the unbroken chain of artistic successes won by Clara Wieck during the troubled years of her girlhood. If, viewed in one light, they appear as the result that was to be expected from an exceptionally favourable training of natural gifts, they seem, in another, almost as prizes snatched from an unwilling destiny. It must be accepted as a rare psychical phenomenon that the young girl who had been more or less consciously struggling from the age of fourteen, alone and unhelped, with the developing phases of an overwhelming passion that threatened to absorb all the energies of her being, should, at eighteen, have reached an artistic eminence on which she stood side by side with the two or

* Litzmann, i. 315.

three most remarkable of her colleagues and seniors. Or, indeed, as we may rather say, in view of her powers as an interpreter of the various schools of art, that she should have attained a summit which the most distinguished of her colleagues had scarcely aspired to climb. And if we are compelled to admiration by the combined force and tenderness displayed by her during the period when, whatever her private anxieties, she was secured from outside cares by her father's protection, must we not almost marvel at the strength that nerved her to go out into the world alone in the fresh bloom of her youth and sustained her there during many months of difficulties hitherto unknown to her, whilst the loving nature, torn between two affections and two duties that could not be reconciled, remained intact?

In a letter to Emilie List, written at the beginning of April, Wieck had threatened that, should his daughter persist in her engagement to Schumann, he would cast her off entirely, disinherit her, keep from her the few hundred pounds' capital that had been saved from her own portion of her earnings, and begin a law process against her and her lover that might drag on for several years.

"If he casts me off, I can justify my action before God," writes poor Clara; "when I think over things as they are, I feel as though I were already without parents, for I hear little of affection from home."

A few days later she received the news of Robert's trouble, and the two letters, arriving so closely one after the other, produced an appreciable effect on her. Then came her concert day, and Clara, though she could express herself bravely as satisfied with the laurels she had won, was nevertheless well aware that her success had not amounted to such a decisive triumph as would constitute an effective prelude to the London campaign on which she had set her heart, and which was to furnish her with the wherewithal to face her first housekeeping cares without grave anxiety. Probably she was beginning to realise the hopelessness of her position as a young artist practically alone in a great city with her name to make. Yet she would not allow herself to be beaten. Already she was deciding to

remain through the summer in or near Paris, to try her luck
in the autumn with a second concert, and to start after
Christmas on another journey that should have England
as its ultimate goal. In this mood, she was surprised, about
a fortnight after the event of her concert, by the arrival of
two more letters from her father, one to herself and a second
addressed to Emilie, both written in a tone completely changed
from that with which she had of late been familiar. It was
the tone of a father appealing against his child's disobedience
and ingratitude to her instinct of filial love. The letters
seemed for the moment to offer a prospect of reconciliation,
and she wrote without delay begging Wieck to join her in
Paris and to associate himself with her plans for the winter
and the following spring and summer; and, whilst she
firmly reiterated her unchanged resolution never to separate
from her lover and pleaded his cause with all the persuasive
power at her command, she promised that she would, under
certain conditions, postpone the date of her marriage.

If Clara's action in this difficult hour may seem to have
been inconsistent with the firm attitude she had maintained
during many previous months of lonely trial, her passing
vacillation, induced by an intense desire for reconciliation
with her father, is easily intelligible. Who shall picture
the unrest of her mind, her longing for the experienced
counsel, the reliable authority that had hitherto shielded and
directed her movements from the point of view of an interest
identical with her own ?—her intense relief in the reawakened
dream that these might ultimately be in some degree available
not only for her father's daughter, but for Schumann's wife ?
Nor does it seem improbable that a conviction of the ex-
pediency of postponing the date of her marriage had for
some few months been forming within her. True, she had
been reassured by Robert as to the safety of his capital; true,
she had, less than a week before proposing travelling plans
to her father for the summer of 1840, renewed her promise
to her lover to become his wife in the spring of the same
year. Clara was not, any more than Robert, under complete illusion as to the chances and possibilities of married
life. If Robert's occasional passing misgivings arose from

the hardly defined presentiment that to share his daily life with a woman of Clara's strongly marked individuality would be to endanger his absorption in art, Clara's more clearly recognised anxieties were centred in the conviction that a conflict with the more sordid cares of existence must end in the paralysis of Robert's creative powers and the ruin of his happiness—possibly even the sacrifice of his life. She was aware that his view of the extent of their joint prospects was apt at times to assume a roseate colour that was derived partly from his wishes. She could not pretend even to herself that she would choose to enter upon a life of embarrassing responsibilities that might be averted by some further delay of the marriage ; she had not been educated for the duties of a housewife of small means and knew she was not prepared to encounter them efficiently. Her fears were, however, in the first place for Robert's ultimate happiness, and it was in the spirit of her devotion to him that she wrote on May 2nd to tell him of her letter to her father, to explain her plans for the ensuing concert season, to deprecate his displeasure in the most moving words of tenderness, and to reiterate her assurances of unchanging love. No doubt this letter, which Schumann could not but regard as a retractation of the promise he had joyfully and confidently accepted from Clara but a few days earlier, would in any case have upset his equilibrium. Its effect was greatly enhanced, however, by the fact of his receiving one by the same post from Emilie, the daily witness of Clara's struggle, which was written at all events with the latter's sanction, if not by her desire :—

" . . . Only my love for Clara and the lively wish to see you happily united," she says, " could induce me to write to you. I regard it as my duty to tell you that Clara's health has been much weakened for some months past. She is in a constant state of agitation, the cause of which you may well imagine. . . . I have long observed the conflict that is going on within her, but should not have ventured to address you if I had not received a heartrending letter from her father this morning which shows me how unhappy he is. His letter has made a deep impression on Clara, and she confessed to me for the first time that she would never feel quite happy know-ing her father unhappy. . . . Herr Wieck says in his letter to me that he does not wish to destroy Clara's love; that he desires, on the contrary, to see her united to you as soon as he is assured of the prospect of a secure future for her. Can you take this demand amiss? . . . Herr Wieck has written to me that he would give you a formal promise to unite you with his daughter as soon as he sees that she would not be compelled by the pressure of care to neglect the art she has acquired with so much exertion. Clara's father wishes to travel with her next year in Holland, Belgium, and England, where she hopes to accumulate a small capital. She would not be able to make this journey successfully, or to command the respect she so greatly deserves, without masculine protection." *

Whether Wieck was really subject to some vacillation of feeling at this date, or whether he was again merely willing to give a pledge on conditions which he had no expectation of seeing fulfilled, remains uncertain. The two letters written and despatched by Clara and Emilie, together with a few lines from Henriette, to Schumann in Leipzig did not fail of their speedy effect. It happened that they crossed a communication prepared and sent off to Paris by Robert in his hot joy at the result of a consultation on ways and means held by him with his friend Reuter, which had convinced him that the joint funds at his own and Clara's disposal would more than suffice for all present needs of married life. It is unnecessary to insist on the feelings of disappointed love, of wounded pride, of fierce anger, roused within him by Clara's appeal and Emilie's well-reasoned arguments, or to dwell on the panic excited in Clara by the storm she had aroused. That she should send Robert a loving, reassuring letter; that he should accept her repentance; and that the matters in question should be speedily readjusted on their former footing, is a foregone conclusion.

"But you will not again allow yourself to be disturbed by fears about our future—promise me not to give way any more to unnecessary anxiety, but to trust and obey me; for

* The entire very long letter is printed by Litzmann, i. 322–326.

the man is above the woman," writes Robert on May 18th in his letter of reconciliation; " and you two other dear girls—I have given you something to remember—may I hope to be forgiven? . . . But do not take it amiss that I have shown I am master in the house and not to be overruled. . . . For the rest, I am particularly pleased with Henriette. She wrote me a few words which are better than all your letters, namely: 'Destiny is deceitful, life is short, swift to the goal.' This says everything. Bravo, Henriette, I admire you! " *

And Schumann, taking advantage of his opportunity, followed Henriette's advice without further demur or delay. The very day after Clara had been restored to something like happiness by his letter of forgiveness, she received for consideration the draft of the petition through which he hoped to obtain, according to the laws of his country, the statutory consent to his marriage with Clara which was refused by her father. She was to study it deliberately, to weigh its every word; for, her signature once obtained to the document itself there would be no drawing back. Should her father refuse to listen to the final appeal which Robert would send him in due course, the matter would be taken from his hands, to be judged according to reason and justice by the tribunal of the law, to whose decree he would have no choice but to submit. And now Clara bowed to necessity. The finally revised document was forwarded to her by Schumann on June 8th, his twenty-ninth birthday, and was signed by her and returned to him on June 15th.† The deed was done. The final turning-point of her girlhood was behind her. She had made her irrevocable choice.‡

Although, as we have already hinted, the first half of the year 1839 was not signalised in Schumann's life by the composition of any work that can be ranked among the pre-eminent efforts of his genius, it was made distinctive by the publication of the Fantasia in C major, Op. 17, which occupies a place among the finest monuments not only of romantic art, but of the entire literature of the instrument to which it

* Litzmann, i. 331.
† Ibid., i. 340.
‡ For the wording of the petition see Litzmann, i. 333.

belongs. The fantasia is, as the reader is aware, to be associated in the first place with one of the darkest periods of the composer's youth, the early summer of 1836, when he had reason to believe that his beloved maiden was lost to him.[*] Its origin was, however, also connected with other special circumstances of the time of considerable, if of less personal, interest which have left marked impress upon the whole composition. At the close of 1835 the idea of erecting a monument to Beethoven in Bonn, the city of his birth, was started by Liszt, a committee was formed to forward the project and a subscription list opened. Schumann, though not at first attracted by the scheme, discussed it characteristically from different points of view in four articles that appeared in the *Zeitschrift* in the beginning of 1836, signed respectively Florestan, Jonathan, Eusebius and Raro, and in December of the year he wrote to the publisher Kistner:—

"ESTEEMED HERR KISTNER,—Knowing your readiness to lend a helping hand to the promotion of a happy idea, I turn to you.

"Florestan and Eusebius desire to contribute to Beethoven's monument, and have written something for the purpose under the following title:—

Ruins. Trophies. Palms.
Grand Sonata for the Pianoforte
For Beethoven's monument
By——

". . . I have my own ideas as to how the work should be brought out, and have imagined something very special, appropriate to the importance of the object. A black cover, or better still, binding, with gold ornamentation, bearing in gold letters the words : Obolus for Beethoven's monument. On the chief title-page palm leaves might, perhaps, droop over the words of the top line. On the next page the dedication :—

For Beethoven's monument
from
Composer and Publisher.

"Pray consider the matter. I am very eager about it and

* See *ante*, p. 175.

can promise you as well as myself honour from the under-taking. The sonata is in itself, too, sufficiently notable. The adagio of the A major symphony [Beethoven] is quoted in the ' Palms.' "

What Kistner answered is not known. The subscriptions fell short of the sum required for the erection of the monu-ment, and no further mention of the "Obolus" occurs in Schumann's correspondence until he tells Clara, in the letter of March, 1838, from which we quoted in an earlier chapter, of the completion of the "Fantasia." He adds, a few weeks afterwards, that this will be the next of his things to appear in print, and that he has called the several movements "Ruins," "Triumphal Arches," and "Star Picture," and the whole composition "Poems": "It took me a long time to find this last word. It seems to me very noble and ex-pressive for music." Probably it was soon afterwards that he sent the work to Breitkopf and Härtel, who accepted it but delayed its publication, and it may have been at their suggestion that the ultimately selected title was decided upon.

There is no doubt that the name "fantasia" is the most suitable that could have been chosen for the composition. Its first movement is, in some respects, suggestive of sonata form, to the statement and recapitulation of which the first and third sections more or less answer. The middle section consists, however, not of the development of foregoing thematic material, but of an independent episode which glances only once, and, as it were accidentally, at the principal motif of the work, while the second and third movements have nothing in common, either essentially or in their order of succession, with what is traditionally accepted as the general plan of a "sonata." As to the character of the feeling that carries the first movement—"To be performed throughout imaginatively and passionately"—irresistibly onward, we have only to add to our previous remarks on the subject that the name "Ruins," chosen by Schumann in 1836 and still deemed appropriate in 1838 for this portion of his com-position, evidently refers to the despair that consumed his soul during the period of his total separation from Clara.

"You can only understand the fantasia by recalling the unhappy summer of 1836 when I believed I had lost you," he wrote to her on the publication of the work ; and he adds—referring to the four lines quoted from Friedrich Schlegel which supplement the title and point to the insistence of the prevailing motif of the first movement :—

" Are you the ' tone ' of the motto ?   I almost believe so." *

That the memory of Beethoven's sorrows was also present within him as he wrote the movement may, however, be inferred from the first of the four articles, " Monument to Beethoven," signed by " Florestan." †

Whilst, however, the first movement of the fantasia belongs primarily to Clara, the second and third sprang no less indubitably from the composer's imaginings on the subject of the proposed Beethoven memorial, and in the third and second of his articles on the subject may be found the clue to the general direction of his thoughts :—

" If I were a prince," exclaims Eusebius, throwing out ideas as to a fitting form for the memorial, " I would build a temple to him in Palladio style. It should contain ten statues. By nine of the statues I would signify that the number of the Muses corresponds with that of his symphonies. The tenth should signify himself, the divine Musagetes. There from time to time the German choirs should assemble ; there competitions, festivals be held ; there his works be given in the most consummate perfection. . . ."

In these words we certainly possess the key to the composer's intention in the superb march of the second movement. Does not the stirring strain of its opening section suggest the inauguration of a great festal ceremony ; the unceasing onward flow of the first episode the gathering together of a multitude of people ever increasing in dignity and importance ; the re-

* " A soft tone, perceptible to him who listens with attuned ear, sounds persistently through the confused sounds of the earthly dream."

† " Gesammelte Schriften," Part 1, 1836.

entry of the march the crowning moment of the assembling—
the arrival of the princely patron or founder of the occasion?
Does not the quieter middle section suggest the commencement of proceedings within closed doors?—the third recapitulation section, with the repetition of the episode, the final
delivery of the glorious march strain, the hurry of the coda,
the movement, and pomp, and finally the press, of departure?
Surely the scene of the dedication of his temple must have been
present to Schumann's imagination when he wrote this movement and placed above it the words " Triumphal arches."

" If some one must, at all hazards, be rescued from oblivion,"
" Jonathan " remarks ironically in another of the articles, " let
this be the fate of Beethoven's critics, especially of him who
wrote in the *Allgemeine Musikalische Zeitung* of 1799, p. 151 :
' If Herr von Beethoven will cease to belie himself and will
follow the course of nature, he will certainly succeed with
his talent and industry in producing much good work for
an instrument which,' &c.   Yes, indeed.   It lies in the course
of nature and in the nature of things.   Thirty-seven years have
passed meanwhile ; the name of Beethoven has expanded like
a heavenly sunflower, while the critic has shrivelled in his
garret to a dry nettle."

In the third movement, the " Star picture," which is of
extraordinary mystic beauty, we seem to follow Schumann's
meditations on the immortality of his great music god ; on the
irresistible penetration of his spirit ever further and higher
until at length the name Beethoven is heard proclaimed from
the last altitude of space.

From the fact that it contains no reference to the allegretto
of the A major symphony we know that the third movement
of the fantasia was rewritten after the first completion of the
work in 1836,* and it is permissible to conclude that the first
and second movements also were subject to drastic revision in
the early part of 1838, when the work was completed in final
form.   The internal evidence of the whole composition, which
in every quality of musicianship greatly transcends the publications of 1836, would in any case lead to this conclusion.   Essentially romantic both in inspiration and workmanship, it unites

* See *ante*, p. 286.

the glowing and varied impulse of Schumann's youth with the greater power of sustained mastery he had acquired by unremitting study and, standing proudly on an eminence of its own, must remain one of the final tests of the executive and imaginative capacity of every pianist who aspires to high artistic rank. The dedication of the fantasia to Franz Liszt proved in every respect appropriate, for it was by his munificence that the memorial scheme was realised after nine years of delay. He provided the balance of the sum required for the erection of the monument from his private purse on the sole condition that he should be allowed to choose the sculptor to whom its execution was to be entrusted. In acknowledgment of the presentation copy of the fantasia in C major sent him by Schumann, with which was enclosed the recently published " Kinderscenen," Liszt wrote on June 5, 1839 :—

" MON CHER MONSIEUR SCHUMANN,—Au risque de vous paraître très monotone, je vous dirai encore que les derniers morceaux que vous avez eu la bonté de m'envoyer à Rome me semblent admirables d'inspiration et de facture. La Fantaisie qui m'est dediée est une œuvre de l'ordre le plus élevé—je suis en vérité fier de l'honneur que vous me faites en m'adressant une si grandiose composition. Aussi veux-je la travailler et la pénétrer à fond afin de tirer tout l'effet possible.

" Quant aux Kinderscenen je leur dois une des plus vives jouissances de ma vie. Vous savez, ou vous ne savez pas que j'ai une petite fille de trois ans que tout le monde s'accorde à trouver *angélique* (voyez quelle banalité !). Son nom est Blandine-Rachel et son surnom *moucheron*. Il va sans dire qu'elle a un teint de rose et de lait et que ses cheveux blonds dorés lui viennent jusqu'au talon tout comme à une sauvage. C'est du reste l'enfant le plus silencieux, le plus doucement grave, le plus philosophiquement gai du monde. J'ai tout lieu d'espérer aussi qu'elle ne sera pas musicienne, ce dont Dieu la garde ! Eh bien ! mon cher Monsieur Schumann, deux ou trois fois par semaine (aux beaux bons jours) je lui joue dans la soirée vos Kinderscenen, ce qui la ravit et moi bien plus comme vous pouvez imaginer, au point que souvent je lui répète vingt fois la première reprise sans aller plus avant.

20

Vraiment je crois que vous seriez content de ce succès si vous pouviez en être temoins ! . . .

"Ce que vous me dites de votre vie intime m'a vivement intéressé et touché. Si je pouvais, je ne sais comment, vous être le moins du monde agréable ou utile dans ces circonstances, disposez complètement de moi. Quoiqu'il advienne comptez sur ma plus absolue discrétion et sur mon sincère dévouement. *Si ce n'est pas trop vous demander*, dites-moi si c'est de *Clara* que vous parlez. Mais pour peu que cette question vous paraisse *déplacée* ne me repondez point. . . .

"Tout à vous amicalement,

"F. LISZT."

Clara passed nearly two months of the summer of 1839 in the country near Paris in the companionship of her pupil, Henriette Reichmann, but the benefit to her health that might have been derived from rest and change of air was to a great extent neutralised by the more unrelieved concentration of her mind on the difficulties besetting her path. Still anxious to gain such a decisive French triumph as might ensure for her in the future the respectful attention of the musical circles of London and Petersburg, the conviction forced itself upon her with constantly growing insistence that to attain it many other conditions besides that of her own artistic excellence were indispensable, conditions which she, as a young, sensitive, unprotected girl, would be unable to fulfil. The idea that, whilst she was spending money without any immediate prospect of return she was going back in her art, began to possess her thoughts and to disturb her pleasure in playing. She longed for her father's vigorous criticism, even for his censure. She had never wished to be independent of his advice, yet perhaps she had never until now fully realised how she had rested on his strength and affection. Her former satisfaction in the exercise of her powers in composition had long been yielding to her consciousness of Robert's overwhelming superiority; yet she had found some distraction in the spring of the year by putting a few of her musical thoughts on paper in the shape of "a little dramatic andante" and an "idyll," and it says much for her feeling of artistic independence that she did not unconditionally adopt the alterations of the "idyll" proposed by Schumann, to whom she submitted the piece at his request for publication in the *Neue Zeitschrift*.

"I have received the idyll and thank you, my dearest," she wrote sweetly, referring to her lover's amendments; "but I am sure you will forgive me if I tell you that I do not altogether like it. You have completely altered the close, which was my favourite part, and which made an impression on every one to whom I played it, and the beginning of the theme seems to me too studied. . . . You have no doubt added to the musical value of the piece, but have made it, I think, too learned for the French; and I wish to ask you if you do not agree that it would be best for me to have it printed here as I first wrote it, with some other little things, whilst you take it with your alterations for the *Zeitung* and call it 'Notturno,' although the name seems rather strange to me; I cannot help feeling it is an 'idyll.' You are not angry with me?"*

But the little piece, during the writing of which Clara had thought "unceasingly" of Robert, was not altered. Another composition, an "Andante and Allegro by Clara Wieck," appeared as a supplement to one of the September numbers of the *Neue Zeitschrift*, which was afterwards sent, by Robert's suggestion, together with the idyll, and a third number composed in July, to Haslinger, of Vienna. He published them in the autumn as Clara's Opus 11 with the title "Trois Romances pour le Piano, dediées à Monsieur Robert Schumann."

* Litzmann, i. 353.

CHAPTER XVIII

1839—1840

Clara's return to Leipzig—The lawsuit—Frau Marianne Bargiel—Clara with her mother in Berlin—Clara's Prussian concerts—Schumann's G minor Sonata—"Three Romances," Op. 28—"Faschingsschwank aus Wien"—An outburst of song—Liszt in Leipzig—Mendelssohn's appreciation of Schumann's songs—Termination of the lawsuit—Marriage of Robert and Clara (September 12, 1840).

THOUGH Clara had cherished the hope that she would be allowed to remain quietly in France until the impending law process to be brought by Schumann and herself as petitioners against her father should have terminated, it is not unlikely that she may, after all, have experienced a feeling of relief on finding that circumstances were to absolve her from the necessity of arranging her own plans for the immediate future. Schumann's final private appeal to Wieck having been unsuccessful, the suit was opened in the middle of July, and the first decision arrived at by the court, that an attempt at reconciliation between the contending parties should be made under official superintendence, rendered her presence in Leipzig indispensable. Leaving Paris, with her pupil, on August 14th, and breaking her journey at Frankfurt, whence Henriette returned to her home in Stuttgart, she arrived on the 24th on a short visit to Schumann's family connections in Schneeberg, and on the 30th found herself again in the town of her birth, the scene of her well remembered childish joys and griefs, her youthful artistic hopes and blissful dreams of love. She was received on her arrival by kind old friends, and moved the next day to the house that was to be her home for the present whenever she might be obliged to stay in Leipzig, that of her own mother's sister, Frau Carl.

Very touching are the words of the diary in which the young girl has recorded her feelings in this troubled hour of her life. Distressed, yet ever persistent filial tenderness ; commiseration of the unhappy father through whose indomitable energy of will her youthful years have been so richly blessed, so harshly smitten ; shrinking dread of the approaching struggle before the world, mingle with a certain misgiving as to her own capacity for the fulfilment of the new duties on which she hopes soon to enter and even as to her power of permanently holding her lover : " His mind is so great and I can satisfy him so little in this respect ! " Yet neither the daughter's pain nor the girl's diffidence can weigh against Clara's deep joy in the consciousness of Robert's love. That she must go to him without a dowry, even from the money she has herself earned, mortifies and saddens her, but : " I will not have learned my art in vain. . . . My greatest desire is to bring it about that Robert may be able to live as he likes— entirely for music ; that his beautiful artist-life may no longer be disturbed by anxiety." *

The order of the court that the two appellants should make a final effort to come to an amicable arrangement with the respondent in the suit was duly carried out, but, as was to be foreseen, it led to no result. Wieck did not appear at the appointed hour at the house of the archdeacon who was selected to preside at the conference, and nothing remained to the lovers but to hope that the successive stages of the law process might be reached with the least possible delay.

We suggested in an early chapter of our narrative that Clara may sometimes, during her childhood, have longed, perhaps half-unconsciously, for the one affection of which she

---

* Compare Litzmann, i. 364. Wasielewsky states, on the authority of Frau Clementina Wieck (" Robert Schumann," p. 260), that Clara's capital amounted, at the close of 1838, to about 7,000 thalers (about £1,050), but that this sum was diminished in the course of 1839 by the sending of the remittances required by her from time to time during her residence in France. Clara herself, however, recording in September, 1839, that her father had proposed to give his formal consent to her marriage with Schumann on certain conditions, mentions as one of them : " I am to renounce the 2,000 thalers (about £300) I have saved from seven years of playing and give them to my brothers."—Litzmann, i. 371.

was deprived; that she may have dreamed wistfully of the mother she had scarcely known. Later on, as she became absorbed in the developing interests of her existence and realised increasingly the place she occupied in her father's heart, his absorption in her talent, his delight in her companionship, his pride in her successes, her sense of something being wanting lost its acuteness and she was no longer saddened by the recollection that her own mother was distant from her life. Though she had frequently visited Frau Bargiel during the visit to Berlin in 1837, she had refused the proposal that she should stay with her mother on the ground that she could not leave her father alone. "The possession of father makes up to me for everything," she had written. But the time had now come when Frau Marianne was to enter into possession of the long-lost treasure of her daughter's love. It had been necessary to obtain her consent to the betrothal, and Robert, paying his first visit to Berlin for this purpose two or three weeks before Clara's return from France, had easily succeeded in his object by his passionate earnestness and simple integrity. "She received me so cordially and seems to like me," he wrote. "As we were walking yesterday evening in the Thiergarten [the chief park of Berlin], I thought so sorrowfully of my lonely distant girl who did not know that her mother and lover were talking together about her."

Frau Bargiel had come from Berlin to support her child through any trouble that might attend the conference and to take her afterwards to her own home. Meanwhile Schumann was made heartily welcome at the aunt's house, and the natural instinct that drew mother and daughter together was strengthened by the affectionate intimacy established at this time between Frau Marianne and himself. Clara made the most of the interval of happiness afforded her by Robert's companionship, but it could only be brief, and once away from Leipzig and settled in Berlin she found little to distract her mind from the strange trials of her lot. To her, affection was life, yet it had been ordained that she should not find complete repose in either of the affections which filled her heart. The refreshment she might have found in the new experience of her mother's love was troubled by her distress on witnessing the hard struggle for existence that shadowed the Bargiel household ; her absorbing devotion to Robert was agitated by grave apprehension on the score of his health, while her unfailing love for her father had become a torturing wound. Then the question of means for present needs was becoming a pressing one, for she naturally shrank from making use of the funds which her lover had, with all delicacy, placed at her disposal. It is, indeed, extraordinarily difficult to reconcile Wieck's behaviour throughout this period with what we have learned of the general rectitude of his character and his unquestionable affection for his daughter. Perhaps the best that can be said for him is that, faced by the ultimate crisis of the one difficulty of his life which had proved unconquerable even by his imperious determination, he did, as we have already suggested, practically lose his reason for the time being. He now not only declined to supply his daughter with funds from the surplus of her own earnings, but actually refused her possession of her personal belongings, and, in particular, of a fine grand pianoforte sent her by the maker Graf, as a "respectful souvenir" of her achievements in Vienna. The shifts employed by him to delay the progress of the lawsuit were completely successful, and throughout the autumn months matters remained at a standstill. Short spaces of happiness were snatched by the lovers between the alternating succession of distracting events and no less trying inaction which marked the three months following the failure of the conference. Schumann managed a visit to Berlin on Clara's twentieth birthday, and surprised her with a copy of the just published sonata in G minor, Op. 22, one of her favourite works. Concerts arranged by her in October in the Prussian capital and provinces, some of the programmes of which included one or more of Schumann's "Noveletten," were very successful, and the presence at the second soirée in Berlin of the King of Prussia, who joined heartily in the applause that followed her performances, gave particular brilliance to the occasion.

It may well be believed, however, that the contemplation of Clara's situation, brought about as it had been by the fidelity

of her attachment to himself, caused Schumann many a torturing pang, and there were times when he was tempted to
bitter self-reproach as having been the cause of her separation
from her father. His short, dubious, infrequent letters when
such moods overcame him added an enigma to Clara's troubles
which was rendered scarcely less painful by her divination that
its solution was to be found in a strained condition of his
nerves resulting from the distressing position of their joint
affairs. That Schumann's self-censure was unmerited has
been shown by the progress of our narrative. Clara's love
for her father's favourite pupil had sprung spontaneously
within her heart when she was a young child, and her spirit
had grown to its beauty and fullness in the sunshine which
Robert's companionship had shed upon her life. Drooping
like a thirsty flower when she had fancied herself separated
from his affection, she had recognised before he had the strange
decree that had linked their lives together. Robert, when he
too had become aware of this mystery, perceived in it the
revelation of an inscrutable law which is granted only now
and then to an elect favourite of the unseen powers, and he
knew that he could not but choose to follow it, however
obscure the places through which it might lead him and his
beloved. He may be pardoned if there were moments when
his courage failed him whilst he was passing through the
thickest tangle of perplexity, for he never lost hold of his
faith in the shining of a light beyond it. Ferdinand Hiller,
who spent the winter of 1839–40 in Leipzig, relates that
Schumann lived during these months as a complete recluse,
only quitting his rooms on absolutely necessary business.
The young composer himself complains of a "total lack of
ideas," of his inability to extemporise at the piano, and of
general intellectual torpor—"sometimes I sit the whole day
silent, without thoughts." Nevertheless, some of his best
work for the pianoforte, and judged by himself as belonging
to his best, is to be associated with this autumn. To the
publication by Breitkopf and Härtel of the sonata in G minor
succeeded that of the Three Romances, Op. 28, by the same
house, and of the "Faschingsschwank aus Wien" ("Carnival
jests in Vienna") by Mechetti (Spina), of Vienna; and if on

the whole the composer has not reached so high a level of imaginative power in these works as in the publications of 1837 and 1838, they contain movements animated throughout by the personal fervour which is Schumann's most fascinating note, whilst two of them denote that he was now rapidly approaching mastery in the particular branch of musical study which had confronted him with special difficulty—the study of sustained development in extended design.   The sonata in G minor is, in a still more comprehensive sense than its elder companion in F sharp minor, to be associated with various stages in Schumann's development.   The andante, the agreeable flow of which is marred in the middle section by a succession of thinly veiled and unpleasant-sounding fifths, was composed as a song (in $\frac{2}{4}$ time and in the key of E flat minor) at Heidelberg in June, 1830.   The first and third movements were sketched in 1833; the rondo was substituted in 1838 for an earlier finale composed in 1835.   The final revision of the entire work for publication was carried out in 1839, and to the period of Schumann's development to which this last date brings us, the sonata must, in virtue of the symmetry and clearness of all its movements, be held essentially to belong.   The present author is not disposed to echo the remarks of those writers who have felt it necessary to depreciate the value of this successful work because its ideas are less ardently emotional than those usually characteristic of Schumann's music.   It is not planned on a grandiose scale. The quality of its thoughts is suitable to the proportions of its design, and its rapid, unwearied impulse rivets the attention of both hearer and performer from beginning to end.   The first movement is effectively written in regular sonata form ; the second in song form ; the scherzo is characterised by its bold rhythmic swing; the finale, an interesting example of rondo-sonata form, contains original features, which do not, however, injure the symmetry of its plan, and is the most musically important portion of the work.*

The " Faschingsschwank aus Wien," with the second title

* The andante, in its first form as a song, and the original finale of the sonata are included in the supplementary edition, edited by Brahms, of the Clara Schumann edition of the complete works.

of " Phantasiebilder," described by Schumann in a letter of 1839 as a " romantic spectacle" (ein romantisches Schaustück) is a reflection of the composer's impressions of the Carnival festivities in the Austrian capital witnessed by him in 1839. The first of its four movements, which has been unaccountably described by more than one distinguished writer as wanting in unity, is written to all intents and purposes in early rondo form, from which it deviates only by the circumstance that the keys G minor and E flat major of the first and second episodes are used again for the third and fifth : the convention being that no two episodes shall appear in the same key. The form, though not traditionally associated with the first movement of an extended work, has been used here with excellent effect, and was no doubt chosen by the composer on account of the opportunity afforded by the episodes for the musical suggestion of the various scenes and moods of the constantly changing picture from which he derived the impulse to write the work. The episodes are in turn playful, stirring, and tender, and the frequently recurring vigorous opening theme in B flat not only invests the movement with complete outward unity, but adds to it an inner cohesion by, as it were, localising itself in the imagination of the listener as the central scene of the show around which the subordinate pictures revolve. An animated coda brings the brilliant movement to a satisfactory conclusion. The Romance, in Lied form, and the Scherzino, in dance form, are attractive in their several ways ; whilst the Intermezzo, in E flat minor, again in Lied form, the gem of the work, heralds the extraordinary outburst of Schumann's genius as a song-writer that was soon to dower the world with some of its rarest musical treasures. In the finale we have an example of sonata form used, with consummate skill, for a romantic purpose. Unfailing in its spontaneous energy, it provides an appropriate counterpart to the first movement and an eminently happy conclusion to the entire series of tone pictures. This genial work would have been not unfitly characterised by the title " Romantic Sonata " which Schumann was inclined to select for it, though the reversal of the tradition of writing a first movement in sonata, and a finale in rondo form, might have offered an easy point for censure to those critics who are concerned only to find fault. The relation in which the "Faschingsschwank aus Wien. Phantasiebilder," Op. 26, stands to the "Carnaval. Scènes Mignonnes," Op. 9, corresponds with the difference in design of the two compositions. Whilst the earlier work portrays for us, in a series of short, vivid flashes, the phantasmagoria of a poet's dream, the later one presents us with pictures of his impressions of certain incidents of actual life. Both are entirely characteristic of Schumann at the several stages of his development as a composer to which they severally belong, and they should be equally cherished, each for its own qualities, in the affection of the true lover of his art. The Faschingsschwank was dedicated to Simonin de Sire, a fine amateur musician, and an early admirer of Schumann's genius.

Of the Three Romances, Op. 28, the first two must be ranked among the most perfect of Schumann's works for the pianoforte in small form. The first is characterised by sustained fervour of inspiration, unity of thought, clearness and finish of workmanship. The second, the lovely little duet in F sharp major, may be regarded as a companion piece to the "Des Abends" and "Warum" of the Opus 12. The final number, though containing many interesting ideas, is, perhaps, a little wanting in conciseness. The opus, dedicated to Count Heinrich Reuss-Köstritz, was published at the end of the year.

At length, about the middle of December, the lawsuit came on again for hearing, and now, no further pretext for postponement being available to Wieck, Clara actually found herself in the position she had so long been dreading : that of appearing before a public tribunal as one of the parties to a petition against her father. Such a situation as that in which she was placed is difficult of realisation in a country where it cannot occur. The contrasted demeanour of the three parties concerned in the case lent emphasis to its dramatic elements. The angry father cast looks of fury on his child and her lover alternately ; the suitor bore himself with dignified self-restraint ; the daughter, feeling as though "nailed to her chair," was trembling and pale with conflicting emotions. Wieck's language was so uncurbed, his denunciations so violent, that he was repeatedly ordered to be silent by the president; "which," writes Clara in her account of the day, "cut me to the soul. I could scarcely endure that he should have to undergo this mortification." He declared his grounds for withholding his consent to his daughter's marriage to be his doubts of the sufficiency of Schumann's means ; of his capacity as composer and author; of the future constancy of the attachment between the lovers; and finally of Schumann's steadiness, coupled with the accusation that he had a propensity for drink.

"This day has separated us for ever," writes Clara the same evening. "At all events, it has broken the tender bond between father and child. I feel as though my heart were broken also."

The decision of the court was announced in the first week of January. All Wieck's contentions were overruled as trivial except the last, and for the accusation against Schumann's stability of character, incontestable proof was to be produced within a given time.

The whole of this pronouncement must have been welcome not only to Clara but Robert, who was aware that Wieck would not find it possible to bring forward evidence in support of his charge and that in the absence of the required testimony the victory in the suit would fall to Clara and himself. If there had been moments in the "unhappy year" 1836 when he had felt tempted in his loneliness and grief to throw up the contest with the adverse influences of his life and surrender himself to despair, they had been moments only. Schumann, whose youth may be said to have been passed in a succession of hardly fought struggles with himself and circumstances, had in every such conflict ultimately proved that his strength was stronger than his weakness. If his innate vigour of mind and his worship of art had been his salvation when he had reason to believe that Clara had forsaken him, the hour that restored to him the assured consciousness of her love rendered him immune from every impulse that could have lured him from his appointed goal. Count Reuss, David, and many others were now anxious to come forward and pledge themselves for their friend. Neither their sympathy, however, nor the prospect of the favourable termination of the lawsuit within a definite period could prevent the young composer from feeling profoundly sensitive to the misery of his position.

" One thing more," he writes to Clara a week after the decision had been made known; " if you imagine that it may become possible later on to reconcile me with your father, renounce all hope of such a thing. The slightest suggestion from you of such a wish would be offensive to me. . . . There are laws of honour as binding as those of love. Promise me that you will recognise them. Make up your mind on this point, which might otherwise endanger our happiness. I am writing strongly, my Clara. . . . I have fallen into a harsh tone in which you do not know me. Bad words and bad men are an abomination to me." *

" Let me only say as regards the matter on which you have expressed yourself so strongly," replies Clara, " that I have long given up the hope of a reconciliation between you. I give you my hand that no word shall ever escape my lips Let that be enough to satisfy you." †

Rising with her usual courage to the practical necessities of her position, Clara arranged a series of public engagements for the opening months of 1840, but they were fulfilled by her under conditions of extreme suffering. The extraordinary trials to which she had been constantly exposed since her return, in the spring of 1838, from her Austrian triumphs had told sensibly on her health, and attacks of exhaustion and giddiness, with severe neuralgia of the kind that makes sound, thought, life itself an agony, to say nothing of a painful accident to her hand, made practising an impossibility through the three first weeks of the year. Her force of will, however, carried her triumphantly through the programmes of her Berlin concerts of January 25th and February 1st, which included Beethoven's B flat and Schubert's E flat trios, solos by Scarlatti, Chopin, and Mendelssohn, several Schubert-Liszt transcriptions, bravura pieces of her own and of Liszt's composition, and "a" sonata by Schumann. Of this work the available press notices of the time give neither key nor Opus number; but from the fact that the

* Litzmann, i. 387.   † Ibid.

mention of Schumann's second and third sonatas to be found in Frau Schumann's complete répertoire (Litzmann, vol. iii.) belongs to the year 1871, we must conclude it to have been the Opus 11 in F sharp minor, and the performance is the first one of this composition of which record can be traced in the press. The Crown Prince of Prussia was present with his consort on both occasions. Clara seems to have been satisfied with the impression produced by the sonata. She writes on February 2nd :—

"Marx called on me to-day. . . . He spoke very enthusiastically about your sonata and I have already heard from several others, connoisseurs of course, that they thought it the most enjoyable thing of the evening. This has greatly delighted me ; also that every one says I played it with so much sympathy it must have been by some one I do not hate." *

The young pianist's arrival, in the companionship of her mother, in Hamburg, Bremen, and other northern towns selected for a short concert journey was embittered in each case by the discovery that it had been anticipated by her father's endeavours to stir up feeling against Schumann and herself on the subject of the lawsuit; yet any prejudice that Wieck may have succeeded in awakening to the detriment of his child seemed to vanish as if by magic on her appearance, whether in public or private circles, and she returned to Berlin early in March encouraged by the consciousness of having achieved financial as well as artistic success. The last week of her tour was brightened by the tidings that Robert had been elected an honorary doctor of philosophy by the university of Jena. The announcement came quite as a surprise to her, though it was not altogether unexpected by Schumann himself, who had for some time been anxious to be the recipient of some such distinction, chiefly on account of the higher status it would give him as the bridegroom of the imperial court pianist Clara. The intelligence that it had been conferred reached him at a moment when he had been goaded by Wieck's public insults into taking proceedings for libel against his future father-in-law and was therefore doubly gratifying.

* Litzmann, i. 392.

Expressions that occur here and there in Schumann's letters show that for the past two years his ambition had been ranging beyond the musical domain within which he had so faithfully served his apprenticeship to musical art—that of composition for the pianoforte—and that he had been attracted by the idea of trying his hand again on a string quartet, a symphony, or a concerto. The beginning of 1840 was to bring these musical stirrings to a definite conclusion and to open a new and great epoch in his career. It was not, however, as the event proved, for the immediate enrichment of a purely instrumental department of art that his inspiration had been quietly gathering force. There is nothing in any previous letter to suggest that he had felt a desire to write for the voice since his university days, but early in February of this year he sends Clara a little song; probably, as Litzmann supposes, "Der Nussbaum":—

"Read the text first," he says, "and think of your Robert. I will only tell you that I have made six books of songs, ballads, large, small, four part. You will like some of them very much." *

Before the end of the month he had "quite completed" "a great cycle of Heine's songs, a ballad, 'Belsazar,' a book from Goethe's 'Westöstlichen Divan,' a book of Burns, two books by Mosen, Heine, Byron, and Goethe, and a book of four-part songs." "I have played and sung some of them to Hiller, Verhülst, and others, and will say, as you do when you have played well: 'and they were quite delighted.'"

To his old university friend Töpken he writes on the same date (February 24th):—

"I have been composing only for the voice lately and could quite succumb to it; the singing and surging within me almost makes me forget ignoble matters outside. I shall be unable to bear this excitement long, but am conscious of having done what was possible in so short a time."

The whole soul of the man had, indeed, found its expression in this new medium. It was as though the finest essence of the fruits of ten years had distilled, unperceived, into a hidden fountain of inspiration that had now suddenly

* Litzmann, i. 404 footnote.

broken forth from the mere impulse of its own vital energy. It was not to be quickly restrained. Throughout the year 1840, Schumann wrote songs and nothing but songs, chiefly for one voice, sometimes for two or more; 138 in all. They are, from first to last, the songs of a poet whose nerves vibrate in sympathy with the lightest wave of emotion that has left its record in the verse he is setting, and of a master musician able to render the subtlest shades of feeling in his own language of tone. They are, too, the songs of a true man, to whom sincerity is a law of being and whose emotional energy proceeds from the experience and conviction of his own life. Schumann's activity as a song composer, upon which he entered at the precise moment of his career that was pre-eminently favourable for its success, marks a new phase in the development of the German Lied. With a rich store of emotional experience garnered within him, he was still a young man, loving and beloved, whilst his ten years' absorbed study of the possibilities of the pianoforte from the standpoint of romanticism had put him in possession of a resource which had been at the command of no previous song composer. It would be trite to write in detail about such beloved and familiar possessions as his settings of Chamisso, Rückert, Eichendorff, and above all, Heine. They are no mere melodies set, with pianoforte accompaniment, to words. They are pictures, expressions, suggested by the most intimate convictions of his spirit, in the utterance of which the pianoforte has an equal share with the voice. In Schumann's songs the ideal of the German romantic poets lives purified and transfigured by the sincerity in which their muse was sometimes lacking; in them German romanticism has attained its most enduring vitality; and it may be said of Clara, that to have given her lover strength, by being what she was, for the luxuriant blossoming time of his genius and his striving which the songs represent, constitutes not the least of her claims to remembrance.

"It rather troubles me that you should have put me in the *second* class in your article on songs," Schumann writes on May 9, 1841, to Kossmaly, an occasional contributor to the *Zeitschrift;* "I should not have asked to be placed in the first, but I believe myself to be entitled to a place of my own."

Opp. 24, 25, 29-31, 33-37, 39, 40, 42, 45, 48, 49, 53, 57, were composed in 1840. Nos. 2, 4, 11 of Op. 37 are Clara's settings.

It had been no small deprivation to Clara to be absent from Leipzig throughout the entire concert season of 1839-40, especially as she had not been able to balance against her sense of what she was losing the consciousness of any substantial advance in her outward career. The reputation of the town as a musical centre had grown in lustre with each of the four seasons that had seen Mendelssohn established as its presiding musical genius, and every successive winter brought an increased number of visitors to participate, whether as performers or listeners, in its glorious activity. Of the distinguished foreign virtuosi who appeared on the Gewandhaus platform in the course of this particular season we may mention in the first place the French pianist, Madame Camille Pleyel, whose brilliant and finished virtuosity created a *furore* wherever she appeared, although her programmes do not claim our attention as having been in any way distinctive in the history of reproductive art. Of more serious interest had been the first public performance of a symphony by Schubert at the subscription concert of December 12, 1839, an event the more interesting to Clara since it had been brought about by Robert's means. An ardent admirer from his youth of Schubert's music, Schumann had taken the opportunity of his visit to Vienna in the season 1838-39 to call on the composer's brother, Ferdinand, and had, to use his own expression, positively "shivered with joy" at the sight of the dusty pile of manuscripts he was permitted to inspect. Selecting from among several symphonies the great one in C major, he arranged that it should be sent to Mendelssohn, who received it joyfully and placed it in the programme of the last concert of the season on March 21, 1839. An alarm of fire arrested the performance near the beginning of the first movement and caused the dispersal of the audience, but the work was heard twice in the season 1839–40, and was published without delay by Breitkopf and Härtel, also on Schumann's initiative.

"Clara, I have been blissful to-day," he wrote on December 11, 1839. "A symphony of Franz Schubert's was played at the rehearsal. If you had only been there! It is impossible to describe it to you. All the instruments are human voices and expressive beyond measure. And the instrumentation—in spite of Beethoven—and the length, the heavenly length, like a romance in four volumes, longer than the ninth symphony. I was perfectly happy and wished only that you were my wife and that I could write such symphonies." *

Poor Clara had not only missed this first performance of the symphony, but its repetition on March 12, 1840, also; and now—Liszt was about to pay his first visit to Leipzig. His coming had been announced in the papers as imminent for weeks past, with the object of raising general interest in the occasion, but when he at length arrived on the morning of his first concert day, March 17th, accompanied by his agent, the action of the latter, who at the eleventh hour reserved more than half the seats in the Gewandhaus Hall at considerably raised prices—a proceeding hitherto unheard of in the musical annals of Leipzig—raised a storm of indignation little less violent than that which had been excited eleven years earlier when Paganini had arrived in the city and quitted it without showing himself to the public. Liszt's concert came off, and the astonishment excited by his marvellous technical powers obtained for him noisy and prolonged demonstrations of applause, but his programme—consisting of his transcription for pianoforte solo of the scherzo and finale from the "Pastoral Symphony," his Pacini variations, chromatic galop, and an *étude* which was played with marvellous delicacy—did not really suit the taste of his audience, and so few tickets were taken for the second concert arranged for the next day, that an hour or two before the hour appointed for the opening of the doors he caused an announcement of his indisposition to be circulated, and, retiring to the seclusion of his room,

* "Jugendbriefe," p. 307.

remained there for a day or two, inaccessible to all visitors except his personal friends, Mendelssohn, Schumann, Hiller, and Count Reuss. This set the seal on the catalogue of his misdemeanours, and it seemed doubtful whether he would be able to venture on another appearance.

"How I wish you were here," writes Robert to Clara. "People seem to have lost their senses. Liszt arrived, much spoilt by the aristocrats, and complained so continually of the absence of toilettes, countesses, and princesses that I became vexed and told him we had our aristocracy also; 150 bookshops, 50 printing presses, and 30 journals, and that he had better take care. He only laughed, did not trouble himself about what is usual here, and now the papers have fallen on him violently. . . ." *

"The newspapers rained down explanations and counter-explanations, criticisms and accusations, and this, that and the other that had nothing to do with music," wrote Mendelssohn a little later on, describing events to his family, "so that one had as much annoyance from his [Liszt's] visit as pleasure, though the pleasure was sometimes very great.

"It occurred to me that the bad feeling might, perhaps, be allayed if the people were to see and hear him privately, and I suddenly determined to give him a soirée in the Gewandhaus with orchestra, chorus, negus, cakes, Meeres-stille, Psalm [Mendelssohn's lately composed 'As the hart pants'], Bach's triple concerto (Liszt, Hiller and I), choruses from 'St. Paul,' Fantasia on 'Lucia,' [Liszt], Erlkönig, the devil and his grandmother, and every one was so delighted and played and sang with such enthusiasm that they said they had never passed a more enjoyable evening and my object was accomplished, and in a very pleasant way." †

Schumann speaks in the *Neue Zeitschrift* of the delightful evening, which in fact restored the Leipzigers so effectually to good humour that Liszt played at his second concert to a crowded room and produced the extraordinary impression which was invariably excited at this period by his performance of Weber's Concertstück, the first piece on the programme.

* Litzmann, i. 416.   † "Mendelssohns Briefe," ii. 225.

It was followed by his own "Huguenot" fantasia and transcriptions of Schubert's "Ave Maria," "Ständchen," and "Erlkönig," the last named "by general desire."

Meanwhile the presence of the concert-giver had completely changed the usual atmosphere of sober Leipzig.

"We have had nothing the last few days but dinners and suppers, music and champagne," reports Robert, who had previously observed to Clara that Liszt, "spoilt by Vienna," had allowed himself too many caprices. "In short, he has overturned our whole life. We all love him boundlessly, and he played again like a god at his [second] concert yesterday. The clamourers and chatterers have been silenced."

For us the most noteworthy of the festivities arranged in Liszt's honour was a dinner-party given by Hiller at which some of the leading residents of Leipzig were present. Who that has sympathetically followed the story of Schumann's brave struggle for the possession of his art will not feel a thrill of affection for Liszt's memory on hearing that after he, as the guest of the evening, had toasted Mendelssohn in his own graceful manner, he rose again to do honour to Schumann, proposing his health in a felicitous speech that paid tribute to the genius he had already unequivocally recognised in another fashion? It must have been a happy moment for the young composer, who found himself frankly recognised for the first time in a society of leading Leipzig musicians as one who counted among them! And Liszt made generous amends for his sins, and still further delighted the Leipzigers, by offering a third concert for the benefit of the pension fund of their orchestra. The programme was to be a very special one; to include the names of Liszt's three friends then in Leipzig, Mendelssohn, Schumann and Hiller, as represented severally by the pianoforte concerto No. 2 in D minor, the Carnaval, and *études* in D flat major and C minor, and to end with the concert-giver's favourite "Hexaméron." Clara received a pressing joint invitation from Schumann and Liszt to come from Berlin to hear it, and of course she could not do otherwise than joyfully accept the proposal. The artistic impression created by the performances was, however, somewhat disappointing.

"It may be recorded here, to the astonishment of many more timorous virtuosi," writes Schumann in his review, after quoting the programme, "that Liszt played nearly all these compositions almost at sight. Probably he had a slight previous acquaintance with the studies and the Carnaval, but he saw Mendelssohn's concerto for the first time only a few days before the concert and could not possibly have had time really to study it. To my openly expressed doubt as to whether the rhapsodical life of the Carnaval could make an impression on a general audience, he answered firmly that he hoped so. I think he was, however, mistaken. . . . Though it may contain things that are attractive to certain people, its musical moods change too rapidly to be followed easily by an entire public, which does not like constant surprises. This had not occurred to my genial friend, and though he played with great sympathy, and may possibly have succeeded in rousing the interest of individuals, the work did not appeal to the mass of listeners. It was otherwise with Hiller's delicate and characteristic studies, which, written in a more familiar form, were received with warm approval. Mendelssohn's concerto had already been introduced by the composer himself with his quiet, clear mastery. Liszt played the work, as we have said, almost at sight. Few could imitate this feat. The full splendour of his virtuosity was displayed in the concluding number, the Hexaméron, a variation cycle by Thalberg, Herz, Pixis, and Liszt himself. One must marvel at the power which enabled Liszt to repeat half the Hexaméron and then to please the audience by adding his galop. I wish, however, that the public could have heard him perform some of Chopin's compositions, which he plays incomparably and with the greatest sympathy. . . ."

Clara, who arrived at her aunt's house on March 28th, two days before the concert, owns to having felt some disappointment at the performance not only of the Carnaval, but of Hiller's and Mendelssohn's works, but attributes it to the magnified expectations she had been induced to form by her recollection of Liszt's playing in Vienna. "He is, however, a phenomenal pianist, there is no other like him. Here in Leipzig his significance is not understood. The public was much too reserved for such an artist."

Of the man himself she speaks with enthusiasm :—

"His conversation is full of animation and life, and though he is a little inclined to show off, one forgets it entirely. . . . I do not feel at all embarrassed with him ; he is so unconstrained himself that every one must feel at ease in his society. I could not be with him for any length of time, however. His restlessness and excitability are too enervating." *

Leipzig was not, in fact, the most suitable place for the display of Liszt's peculiar gifts. The feverish desire for sensational effect of one kind or another generally characteristic of French romanticism was accentuated in him by the fact that his career was one of personal publicity. He did not sufficiently discriminate between one audience and another, but sought to subdue by his astounding virtuosity those who had been educated to higher ideals. It is probable that he would have left a more enduring impression behind him in the North German city if he had given his hearers better opportunity of appreciating his gifts as an interpreter than was afforded by his performances of the two insufficiently studied works by Mendelssohn and Schumann. We, however, as loyal Schumann lovers, can only feel that we, too, "love him boundlessly" for his generous and spontaneous recognition of the genius to which we owe so many happy hours, even though his artistic proclivities may not command our entire sympathy.

The month of April was one of great happiness to the lovers, in spite of the suspense to which they were still condemned as to the issue of the lawsuit. Clara remained in Leipzig for more than a fortnight after Liszt's departure, blissful in the sense of Robert's nearness and in the constant opportunity of making music with him. And this opportunity brought a new conviction to her mind. The wealth of Schumann's genius and the extent and certainty of his acquirement, as she now learned to appreciate them, excited a feeling of surprise even in her, and it became clear to her

* Litzmann, i. 421.

that in the new domain of art upon which he had entered so suddenly he had, in the space of a few short weeks, already proved himself the pre-eminent master among the musicians of his time. To us who have been born and bred, so to speak, in the knowledge and appreciation of the surpassing beauty of the songs, the discovery may not seem particularly noteworthy, yet it was one which, at the period when Mendelssohn was near the height of his fame as a creative musician, whilst Schumann was known only to a circumscribed circle as a promising composer for the pianoforte, of somewhat eccentric tendencies, must have caused Clara strong thrills of wonder and delight.

Schumann accompanied his fiancée to Berlin on April 17th, and stayed on for the remainder of the month as her mother's guest, and perhaps on one or other evening of his visit the "bride's concert" may have taken place which he had bespoken a month previously, writing the express order of the programme. Though it had been arranged as a strictly private entertainment, its memory has an interest for the general music-lover, for Robert had desired Clara to be ready to play him the great Beethoven sonata in B flat, Op. 106—not one or two of its movements, but all four of them—and Bach's C sharp minor fugue from the first book of the "Well-tempered Clavier," and the choice of these two works clearly illustrates the nature of the studies and recreations of the lovers. Then they visited the sights of Berlin together and made excursions to Potsdam and other environs. "Ah, I have been so happy!" exclaims Clara in her diary, unconsciously echoing the words overheard from her by Robert when, as a young girl of fourteen, she had saved him from stumbling over the stones that lay on the road to Connewitz.* Perhaps, however, no occasion brought them such felicity as that on which Mendelssohn, who was staying at the time with his family in Berlin, paid them a long visit for the express purpose of hearing Robert's songs. He had not, so far as can be ascertained from the literature of the time, acknowledged any sympathy with Schumann's strivings since the birthday party at Wieck's

* See *ante*, p. 85.

house in September, 1835, when he had asked Clara for a repetition performance of the scherzo from the F sharp minor sonata. But now he sat for two hours with the colleagues who had always shown him such loyal recognition, and sang all the songs they put before him to Clara's accompaniment, so that Schumann wrote a few days later, "it filled me with happiness." *

Probably Mendelssohn's reserve, which had doubtless been conscientious, was effectively broken down on this occasion. Whatever personal liking he may have felt for Schumann gradually widened from now into considerable interest in his music. He conducted, or attended, the Leipzig performances of Schumann's great works in the years to come, showing his interest in them by every means in his power, and it was on his initiative that Jenny Lind, the most perfect interpreter of Schumann's songs, first made herself acquainted with them, as the present author was assured by Otto Goldschmidt, the husband of the great singer. We have been able in the course of our story to afford the reader occasional glimpses of the friendly relations with Chopin and Liszt which were cultivated as opportunity occurred alike by Schumann and Mendelssohn, and it is pleasant to be able at length to present the two great German representatives of musical romanticism in the enjoyment of an hour's intimate intercourse, in which the appreciation felt by the one for the other's art appears to have been mutual.

Schumann returned to Leipzig on the last day of April, and May ran its course in quiet fashion. The end of the lawsuit seemed to recede ever further from view as the weeks passed on, and the question of ways and means for the summer months, conceivably even for the ensuing winter— the only trouble she would not share with Robert—pressed painfully on Clara's thoughts. She went again to Leipzig in June for a visit of several weeks, and enjoyed whatever there was to enjoy of musical interest during the quiet season of the year, but her ever-present consciousness of the miserable feud existing between her father and lover

* "Briefe," 188. Letter to Dr. Krüger.

disturbed her peace, and she could not cease her longing for the reconciliation of the two people she loved best. Wieck's position was at this time lamentable indeed. The private judgment of his world was against him. The sympathies of the leading musicians, not of Leipzig alone but generally of the towns where he had taken pains to circulate invectives against his daughter and her lover, were with Clara and Schumann, whilst the ultimate verdict of the law, delayed as it might be, was a foregone conclusion. Wieck had suffered many rebuffs during the past few months, which had given him perhaps the first serious set-back in his calling that he had experienced since settling in Leipzig a quarter of a century earlier. Liszt, in pursuance of the desire expressed in his letter of June, 1839, to be of service to Schumann, had not only refused to accept Wieck's call, but had used a pianoforte by Härtel for his concerts instead of choosing one from Wieck's show-rooms, as he would have done under ordinary circumstances. His agent had been successful in an action for libel against Wieck, who, irritated by Liszt's attitude towards himself, had been one of the most active parties to the newspaper agitation of which we have related a few of the circumstances, and Wieck, failing in an appeal against the decision of the court of first instance, had been mulcted in damages. Other lesser occasions of annoyance had not been wanting, and now he was confronted by the imminence of the next hearing of the lovers' suit and the impossibility of finding any evidence to support his charge against Schumann's character. The end of the long struggle between father and daughter was, indeed, much nearer at hand than Clara had dared to dream.

"Robert surprised me with cheering news to-day!" she writes on July 7th. "Father has refused to bring testimony in proof of his assertions. . . . We expect the consent within eight days. I hardly know how I felt on receiving the tidings." *

But the law has its own mysterious processes of delay. It was not until August 1st that the document containing the legal sanction of the marriage was in the hands of the long-

* Litzmann, i. 426.

tried pair, and even then it was subject for the space of ten more days to the possibility of an appeal from Wieck. Clara was helped through the agitation of this last suspense by the activities of a short concert journey arranged by her in Thuringia. She was finally set free from anxiety on August 12th, the day after her appearance at a private state concert given by the Grand Duke and Grand Duchess of Weimar to the Empress of Russia and other august personages who were their guests at the time. At Jena, Weimar, and Castle Altenstein, the country residence of the Duke of Saxe-Meiningen, the young artist was received with the appreciation and even affection which her personal charm, her musical gifts, and her romantic story could hardly fail to arouse. Concerts in Gotha and Erfurt were followed by a second appearance in Weimar, her last as Clara Wieck, at which her lover was present, and on the following day, September 7th, Robert and Clara returned together to Leipzig, quietly, almost solemnly blissful in the consciousness that they had, after many difficult years of struggle, inalienably proved their right to the possession of each other. Robert's libel action against Wieck was withdrawn and the marriage was to take place without delay. They had already chosen their home: " a quiet but pleasant dwelling in Inselstrasse," and Robert pleaded that his bride should come to him on September 12th, the day before her twenty-first birthday.

The imps of the Polterabend comported themselves with decorum on the eve of this wedding, which was passed by the bridal pair in the midst of a few intimate friends, in the quiet happiness that seemed most suitable to the peculiar circumstances of the occasion. Its memory is enshrined in one of the familiar possessions of the musical world—in the special and unique gift presented by Schumann to his beloved. He brought her a specially bound copy of the just published Liederkreis, Op. 25, twenty-six songs in all, which he had called "Myrthen." A special leaf following the title-page contained the dedication, surrounded by a wealth of myrtle leaves, "To his beloved bride." And when we remember that the volume contained not only "Der Nussbaum," "Die Lotosblume," "Du bist wie eine Blume," but, as its first number, the great, passionate " Du meine Seele," we may well wonder whether ever bride before or since has received so rich and rare a tribute.*

The wedding took place at Schöneberg early in the morning of the 12th. Pastor Wildenhahn, an old friend of Schumann's, officiated, and only Clara's mother and the good friend Becker, who had arrived in Leipzig a few days previously, were present at the ceremony. Two or three friends joined the bridal party later in the day and in the evening:—

" There was a little dancing, and on every countenance an expression of quiet content. It was a beautiful day, and even the sun, which had lately been obscured, shone mildly on us as we drove to the wedding, as though to bless our union. Nothing occurred to disturb us during the day, and so let it be noted in this book [the diary] as the happiest and most significant of my life. . . . I always had great faith in God and will ever retain it." †

* As in England the orange flower, so in Germany the myrtle is the bride's symbol.

† Litzmann, i. 430.

CHAPTER XIX

1840–1907

Afterwards

A ND so the romance of Clara Wieck ended and the life of Clara Schumann began; a life that was a continued romance in which gladness and sorrow, trial and victory, love and loss, were blended in such sharp contrasts as have marked the careers of but few of those whose eminence has given us in some sort the right to enter into the memory of the joys and griefs that helped to make them what they were. That Clara's marriage had the immediate result of withdrawing her from the conspicuous public position she had occupied as Clara Wieck in the musical world of Germany, and of postponing her achievement of the European fame for which her father had destined her, resulted necessarily from the fact that henceforth she was first a wife and then an artist. If the conflicting claims of her wifehood and her profession caused her some inward struggle during her first years of wedded life, she remained intensely aware that her husband's happiness and, to a great extent, the ultimate fate of his genius were in her hands and, never flinched from the allegiance she had yielded during her girlhood to love rather than art as the supreme law of her being. She continued to practise her calling, adding important works to her répertoire year by year, and frequently appearing before the public of certain German towns, and especially of her native Leipzig, but made few prolonged or distant tours during her married life; those to Russia in 1844 and Holland in 1854, undertaken in her husband's company, and both very successful, being, perhaps, the most important. The constant development of Robert's career, both in

respect to the marvellously rapid advance of his creative powers
and to their growing acceptance by the musical world, soon
brought it about that whilst Schumann's standing in the eyes
of casual acquaintances ceased to be that of Clara Wieck's
husband, a position he rightly resented, Clara's came to be
in the first place that of Robert Schumann's wife, a change
which, had she had a choice in the matter, she would gladly
have endorsed.   Ripening in musicianship and musical feeling
with the years she spent at Robert's side, she ministered to
his successes and made them her own, whether by her inspired
performances or her comprehensive sympathy, at every new
stage of the achievement of his ripe mastership.   And with
the date of his marriage the period of his full mastership
opens.   Ten years of unwearied striving, during which he had
enriched the literature of the pianoforte by the composition
of a number of large and small works, many of which are
permanently enshrined in the prime affection of music-lovers,
had resulted in the luxuriant outburst of lyrical genius that
had carried him to a place of his own by Schubert's side as
one of the two pre-eminent masters of song, a fact that was
soon to obtain general recognition.   The following decade
witnessed those achievements in the larger forms of art which
confirmed the right he had founded by the publication of the
Études Symphoniques and the Fantasia, Op. 17, to be regarded
—not as a second or lesser Beethoven—but as the Beethoven of
the new musical romanticism in the sense that has been defined
in an earlier chapter of this volume.*   Throughout this period
and during the four sad years that followed it, in the course of
which the master's overtasked energies gradually waned, Clara,
sinking her own artistic individuality to a certain extent, was,
and was content to be, in the first place Schumann's companion
and helpmate.   To enter in detail upon the events of those
fourteen years, or of the epoch lying beyond them, whether in
respect to the advance of Clara's history, the progress of
Schumann's career, or the continued development of interpretative art, is not part of our design.   We have noted the
evolution of the era of so-called musical romanticism from
dawn to maturity, studying it especially as represented by

* See *ante*, p. 121.

Schumann's genius; have followed the course of reproductive art as it was guided to the high ideals of interpretation now familiar to musicians and amateurs, in the first place by Mendelssohn and Clara; and have seen that the musical leadership of Europe, which had passed in the course of the centuries from north to south, had returned to the north. Leipzig reached the consummation of its long progressive development in 1843, when Mendelssohn succeeded in establishing the music school which, under his direction, became a centre within a centre whence something of his own artistic aims was conveyed far and wide through the world by those who had been educated under his influence. He was spared only for four years to rejoice in the prosperity of his achievement, but the musical activity of Leipzig preserved for a while much of the fresh vitality which he had imparted to it, and he left behind him those whose artistic endeavour, guided through life by his spirit, was mighty in the world for good. He died at his house in Leipzig on November 4, 1847, from overwork and the nervous shock caused him by the sudden death of his sister Fanny, in the presence of his wife, brother, and one or two intimate friends, at the age of thirty-eight.

Not as his contemporaries and admirers must confidently have expected has his fame as a composer endured, nor may we look forward with confidence to its vigorous revival. Mendelssohn, gifted with genius, educated with care, filled with the noblest aims, was, throughout his life, too far removed from the struggle that seems indispensable to the development of the sublimest qualities of the creative faculty to produce works entirely representative of his age. Though touched to some extent by the spirit of his time, he was never forced either by circumstances or conviction to grapple with it, or so to wrestle with his own ideas as to compel from them the musical utterance which, corresponding with the thought of the day, might have given immortality to his art as a whole. Whilst his music cannot be seriously considered by the side of that of the great masters who preceded him, it is less representative of the romanticism of the thirties than that either of Chopin or Schumann. Yet though we may perceive that his creative achievement, noble and harmonious as it was, does not possess those supreme qualities attributed to it when its clearness and brilliancy first fascinated the world, we may believe that it has since been unjustly depreciated. Perhaps we may be justified in hoping that in time to come Mendelssohn's name will be remembered with something more than historical interest, and that, in particular, certain of his orchestral and chamber music compositions may be reserved for enduring life.

Not quite two years after Mendelssohn's death, on October 17, 1849, Frédéric Chopin passed away in his rooms in Paris, 12, Place Vendôme at the age of forty, supported in his dying hours by the ministrations of his sister and a few friends and favourite pupils, and having been provided with the necessities and comforts of his last weeks on earth by the generosity of a Scotch lady, Miss Stirling. His naturally delicate constitution had never completely recovered from the hardships of the winter 1838–39, passed in Majorca, and the seeds of consumption which had declared themselves soon afterwards had been fostered by his participation in the life of Paris *salons*, the morbid excitability of his musical imagination, and later, by his disturbed relations and final break with George Sand, from whom he parted in 1847 after a friendship of more than nine years. Chopin's place amongst musicians, which, as we have seen, was a matter of controversy during his life, has gradually become recognised in the sixty odd years that have passed since his death as that of one of the few preeminent writers for the pianoforte of all time, and, on his own lines, unapproached and unapproachable. Romantic in every tone and phrase, the peculiar quality of his genius presents itself to us as the spontaneous product of the time and place of his birth. Fortunately its guidance was entrusted from his childhood to experienced and able hands, by which it was developed to the best advantage. Chopin has sometimes been erroneously classed, as a musician, with the French romanticists with whom the chance of circumstances associated him in friendship. His artistic temperament was, in truth, completely different from theirs, though it was no doubt from Chopin that Liszt learned some of the most fascinating qualities of his playing. Violent contrast, startling sensationalism, on which the French romanticists, in whatever branch of art, relied for their characteristic effects, were abhorrent to Chopin's sensitive nature that delighted in refinement of detail, symmetry of form, and perfection of style. Not a little striking is it that the wave of national feeling which spread through Teutonic Europe in the beginning of the nineteenth century, leading to the revival of myth and legend and folklore that inspired much of the work of Weber and those he represents, should have reappeared in the young Polish composer of the next generation, manifesting itself from his childhood in his fondness for the Slavonic tunes of his own country, his curiosity as to their origin, his interest in adapting them to his own musical purposes. The attractiveness of his melodies and rhythms is partly to be traced to his nationality; and, whether in the forms of his own invention, as in the independent scherzi and ballades—the latter inspired by works of the Polish poet Mickiewicz—or in those of the characteristic dances of Poland, the Polonaise and Mazurka, which he has idealised and extended, or in others that he found ready to his hand, he was above all the tone-poet of his people. The entire fruits of Chopin's genius do not occupy a large space upon our library shelves. The opus numbers of the works, most of them in small form, which he published during his life reach sixty-five, to which eight sets of pianoforte pieces, many of them belonging to his early youth, and seventeen Polish songs were added after his death. They represent, however, the fulfilment of an ambition expressed by Chopin in a letter of December, 1831, to his teacher, Joseph Elsner, of Warsaw. They helped to " bring about a new era " in the art of the pianoforte which, so far as can be seen, will not yet be superseded.

Schumann, then, was the survivor of the three pre-eminent composers who brought to its matured expression the musical romanticism that had been born of the word and tone-poets of the generation that preceded them. That his development from the year 1840, which marks the close of the inward and outward, the personal and artistic, struggles of his youth brought him into closer outward harmony with tradition,

and that his symphonic period found him successfully treading
the paths of the Vienna masters, has been matter for frequent
comment, varying according to the various standpoints of
those who have made a study of the progressive phases of
his career. Perhaps the uncompromising disciples of modern
tendencies who see in his later achievement a falling away
from the promise of his youth have not entirely entered into
the intention of his early striving. It is certain that the
young Schumann believed it probable that the development
of the art of music might proceed in the direction of adding
to its power of distinctness and detail as the reflection of
life, but apart from one or two passages in his youthful
correspondence there is nothing in his early work, whether
as author or composer, to show that he ever looked forward
to the achievement of this end by revolutionary means. That,
on the contrary, he desired almost from the commencement
of his artistic career to make himself master of classical form
is evident from the details of his progress ; and acquaintance
with the youthful works in which he attempted it and of
the later ones in which he mastered it, leads to the conviction
that he must have devoted much strenuous labour to its
acquirement of which we do not possess the record. Meanwhile he gave expression to his inexhaustible musical ideas
in forms of his own invention which, proving more or less
adequate for his purpose, enabled him to speak to music-
lovers in an absolutely new idiom that they gradually learned
to appreciate and that was rendered continually clearer and
more significant by his growing command of resource. One
might almost say of the first years of Schumann's career that
the desires and ardours of his temperament, by forcing themselves into articulate musical utterance in one shape or another
as they were affected by the outward events of his life,
served him in some sort as the substitute for the power of
symmetrical design which he had not as yet acquired. But
we, at least, cannot share the apparent regret of some of
his later critics that, having once attained to full knowledge
of the law, he availed himself of the freedom and support
he obtained by moulding his ideas to its demands. Are the
thoughts of the pianoforte quintet less glowing from being

arranged as a symmetrical whole, the parts and proportions of which are readily evident to the mental vision? Are the themes less valuable in themselves because they are combined into a perfected unity? That the passionate outburst of the Fantasia Op. 17 is not arranged in quite clearly defined shape and is none the less impressive on this account, is, in our opinion, only one of those exceptions which go to prove a truth. And the truth which concerns us here is that neither life nor art, which should be at once the reflection and inspiration of life, can be developed to any high significance except under ordered restraint. Schumann's matured principles did not lead him in the direction of so-called "programme music," nor, if they had done so, would they have been consistent with the convictions of his youth.

His acquaintance with Liszt did not advance to permanent intimacy. Resembling each other in noble generosity of nature, the two musicians were too radically dissimilar in all other respects to become closely united in personal or artistic friendship. Liszt's standpoint as a virtuoso is well described in his words to Wasielewski :—

" The repeated failure of my public and private performances of Schumann's works discouraged me from placing and retaining them in my concert programmes. . . . It was an error which I have since recognised and heartily regretted, as I have become aware that, for an artist worthy to be so called, the danger of displeasing the public is far less serious than that of allowing himself to be guided by its caprices. . . . Though my faintheartedness in regard to Schumann's works may, perhaps, be to some extent extenuated in view of the prevailing bad taste of the time, I am aware of having shown an unfortunate example which I am scarcely in a position to rectify. The force of habit and the slavery of the artist who depends for his existence and renown on the encouragement and applause of the public are so restrictive as to make it extremely difficult even for the more intelligent, of whom I am proud to count myself one, to maintain their better *I* against the vehement, indiscriminate *we*." *

Liszt finally abandoned his virtuoso career in 1847, when

* Wasielewski, Appendix F.

at the zenith of his fame. For the achievement of its highest
victories, those of the artist who becomes the leader, rather
than the entertainer, of the public, he had not, as we perceive
by his own confession, the moral strength. In the illusory
triumphs of the phenomenal executant who dazzles his
audience with prodigious technical feats, neither his intellect
nor his feelings could find satisfaction. The most fruitful
period of his career was still before him when, at the age
of thirty-eight, he settled in Weimar as Kapellmeister of
the court theatre with the declared purpose of championing
the cause of musical progress by producing works of talent
not written with a view to immediate success and having
little prospect, therefore, of being brought to a hearing
elsewhere. In this capacity Liszt's rare gifts as an interpreter
found adequate scope. He identified his name in the first
place with the works of Berlioz and Wagner, but preserved
his interest in the art of Schumann, whose " Manfred " music
was heard for the first time on June 13, and repeated on
June 17, 1852, at Weimar under Liszt's direction, and whose
opera " Genoveva," first performed in Leipzig, he gave later
on. Liszt became known, during the twelve years of his
residence in Weimar, as the leader of the " New-German "
party, whose warfare with the classicists of Leipzig became
notorious and embittered about the middle of the nineteenth
century, and to his efforts must be ascribed in the first
instance the ultimate triumph of Wagner's art.

That Schumann, having fought his way alone, yet ardently
and hopefully, through the preliminary stages of musicianship,
should, on his achievement of ripe mastership, perform
rapid and glorious deeds for the enrichment of his beloved
art was to be expected from his passionate genius. Nevertheless, as we look back from the height of his performance
on the two main periods into which his career naturally
falls and which are linked together by the year of his marriage
—the song year—we may well marvel both at the nine
years of study with their immediate results, and the ten
or eleven of richest fruition which teach us to realise what
the studies had been. These pages are concerned with
Schumann's activity as a composer for the pianoforte, and

the space at our disposal only allows us to remind the reader that the great list of works produced during the two years following that of his marriage includes the symphonies in B flat and D minor (first form), the symphony movements Op. 52, the first movement of the pianoforte concerto, the three string quartets, the pianoforte quartet and quintet, and smaller pieces. To his compositions for pianoforte alone he added nothing, during his mature period, that can be considered as important in comparison with the productions of the earlier half of his career—the six fugues on the name of Bach being written for the organ—but in the domain of chamber music for pianoforte and strings, in which he won such triumphant victories in 1842, and which he further enriched later, notably with the D minor and F major trios, his achievements rank amongst those of the greatest masters of his art. And not only in this domain. The concerto for pianoforte and orchestra is a gem of art. Romantic in thought, masterly in design, and written throughout with the freedom that only mastery can give; rich in poetic ideas that are exhibited in continual variety of aspect; rhythmically interesting; effective for the soloist's display, though its passages are never constructed merely with a view to the requirements of virtuosity, it occupies a distinctive place amongst the few pre-eminent works of its class, and examination of its parts and details and of their combination into an artistic whole furnishes in itself sufficient answer to those who have seen in the composer's later employment of classical form the abandonment of his youthful ardour for progress.

That Schumann consistently looked forward to a new musical era, to be brought about not by the destructive, but by the adaptive energy of the years to come, is borne out by the circumstances of his welcome to Johannes Brahms, who visited him in the autumn of 1853 bringing a packet of MSS. for the master's inspection, and by the terms of his introduction of the obscure young stranger from Hamburg to the musical world in his essay "New Paths." That Brahms' youthful works already exhibited the combination of freedom with mastery in the art of design which was one of the characteristics of his maturity, that they showed unusual command of resource acquired by the study of traditional learning and applied to modern purposes, that they were rich in original harmonic and rhythmic combinations, and that their ideas were to a great extent romantic, fully explains the enthusiasm which caused Schumann to overlook their defects of imma- turity. He perceived, in the youthful genius, the fully equipped musician already in a position to carry to a further point the realisation of his own dream and to give musical expression to the spirit of the age in forms expanded to meet its requirements. The coming of Brahms was one of the last great pleasures of Schumann's life. The strain of twenty-four years of incessant musical activity, during which he lived successively in Leipzig, Dresden, and Düsseldorf, had told permanently on his vital powers. He became more and more frequently subject to the attacks of morbid depression from which he had occasionally suffered from youth, and was struck down in February, 1854, by the crisis of his nervous malady. He passed the last two years and five months of his life under the care of Dr. Richarz, of Endenich, near Bonn, comforted as far as might be by the loving solicitude of his wife and the affection of his dear young musicians, Brahms and Joachim, and sank peacefully to rest on July 29, 1856, soon after completing his forty-sixth year.*

It was in the first year of her husband's last illness that Frau Schumann, deriving strength from the necessities of her position, nerved herself for the resumption of the virtuoso's duties, from which she had in some measure withdrawn on her marriage. The date of her lonely departure in the autumn of 1854 on a prolonged tour in Germany, undertaken in the interests of her young children, who were now dependent on her exertions, was to prove to all intents and purposes the date of the continuation of the career that had virtually been suspended when, as Clara Wieck, she had returned in April, 1838, from her successes in Austria. Not again till the close of a long and strenuous life was she to know pause or rest from the victories and cares of the successful executive artist.

---

* The author has given details of the last two years of Schumann's life in her " Life of Johannes Brahms."

For the joy of ministering to her husband's needs, of constituting his home as the temple of his genius, of intervening as far as possible between him and every untoward occurrence that might disturb the current of his creative impulse, she was to exchange the sacred duty of spreading far and wide, by means of her own powers of enchantment, the appreciation of his art. And throughout the vicissitudes of her chequered lot, Frau Clara fought gloriously and won nobly. The wounds which had torn her heart when, standing as a young girl between father and lover, she had remained indomitably loyal to both, were healed as far as might be in the third year of her marriage. The outstanding business affairs between her father and herself were taken in hand and brought to a settlement by Major Serre in 1841,* a reconciliation took place in 1843, on Wieck's initiative, first between his daughter, and afterwards between her husband and himself, and Clara had the satisfaction of knowing her father happily occupied with the musical education of his second daughter, her young sister, Marie Wieck, who, growing up to be a pianist of distinction, successfully practised her art until her ripe old age. Throughout life, however, sorrow dogged Clara's footsteps in the train of joy. Three times was her mother's heart—abundantly satisfied by the youthful promise and devotion of her children —pierced by the hand of death, whilst the progress of an incurable mental infirmity obliged her to place her eldest son, who was to survive her, under a doctor's care when he was on the threshold of his manhood. Yet, upheld by her own strong nature and the devotion of the daughters who remained at her side, she endured and battled on and conquered, confirming ever, with the progress of the years, her glorious renown as an artist whose art had been sanctified by the fullness of an unchanging love.

The first artistic journey undertaken by Frau Schumann after the tragedy of her life fell upon her, was succeeded in the immediately following years by tours in Holland, Austria, Great Britain and Ireland. These laid the foundation of a world-wide fame that gradually placed her alone with Anton Rubinstein, her junior by ten years, at the head of the great

* " Schumann's Briefe," 512, note 263,

pianists of Europe. The long period of her mature career was the period of the triumph of interpretative art. In its great high priest, the unparalleled violinist and reproductive musician Joseph Joachim, she found a colleague whose aims she shared, and in the innumerable engagements and concert journeys in which they were associated these two incomparable executants led to its consummation the rapidly proceeding popularisation, of which we have traced the beginnings in our early chapters, of the instrumental art of the great masters of all periods. Joachim, passing at the age of twelve from the Konservatorium of Vienna to live for four or five years under the influence and protection of Mendelssohn in Leipzig, became fired at an early age with Mendelssohn's ideals, for the appreciation of which the earnest bent of his own genius made him peculiarly fitted. A temporary alliance, after Mendelssohn's death, with Liszt and his party produced in him a feeling of profound dislike for the tendencies of the New-German group, and he was led to make special overtures of artistic friendship to Schumann, whom he had learned to recognise as the living representative of the masters of tradition revered by him from childhood as the prophets of musical art. The intimacy thus formed between the great composer of forty-two and the famous young violinist of twenty-one established a permanent bond between Frau Schumann and Joachim, who, as time passed on, became invested in the eyes of the public with the halo of special authority, the one in virtue of her position as Schumann's widow, the other of the close relation in which he had stood to Mendelssohn, which combined with the artistic genius and magnetic personality possessed in different degrees by either artist to render their influence paramount in the musical world of Europe. The particular characteristics of Frau Schumann's style were : beauty of tone, which combined great fullness of sound with roundness of quality ; rhythmic clearness and decision ; broadness of phrasing ; passionate impulse that could give place to delicate tenderness ; and unswerving sincerity of interpretation. Her technique was not always perfectly " clean." The enthusiasm that bore her irresistibly onward when she was interpreting a favourite work engrossed her so completely that she occasionally struck wrong notes, especially when under the agitation of public performance; but she was herself more sensible [of this liability—hardly to be called a defect—than the audiences whom she carried away by her inspiration. Her hands, which, as we have seen, had been carefully trained for the pianoforte from her early childhood, were finely developed and had an unusual "stretch." She could perform passages of tenths with as much ease as the ordinary pianist can play octaves. This feature of her technique has its memorial in some of Schumann's compositions, notably in the finale of the "Études Symphoniques." Gradually discarding from her répertoire, from the date of her marriage, the mere virtuoso pieces which, as we have seen, had formed a necessary part of her early programmes, she was perhaps at her finest in works of Beethoven and Schumann. Of Beethoven's sonatas, beside the Op. 53 in C major, and the Op. 57 in F minor, Op. 101 in A major and Op. 109 in E major were particular favourites with her during the middle and later years of her career. Of Beethoven's concertos her playing of the poetic No. 4 in G major was especially memorable. All Schumann's works, large and small, were in her répertoire. Among her most vividly remembered English performances of his unaccompanied pianoforte solos, from 1867 (her first season at the St. James's Hall "Popular Concerts"), are those of the F sharp minor sonata, Études Symphoniques, Carnaval, Davidsbündler Tänze, Kreisleriana, Fantasiestücke Op. 12, Romance in F sharp major from Op. 28, Novelette No. 1 in F major. Probably no such fine interpretations of the masterpieces of chamber music for pianoforte and strings have been heard since Mendelssohn's death as those given by her in association with Joachim, Piatti, and their colleagues in London and the British provinces during the palmy years of the Monday and Saturday "Pops."

And as the career of Clara Wieck had been historically distinctive in the annals of musical art, as to Clara Wieck attaches the glory of having been the first pianist to lead her musical public to the appreciation of the masterpieces for her instrument of Bach and Beethoven, Schumann and Chopin, so did it fall to the lot of Clara Schumann to be the pioneer of the pianoforte works of Brahms. She it was who introduced his name in the first instance not only to the music-lovers of many German towns, but to the public of Vienna and London. Hers were the first public performances of the Andante and Scherzo from Brahms' F minor sonata, Op. 5, of selections from the Ballades, Op. 10, of the variations on an original theme, Op. 21, No. 2, the Handel variations and fugue, Op. 24, the G minor pianoforte quartet, Op. 25, and of an unpublished sarabande and gavotte not now in existence. Bach, Beethoven, Schumann, Chopin, Brahms. A goodly list!

Frau Schumann retained to the end of her artistic life the simplicity of manner that had characterised her in her girlhood when before the public, combining with it in her maturity the unconscious dignity of bearing that comes insensibly to those who have faced and conquered the sorrows of life, and the pathetic attractiveness of her appearance in middle age, with the atmosphere of romance that surrounded her, added a touch of reverence to the affection with which she was regarded that seemed to place her on terms of sympathetic affection with the great audiences that used to assemble to hear her play. In private life she was regarded with profound veneration and esteem, which she justified by her great goodness of heart and devotion to duty. That prolonged intimate association with her was always easy cannot be said. Her naturally sensitive nerves had been rendered acutely susceptible to passing impressions by the conflicts of her life and the strain of a long public career, and she became apt to see slights and insults where none were intended. She could not easily be induced to believe there might be another side to a question on which she had formed a strong opinion, nor, once seriously offended, did she readily forget and forgive. Her innate power of commanding affection was, however, so great that those who had once loved her could not choose but love on, even though they might know themselves misjudged by her. The position she occupied during her forty years of widowhood in the large circle of her personal friends, among whom Schumann's beloved Johannes Brahms and Joseph Joachim stood foremost, is best estimated by perusal of the selection from her correspondence contained in the third volume of her biography: " Clara Schumann und ihre Freunde," by Berthold Litzmann.

Frau Schumann occasionally exercised her talent for composition after her marriage, and her published works, reaching to the number of twenty-three, include a trio for pianoforte and strings, three preludes and fugues for pianoforte alone, and three romances for pianoforte and violin.

She gave private lessons to pupils of talent at certain seasons of the year throughout her long career, and in 1878 accepted an appointment at the Konservatorium founded by Dr. Hoch in Frankfurt, where she trained many musicians who have attained distinction and have carried to various parts of the world the traditions of the great art of pianoforte playing acquired by them from her teaching and influence. She suffered much during her last ten years of life from failing health, and especially from increasing deafness, but retained till the end her vivid interest in her art. The last tones she heard were those of Nos. 4, 5, 6 from Schumann's Intermezzi, Op. 4, and finally the beautiful F sharp romance from Op. 28. These were played to her on May 9, 1896, by her grandson, Ferdinand Schumann, as she lay between life and death after making a partial recovery from a slight paralytic seizure by which she had been attacked some weeks before. She passed away in the presence of her daughters in the afternoon of May 20th in the seventy-seventh year of her age, and was borne to her rest by her husband's side in the cemetery of Bonn on May 24th, attended by her children and grandchildren and a crowd of personal friends and of admirers of her art, leaving a great memory behind her and a vacant place to which there can be no successor. In less than a year after her death Brahms followed her to the unknown spaces beyond the limits of time, and in August, 1907, Joachim also departed. Thus a glorious period of art which had brought to its fruition the evolution of the ages finally closed, and the future calls to us with uncertain voice.

APPENDIX

LIST OF THE PUBLISHED WORKS

OF CLARA WIECK.

Op.
1 Quatres Polonaises ... ... For Pianoforte Solo
2 Caprices en forme de Valses... ... ... ,, ,, ,,
3 Romance varié... ... ... ,, ,, ,,
4 Valse romantique ... ... ,, ,, ,,
5 Quatre Pièces caractéristiques ... ... ,, ,, ,,
6 Soirées musicales, contenant :
    Toccatina, Ballade, Nocturne ... ... ,, ,, ,,
    Polonaise et deux Mazurkas ... ... ,, ,, ,,
7 Premier Concert ... ... For Pianoforte with
    orchestral accompaniment
8 Variations de Concert sur la Cavatina du Pirate
    de Bellini ... ... For Pianoforte Solo
9 Souvenir de Vienne. Impromptu ... ... ,, ,, ,,
10 Scherzo ... ... ,, ,, ,,
11 Trois Romances ... ... ,, ,, ,,

OF CLARA SCHUMANN.

12 Three Songs (originally published as Nos. 2, 4, 11, of Robert Schumann's Op. 37).
13 Six Songs.
14 Second Scherzo ... ... For Pianoforte Solo
15 Four Fugitive Pieces ... ... ,, ,, ,,
16 Three Preludes and Fugues ... ... ,, ,, ,,
17 Trio for Pianoforte, Violin, and Violoncello.
20 Variations on a Theme of Robert Schumann ... ,, ,, ,,
21 Three Romances ... ... ,, ,, ,,
22 Three Romances for Pianoforte and Violin.
23 Six Songs.
    Cadenzas to Beethoven's concertos in C minor and G major.
    Cadenza to Mozart's concerto in D minor.

N.B.—Opp. 18 and 19 do not appear in any publisher's catalogue. They are probably to be identified as the works which appeared without opus number :
    Andante and Allegro for Pianoforte.
    Song ' Am Strande ' (compare Litzmann, iii. 614).

LIST OF ROBERT SCHUMANN'S PUBLISHED WORKS FOR KEYED INSTRUMENTS

The references are to the pages of this work.

Op.	Title of Work.	Published	Pages
	For Pianoforte Solo.		
1	Theme on the name "Abegg" with variations	1831	57, 58
2	Papillons	1832	57, 58, 59, 75, 76, 84
3	Studies after caprices by Paganini	1832	76, 82, 83, 84
4	Intermezzi	1833	84
5	Impromptus on a theme by Clara Wieck	1833	86
6	Davidsbündlertänze	1838	217–219, 328
7	Toccata	1834	125
8	Allegro	1834	75, 109
9	Carnaval, Scènes mignonnes sur quatre notes	1837	110–115, 219, 222, 238, 251, 252, 299, 308, 309
10	Six Concert Studies after caprices by Paganini	1835	168, 169
11	Sonata. F sharp minor	1836	130, 131, 149, 150, 151, 167, 168, 169–172
12	Phantasiestücke	1838	216, 217, 251, 257, 269, 328
13	Études en forme de variations (XII Études Symphoniques)	1837	115–123, 203, 204, 205, 206, 233, 234, 328
14	Grand Sonata. No. 3. F minor	1836	166, 175–178
15	Kinderscenen	1839	257, 258, 289, 290
16	Kreisleriana	1838	257
17	Phantasie. C major	1839	175, 284–289, 317, 322
18	Arabesque	1839	275
19	Blumenstück	1839	275
20	Humoresque	1839	276
21	Novelletten	1839	256, 257, 295, 328
22	Sonata No. 2. G minor	1839	275, 295, 296, 297
23	Nachtstücke	1840	277
26	Faschingsschwank aus Wien. Phantasiebilder	1840	296, 297–299
28	Three Romances	1840	296, 299
32	Four Pieces: Scherzo, Gigue, Romance, and Fughetta	1841	275
68	Album for the Young	1849	
72	Four Fugues	1850	
76	Four Marches	1849	
82	Waldscenen	1851	
99	Bunte Blätter. Fourteen pieces	1852	275
111	Three Phantasiestücke	1852	
118	Three Pianoforte Sonatas for the Young. G, D, and C major	1854	
124	Albumblätter. Twenty pieces	1854	275
126	Seven Pieces in Fughetta form	1854	
133	Gesänge der Frühe. Five pieces	1855	

Op.	Title of Work.	Published.	Pages

For Pianoforte Duet.

66	Bilder aus Osten	1849	
85	Twelve pieces	1850	
109	Ballscenen	1853	
130	Kinderball. Six easy pieces	1854	

For Two Pianofortes.

46	Andante with variations. B flat major	1844	

For Pianoforte with Orchestral Accompaniment.

54	Concerto. A minor	1846	324
92	Introduction and Allegro appassionato. G major	1852	
134	Concert Allegro with Introduction. D minor	1855	

For Pianoforte with Various Instruments.

44	Quintet for Pianoforte, two Violins, Viola, and Violoncello. E flat	1843	321, 322, 324
47	Quartet for Pianoforte, Violin, Viola, and Violoncello. E flat	1843	324
63	Trio for Pianoforte, Violin, and Violoncello. D minor	1848	324
80	Trio for Pianoforte, Violin, and Violoncello. F major	1850	324
110	Trio for Pianoforte, Violin, and Violoncello. G minor	1852	
132	Märchenerzählungen for Pianoforte, Clarinet, and Viola	1854	
88	Phantasiestücke for Pianoforte, Violin, and Violoncello		
105	Sonata for Pianoforte and Violin. A minor	1852	
121	Sonata for Pianoforte and Violin. D minor	1853	
70	Adagio and Allegro for Pianoforte and Horn	1849	
73	Phantasiestücke for Pianoforte and Clarinet	1849	
94	Romances for Pianoforte and Oboe	1851	
102	Stücke im Volkston for Violoncello and Pianoforte	1851	
113	Märchenbilder for Pianoforte and Viola	1852	

OP.	TITLE OF WORK.	PUBLISHED.	PAGES
	FOR PEDAL PIANOFORTE.		
56	Studies	1845	
58	Sketches	1846	
	FOR ORGAN.		
60	Six Fugues on the name "Bach"	1850	

INDEX OF NAMES

ERRATA.

P. 82, l. 22, *for* Dr. C. F. Pohl *read* M. Pohl.
P. 249, l. 24, *for* Haslinger *read* Hofmeister.

UNWIN BROTHERS, LIMITED, THE GRESHAM PRESS, WOKING AND LONDON.

Telegrams :
" Scholarly, London."
Telephone :
No. 1883 Mayfair.

41 and 43 Maddox Street,
Bond Street, London, W.
February, 1912.

Mr. Edward Arnold's
LIST OF NEW BOOKS,
Spring, 1912.

————•◄►•————

SERVICE MEMORIES IN FOUR CONTINENTS.

By Surgeon-General Sir A. D. HOME, V.C., K.C.B.

Demy 8vo.   With Portrait.   **12s. 6d. net.**

These interesting reminiscences of an Army Surgeon on active service cover a wide field of work. Beginning with early years of service in the West Indies, the author soon proceeded to the Crimea, where he remained until peace was declared. A year or two afterwards he joined the expeditionary force destined for China, which was deflected to India by the news of the Mutiny. He was present at the Relief of Lucknow, and won the Victoria Cross for his " persevering bravery and admirable conduct " on that occasion. In 1860 we find him in the East again during the China War, advancing with the Allied Forces to Pekin. At the close of 1861, when the Civil War in America seemed likely to embroil Great Britain, Surgeon Home was sent out to Canada, in readiness for anything that might occur. Fortunately the clouds lifted, and before his return to England the author was able to visit Baltimore and Washington, where he gained many interesting impressions of the war then in progress. The volume concludes with an episode in the Maori War in New Zealand in 1864.

LONDON : EDWARD ARNOLD, 41 & 43 MADDOX STREET, W.

THE PACIFICATION OF BURMA.

By Sir CHARLES CROSTHWAITE, K.C.S.I.,

CHIEF COMMISSIONER OF BURMA, 1887-1890 ; MEMBER OF THE COUNCIL OF INDIA, ETC.

With Maps and Illustrations.   *One Volume.*   *Demy 8vo.*   **16s. net.**

Sir Charles Crosthwaithe succeeded the late Sir Charles Bernard as Chief Commissioner of Burma in March, 1887. From that date until December, 1890, he administered Burma, and he had every opportunity, therefore, of knowing what was done. The measures by which, in four years and in a country which has been described by a soldier as " one vast military obstacle," order and law were established, are narrated. After the military measures, without which no attempt at a Civil Government would have been possible, the constitution of the Indian military police and the establishment on a legal basis of the indigenous village system were the chief means of restoring peace. These measures are explained, and the way in which order was gradually evolved out of confusion is told.

CURRENT POLITICAL PROBLEMS.

By Sir J. D. REES, K.C.I.E.

One Volume.   **5s. net.**

In this book Sir J. D. Rees, K.C.I.E., ex.-M.P., surveys the more important political problems at present before the nation from the points of view of both great parties in the State. The following subjects are dealt with : Imperial Organization, Defence, Foreign Policy, Indian and Colonial Problems, Trade Relations and Tariff Reform, Suffrage, Home Rule, Education, Disestablishment, Finance, Socialism, Labour Questions, Land Reform, and the Constitutional Problems at present before the country. To each great question a chapter is devoted which gives the reader a concise survey of the points at issue and a summary of the position at the present day, and to every chapter are appended the arguments for and against : in the hope that the reader in a few pages may find a guide to the reasons upon which political parties base their case. The information has been compressed into a volume of handy size so as to be of use to speakers and politicians. It is not, however, merely a work of reference—although an excellent index and the sub-division of the chapters make reference easy—but is intended to be read.

REMINISCENCES OF THE YUKON.

By the Hon. STRATFORD TOLLEMACHE.

With 16 full-page Illustrations from drawings by
J. F. HARRISON DUTTON.

One Volume. Demy 8vo. **12s. 6d. net.**

The author's experiences in the Yukon region covered the period from 1898 to 1909. For the first three years he was employed principally in mining, until a severe accident, which resulted in permanent lameness, compelled him to abandon it. For the next two years he lived in Dawson, and then moved to the Pelly River, and remained in the vicinity for about six years, engaged in exploring, hunting, and trapping. His knowledge and experience of a trapper's life enable him to give extremely interesting information about the habits of fur-bearing animals, and the adventures and hardships attendant on their pursuit. Many good yarns are narrated of the early days on the Yukon, and there are a number of graphic illustrations.

OXFORD MOUNTAINEERING ESSAYS.

Edited by ARNOLD LUNN.

With Contributions by M. SADLER, JULIAN HUXLEY, N. EGERTON YOUNG, H. K. LUNN, H. E. G. TYNDALE, and H. R. POPE.

Crown 8vo. **5s. net.**

Periodically the cry goes up that " the Alps are exhausted," but always the rising generation of mountaineers has protested against this opinion, maintaining that the exhaustion was in those who uttered it, and that the fascination of the Alps was, not unchanged perhaps, but as potent and multiform as ever. This collection of Essays, all the authors of which either still are, or have only recently ceased to be, undergraduates, is for the most part an attempt to give literary expression to this protest, by describing, as matter of individual experience, some of the less tangible and obvious elements which enter into the perennial charm exerted on climbers by the mountains. Narratives of new or unrecorded expeditions—except, indeed, those accomplished on the roofs of Oxford Colleges—of course find no place in it, but new ground is broken in two of the Essays, dealing respectively with the painting of mountains and mountains in Greek poetry.

THE GIRLHOOD OF CLARA SCHUMANN.

Clara Wieck and her Time.

By FLORENCE MAY,

AUTHOR OF "THE LIFE OF JOHANNES BRAHMS."

One Volume. Demy 8vo. With Portraits. **12s. 6d. net.**

The years covered by the early career of the great pianist who is remembered as Clara Schumann, but who, during her girlhood, became famous in Germany and Austria as Clara Wieck, coincide with an interesting period of musical history; and it is one of the purposes of this book to show that Clara Wieck's artistic activity was epoch-making in the annals of executive art; a fact not definitely recognized in any work bearing on the subject that has hitherto been published, whether in England or Germany.

The musical friendships formed by the youthful Clara with Chopin, Mendelssohn, Liszt, and other great musicians of her day, are noted in the course of the narrative, whilst the progress of the attachment that was to result in her marriage is sketched in an account—presented side by side with that of her own special development—of Schumann's early period. In this are included details of the outward circumstances that were associated with the composer's production of the majority of his works for pianoforte alone.

"FATHER WILLIAM."

By S. L. BENSUSAN,

AUTHOR OF "A COUNTRYSIDE CHRONICLE," ETC.

With Illustrations. Crown 8vo. **5s. net.**

The book is made up of dialogues, impressions, and character studies; it is the record of many years' quiet observation in a corner of the country that no man of letters knows better than the author. Formerly given over to wheat-raising and smuggling, it is only now beginning to recover from a long period of depression that availed to keep the old men and the old customs free from contact with modern thought and enterprise. Here we obtain a vivid picture of a generation that is passing rapidly, and will leave no survivors. "Father William," the aged and choleric shepherd; "Granfeyther," his great rival; Ephraim the carrier; and Elijah Bird, the much-married man, appear in their habit as they live, and supply the author with admirable types of the sturdy East Anglians he loves to portray.

THE PERFECT GENTLEMAN.

A Guide to Social Aspirants.

Compiled from the Occasional Papers of Reginald Drake Biffen.

By HARRY GRAHAM,

AUTHOR OF "LORD BELLINGER," "THE BOLSTER BOOK," ETC.

Illustrated by LEWIS BAUMER.

Crown 8vo. **6s.**

In this volume the author of "Lord Bellinger" and "The Bolster Book" sets out to supply a longfelt want by providing his readers with much excellent, if somewhat frivolous, advice upon a variety of interesting social topics. In these pages a number of interesting subjects, ranging from Art to Table-Manners, from Social Intercourse to Foreign Travel, from Dancing to Country-House Visiting, are dealt with in a light and satirical vein, and the author's lively style should recommend the work, not only to aspirants after social success, but also to every lover of humour. The value of these amusing essays is greatly enhanced by the presence of some sixty clever drawings by Mr. Lewis Baumer, the famous *Punch* artist, which are lavishly scattered throughout the text.

MONETARY ECONOMICS.

By WILLIAM WARRAND CARLILE, M.A.,

AUTHOR OF "ECONOMIC METHOD AND ECONOMIC FALLACIES."

One Volume. Demy 8vo. **10s. 6d. net.**

This book endeavours to demonstrate the futility of the view largely current among the economists to the effect that the more completely money is ignored in economics the better and more philosophically can the subject be treated; and contends that, on the contrary, all economic phenomena are the offspring of the evolution of money. This conception, again, as the writer endeavours to show, is calculated to clear the slate of the mass of tiresome technicalities with which the science has recently become invested; and is calculated, at the same time, to bring into relief those aspects of economic truth which are most thoroughly irreconcilable with Socialistic teaching. In the latter connection the chapters on the Nature of Wealth and the Creation of Wealth are, perhaps, specially worthy of attention.

FROM RELIGION TO PHILOSOPHY.

By FRANCIS MACDONALD CORNFORD,

FELLOW AND LECTURER OF TRINITY COLLEGE, CAMBRIDGE ;
AUTHOR OF " THUCYDIDES MYTHISTORICUS," ETC.

Demy 8vo. **10s. 6d. net.**

Mr. Cornford's theory is that the originators of Greek philosophy
did not, as is usually supposed, turn their backs wholly on religion
and go direct to their own consciousness and the world around them
for data for an explanation of the universe, but that at the very outset
of their investigations they in fact, though unconsciously, took over
certain fundamental conceptions—those of Nature, God, and Soul—
from the religious system which they believed themselves to have
got rid of.   In an elaborate and brilliant argument he traces back
these conceptions to their roots in the " collective mind " of primitive
pre-religious man, and then, having established his theory, applies it
to the explanation of the subsequent history of religious and philo-
sophic thought, on which it throws a flood of new light.

CATHOLICISM AND THE MODERN MIND :

A Contribution to Religious Study and Progress.

With a Prefatory Letter to Pope Pius X.

By MALCOLM QUIN,

AUTHOR OF " AIDS TO WORSHIP," " NOTES ON A PROGRESSIVE CATHOLICISM," ETC.

Crown 8vo. **7s. 6d. net.**

The author of this book was for thirty years an adherent and
advocate of the religious system of Auguste Comte, and head of one
of the communities formed to give effect to the religious conceptions
of that celebrated thinker.   In a Prefatory Letter, addressed to
Pope Pius X., he explains how, as a result of his life's study and
work, he has been led to the conclusion that the religious unity and
advance of mankind cannot be brought about by any revolutionary
attempt to establish a new " religion," or new sect, but depend upon
the common acceptance of Catholicism, so interpreted and expanded
by the modern mind as to render it capable of overcoming the existing religious disorder, and of ultimately unifying all forms of faith
and culture.   From this point of view the writer analyses the
religious and social conditions due to the rise of Protestantism and
unbelief, and seeks to show how the chief Catholic conceptions and
doctrines admit of a construction at once conservative and progressive, in harmony both with the fundamental aims of Catholicism and
with the developing thought and needs of the world.

THE PARTING OF THE ROADS :
Studies in the Development of Judaism and Early Christianity.

By MEMBERS OF JESUS COLLEGE, CAMBRIDGE.

With an Introduction by W. R. INGE, D.D.,
LATE PROFESSORIAL FELLOW, NOW HONORARY FELLOW OF THE COLLEGE AND DEAN OF ST. PAUL'S.

Edited by F. J. FOAKES JACKSON, D.D.,
FELLOW AND DEAN OF THE COLLEGE.

Demy 8vo.   **10s. 6d. net.**

This volume has the distinction of being essentially a young man's book, and the work of a single college, instead of representing the collective opinion of a University.

The essays are not the product of any school, but represent all shades of thought in the Church of England, whilst one is written by a Nonconformist, and another by a Jewish scholar.

With the exception of the introduction by the Dean of St. Paul's and the first essay by the editor, the volume is the work of young men. Although the plan of the volume was sketched by the editor, there has not been any attempt to make it a mere echo of his opinions. The essayists are of very different schools of thought, and have always been encouraged at Cambridge to give full play to their individuality ; and the editor has met with a gratifying determination on the part of his fellow-workers to express their own opinions in their own words.

The object of the work is to trace the origin of Christianity from Judaism, and its development till the final parting of the two religions.

THE OLD TESTAMENT.

By the Rev. H. C. O. LANCHESTER,
RECTOR OF SALL.

Crown 8vo.   **2s. 6d. net.**

An attempt to place the general reader in a better position for the intelligent study of the Old Testament. The main results of the Higher Criticism are frankly accepted, and it is recognized that this movement has been fraught with considerable perils to faith ; but the writer endeavours to point out that modern studies have resulted in a broadening, rather than in an evaluation, of a reasonable faith. Some account is given of the historical background of the Old Testament, and of the assistance which recent researches have afforded to the study of it. The several books are, with few exceptions, briefly reviewed, and a chapter is added on the principles of interpretation which have obtained in different ages.

AN INTRODUCTION TO THE SYNOPTIC PROBLEM.

By the Rev. ERIC REDE BUCKLEY,
VICAR OF BURLEY-IN-WHARFEDALE, PROCTOR IN CONVOCATION.

Crown 8vo. **5s. net.**

This book gives the main results of recent research as to the literary origin and composition of the Gospels of St. Matthew, St. Mark, and St. Luke. A distinctive feature of it is that all the more important passages on which the arguments rest are printed in full in English, thus relieving the reader of the necessity of constant reference to his Bible or Greek Testament. Besides giving a careful explanation of the theories most widely accepted by contemporary critics, the author has stated some alternative theories which seem worthy of consideration. An interesting feature of the book is the discussion of the light thrown on the matter by the Gospel quotations in the Apostolic Fathers, and by the extant fragments of the Gospel according to the Hebrews.

JESUS SALVATOR MUNDI:
Some Lenten Thoughts on Salvation.

By the Rev. J. H. BEIBITZ,
RECTOR OF SHELSLEY BEAUCHAMP AND SHELSLEY WALSH, WORCESTER;
LATE VICE-PRINCIPAL OF THE THEOLOGICAL COLLEGE, LICHFIELD.

Crown 8vo.   Cloth. **2s. 6d. net.**

There are few tasks more important than that of subjecting our ordinary religious ideas to a thoroughgoing analysis. Only so can they become real to us, and gain, or regain, the power of directing and moulding our lives. This little book represents an attempt to fulfil this task in regard to the fundamental Christian conception of our salvation through and in Jesus Christ; in other words, to answer the question in what sense, and by what means, are we " saved "? It is divided into seven sections, or chapters. The first deals with the Lenten season as presenting a great opportunity for clarifying our religious notions; the second, with the New Testament idea of salvation. The third and fourth chapters are concerned with salvation through the Cross and in the Church. The fifth and sixth discuss the meaning of salvation as applied to the social and individual life respectively. The seventh is a meditation on the two-fold sign of the Water and the Blood. It is hoped that the final, practical aim of the whole investigation is borne in mind throughout—namely, that with fuller, clearer conceptions we may be able to enter yet more completely into the riches of our spiritual inheritance.

THE SAINTS' APPEAL.

By the Rev. S. A. ALEXANDER,
CANON AND TREASURER OF ST. PAUL'S;
AUTHOR OF "THE MIND OF CHRIST," ETC.

Fcap. 8vo.   Tastefully bound.   2s. net.

It is hoped that, while suitable for devotional reading throughout the year, the book will be found especially helpful as a companion for quiet hours in Lent. It consists of a selection of the sermons preached by Canon Alexander last year to very large congregations in St. Paul's Cathedral on Sunday afternoons. They are an attempt to show the romance and heroism of the Christian life, to bring the mystical and spiritual side of it into closer touch with ordinary, practical affairs, and to illustrate in general ways the power and fascination both of the belief and of the character of those who have endeavoured to live that higher life under many different conditions of society.

THE "SEVEN AGAINST THEBES" OF ÆSCHYLUS.

Rendered into English Verse by EDWYN BEVAN.

Crown 8vo.   Cloth.   2s. net.

MODERN THEORIES OF DIET,

And their Bearing upon Practical Dietetics.

By ALEXANDER BRYCE, M.D., D.P.H. (Camb.),
AUTHOR OF "THE LAWS OF LIFE AND HEALTH," ETC.

Large crown 8vo.   7s. 6d. net.

The author offers an interesting and informing survey of the important subject of dietetics. He deals fully with all the important systems of diet which are entitled to serious consideration. Questions which have long been much debated are discussed, and the author gives clearly and concisely his own views and those of eminent authorities concerning the different systems of diet. He discusses the problems in relation to the amount and the kind of food required in health and also in disease, and endeavours to arrive at some rational decision which may guide us in the application of dietetic principles in everyday life.

THE
CHEMISTRY OF BREADMAKING.

By JAMES GRANT, M.Sc.Tech., F.I.C., F.C.S.,
HEAD OF THE FERMENTATION INDUSTRIES DEPARTMENT IN THE MUNICIPAL SCHOOL OF TECHNOLOGY, MANCHESTER.

viii + 224 pages. Crown 8vo. **5s. net** *(inland postage 4d.).*

A handbook describing simply and clearly the chief points where breadmaking is brought into contact with Chemistry, Physics and technical Mycology.

SMOKE : A STUDY OF TOWN AIR.

By J. B. COHEN, F.R.S.,
PROFESSOR OF ORGANIC CHEMISTRY IN THE UNIVERSITY OF LEEDS ;

And A. G. RUSTON, B.A., B.Sc.

Demy 8vo.   With 35 Figures. **5s. net.**

An account of experiments and observations carried on during the last twenty years on the effects of the solid and gaseous products of combustion, especially in regard to vegetation.   The daily soot-fall in industrial centres and the causes of town-fog are discussed.

THE THEORY AND DESIGN OF REINFORCED CONCRETE.

By OSCAR FABER, B.Sc. (Lond.), A.M.Inst.C.E.,
And P. G. BOWIE, A.C.G.I.

'Demy 8vo., with 155 Figures. **12s. 6d. net.**

The scientific design of all kinds of structures in reinforced concrete is here treated by two expert engineers.   The mathematical results of the calculation of stresses in a large variety of difficult cases are put into a practical form for practical use.

NEW AND CHEAPER EDITION.

ACROSS THE BRIDGES.
A Study of Social Life in South London.

By ALEXANDER PATERSON.

With Preface by the BISHOP OF SOUTHWARK.

Cloth, **2s. net**; *paper,* **1s. net.**

BOOKS LATELY PUBLISHED.

MEMOIRS AND LETTERS OF THE RIGHT HON. SIR ROBERT MORIER, G.C.B.,

FROM 1826-1876.

Edited by his Daughter, Mrs. ROSSLYN WEMYSS.

In Two Volumes. With Portraits. Demy 8vo. **32s. net.**

"A continuous inner history of Europe. Mrs. Wemyss has concentrated her attention upon the greater matters, but the book is full also of good entertainment. Morier was the most vivacious of letter-writers and a master of apt characterization. We congratulate Mrs. Wemyss on a work which is not only a worthy memorial of a great man, but one of the most valuable political treatises of recent years."—*Spectator.*

"Two well-filled volumes packed with material of the very highest interest to the political student, commendably devoid of padding and decoration, and admirably frank in their comment upon the European history of the second half of the Nineteenth Century."—*Daily Telegraph.*

"These two volumes are indeed a very great record, not only of the service of the man who wrote it, but of the high politics of Europe set down in the most discerning and comprehensive manner."—*Daily News.*

THE FRAMEWORK OF HOME RULE.

By ERSKINE CHILDERS,

AUTHOR OF "WAR AND THE ARME BLANCHE," "THE RIDDLE OF THE SANDS," ETC.

One Volume. Demy 8vo. **12s. 6d. net.**

"It is a work of great ability, and will amply repay either Unionists or Home Rulers for the effort for which it calls."—*Times.*

"This is the ablest and most clear-sighted book that has ever come from any English writer on the subject of Home Rule. It is at once bold and practical, careful in its study of human nature, and daring in its faith in human nature's possibilities. It is certain that 'The Framework of Home Rule' will impress and influence every intelligent man who reads it."—*Daily News.*

"By far the most important contribution to the study of the Irish political problem which has appeared since Home Rule re-emerged into the region of practical politics."—*Irish Times.*

FROM PILLAR TO POST.

By Lieut.-Colonel H. C. LOWTHER, D.S.O., M.V.O.,
SCOTS GUARDS.

With Illustrations. Demy 8vo. **15s. net.** *Third Impression.*

"Colonel H. C. Lowther owes his readers no apology for publishing in 'From Pillar to Post' his reminiscences of a crowded and many-sided life. Very few men of our generation have contrived in the space of a few years to see more of the world, or to see it with so observant and humorous an eye."—*Times.*

"His chapters are so full of good things that 'From Pillar to Post' should prove one of the reminiscence-books most in demand this season."—*Daily Telegraph.*

"Colonel Lowther has written a very delightful book which, from its very unpretentiousness, impresses the mind with a sense of actuality. His careless yarns about the war have more of the real ring about them than acres of florid and bombastic description. We can only urge everyone to beg, borrow, or steal the book and read it."—*Evening Standard.*

MY LIFE STORY.

By EMILY, SHAREEFA OF WAZAN.

With Illustrations. Demy 8vo. **12s. 6d. net.** *Second Impression.*

"This is a very remarkable book, and one that should interest alike those who are fascinated by the romance of reality and those who are always glad to learn about other races from those possessed of intimate knowledge."—*Daily Telegraph.*

"The book is much more than the story of a very exceptional life. It is a mirror of Moorish society in its feminine aspect."—*Times.*

"A remarkable book, and bears on every page the evidence of unvarnished truth."—*Daily News.*

"It may honestly be said that there is not a dull page in it."—*Pall Mall Gazette.*

MY ADVENTURES IN THE CONGO.

By MARGUERITE ROBY.

With Illustrations and a Map. Demy 8vo. **12s. 6d. net.**

"Mrs. Roby not only writes well, with an engaging candour and vivacity, but she has genuinely stirring episodes to describe. She has given us one of the best travel books we have read for a long time."—*Liverpool Courier.*

"A brilliant exposure of humanitarian humbug. After reading the book I have taken every means in my power to test the good faith of the writer. She is a woman whom I cannot describe otherwise than as a born leader. Read the book and you will know some of the qualities required for leadership."—VANOC in the *Referee.*

THE GREAT PLATEAU OF NORTHERN RHODESIA.

By CULLEN GOULDSBURY AND HERBERT SHEANE,
OF THE BRITISH SOUTH AFRICA COMPANY'S SERVICE.

With Preface by Sir ALFRED SHARPE, K.C.M.G., C.B.

With 40 pages of Illustrations and a Map. **16s. net.**

"The most minute, thorough, and interesting description that has yet been written of the vast territory that is called Northern Rhodesia. We thoroughly recommend the book."—*Standard.*

"Not the least interesting of the twenty chapters, each packed with the most valuable material of native African history, is the one dealing with 'animism and witchcraft,' which throws light on the phenomena of black magic and totemism."—*Daily Telegraph.*

THE WILDS OF PATAGONIA.

A Narrative of the Swedish Expedition to Patagonia, Tierra del Fuego, and the Falkland Islands in 1907=1909.

By CARL SKOTTSBERG, D.Sc., etc.

With Illustrations and Maps. One Volume. Demy 8vo. **15s. net.**

"Few books of the kind that I have read in recent years are half as interesting. Instead of bloody records of the butchering of defenceless beasts (for it should never be forgotten that even tigers and rhinoceroses are practically without defence against quick-firing guns) we have an interesting account of plants, stones, natural history, and scientific problems, all set down by a young, well-educated and adventurous man. The book reads like what Captain Cook's adventures might have been had they been written by Sir Joseph Banks, and still preserved Cook's charm."—Mr. R. B. CUNNINGHAME GRAHAM in the *Saturday Review.*

ROUGHING IT IN SOUTHERN INDIA.

By Mrs. M. A. HANDLEY.

With Numerous Illustrations. Demy 8vo. **12s. 6d. net.**

"The scope of Mrs. Handley's book is quite inadequately indicated by the title; it really forms a welcome addition to our knowledge of the vast and complex subject of India in that it contains the impressions of a keen and shrewd observer on many Indian races, their manners, customs, religions, virtues, vices, and idiosyncrasies, as well as admirable descriptions of scenery, vivid accounts of hunting incidents and travel episodes, and instructive little asides on the political and economical, social and racial problems of the great peninsula. We recommend the book thoroughly; it is well written in a style that is as attractive as it is sound, and the matter is worthy of all consideration."—*Standard.*

HANDLEY CROSS;

OR,

MR. JORROCKS'S HUNT.

Illustrated by CECIL ALDIN.

In Two Volumes, with 24 Coloured Plates and about 100 Black-and-White Illustrations. The Ordinary Edition. **21s. net.**

Also a limited Edition de Luxe of 250 copies only for the British Empire, each Copy Numbered and Signed by the Artist. **£3 3s. net.**

THE HORSE :

𝔍ts 𝔒rigin and 𝔇evelopment, combined with 𝔖table 𝔓ractice.

By Colonel R. F. MEYSEY-THOMPSON,

AUTHOR OF "A HUNTING CATECHISM," "REMINISCENCES OF CAMP, COURSE, AND CHASE," ETC.

With Illustrations.   One Volume.   Demy 8vo. **15s. net.**

"All who love horses will find much of absorbing interest in 'The Horse,' for the book contains some of the life experiences of one of the greatest experts on a subject which appeals strongly to most of us.   The author imparts many secrets of training, and gives sound and practical advice all the time.   Especially may the book be commended to the notice of horse show judges."—*Referee.*

THE SPORT OF SHOOTING.

By OWEN JONES,

AUTHOR OF "TEN YEARS OF GAME-KEEPING," ETC.

With Illustrations.   One Volume.   Demy 8vo. **10s. 6d. net.**

"What Mr. Jones does not know about 'Game' and 'Shooting' is, in the vernacular, not worth knowing.   'The Sport of Shooting' is a book which every shooting man should study."—*World.*

"A very readable and informing book."—*Morning Post.*

"Not only a useful manual for boys entrusted with their first gun, but is very interesting to sportsmen of more mature years, the descriptive passages being excellent."—*Standard.*

THE LIFE OF A TIGER.

By Sir S. EARDLEY-WILMOT, K.C.I.E.,
AUTHOR OF "FOREST LIFE AND SPORT IN INDIA."

With nearly 150 *Original Illustrations. Medium 8vo.* **7s. 6d. net.**

"A book which is well worthy to be placed on the same shelf as the chronicle of Mowgli's adventures."—*Morning Post.*

A LITTLE HISTORY OF MUSIC.

By ANNETTE HULLAH.

With Numerous Illustrations. One Volume. Medium 8vo. **5s.**

"The clear-sightedness of the whole book makes it valuable and interesting."—*Morning Post.*

HINTS TO SPEAKERS AND PLAYERS.

By ROSINA FILIPPI.

One Volume. Crown 8vo. **3s. 6d. net.**

"An immensely helpful little book. It is as shrewd as it is sympathetic, and many besides stage-pupils should read it."—*Morning Leader.*

THE GRAVEN PALM.

A Manual of the Science of Palmistry.
By Mrs. ROBINSON.

With about 250 *Original Illustrations. Medium 8vo.* **10s. 6d. net.**

A GOODLY FELLOWSHIP

Thoughts in Verse and Prose from many Sources.

Collected by ROSE E. SELFE.

With a Preface by
His Grace the ARCHBISHOP OF CANTERBURY.

One Volume. Small 8vo. **2s. 6d. net.**

RECENT FICTION.

TANTE.

By ANNE DOUGLAS SEDGWICK,

AUTHOR OF "FRANKLIN KANE," "AMABEL CHANNICE," ETC.

Crown 8vo. **6s.** *Fourth Impression.*

"I stand amazed by the qualities of the author's genius. She really can create characters, quite original, and, as it were, not fanciful, not fantastic, but solid samples of human nature. When one lights on something really good in contemporary fiction one has pleasure in saying how excellent one finds the rarity."—Mr. ANDREW LANG in the *Illustrated London News.*

"'Tante' is a fine piece of work, well thought out, well constructed, and full of human nature. There is no possible doubt that it will stand out among the most distinguished novels of the year."—*Daily Telegraph.*

"There can be but one opinion as to the merits of this entirely fascinating and able novel, which marks a fresh stage in the development of one of the most remarkable writers of the present day."—*Westminster Gazette.*

"One does not know of any woman writing novels in England to-day who is capable of anything so imposing in invention and so refined in execution as 'Tante.' 'Tante' is a remarkable novel, full of brilliant things and of beautiful things—the strongest work of a very distinguished writer."—*Manchester Guardian.*

THE BRACKNELS.

By FORREST REID.

One Volume. *Crown 8vo.* **6s.**

"A work of rare distinction. 'The Bracknels' is more than brilliant; it is actual; it is true; it is an accurate reproduction of an experience."—*Daily News.*

"An admirable novel, from which one has had no ordinary amount of pleasure."—*Manchester Guardian.*

"A remarkable novel and a novel of character. It is as fine a piece of work as we have come upon for a long time."—*Daily Chronicle.*

MORE GHOST STORIES.

By Dr. M. R. JAMES,

PROVOST OF KING'S COLLEGE, CAMBRIDGE.
AUTHOR OF "GHOST STORIES OF AN ANTIQUARY," ETC.

Medium 8vo. **6s.** *Second Impression.*

"I wish to place myself on record as unreservedly recommending 'More Ghost Stories.' It is Dr. James's method that makes his tales so fascinating. As he puts it in his preface, a ghost story ought to be told in such a way that the reader shall say to himself: 'If I am not very careful something of this kind may happen to me.'"—*Punch.*

LONDON: EDWARD ARNOLD, 41 & 43 MADDOX STREET, W.

Music and Books published by Travis & Emery Music Bookshop:

Anon.: Hymnarium Sarisburiense, cum Rubricis et Notis Musicis.

Agricola, Johann Friedrich from Tosi: Anleitung zur Singkunst.

Bach, C.P.E.: edited W. Emery: Nekrolog or Obituary Notice of J.S. Bach.

Bateson, Naomi Judith: Alcock of Salisbury

Bathe, William: A Briefe Introduction to the Skill of Song

Bax, Arnold: Symphony #5, Arranged for Piano Four Hands by Walter Emery

Burney, Charles: The Present State of Music in France and Italy

Burney, Charles: The Present State of Music in Germany, The Netherlands ...

Burney, Charles: An Account of the Musical Performances ... Handel

Burney, Karl: Nachricht von Georg Friedrich Handel's Lebensumstanden.

Cobbett, W.W.: Cobbett's Cyclopedic Survey of Chamber Music. (2 vols.)

Corrette, Michel: Le Maitre de Clavecin

Crimp, Bryan: Dear Mr. Rosenthal ... Dear Mr. Gaisberg ...

Crimp, Bryan: Solo: The Biography of Solomon

d'Indy, Vincent: Beethoven: Biographie Critique

d'Indy, Vincent: Beethoven: A Critical Biography

d'Indy, Vincent: César Franck (in French)

Frescobaldi, Girolamo: D'Arie Musica'i per Cantarsi. Primo & Secondo Libro.

Geminiani, Francesco: The Art of Playing the Violin.

Handel; Purcell; Boyce; Geene et al: Calliope or English Harmony: Volume First.

Hawkins, John: A General History of the Science and Practice of Music (5 vols.)

Herbert-Caesari, Edgar: The Science and Sensations of Vocal Tone

Herbert-Caesari, Edgar: Vocal Truth

Hopkins and Rimboult: The Organ. Its History and Construction.

Hunt, John: Adam to Webern: the recordings of von Karajan

Isaacs, Lewis: Hänsel and Gretel. A Guide to Humperdinck's Opera.

Isaacs, Lewis: Königskinder (Royal Children) A Guide to Humperdinck's Opera.

Lacassagne, M. l'Abbé Joseph : Traité Général des élémens du Chant.

Lascelles (née Catley), Anne: The Life of Miss Anne Catley.

Mainwaring, John: Memoirs of the Life of the Late George Frederic Handel

Malcolm, Alexander: A Treaty of Music: Speculative, Practical and Historical

Marx, Adolph Bernhard: Die Kunst des Gesanges, Theoretisch-Practisch

May, Florence: The Life of Brahms

Mellers, Wilfrid: Angels of the Night: Popular Female Singers of Our Time

Mellers, Wilfrid: Bach and the Dance of God

Mellers, Wilfrid: Beethoven and the Voice of God

Travis & Emery Music Bookshop
17 Cecil Court, London, WC2N 4EZ, United Kingdom.
Tel. (+44) 20 7240 2129

Music and Books published by Travis & Emery Music Bookshop:

Mellers, Wilfrid: Caliban Reborn - Renewal in Twentieth Century Music
Mellers, Wilfrid: François Couperin and the French Classical Tradition
Mellers, Wilfrid: Harmonious Meeting
Mellers, Wilfrid: Le Jardin Retrouvé, The Music of Frederic Mompou
Mellers, Wilfrid: Music and Society, England and the European Tradition
Mellers, Wilfrid: Music in a New Found Land: ... ... American Music
Mellers, Wilfrid: Romanticism and the Twentieth Century (from 1800)
Mellers, Wilfrid: The Masks of Orpheus: ...... the Story of European Music.
Mellers, Wilfrid: The Sonata Principle (from c. 1750)
Mellers, Wilfrid: Vaughan Williams and the Vision of Albion
Panchianio, Cattuffio: Rutzvanscad Il Giovine
Pearce, Charles: Sims Reeves, Fifty Years of Music in England.
Playford, John: An Introduction to the Skill of Musick.
Purcell, Henry et al: Harmonia Sacra ... The First Book, (1726)
Purcell, Henry et al: Harmonia Sacra ... Book II (1726)
Quantz, Johann: Versuch einer Anweisung die Flöte traversiere zu spielen.
Rameau, Jean-Philippe: Code de Musique Pratique, ou Methodes.
Rastall, Richard: The Notation of Western Music.
Rimbault, Edward: The Pianoforte, Its Origins, Progress, and Construction.
Rousseau, Jean Jacques: Dictionnaire de Musique
Rubinstein, Anton : Guide to the proper use of the Pianoforte Pedals.
Sainsbury, John S.: Dictionary of Musicians. Vol. 1. (1825). 2 vols.
Simpson, Christopher: A Compendium of Practical Musick in Five Parts
Spohr, Louis: Autobiography
Spohr, Louis: Grand Violin School
Tans'ur, William: A New Musical Grammar; or The Harmonical Spectator
Terry, Charles Sanford: Four-Part Chorals of J.S. Bach. (German & English)
Terry, Charles Sanford: Joh. Seb. Bach, Cantata Texts, Sacred and Secular.
Terry, Charles Sanford: The Origins of the Family of Bach Musicians.
Tosi, Pierfrancesco: Opinioni de' Cantori Antichi, e Moderni
Van der Straeten, Edmund: History of the Violoncello, The Viol da Gamba ...
Van der Straeten, Edmund: History of the Violin, Its Ancestors... (2 vols.)
Walther, J. G.: Musicalisches Lexikon ober Musicalische Bibliothec

Travis & Emery Music Bookshop
17 Cecil Court, London, WC2N 4EZ, United Kingdom.
Tel. (+44) 20 7240 2129

Discographies by Travis & Emery:

Discographies by John Hunt.

1987: 978-1-906857-14-1: From Adam to Webern: the Recordings of von Karajan.

1991: 978-0-951026-83-0: 3 Italian Conductors and 7 Viennese Sopranos: 10 Discographies: Arturo Toscanini, Guido Cantelli, Carlo Maria Giulini, Elisabeth Schwarzkopf, Irmgard Seefried, Elisabeth Gruemmer, Sena Jurinac, Hilde Gueden, Lisa Della Casa, Rita Streich.

1992: 978-0-951026-85-4: Mid-Century Conductors and More Viennese Singers: 10 Discographies: Karl Boehm, Victor De Sabata, Hans Knappertsbusch, Tullio Serafin, Clemens Krauss, Anton Dermota, Leonie Rysanek, Eberhard Waechter, Maria Reining, Erich Kunz.

1993: 978-0-951026-87-8: More 20th Century Conductors: 7 Discographies: Eugen Jochum, Ferenc Fricsay, Carl Schuricht, Felix Weingartner, Josef Krips, Otto Klemperer, Erich Kleiber.

1994: 978-0-951026-88-5: Giants of the Keyboard: 6 Discographies: Wilhelm Kempff, Walter Gieseking, Edwin Fischer, Clara Haskil, Wilhelm Backhaus, Artur Schnabel.

1994: 978-0-951026-89-2: Six Wagnerian Sopranos: 6 Discographies: Frieda Leider, Kirsten Flagstad, Astrid Varnay, Martha Moedl, Birgit Nilsson, Gwyneth Jones.

1995: 978-0-952582-70-0: Musical Knights: 6 Discographies: Henry Wood, Thomas Beecham, Adrian Boult, John Barbirolli, Reginald Goodall, Malcolm Sargent.

1995: 978-0-952582-71-7: A Notable Quartet: 4 Discographies: Gundula Janowitz, Christa Ludwig, Nicolai Gedda, Dietrich Fischer-Dieskau.

1996: 978-0-952582-72-4: The Post-War German Tradition: 5 Discographies: Rudolf Kempe, Joseph Keilberth, Wolfgang Sawallisch, Rafael Kubelik, Andre Cluytens.

1996: 978-0-952582-73-1: Teachers and Pupils: 7 Discographies: Elisabeth Schwarzkopf, Maria Ivoguen, Maria Cebotari, Meta Seinemeyer, Ljuba Welitsch, Rita Streich, Erna Berger.

1996: 978-0-952582-77-9: Tenors in a Lyric Tradition: 3 Discographies: Peter anders, Walther Ludwig, Fritz Wunderlich.

1997: 978-0-952582-78-6: The Lyric Baritone: 5 Discographies: Hans Reinmar, Gerhard Huesch, Josef Metternich, Hermann Uhde, Eberhard Waechter.

1997: 978-0-952582-79-3: Hungarians in Exile: 3 Discographies: Fritz Reiner, Antal Dorati, George Szell.

1997: 978-1-901395-00-6: The Art of the Diva: 3 Discographies: Claudia Muzio, Maria Callas, Magda Olivero.

1997: 978-1-901395-01-3: Metropolitan Sopranos: 4 Discographies: Rosa Ponselle, Eleanor Steber, Zinka Milanov, Leontyne Price.

1997: 978-1-901395-02-0: Back From The Shadows: 4 Discographies: Willem Mengelberg, Dimitri Mitropoulos, Hermann Abendroth, Eduard Van Beinum.

1997: 978-1-901395-03-7: More Musical Knights: 4 Discographies: Hamilton Harty, Charles Mackerras, Simon Rattle, John Pritchard.

1998: 978-1-901395-94-5: Conductors On The Yellow Label: 8 Discographies: Fritz Lehmann, Ferdinand Leitner, Ferenc Fricsay, Eugen Jochum, Leopold Ludwig, Artur Rother, Franz Konwitschny, Igor Markevitch.

1998: 978-1-901395-95-2: More Giants of the Keyboard: 5 Discographies: Claudio Arrau, Gyorgy Cziffra, Vladimir Horowitz, Dinu Lipatti, Artur Rubinstein.

1998: 978-1-901395-96-9: Mezzo and Contraltos: 5 Discographies: Janet Baker, Margarete Klose, Kathleen Ferrier, Giulietta Simionato, Elisabeth Hoengen.

1999: 978-1-901395-97-6: The Furtwaengler Sound Sixth Edition: Discography and Concert Listing.

1999: 978-1-901395-98-3: The Great Dictators: 3 Discographies: Evgeny Mravinsky, Artur Rodzinski, Sergiu Celibidache.

1999: 978-1-901395-99-0: Sviatoslav Richter: Pianist of the Century: Discography.

2000: 978-1-901395-04-4: Philharmonic Autocrat 1: Discography of: Herbert Von Karajan [Third Edition].

2000: 978-1-901395-05-1: Wiener Philharmoniker 1 - Vienna Philharmonic and Vienna State Opera Orchestras: Discography Part 1 1905-1954.

2000: 978-1-901395-06-8: Wiener Philharmoniker 2 - Vienna Philharmonic and Vienna State Opera Orchestras: Discography Part 2 1954-1989.

2001: 978-1-901395-07-5: Gramophone Stalwarts: 3 Separate Discographies: Bruno Walter, Erich Leinsdorf, Georg Solti.

2001: 978-1-901395-08-2: Singers of the Third Reich: 5 Discographies: Helge Roswaenge, Tiana Lemnitz, Franz Voelker, Maria Mueller, Max Lorenz.

2001: 978-1-901395-09-9: Philharmonic Autocrat 2: Concert Register of Herbert Von Karajan Second Edition.

2002: 978-1-901395-10-5: Sächsische Staatskapelle Dresden: Complete Discography.

2002: 978-1-901395-11-2: Carlo Maria Giulini: Discography and Concert Register.

2002: 978-1-901395-12-9: Pianists For The Connoisseur: 6 Discographies: Arturo Benedetti Michelangeli, Alfred Cortot, Alexis Weissenberg, Clifford Curzon, Solomon, Elly Ney.

2003: 978-1-901395-14-3: Singers on the Yellow Label: 7 Discographies: Maria Stader, Elfriede Troetschel, Annelies Kupper, Wolfgang Windgassen, Ernst Haefliger, Josef Greindl, Kim Borg.

2003: 978-1-901395-15-0: A Gallic Trio: 3 Discographies: Charles Muench, Paul Paray, Pierre Monteux.

2004: 978-1-901395-16-7: Antal Dorati 1906-1988: Discography and Concert Register.

2004: 978-1-901395-17-4: Columbia 33CX Label Discography.

2004: 978-1-901395-18-1: Great Violinists: 3 Discographies: David Oistrakh, Wolfgang Schneiderhan, Arthur Grumiaux.

2006: 978-1-901395-19-8: Leopold Stokowski: Second Edition of the Discography.

2006: 978-1-901395-20-4: Wagner Im Festspielhaus: Discography of the Bayreuth Festival.

2006: 978-1-901395-21-1: Her Master's Voice: Concert Register and Discography of Dame Elisabeth Schwarzkopf [Third Edition].

2007: 978-1-901395-22-8: Hans Knappertsbusch: Kna: Concert Register and Discography of Hans Knappertsbusch, 1888-1965. Second Edition.

2008: 978-1-901395-23-5: Philips Minigroove: Second Extended Version of the European Discography.

2009: 978-1-901395--24-2: American Classics: The Discographies of Leonard Bernstein and Eugene Ormandy.

Discography by Stephen J. Pettitt, edited by John Hunt:

1987: 978-1-906857-16-5: Philharmonia Orchestra: Complete Discography 1945-1987

Available from: Travis & Emery at 17 Cecil Court, London, UK. (+44) 20 7 240 2129. email on sales@travis-and-emery.com .

www.ingramcontent.com/pod-product-compliance
Lightning Source LLC
Chambersburg PA
CBHW060239100426
42742CB00011B/1583